Psychology Revivals

Infant Development: Recent Advances

Originally published in 1997, this edited volume provided an authoritative account of research into infant development at the time, containing 13 chapters written by leading British and North American infancy researchers. Editorial sections are used to provide an integrated whole and to point the reader to similarities and contrasts between arguments developed by different authors. Although the chapters are organised along conventional lines into sections on perceptual, cognitive and social development, the emphasis (appearing both within chapters and in the linking editorial passages within sections) is on links between perceptual, cognitive and social aspects of development. Thus, exciting new findings on infant perception are related to both old and new accounts of cognitive development, and links are drawn between these topics and the development of social interaction and language. There is a strong theoretical component in all sections of the book, with particular attention given to both traditional approaches such as Piagetian theory and more recent approaches such as direct perception and dynamic systems theory. There is also a chapter devoted to interpreting infant development from a psychoanalytic perspective.

A particular feature of this book is its aim to make recent findings and theoretical developments accessible to a student audience with little advanced knowledge of the area. Thus, the book should appeal to a wide readership ranging from advanced undergraduate psychology students to established infancy researchers.

Infant Development: Recent Advances

Edited by

Gavin Bremner, Alan Slater and George Butterworth

Routledge
Taylor & Francis Group
LONDON AND NEW YORK

First published in 1997
by Psychology Press

This edition first published in 2026 by Routledge
4 Park Square, Milton Park, Abingdon, Oxon, OX14 4RN

and by Routledge
605 Third Avenue, New York, NY 10158

Routledge is an imprint of the Taylor & Francis Group, an informa business

Publisher's Note
The publisher has gone to great lengths to ensure the quality of this reprint but points out that some imperfections in the original copies may be apparent.

Disclaimer
The publisher has made every effort to trace copyright holders and welcomes correspondence from those they have been unable to contact.

For Product Safety Concerns and Information please contact our EU representative GPSR@taylorandfrancis.com. Taylor & Francis Verlag GmbH, Kaufingerstraße 24, 80331 München, Germany

A Library of Congress record exists under ISBN: 9780863774621

ISBN: 978-1-041-27165-9 (hbk)
ISBN: 978-1-003-75306-3 (ebk)
ISBN: 978-1-041-27170-3 (pbk)

Book DOI 10.4324/9781003753063

Infant Development: Recent Advances

Edited by

Gavin Bremner
Department of Psychology
Lancaster University

Alan Slater
Department of Psychology
University of Exeter

George Butterworth
Division of Psychology
University of Sussex

Psychology Press
An imprint of Erlbaum (UK) Taylor & Francis

Psychology Press
27 Church Road
Hove
East Sussex, BN3 2FA
UK

British Library Cataloguing in Publication Data

A catalogue record for this book is available from the British Library

ISBN 0–86377–463–6 (Pbk)

Typeset by DP Photosetting, Aylesbury, Bucks.
Printed and bound by Biddles Ltd., King's Lynn

Contents

Contributors

Jacqueline Barrett, Department of Psychology, University of Exeter, Washington Singer Laboratories, Exeter EX4 4QG, UK.

Marc H. Bornstein, Child and Family Research, National Institute of Child Health and Human Development, Building 31, Room B2B15, 9000 Rockville Pike, Bethesda, MD 20892-2030, USA.

J. Gavin Bremner, Department of Psychology, University of Lancaster, Lancaster LA1 4YF, UK.

Elizabeth Brown, Department of Psychology, University of Exeter, Washington Singer Laboratories, Exeter EX4 4QG, UK.

George Butterworth, Division of Psychology, University of Sussex, Falmer, Brighton BN1 9QN, UK.

Gillian Harris, School of Psychology, The University of Birmingham, Edgbaston, Birmingham B15 2TT, UK.

Margaret Harris, Department of Psychology, Royal Holloway and Bedford New College, Egham Hill, Egham, Surrey TW20 0EX, UK.

Dale Hay, Faculty of Social and Political Sciences, University of Cambridge, New Museum Site, Cambridge CB2 3RQ, UK.

R. Peter Hobson, Development Psychopathology Research Unit, Adult Department, The Tavistock Clinic, 120 Belsize Lane, London NW3 5BA, UK.

Brian Hopkins, Department of Psychology, University of Lancaster, Lancaster LA1 4YF, UK.

Jean M. Mandler, Department of Cognitive Science, University of California – San Diego, La Jolla, CA 92093-0515, USA; and MRC Cognitive Development Unit, 4 Taviton Street, London WC1H 0BT, UK.

David Messer, Department of Psychology, University of Hertfordshire, Hatfield Campus, College Lane, Hatfield AL10 9AB, UK.

Lynne Murray, Winnicott Research Unit, Department of Psychology, University of Reading, 3 Earley Gate, Whiteknights, Reading RG6 2AL, UK.

Vasudevi Reddy, Department of Psychology, University of Portsmouth, King Henry Building, King Henry I Street, Portsmouth PO1 2ER, UK.

Elizabeth Roberts, Department of Psychology, University of Exeter, Washington Singer Laboratories, Exeter EX4 4QG, UK.

Julie C. Rutkowska, COGS, Physics Building, University of Sussex, Falmer, Brighton BN1 9QH, UK.

Alan Slater, Department of Psychology, University of Exeter, Washington Singer Laboratories, Exeter EX4 4QG, UK.

Colwyn Trevarthen, Department of Psychology, University of Edinburgh, 7 George Square, Edinburgh EH8 9JZ, UK.

Peter Willatts, Department of Psychology, University of Dundee, Dundee DD1 4HN, UK.

Preface

Infancy is the time of life during which enormous changes take place. The newly born, incompetent infant is almost a different species from the inquisitive 18-month-old toddler who has a command of language and is becoming increasingly independent. Psychologists have long recognised that developments in infancy are some of the most exciting and important to be found in human development. The last 30 years has seen an enormous increase in our understanding of these developments: the aim of this book is both to reflect current knowledge and to point to some of the many questions that remain unanswered.

The contents of the book stem from two ESRC funded meetings of the British Infancy Research Group in 1992 and 1993, whose focus was recent developments in theory and findings. The chapter topics were selected to reflect the breadth of psychological research on infancy, and our contributors were approached with clear suggestions about the chapters we hoped they would write, with a view to producing authoritative accounts of key topics in the major areas of infant development, namely, perceptual, cognitive, social and language development.

In some respects the aims of the book are similar to those of an earlier book, *Infant Development*, edited by two of the present editors (Slater and Bremner) and published by Lawrence Erlbaum in 1989. However, the present book is not simply an update, since many of the contributors are different and in those cases where the same authors have contributed chapters to both books their contributiions, and topic areas, are different.

Our contributors have served us well in producing clear accounts of exciting and at times difficult issues in infancy research. In order to enhance the reader's integration of the contents of the separate chapters, each of the major sections is prefaced by introductory comments. The book is intended for an advanced undergraduate readership, but it will also be useful for postgraduates, lecturers, researchers, and other professionals with an interest in infancy.

J. Gavin Bremner
Alan Slater
George Butterworth
3 June 1996

1

PERCEPTUAL AND MOTOR DEVELOPMENT

Perceptual and Motor Development: Introduction

The four chapters in Part 1 look at different areas of perceptual development. Infant feeding, and taste perception are areas that have always been considered to be of great interest to parents, to health visitors, and to medical research. In Chapter 1 Harris shows how these areas are also of great interest to psychology, and discusses ways in which the infant becomes able to monitor and regulate food intake so that the intake is appropriate both for energy output and for growth. She notes that an individual's growth trajectory is not determined solely by food intake but that there is also a major genetic component.

At birth, and for a month or so, regulation of food intake seems primarily to be determined by the primitive peripheral stimulus of stomach distension, but beyond this age more sophisticated central regulatory mechanisms develop, based on the monitoring of blood sugar levels and calorie intake. Infants become increasingly able to regulate their food intake according to the energy levels of the food, ingesting, for example, greater amounts of dilute formulae in comparison with standard formulae milk. Solid foods are usually introduced between the ages of 3 and 6 months. While the best predictor of the age of introduction is the age at which the mother *expects* to have to introduce them, there are complex interactions in that mothers usually give changes in their infants' behaviour as the main reason. The introduction of solid foods suddenly brings with it variety, and the infant has quickly to learn and develop a set of taste preferences, based on exposure to the foodstuffs available to him. Harris illustrates the development of these preferences, and their interaction with innately determined preferences, using the examples of sweet and salty solutions: an innate preference for sweet can be overcome by ingesting salty solutions if the latter have positive nutritional consequences—the inevitable result is the later preference for ready-salted crisps!

Harris deals with a range of variables, such as temperament, early exposure, and cognitive factors that influence food acceptance and "faddiness", and discusses some of the factors that may lead to food aversion. The chapter describes the ways in which, as infancy progresses, there is a change from the predominance of intrinsic cues to extrinsic ones; from hunger/satiety-driven feeding to the acquisition of cultural norms and expectations about appropriate meal spacing and appropriate foods for particular times of day.

In Chapter 2 Slater considers some of what is known about the organisation of visual perception in early infancy. Not so many years ago the predominant view of visual development, expressed by theorists such as Hebb and Piaget, was that the infant's awareness of the world is initially extremely limited, and that an organized visual world is gradually and laboriously constructed as development proceeds. However, an intensive period of research over the last 30 years or so has had the effect of changing the stereotype of the young infant from one of "incompetence" to one of "competence".

Slater's chapter has an emphasis on "what sense can the infant make of what she sees?" The first topic discussed is shape and size constancy. As objects move in space relative to the observer, or as the observer moves relative to objects, the objects' retinal images will change in complex ways. In order for the baby to make sense of these otherwise bewildering retinal changes some degree of shape and size constancy—perception of objects' real shapes and sizes regardless of the retinal changes that accompany changes in orientation and distance—needs to be present in visual perception. Empiricist and constructivist views of perceptual development have long held that such constancies are learned, perhaps as a consequence of seeing the same objects at different distances and different retinal eccentricities, or by the mediation of the sense of touch ("touch teaches vision"). However, there is now convincing evidence that shape and size constancy are organising features of perception that are present at birth, and that newborn infants perceive the objective, real shapes and sizes of objects.

Slater considers other aspects of visual perception that seem to be present at, or soon after birth. Topics include the perception of simple shapes and of stimulus compounds, appreciation of subjective contours, the developing ability to categorise perceptual input, and detection of form from moving displays. Finally, some of the recent findings on infants' developing understanding of objects are presented.

It is clear that the newborn infant is possessed of many inbuilt means with which to make sense of the visual world. Many of the newborn's perceptual limitations, such as an apparent inability to "fill in", or complete, parts of an object that are occluded by a nearer object, are overcome within a few months, and the weight of evidence suggests that young infants perceive the world objectively: in other words, young infants are sophisticated perceivers of the world.

This conclusion constitutes the starting point of Bremner's chapter, and he begins by raising an important theoretical point: "If the world is objectively perceived, is there any need to postulate the development of cognitive structures that conventional theory suggests are needed to interpret subjective sense data?" Bremner begins an answer to this question by introducing one obvious fact, and an apparent paradox: the fact is that during infancy much does develop, and the apparent paradox is that perceptual competencies do not appear in self-initiated behaviour in early infancy. For instance, if infants perceive the world objectively, this should be sufficient to specify the continued existence of hidden objects, and evidence from recent studies of object knowledge indicates that quite young infants have object permanence. However, it is only around 8 months that they begin to search for hidden objects, and even then, they make particular systematic errors in search. In perceptual development (perhaps in all development) there must be an interplay or balance between what the organism brings to the encounter—processes and structures internal to the individual—and what is objectively "out there"—environmental structures. Bremner argues that major theories that have been applied to perceptual development, such as Piaget's and Gibson's, have not got this balance right; and he develops the view that dynamic systems theory, which is also the focus of Chapter 14, offers the possibility of new explanatory power.

The main thrust of this chapter is to argue that much development in infancy is to be explained in terms of the formation of links between *pre-existing* perceptual competencies and *emerging* action, so that knowledge of the world that is initially implicit in perception ultimately becomes explicit knowledge in the sense that it can guide action. In other words, as the infant develops new actions and new capacities for action there is a need to acquire knowledge of how these actions relate to the perceptual world.

This theme is illustrated with respect to the onset of self-induced locomotion—crawling. The infant is in possession of a new-found freedom of movement, which brings with it a number of changes and developments. For example, at a perceptual level the changes to the visual world that accompany crawling result from the infant's own actions, unlike those that occur when the infant is carried by an adult: in the former case visual changes are correlated with vestibular information, while in the latter they are not. The consequences of these changes are many and far reaching. One set of changes is to do with spatial orientation and awareness, while another is emotional: while the infant was previously perfectly able to perceive vertical drops, *wariness* of such drops does not develop until the infant crawls. From Bremner's analysis it is apparent that we should view early perceptual competencies as existing within a system, which includes the whole infant and her social and physical environment. These competencies become realised in a meaningful sense only when they are used to guide actions, and to facilitate cognitive and emotional development.

The terms "perception" and "cognition" are often distinguished in that the former refers to the basic detection and processing of sensory information, while the latter refers to the ability to extract sense, meaning and understanding from this information. It is often not easy to draw a clear distinction between them, and in any event it is clear that perceptual abilities inform and are an integral part of cognitive and social abilities. This theme is further illustrated in Part 2, Cognitive Development, where Mandler distinguishes between perceptual and conceptual categories in infant development, and discusses the implications of these distinctions for different types of categorical knowledge, and in Part 3, Social and Language Development, where Slater and Butterworth consider how face perception in early infancy is linked with early representational abilities, and leads to detection of facial expressions and to categorisation of faces.

The final chapter in this section enlarges on the point made by Bremner about the need to consider the relationship between perception and action. And it does this by presenting a radical alternative to more conventional accounts of early development. Dynamical systems approaches derive from certain approaches in the physical sciences which view complex systems as self-organising. Butterworth and Hopkins show how this type of approach can be applied productively to developmental questions. A full understanding of this type of approach requires considerable background knowledge of mathematics and physics, and so much of the detail is relatively inaccessibly to most readers. However, this same mathematical sophistication constitutes the strength of this sort of approach, since it promises to provide a rigorous analysis of developmental processes.

Despite the complexity of this approach, some fairly simple principles emerge that mark it as a radical departure from conventional thinking. First of all, the principle of self-organisation can be identified as a clear challenge to approaches that conceptualise development as underpinned by changes in mental structures. Instead, this approach identifies the structure of behaviour as a property of the whole system and not just whatever part of the system resides in the head. Thus, in considering motor development, the approach denies the need to invoke neural pattern generators, since much of the structure of behaviour is determined by the biomechanics of the limbs concerned. Of course, the approach does not deny a role for neural structures, but it very much reduces it.

A second principle relates more directly to developmental questions. The claim is made that complex changes in the system can be brought about by quite simple changes in component factors of the system. For instance, a simple change in muscle strength or limb weight can lead to a change from one stable state of the system to another stable state, and although the causal factor may be very simple, the change to the new state may be complex. This might appear to be a case of getting something for nothing (or for very little). But the point is that the complexity of behaviour is a property of the interaction of all the components of the system, and a change in one of these components may change completely the overall interaction of parts. Again, the implication is that it is inappropriate to propose developmental mechanisms based on mental or neural processes that constitute some sort of internal copy of behaviour. To the extent that representation is involved, it is very much a distributed representation that resides in the system as a whole rather than in the head.

The promise of dynamic systems is that its scope is essentially boundless; that is, the system under consideration can be sensibly extended beyond the individual to incorporate the individual's physical and social environment. When we do that, the truly radical nature of the approach becomes apparent, since the processes leading to particular behaviours of the system can no longer be identified as residing in the individual, even in a distributed form. Instead, behaviour has to be viewed as a property of the interaction between properties of individual and environment. It is of interest to note that there are clear points of contact here with Vygotskian social construction approaches; and one exciting path for future research will involve investigation of the extent to which dynamic systems approaches can be applied to the social domain rather than simply in the field of motor development where they have been applied with most success to date.

1 Development of Taste Perception and Appetite Regulation

Gillian Harris
School of Psychology, University of Birmingham, UK.

INTRODUCTION

Relatively few studies have been carried out on the psychology, or psychophysiology, of infant feeding. It is an area that is not thought relevant to theoretical research on infant development, but more an area of interest to those involved in medical or health related research. Perhaps because of this, the direction of the research has mainly been into health or childcare-related issues, such as studies that aim to help parents decide how much food, or which foods, an infant should be taking at any particular age for optimal health and growth. These decisions are then handed on to the health worker or parent as goals that must be achieved, and are imposed upon the infant by the adult. This means that many parents are given the idea that "growing" an infant can be achieved almost in the same way that one would make a cake; add four ounces of milk, two teaspoons of grated carrot and leave for four hours.

There is a further misunderstanding prevalent amongst parents that growth is dependent purely on food intake; that is, an infant's growth trajectory can be determined by the amount of food the parent can get into the infant. There is often no realisation that growth is also determined by genetic factors. These ideas, common in both parents and health workers, can be summarised as an inability to appreciate that the infant might have something to contribute to the feeding process.

If we wish to understand developmental processes that might be taking place within the infant—that is, to look at infant feeding from anything other than a medical perspective—we have but few studies in disparate areas to work from. This chapter then, has to be largely theoretical; outlining models that we are currently testing, and drawing frequently on clinical observations to support these, as yet, not fully tested models.

Growth and feeding

If we discard the idea that an infant's growth is solely determined by what others choose to put in to the infant, then we have to accept that in feeding, as in areas of cognitive and social development, the infant needs to be able to act upon the world in order to regulate its own feeding behaviour to accord with both internal and external factors. In which case we have to ask the question: what does a newborn infant have to achieve when first trying to regulate feeding and growth?

Firstly, the infant needs to take in sufficient calories to fulfil its growth potential, given its metabolic rate and energy output. Secondly, the infant needs to learn how to obtain sufficient calories from the environment. To do this, the infant has to learn to differentiate between food and non-food; that is, which eatable substances are considered by the caregiver to be both safe and culturally appropriate. The infant also has to learn which foodstuffs are associated with positive nutritional consequences.

APPETITE REGULATION

Achievement of the first need, taking in sufficient calories to fulfil growth potential, is dependent upon four things:

1. The infant needs to be able to monitor calorie intake.
2. The infant needs to be able to regulate intake to enable the genetically determined growth trajectory, and to accord with metabolic rate and energy output; the regulatory system involved here must also trigger the sensations of hunger and satiety.
3. The infant needs the ability to signal the sensations of hunger and satiety to the caregiver.
4. The infant needs sufficient oral-motor skills to ingest food at an appropriate rate when food is presented.

A further component in the feeding interaction is, of course, the caregiver's interpretation of the infant's signals of hunger and satiety, and the caregiver's behaviour based upon that interpretation. This is possibly one of the most complex and crucial chain of behaviours to the newborn infant; failure in one of the links in the chain would result in malnutrition and eventual death. Possibly because of the critical nature of this chain of events, the system is amazingly robust. The first response of the neonate is to orient towards, and suck on, any physical stimulus presented near to the mouth.

The first response of the parent to a crying infant is to feed it; if the infant feeds slowly, parents will feed for longer. Even in those infants where the internal regulatory system does not seem to function well—that is, the infant will go for long periods without food, and does not signal hunger by crying—failure to thrive occurs ONLY in those dyads where the parent does not impose a feeding schedule upon the infant (Davies & Evans, 1976; Skuse, Wolke, and Reilly, 1992). Most parents will feed an infant at regular intervals in the first weeks of life even though the child does not cry. Leaving a infant without feeding it is of course less likely to happen where the infant is breastfed, and where discomfort drives the mother on to feed, whether or not the infant is signalling hunger.

Perhaps the one element of this chain that is most frequently misunderstood is the infant's ability to regulate its own calorie intake to accord with its own growth velocity and metabolic rate, a system which is, of course, most often called into question when it is seen to be failing, and the infant is not growing or feeding at a rate which accords with others' expectations. The regulatory system cannot, of course, be "hard-wired" because the calorie content of food taken in must increase with the growth of the infant. There must be feedback to ensure that calorie intake increases according to growth needs. In adults, the utilisation of stored or available energy partly determines the sensation of hunger and the onset of eating behaviour (Logue,1991). However, in children there needs to be another component in the equation. Adults might be thought to regulate their weight to accord with a part learned, part genetically determined "set-point" (Keesey, 1978); children, however, have to regulate intake according to a largely genetically determined "set" growth trajectory. Growth, or the production of growth hormones, can be seen to be involved in feedback to the intake regulatory system because children with growth hormone dysfunction have reduced appetites which increase when growth hormones are given. Similarly, children with genetic disorders, such as Silver–Russell syndrome, who have congenital short stature, are frequently diagnosed on the basis of "poor" appetite. However, self-regulation based upon the monitoring of calorie intake cannot be present at birth, because the infant needs to learn the consequences of ingesting specific foods. It would seem safe to assume that the co-ordination of all the components involved in maintaining the regulatory system develop over the first months of life, and there are some research studies which seem to support this assumption.

Peripheral regulators

It is often assumed that the primary regulator of appetite in infancy is the stomach or, to be more precise, the degree of stomach distension experienced by the infant. In fact, infancy *is* possibly the only time in our lives, apart from major celebrations such as Christmas, when stomach distension is used to regulate intake. Sufficient food is rarely taken at any other time to extend the stomach to full capacity. The regulation of intake by stomach distension probably serves in the early weeks of infancy until a more sophisticated regulatory system based on monitoring of blood sugars and other, more peripheral, mechanisms has developed. Whilst the infant is still relatively small, sufficient milk can be taken at one feed both to fill the stomach and adequately satiate the infant. Subsequent feeds are initiated quite quickly because of the rapid gastric-emptying rate of a food such as breast milk. Gastric-emptying rate is a peripheral regulator of appetite even in adults. Rapid gastric emptying may lead to an earlier sensation of hunger than does slow gastric emptying, (Hunt, 1980).

Many assume, quite wrongly, however, that stomach distension is the only regulator of hunger and satiety in infancy and do not consider that more central mechanisms might form part of the developmental agenda. Parents and health professionals alike often favour the "concrete" approach to infant feeding. The fuller the stomach, for longer, the less likely the infant is to cry as frequently for feeds. Many of the infant formulae which are advertised as "satisfying" hungry babies (that is pacifying them or stopping them from crying), are formulae which form curds in the stomach. Curded milk is less quick to empty from the stomach, and therefore should give the feel of stomach distension for longer. However, the consequences of adopting such an approach, should it work, have not been thought through. If we were able to "fool" an infant in such a way, by maintaining stomach distension which would in turn maintain a sensation of satiety, then we could, quite easily, starve an infant, by making it feed less frequently than it would otherwise have done. However, infants, and their stomachs, are not fooled for long. There is evidence to support the idea that the monitoring of calories begins at least by about six weeks of age, and that this monitoring overrides stomach distension in the regulation of feeds.

Calorie regulation

Infants, and adults, regulate their intake according to the energy density of the food, or formula (Fomon et al., 1976). There is as yet no evidence to suggest that the physiological regulation of intake can occur for any other property of food; we do not seem to be able to monitor and regulate fat, protein, vitamin or mineral intake. For the infant, the consequence of the regulation of energy intake is to maintain a balanced nutritional intake, because breast milk should provide all the infant's nutritional needs. In later childhood, balance of nutrients comes from the wide range of foods that might be seen to be appropriate and available. When infants were given formula milks that were similar in energy density, but differed in composition—that is, energy was provided either as fat or carbohydrate—no difference was observed in intake. Intake was regulated by energy density alone (Fomon et al., 1976). The way in which energy intake is monitored does, however, seem to change over the first weeks of life. Fomon et al. (1969) fed infants dilute formula milk and compared intake with that of standard formula milk. The infants fed the dilute formula took in more milk, but not enough in the early weeks to compensate for the reduction in calories. Not until they were around seven weeks old did milk consumption entirely compensate for the difference in the energy density of the milk. Increased consumption of the dilute milk in the early weeks could be explained in terms of the more rapid gastric emptying of the less energy-dense formula. Slow gastric emptying inhibits feeding. However, after the age of seven weeks the infants were able to compensate for the low energy density by increasing consumption until energy needs were met.

In as yet unpublished data, Anna Thomas and I have observed that infants fed formulae of similar energy density but with different gastric emptying rates, show compensatory feeding by the age of six weeks. That is, infants fed formulae with slow gastric-emptying rates feed for a shorter period than infants fed formulae with faster gastric-emptying rates. However, the infants fed the slow gastric-emptying formulae inititate a subsequent feed sooner than the infants fed on the fast emptying formulae. Where energy intake at any one feed is low then feed spacing is more frequent. This compensation was not observed prior to six weeks.

The data suggest that infants are able to regulate intake according to the "long-term" consequences of ingestion, and that this co-ordination of central and peripheral regulation of energy intake does not occur until the second month of life. Such regulation of intake involves both monitoring, and learning, the calorific consequences of ingesting specific foods. This is an ability observed in both adults and children (Birch et al., 1991), and often such learning involves the association of a specific calorie load with a certain taste. Birch and Deysher (1985;1986) found that three- and four-year-old children would eat more food *ad libitum* following a low-calorie first course than they did following a high calorie first course. This compensation followed a series of conditioning trials where specific flavours were paired with certain calorie loads. Learning to associate flavours with energy density is also, of course, important given that the infant needs to consume energy-dense foods to grow at the rapid rate normal and necessary in the first weeks of life. The infant's preference for flavours associated with energy density is discussed further in this chapter, when innate and learned taste preferences are considered.

The infant rapidly develops intrinsic cues to satiety. In the first weeks these cues are mainly those provided by peripheral sensors, such as stomach distension and gastric-emptying rate. From the second month, however, central mechanisms seem to be active. The infant can both monitor and regulate intake so that energy intake is appropriate for growth and energy output (Waterlow & Thomson, 1979). This regulatory system, based on internal cues, determines feeding patterns until extrinsic cues which regulate feeding come into play. The first of these extrinsic cues is probably culturally appropriate meal spacing, and achievement of a diurnal feeding pattern.

Hunger, and the introduction of solid foods

We might then assume that the development of energy regulation is perceived as a key issue in infant development; the gradual acceding to the infant of the power to regulate at least the amount of food which is taken in. However, few who care for infants, or work with them professionally, are aware that such a system exists. Most caregivers rely on extrinsic cues to determine whether or not their infant is taking in enough food (Birch, 1993). They use comparisons between children to aid their judgements, or concentrate upon the child's growth rate or body shape. These measures are harmless, or even useful, if the infant takes in a large amount of food and grows well. If, however, the infant is genetically of small stature, we often find that the caregivers will force-feed, or attempt to overfeed (Harris & Booth,1992), on the assumption that there is a linear relationship between food intake and growth. That is, the parents assume that the more food that they feed to the child, the taller the child will be, regardless of genotype. Many parents also assume that there is no physiological "limiter" to intake, that the infant does not have a feeling of satiety. However, most parents do seem to assume that the *onset* of the infant's feeding behaviour is determined by hunger. The first impulse is to feed a crying infant, and perhaps because of this behaviour by the parent the infant is able to learn to recognise intrinsic hunger cues, and differentiate between hunger and other sources of discomfort. Parents also assume that a hungry infant will not sleep; they assume, in fact, that sleep patterns are determined by feeding patterns (Eaton-Evans & Dugdale, 1988). This is especially true with night sleep; extra "thickened" (calorie dense) feeds are often given at the last feed of the day in order that the infant should sleep through the night (Matheny, Birch, & Picciano, 1990) The organisation of sleep/ wake patterns seems, however, to be associated as much with maturational factors as with environmental factors (Zaiwalla & Stein,1993). When sleep patterns change, and the infant wakes more frequently than before, this is also perceived by the mother to indicate hunger in the child; and might be perceived as an appropriate time to add solid food to the infant's diet (Harris, 1988).

The timing of the introduction of solid food is another stage in infant feeding that is prescribed by the experts (DHSS, 1983); an age at which solid food should be introduced is suggested, rather than a weight or developmental stage. Whitehead (1985) suggests that, given the usual rate of growth of an infant and the energy density of breast or formula milk, the infant should need to be fed solid foods at some time between the ages of three and six months, dependent upon growth velocity. The actual age-point at which health professionals suggest that solid food should be introduced does, however, tend to vary according to prevailing health concerns. In addition, the age at which mothers *do* introduce solid foods also varies according to the social class of the parent (McIntosh, 1986), middle-class mothers tend to introduce solid foods later than do working-class mothers (Harris, 1988). This could be because middle-class mothers tend to be aware of prevailing health-related issues, or at least to act on them, before working-class mothers do; and within recent years there has been a tendency for health professionals to promote the later introduction of solids.

The best predictor of the age of the introduction of solids was found to be the age at which the mother expected to have to introduce solid foods (Harris,1988). These expectations were present at the time of the birth of the child and were determined by cultural or sub-cultural norms. However, in this study, mothers also reported that the introduction of solid foods had followed a change in the infant's behaviour; in fact 75% of the mothers gave this as their reason for giving their infant supplementary solid food. The changes that the mothers observed, and independently reported, were of crying more frequently for feeds during the day, or showing hunger by fist sucking, and the return of night waking. Although most mothers had said that they intended to introduce solids, on average, at the age of 17 weeks, the median age of introduction was 14 weeks. Behavioural change in the infant coincided with, or preceded, maternal expectations about the age of introduction.

The infants' behaviour seemed to have a regulatory function: as growth velocity exceeded energy intake so the infants changed the pattern of feeds already established, the effect of which was to increase overall intake. The greater the weekly weight increase of the infant, the earlier the infant was likely to receive additional solid food. The infants were able to signal to the mother that their energy needs were changing, and most mothers responded appropriately. In fact, at this age, infants are also able to give behavioural signals which indicate food preference. Infants as young as 16 weeks, who had just started spoon-feeding, were observed to signal both appetite and food preference, behaviourally (Harris, Thomas, & Booth, 1990).

FOOD AND TASTE PREFERENCES

The infant does seem able both to monitor and regulate energy intake, and to communicate energy needs to the parent. We might not say that the communication of hunger is at first intentional on the part of the infant; it is probably better described as reactive. But, whether or not the infant's behaviour is intentional or reactive, the infant depends upon the parent being able to interpret the behaviour in an appropriate manner. Problems that occur along this chain of communication between parent and infant are most likely to occur as the regulatory mechanism develops and as the parent accedes, or fails to accede, control of intake to the infant. Failure-to-thrive, (growth faltering where there is no obvious organic cause for the failure to gain weight), is most likely to be observed in onset at the age of 3 months (Harris, 1993a). This is the age, as we have already observed, at which most infants are first given solid foods (Harris,1988).

The age of three months heralds a transitional stage, during which the main source of calories for the child changes in the method of delivery, coming on a spoon rather than in a bottle. Perhaps one of the major problems with the change from milk to solid food is the sudden introduction of variety, and the need for real communicative intent between infant and parent if food preferences are to be learned, and energy intake regulation maintained.

It is clear that there is a need for a system of appetite regulation, other than that of stomach distension, to develop quite rapidly within the first weeks of life so that growth can be adequately maintained. It is also necessary for infants to develop a set of taste preferences. Children have to learn which substances within their environment are safe and have positive nutritional consequences. Given the differences in climate of the environments which humans inhabit, and therefore the difference in flora and fauna in their immediate environment, humans depend upon a wide range of foodstuffs to sustain life. Because of this great variabilty in available foodstuffs, food preferences cannot be genetically determined; they must instead be culturally transmitted, or dependent upon rapid learning about negative consequences of ingestion. Infants cannot, therefore, have food preferences that are "hard-wired", their preferences must eventually be determined by the foodstuffs available to them. Food preferences must be learned; taste preferences, however, can be innate.

Taste preferences

The safest method of obtaining a preference for a varied and appropriate diet is to learn to like those foods that are given most frequently in early infancy before the child becomes mobile. The infant learns about foods and tastes that are appropriate to its particular sub-culture, and it is certainly true that a preference for most foods is gained as a function of exposure (Pliner, 1982). However, although a period of rapid learning about food to which the infant is exposed would seem to have to occur at the period of transition from milk to solid food diet, this does not mean that the infant does not also have innate taste preferences, or aversions. These are necessary to ensure that, in the early weeks, food that is high in energy is likely to be ingested as opposed to food that is likely to be toxic. Food that is high in energy is likely to have a sweet taste, food that is toxic is likely to have a bitter taste (Rozin, 1989). Neonates seem to have an innate preference for sweet tastes. This innate preference for a sweet taste, commonly observed in all neonates (Crook, 1978), means that they have a preference at birth for the taste of breast milk, which is inherently sweet. This innate preference is, however, still open to rapid modification when necessary.

We might expect that the developmental stages of taste perception and preference would be similar to that of other perceptual modalities, such as vision and hearing. In these modalities we might roughly summarise the rules of development for the neonate as:

1. Firstly, attend to, or show preference for, that for which there is an innate predisposition.
2. Secondly, attend to, or show preference for, that which has been experienced before.
3. Thirdly, get bored with that which has been experienced before and attend to new stimuli, especially those stimuli which have some properties in common with known stimuli, that is, they differ only slightly from known stimuli.

The effect of these three rules is to direct the infant's attention to salient stimuli within the environment, stimuli that, if attended to, will increase the infant's chances of survival. This usually means that the infant attends to, or shows preferences for, properties of the caregiver or stimuli likely to be associated with the caregiver. The human infant is totally dependent upon the care and protection of an older human for many years of life; it is, therefore, important that the infant is preprogrammed to respond to or learn rapidly about stimuli which are normally properties of, or associated with, other human beings.

The development of taste preferences

The neonate has an innate preference for sweet solutions, whatever the method of measuring preference. The neonate's response to other tastes does, however, vary according to the method of data collection, (facial expression, sucking rate, ingestion) and, perhaps more importantly, according to the strength of the solution used as a tastant. In Crook's 1978 study, infants' bursts of sucking triggered by salt solutions (0.1–0.6m) were shorter than those triggered by comparable sucrose solutions. Maller and Desor (1973), however, looked at the amount of water plus salt *ingested* by the infant, and consequently did not use a solution higher than 0.2m NaCl.

Using this solution strength they found that the addition of salt did not significantly inhibit the infants' ingestion of water. From this we might conclude two things: (1) that infants already inhibit the ingestion of water, therefore, the addition of sodium does not inhibit the ingestion of water further below baseline; or (2) that the solution strength was not strong enough to be aversive. The first point is supported by a subsequent intake study by (Desor, Maller, & Andrews, 1975) who added 0.2m NaCl to a sucrose solution and found that intake was not suppressed, although it was suppressed when a sour stimulus (citric acid) was added to the sucrose solution. The second point is supported by our own observations of infants' facial expression of disgust. In recent pilot studies, and in response to 5ml of saline solution placed on the tongue, we have observed no disgust response to a 3% solution but a clear disgust response to a 7.5% solution (Fig 1.1a). The latter solution tastes mildly aversive to an adult. The former solution (3%) is, however, isotonic and similar to that used in oral rehydration salts. In addition, when observing the infant's response to the milder solution, we must remember that the infant has experienced a similar saline solution when in the womb, in the form of amniotic fluid.

We can conclude from these data that the infant inhibits the intake of water in comparison to a sweet solution and that the addition of low levels of other tastants, with the possible exception of a sour tastant, does not increase or further inhibit water ingestion. However, the addition of sucrose does increase intake (Desor et al., 1975). Similarly, sucrose has a positive effect on sucking rate and does not produce facial expressions of disgust or distaste (Fig. 1.1b), whereas higher concentrations of salt do inhibit sucking rate and do elicit facial expressions indicative of aversion. Such facial expressions have also been observed by Rosenstein and Oster (1988) who noted negative facial expressions in response to quinine (bitter), and citric acid (sour) tastants, in comparison with infants' facial expressions in response to sucrose solutions. Rosenstein and Oster also observed a less marked, but still aversive, response to sodium chloride (but once again the solution used was less "strong" than the solution used for the bitter taste test). It is interesting to note, that if the facial response to a sweet solution is observed carefully there is an initial negative response, followed rapidly by a more positive facial expression and sucking response.

The simplest interpretation of these data is that the neonate responds positively on all measures to sweet solutions but will not preferentially ingest water, or solutions which have a bitter, sour or salt taste. Strong solutions of quinine, citric acid and sodium chloride will also elicit an aversive response. (It could also be true that a very concentrated sucrose solution would elicit an aversive response; the upper end of this range has not yet been tested). The neonate, therefore, seems to have an innate preference for a sweet taste. Newborn infants can also discriminate between a sweet taste and sour, salt

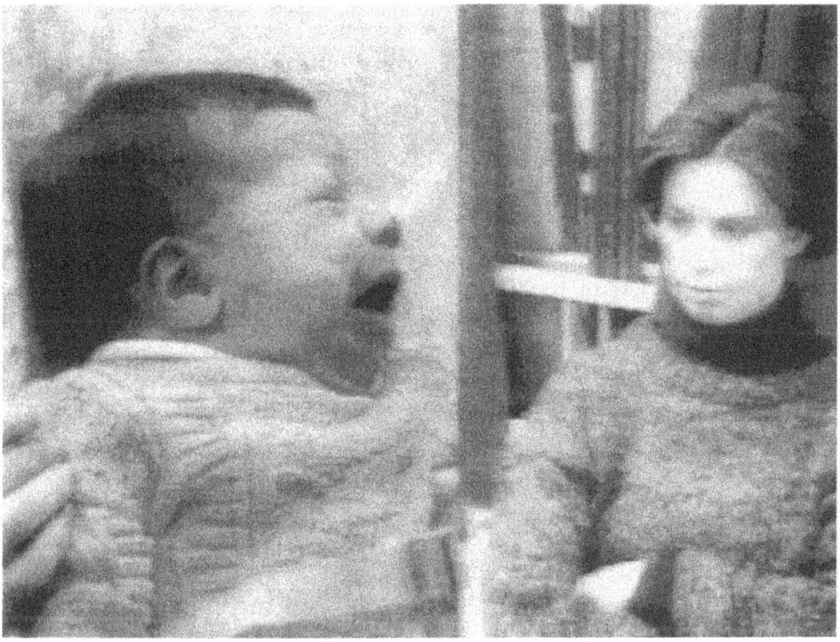

FIG. 1.1a. Neonatal facial expression in response to salt solution.

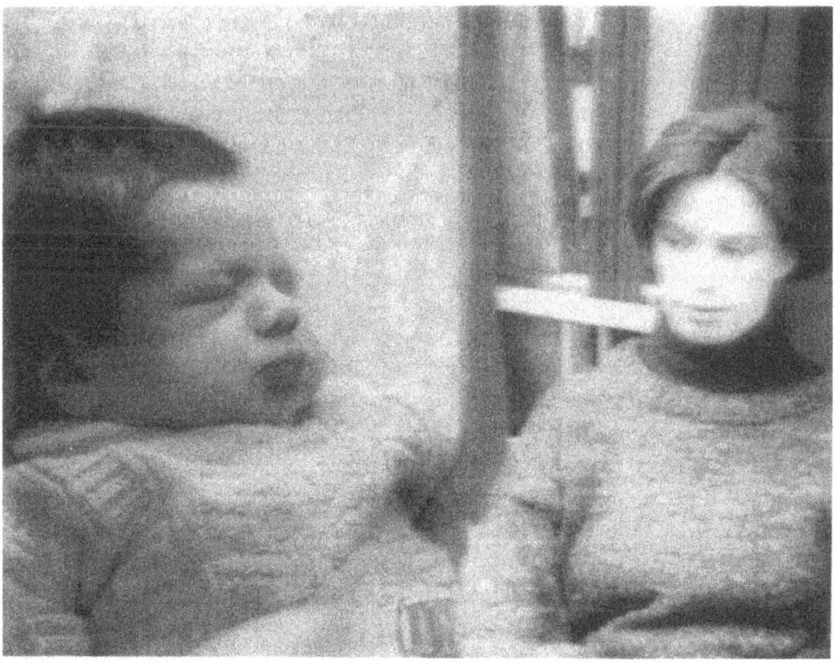

FIG. 1.1b. Neonatal facial expression in response to sucrose solution.

and bitter tastes. They also seem to respond differently to different concentrations of the "aversive" stimuli. It is not clear from the research data whether neonates can actually differentiate between the aversive stimuli, sour, bitter and salt, although it is assumed that they can. The seeming differentiation could be caused by differences in perceived strength of the different stimuli.

In summary, the neonate responds preferentially to a sweet taste, a taste frequently associated with energy dense food, and a taste that corresponds most closely to that of breast milk. Breast milk traditionally would have been the only source of nutrition available to the newborn infant. In contrast, the neonate does not ingest, or responds negatively to those tastes which are not likely to be associated, at this time of life, with sources of nutrition. Weak saline solutions are not found aversive, but then neither are they ingested, because they have been experienced before birth, as amniotic fluid.

Early learning

The young infant would seem to have innate preferences and aversions for specific tastes, but this is not to say that these innate preferences and aversions cannot be modified very rapidly by experience. Just as the neonate will modify the sucking reflex to accommodate the teat of a bottle rather than the nipple of a breast, so the singular, innate preference for a sweet taste can be modified by experience to accommodate other taste stimuli. There is at the moment only anecdotal evidence to support this claim, but this anecdotal evidence is readily available. Infants who are at risk for, or showing signs of atopic disorders, or have a gastro-intestinal intolerance of cow's milk, are often changed from standard cow's milk formula feeds to soya-milk, or a vegetable hydrolosate (Dobbing, 1987). Both of these two "alternative" milk feeds have a strong, and not very sweet, taste. The vegetable hydrolosate formula, in particular, has a very strong bitter taste. However, if infants are changed to these formulae quite soon after birth, there seems to be only a short period of adjustment before the feed is not only accepted, but preferred to other standard feeds (Harris, 1993b). We might say that the neonate learns or forms a conditioned preference for a normally aversive taste when it is paired with positive nutritional consequences. The rule would, therefore, seem to be that all responses towards a sweet taste should be positive, because a sweet taste is most likely to be paired with calorie density, but if normally aversive stimuli should prove to be paired with a high calorie intake, then the infant should form a preference for that taste. Given that even the taste of breast milk can change according to the food that the mother might have eaten, this would seem to be a good strategy (Menella & Beauchamp, 1991). In later childhood, of course, the flavours that are often found aversive by the infant, are preferred by the child; the acquired taste for salty foods (crisps) is probably the best example of this (Beauchamp, 1987).

Later learning

It is difficult to move from studies which observe the neonate's response to tastants in solution to studies which observe infants' responses to tastants in food. A linear model of development is often assumed: that which determines preference for a tastant added to water, will determine preference for tastants added to food. This is, however, an assumption that must be made with caution; a tastant added to food will enhance or change the inherent taste of that food, but there is no interaction effect when a tastant is added to water. It is also difficult to carry out the research which might disconfound the factors of development and medium, for although we can test older infants' responses to the taste of fluids, we cannot test young infants' responses to the taste of foods. It is not ethically acceptable to introduce solid foods to an infant before the age at which the parent would wish to start feeding the child such foods, or at an age when medical advice would proscribe it.

When testing infants to whom solid foods had been introduced we did, however, come up with some quite surprising data. Our first study, carried out when infants were 6 months old (Harris & Booth, 1987), found that some very rapid learning by exposure seemed to be taking place. We were primarily interested in this study in finding out how tastes found aversive by the neonate came to be preferred by the older child. Beauchamp, Cowart, and Moran (1986) noted that after 4 months of age infants seemed to prefer moderate concentrations of NaCl in solution to water, although before this age they would have found both the saline solution and the water equally aversive. Whereas the neonate finds a fairly strong salt solution aversive, the toddler finds a packet of salted crisps desirable. We concentrated, therefore, on 6-month-old infants' preference for the taste of salt. Using a tasteless rice based medium, infants' intake of cereal, with or without added salt, was measured across a four-day period. The infants were fed by the parent, who was given behavioural criteria upon which to base the decision to end the feed. The criteria were that the infant either refused a proffered spoonful on three consecutive offers, or cried. The amount of salt added to the cereal was equivalent to the upper level usually experienced in commercially available baby food. Most infants preferred the salted to the unsalted cereal. The infants' intake of the salted cereal was then correlated with the number of experiences of salty foods that the infant had had in the week prior to testing. Salty foods were defined as those with a salt content equal to, or greater than, that used in the test cereal. It was found that the number of experiences of salty foods in the week prior to testing correlated positively with the infants' preference for salted cereal in the test situation, $p < 0.001$ (Fig. 1.2).

Some form of change seemed, therefore, to have taken place over the first 6 months of life in the infant's preference for a salt taste. We assumed at first that the preference observed was merely a function of exposure, an effect noted anecdotally in young infants changed to bitter tasting milk. A learned preference takes place, of course, only where the effect of ingestion is positive; that is, it has positive nutritional consequences. Where the effect of

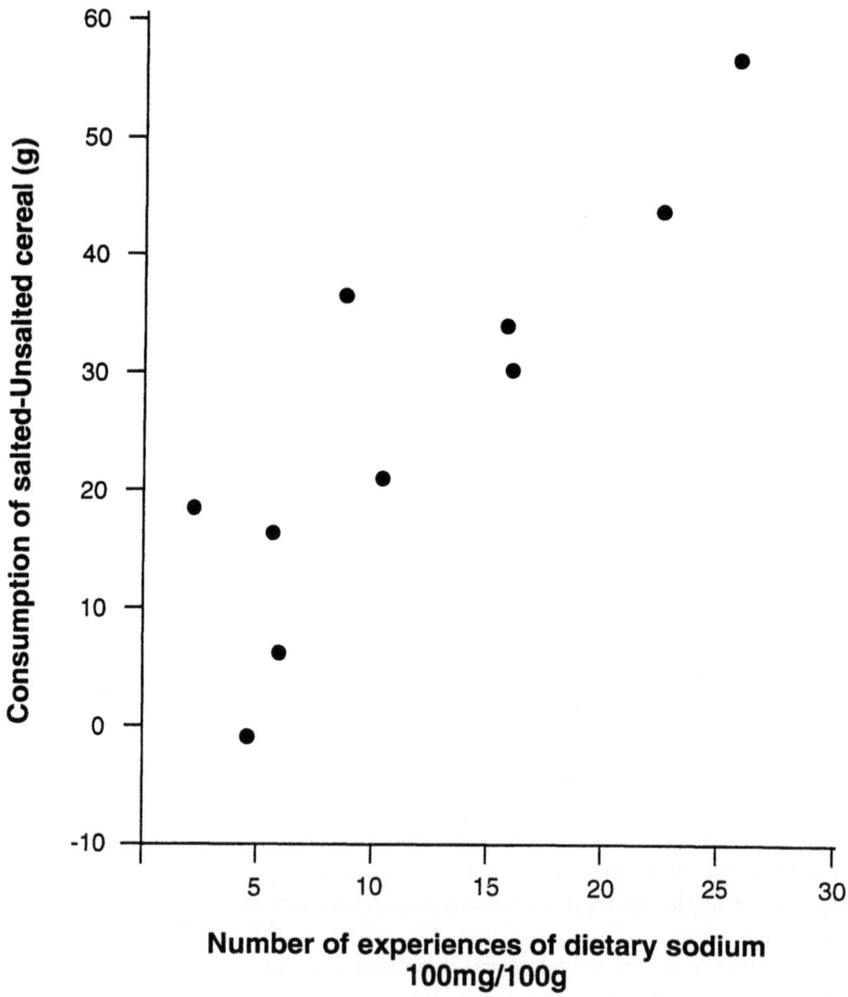

FIG. 1.2. Preference for salted cereal, and dietary experience, at 6 months. From Harris and Booth (1987). Copyright © John Wiley & Sons Ltd. Reproduced with permission.

ingestion is negative, where ingestion is paired with nausea or vomiting, then a learned aversion occurs (Pelchat & Rozin, 1982).

When we extended our studies to look at older and younger age groups, however, we found that this effect, of preference as a function of exposure, was not a linear trend. Children tested at one year of age, not this time with cereal which most of them refused, but with salted or unsalted mashed potato, still showed a preference for salted rather than unsalted food. This effect, however, was apparent only if the food medium was relatively novel to them (Harris & Booth, 1987). Those infants who had been fed mashed potato as part of their normal everyday diet, preferred the potato in the form in which it was usually fed to them; either salted or unsalted. This differs from the effect observed in the younger infants, all of whom had been fed rice-based cereal, and none of whom had been fed salted rice-based cereal. In the younger infants we could say that the preference for a salt taste generalised to all other foods offered to the infant. However, this generalisation was not observed in the older infants, or at least the generalisation was observed only with new foods; with known foods, the effect was different. The infants had learned to like foods in the form known to them, with the inherent taste, texture and smell. This phenomenon is noticed by many parents who feed their infant on a commercial baby food form of, say, cauliflower cheese, and then try to feed the child their own home-cooked version; the result is usually rejection. The infant already has an idea of how cauliflower cheese "should" taste, and will be reluctant to accept variations on the ideal. Indeed, most adults retain memories of how a specific recipe "should" taste, based on earlier or habitual experience.

In this learned preference for foods that have been fed habitually during the first year, we can observe the beginnings of neophobia, the reluctance of infants between the ages of 1 to 2 years even to taste unfamiliar foods (Birch & Marlin, 1982). Neophobia at this age might, at one time, have had survival value, in that the infant when mobile would be less likely to taste possible foodstuffs that had not already been given by adults within the social group, and would therefore be less likely to poison itself.

Late maturing innate preference

Research carried out on still younger infants than our 6-month-old group, also yielded data that did not fit in with the linear model. We might have assumed from our data on the taste preferences of 6-month-old infants, that gradual exposure to different tastes would increase the infant's preference for that taste. If this were true, young infants, with no experience of tastes other than those provided by breast milk, should show a preference for sweet or neutral tastes rather than a preference for a salt taste. A salt taste would be novel to them. When we tested breastfed infants for their preference for non-salted as opposed to salted cereal we found, however, that the reverse was true. Infants aged 16 to 25 weeks, and tested for their salt preference in the first solid food ever fed to them, showed a preference for salted cereal (Harris et al., 1990). This preference was, however, stronger in the younger infants; preference for salted cereal declined with age. Infants who had been breastfed until 19 weeks showed little difference in their intake of salted or unsalted cereal.

There are two possible explanations for these data. The first is that there is a late maturing innate mechanism, occurring somewhere around the third month of life, which facilitates acceptance of any new tastes. These preferences are then subsequently modified, and narrowed, by learning. The second hypothesis is that preferences for tastants in food are present from birth, but that we are unable to measure these because we are able to test the neonate only for their preferences for tastants in solution. The first hypothesis does fit in with some of the other "U"-shaped preference curves noted in other areas of perceptual preference. However, in contrast with other postulated "U"-shaped curves, such as that observed in schematic face preference, the change in taste acceptance of new, non-sweet stimuli, is from aversion at birth to acceptance at 3 months, and subsequently returning to aversion. One similarity, however, between taste and other perceptual modalities, is that the neonate will show a rapidly learned preference in the first days of life for salient stimuli to which they are frequently exposed.

If there is a late maturing innate acceptance of hitherto aversive tastes, then it is interesting to note that this developmental change occurs at the

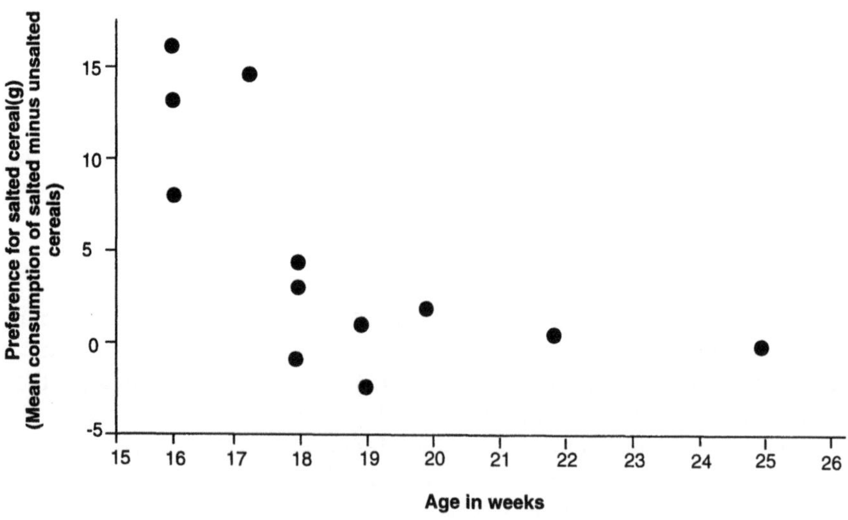

FIG. 1.3. Infant age and intake preference for salted cereal in 12 infants. From Harris et al., 1990. Copyright © (1990) by the American Psychological Association. Reprinted with permission.

same time (around 16 weeks) as most mothers are introducing solid foods to their infant. This introduction usually occurs at a time at which the infant needs to take in additional sources of energy. So, at the time new foods are usually introduced to the infant, there seems to be a heightened acceptance of new tastes.

FOOD ACCEPTANCE AND FADDINESS

The range of foods that we will accept and eat narrows as we get less hungry; that is, we will eat stale bread when starving but at the end of a large meal might be tempted only by a chocolate mint. It might be assumed, therefore, that the food refusal and food faddiness often observed in young children are merely points along the same continuum. As the child's appetite reduces so does the number of foods that the child will accept and eat. Clinical observation of children with eating problems does not, however, support this hypothesis. The dimensions small to large appetite, and narrow to wide range of foods accepted, seem to be orthogonal.

One dimension, poor to good appetite, is determined by the system which regulates appetite. Movement along this dimension indicates how well the infant is able to regulate intake according to energy needs, metabolic rate and growth velocity. The other dimension describes the continuum that

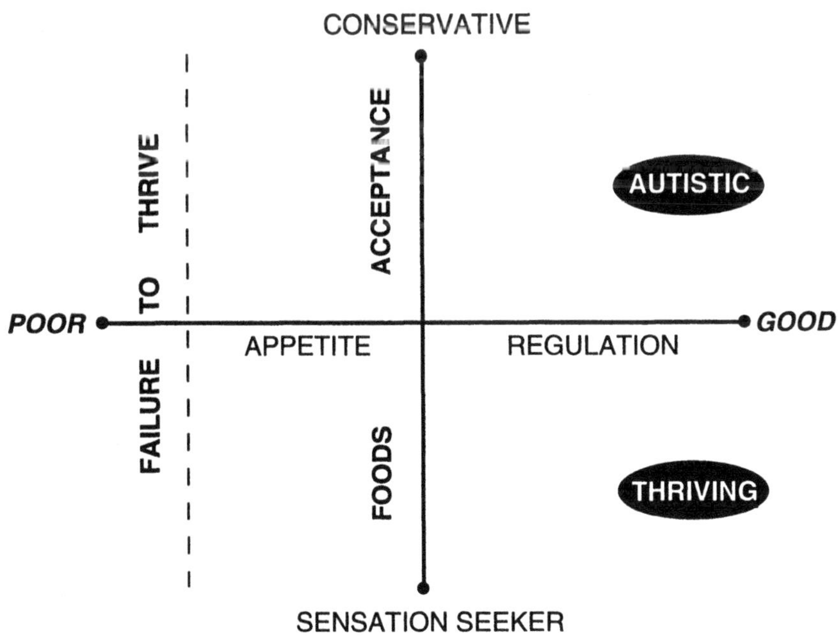

FIG. 1.4. Dimensions of appetite regulation and food acceptance.

ranges from those who will preferentially accept only a few foods to those (usually adults) who will seek out and eat foods usually prohibited by the disgust response. Whereas the first dimension might be seen as a function of the appetite regulatory system, the second could be seen as a dimension in temperament, perhaps akin to sensation-seeking and conservativism. Conservativism, or perseverance, in the types of food eaten can be observed in some children with autism. Such children will maintain an adequate calorie intake whilst restricting their diet to very few foods. Clinically one can also observe both children with small appetites and failure to thrive who eat a wide range of foods, and children with small appetites and failure to thrive who eat a very limited range of foods. This would suggest that food acceptance is not totally a function of appetite. In addition, non-clinical observations can be made of children with good appetites who eat all foods offered to them. However, very few pathologically hyperphagic children show dietary discrimination; they are, in fact, renowned for their lack of discrimination in that they will scavenge for food in waste bins. The general model of orthogonal dimensions must therefore be subject to modification by other environmental factors. In times of famine, or induced famine where satiety is not signalled, temperamental conservatism might be overridden, and anything edible will be eaten.

If we think of movement along either dimension as reflecting innate dispositions, we must still accept that both will be subject to modification by extrinsic, environmental factors. For example, if an infant finds mealtimes aversive then hunger signals might be ignored; food preferences can also be modified by availability or restraint. In early infancy, food preference is a function of exposure (Harris & Booth, 1987), and the more foods offered to the infant the more will be accepted as part of their diet, although of course this learned acceptance will show an interaction with the hypothesised temperament dimension. In later infancy, in the second year, cognitive factors also begin to operate. By this age children will imitate adults and eat new foods that they have seen an adult eat, although they might not have eaten the new food had it been offered to them without first observing adult modeling (Harper & Sanders, 1975). At this age we also see the beginning of such effects observed by Birch and Marlin (1984) and Shakespeare, Johnson, and Harris (1994) . Food which is cognitively "enhanced", either by being withheld or given as a reward food, or by being given in a positive social environment, is rated as nicer or consumed preferentially. However, food which is used as the instrumental component in a task/reward paradigm ("Eat up your vegetables and then you can have some icecream."), or food which is made freely available, is cognitively devalued and consumption decreases. Even infants who eat only a narrow range of foods often eat those foods which do not form part of a culturally "normal" meal, but which are given in "reward" situations and outside of the usual interactive mealtime. Crisps, grapes and ice-lollies are often the main components of the diet of the "few foods" child. These foods are not only given at first but rarely, they are also never forced upon the child.

Food acceptance in infancy can therefore be a function of temperament, early exposure, interactive and cognitive factors.

Food aversion

Specific food phobias, the disgust response and contamination fears, are not usually observed in children until they are older than 2 years of age. In fact Rozin (1989) suggests that children do not show the disgust response to foods for which their culture shows disgust, and contamination fears, until they are at least 5 years old. However, conditioned aversions can occur in the neonate. Humans will rapidly learn the association between the flavour of a food and its consequence (Rozin, 1986): a food which is paired with negative outcome will subsequently be avoided (Pelchat & Rozin, 1982). The most powerful "negative outcome" of ingestion is of course vomiting, often also associated with stomach pain and diarrhoea. In a recent pilot study, Ben Smith and I observed that the best predictor of feeding problems in later infancy in a clinical group was the presence of gastro-intestinal problems, such as vomiting and diarrhoea, in the neonatal period. One explanation for these data is that conditioned food aversions occur in early infancy which affect food acceptance in later infancy. Similar feeding problems seem to occur in clinical groups where there has been early and prolonged intubation or other medical procedures involving the mouth (Monahan, Shapiro, and Fox, 1988); or in both clinical and non-clinical groups where there has been force-feeding (Harris & Booth, 1992). An aversion to solid foods as opposed to milk can often be observed in children to whom solid foods have been introduced late in the first year (Harris et al., 1990; Illingworth & Lister, 1964). This could be because the period in which new foods and tastes are readily accepted has been missed, and the onset of neophobia has begun. Children to whom solid food has been introduced quite late can show both food aversion and failure to thrive. The ability to take in sufficient food to meet energy and growth needs is affected by an aversion to food, which stems not from negative association, but which is based upon the lack of early experience and exposure to foods.

CONCLUSION

There are quite clear stages in the development of appetite regulation, and taste and food acceptance, which are neccessary to accommodate the uncertain interaction between available energy and individual growth trajectories. It is also clear that the two systems are interdependent; infants require additional energy-dense foods at a time when they are prepared to accept such foods quite readily. If infants are not prepared to accept the foods available, then they cannot grow to their full potential, neither can they take the range of foods required by humans to achieve a "balanced" diet. There is also the possibility that although, at first, appetite is driven by growth needs, should there be insufficient food available, then the growth trajectory is reset. Infants who experience short-term disruptions to feeding will achieve "catch-up" growth and fulfil their original potential (Ashworth, 1969). Infants who experience long term calorie deprivation for a period prolonged past the first year appear not to make "catch-up" growth. This effect is often attributed to emotional deprivation (Skuse et al., 1992), but is also observed as an effect of famine within populations. We could hypothesise that the infant's set trajectory might recalibrate in response to an energy deficit; it is more important for life to be sustained than growth potential to be fulfilled. There might, therefore, be a three-way interaction between energy regulation, food acceptance and growth.

The development of taste and food preferences seems to follow stages observed in other areas of perceptual development. The infant has innate preferences and aversions which direct it towards salient environmental stimuli. In addition to this, and still in the neonatal period, the infant can rapidly learn a preference for tastes to which it is exposed, even if these are not initially preferred. By the age of at least 14 weeks, the infant is more active and open in acceptance. Many objects, including food, are explored with the mouth; other people eating are watched with close interest. A range of foods will eventually form the basis of the infant's diet and new foods will be less readily accepted. The acceptance of subsequent foods by older children is dependent then upon cognitive factors, although preference is still observed to be a function of exposure.

In both appetite regulation and the acquisition of food preferences, there is, therefore, a change in the first two years in the predominance of intrinsic or extrinsic cues. There is a change from hunger-driven feeding to an acceptance of cultural expectations about appropriate meal spacing and appropriate foods for different times of day. There is a change from innate or exposure-based learned preferences to preferences determined by cognitive factors. This is not to say, of course, that extrinsic and intrinsic factors do not both operate to some extent throughout life. One aspect of early feeding that this chapter has not addressed is the interaction between infant and parent, and its effect on the regulation of feeding and acquisition of food preference. The parent is, of course, usually active in providing extrinsic cues for the infant: "This is the time to eat"; "This food is nice". And such extrinsic cues are made available to the infant from birth. However, similar omissions are frequently made in other areas of developmental psychology; the aim of this chapter has been to concentrate on the infant's own contribution to food acceptance and appetite regulation.

REFERENCES

Ashworth, A. (1969). Growth rates in children recovering from malnutrition. *British Journal of Nutrition, 23*, 799–804.

Beauchamp, G.K. (1987). The human preference for excess salt. *American Scientist, 75*, 27–32.

Beachamp, G.K., Cowart, B., & Moran, M. (1986). Developmental changes in salt acceptability in human infants. *Developmental Psychology, 19*, 17–25.

Birch, L.L. (1993). Children, parents and food. *British Journal of Food, 95* (9), 11–16.

Birch, L.L. & Deysher, M. (1985). Conditioned and unconditioned caloric compensation: Evidence of self-regulation of food intake by young children. *Learning and Motivation, 16*, 341–55.

Birch, L.L. & Deysher, M. (1986). Caloric compensation and sensory specific satiety: Evidence of self-regulation of food intake by young children. *Appetite, 7*, 323–31.

Birch, L.L., Johnson, S.L., Andresen, G., Peters, J., & Schulte, M. (1991). The variability of young children's energy intake. *New England Journal of Medicine, 324*, 232–35.

Birch, L.L. & Marlin, D.W. (1982). I don't like it, I never tried it: Effects of exposure to food on two-year-old children's food preferences. *Appetite, 3*, 353–60.

Birch, L.L. & Marlin, D.W. (1984). Eating as a "means" activity in a contingency: Effects on young children's food preferences. *Child Development, 55*, 431–39.

Crook, C.K. (1978). Taste perception in the newborn infant. *Infant Behaviour and Development, 1*, 52–69.

Davies, D.P. & Evans, T.I. (1976). Failure to thrive at the breast. *Lancet, 11*, 1194–5.

Desor, J.A., Maller, O., & Andrews, K. (1975). Ingestive responses of human newborns to salty, sour and bitter stimuli. *Journal of Comparative and Physiological Psychology, 89* (8), 966–70.

DHSS (1983). *Present day practice in infant feeding*. Report on Health and Social Subjects, No. 20, HMSO, London.

Dobbing, J. (1987). *Food intolerance*. London: Balliere Tindal.

Eaton-Evans, J. & Dugdale, A.E. (1988). Sleep patterns of infants in the first year of life. *Archives of Diseases in Childhood, 63*, 647–9.

Fomon, S.J., Filer, L.J., Thomas, L.N., Anderson, T.A., & Nelson, S.E. (1969). Relationship between formula concentration and rate of growth of normal infants. *Journal of Nutrition, 98*, 241–54.

Fomon, S.J., Thomas, L.N., Filer, L. J., Anderson, T. A., & Nelson, S. E. (1976). Influence of fat and carbohydrate content of diet on food intake and growth of male infants. *Acta Paediatrica Scandinavica, 64*, 136–44.

Harper, L. & Sanders, K. (1975). The effects of adult's eating on young children's acceptance of unfamiliar foods. *Journal of Experimental Child Psychology, 20*, 206–14.

Harris, G. (1988). Determinants of the introduction of solid food. *Journal of Reproductive and Infant Psychology, 6*, 241–49.

Harris, G. (1993a). Feeding problems and their treatment. In I. St James Roberts, G. Harris, & D. Messer, *Infant crying, feeding and sleeping: development, problems and treatment*, 118–132. Herts: Harvester Wheatsheaf.

Harris, G. (1993b). Introducing the infant's first solid food. *British Food Journal, 95* (9), 7–10.

Harris, G. & Booth, D.A. (1987). Infants' preference for salt in food: Its dependence upon recent dietary experience. *Journal of Reproductive and Infant Psychology, 5*, 97–104.

Harris, G. & Booth, I.W. (1992). The nature and management of eating problems in preschool children. In P.J. Cooper & A. Stein (eds), *Feeding problems and eating disorders in children and adolescents* (pp. 61–84). Chur: Harwood Academic Publishers.

Harris, G., Thomas, A., & Booth, D.A. (1990). Development of salt taste in infancy. *Developmental Psychology, 26* (4), 534–8.

Hunt, J.N. (1980). A possible relation between the regulation of gastric emptying and food intake. *American Journal of Physiology, 2*, 1–4.

Illingworth, R.S. & Lister, J. (1964). The critical or sensitive period with specific reference to certain feeding problems in infants and children. *Journal of Pediatrics, 65*, 839–48.

Keesey, R.E. (1978). Set-points and body weight regulation. *Psychiatric clinics of North America, 1*, 523–43.

Logue, A.W. (1991). *The psychology of eating and drinking*. New York: Freeman.

McIntosh, J. (1986). Weaning practices in a sample of working-class primaparea. *Childcare, health and development, 12*, 215–26.

Maller, O. & Desor, J.A. (1973). Effect of taste on ingestion by human newborns. In J.F. Bosna, (ed.) *Fourth symposium on oral sensation and perception* (pp. 292–303). Washington DC: US Government Printing Office.

Matheny, R.J., Birch, L.L., & Picciano, M.F. (1990). Control of milk intake by human milk fed infants: Relationship between feeding size and interval. *Developmental Psychobiology, 23*, 511–18.

Menella, J.A. & Beauchamp, G. K. (1991). Maternal diet alters the sensory qualities of human milk and the nursling's behaviour. *Pediatrics, 88* (4), 737–44.

Monahan, P., Shapiro, B., & Fox, C. (1988). Effect of tube feeding on oral function. *Developmental Medicine and Child Neurology, 57*, 7–12.

Pelchat, M.L. & Rozin, P. (1982). The special role of nausea in the acquisition of food dislikes by humans. *Appetite, 3*, 341–51.

Pliner, P. (1982). The effects of mere exposure on liking for edible substances. *Appetite, 3*, 353–60.

Rosenstein, R. & Oster, H. (1988). Differential facial responses to four basic tastes in newborns. *Child Development, 59*, 1555–68.

Rozin, P. (1986). One trial acquired likes and dislikes in humans: Disgust as a US, food predominance and negative learning predominance. *Learning and Motivation, 17*,180–89.

Rozin, P. (1989). The role of learning in the acquisition of food preference by humans. In R. Shepherd (ed.), *Handbook of the psychophysiology of human eating* (pp. 205–230). Chichester: Wiley.

Shakespeare, A., Johnson, R., & Harris, G. (1994). *Naughty but Nice*. Paper given at BPS Annual Developmental Section Conference, Portsmouth, September.

Skuse, D., Wolke, D., & Reilly, S. (1992). Failure to thrive: Clinical and developmental aspects. In H. Remschmidt and M. Schmidt (eds), *Child and youth psychiatry: European perspectives*, Vol. II. *Developmental psychopathology*. Lewiston: Hogrefe & Huber.

Waterlow, J.C. & Thomson, A.M. (1979). Observations on the adequacy of breast-feeding. *Lancet, 2*, 238–41.

Whitehead, R.G. (1985). Infant physiology, nutritional requirements and lactational adequacy. *American Journal of Clinical Nutrition, 41*, 447–58.

Zaiwalla, Z. & Stein, A. (1993). The physiology of sleep in infants and young children. In I. St James Roberts, G. Harris, & D. Messer (eds), *Infant crying, feeding and sleeping: development, problems and treatment*, 135–149. Hemel Hempstead: Harvester Wheatsheaf.

2 Visual Perception and its Organisation in Early Infancy

Alan Slater
Department of Psychology, Washington Singer Laboratories, University of Exeter, UK.

INTRODUCTION

With respect to visual perception, the world that we experience is immensely complex, consisting of many entities whose surfaces are a potentially bewildering array of overlapping textures, colours, contrasts and contours, undergoing constant change as their position relative to the observer changes. However, we do not perceive a world of fleeting, unconnected retinal images; rather, we perceive objects that move and change in an organised and coherent manner.

Speculation about the many organisational principles that contribute to the perceived coherence and stability of the visually perceived world has been around for hundreds of years, and these speculations gave rise to one of the longest running debates in psychology and vision research, concerning the question of whether perception is innate or learned. The oldest theory of perceptual learning was put forward by the philosopher George Berkeley in *A new theory of vision* published in 1709. He claimed that the distance of objects, or "distance of itself", cannot be perceived directly, because the image on the retina is flat and two-dimensional. Given that the retinal image of an object changes "as you approach to, and recede from the tangible object'" such that "it has no fixed or determinate greatness", it follows that the sense of vision provides constantly changing and ambiguous information both about distance and about an object's true size. Therefore, the argument continues, "the judgement we make of the distance of an object, viewed with both eyes, is entirely the result of experience".

More recent theorists, who similarly emphasised the extreme perceptual limitations of infants, were Hebb and Piaget. Hebb (1949) acknowledged that "the idea that one has to learn to see a triangle must sound extremely improbable" (p. 31) but argued that perception of even such simple shapes is a result of complex learning. Piaget said of the young infant: "The world is a world of pictures, lacking in depth or constancy, permanence or identity which disappear or reappear capriciously." (1954, p. 3); and: "Perception of light exists from birth and consequently the reflexes which insure the adaptation of this perception (the pupillary and palpebral reflexes, both to light). All the rest (perception of forms, sizes, positions, distances, prominence, etc.) is acquired through the combination of reflex activity with higher activities." (1953, p. 62).

The obvious alternative to a perceptual learning account of visual development is to adopt a nativist view that the ability to perceive a stable, organised world is an innate property of the visual system, and to claim that babies perceive the world in much the same way that adults do. One of the first researchers to carry out scientific investigations into perceptual organisation in infancy was Bower (1966), and he concluded "that infants can in fact register most of the information an adult can register but can handle less of the information than adults can." (p. 10).

Answers to the many questions about the origins and development of visual organisation awaited the development of procedures and methodologies to test infants' perceptual abilities, and in the last 30 years a large number of relevant infant studies have been reported. In general, these studies have given rise to conceptions of the "competent infant", since the perceptual world of young infants has been found to be surprisingly well organised. While we can now reject extreme empiricist views of perceptual development, the picture of infant visual perception that is emerging is complex: some aspects of perceptual organisation are present at birth, while others show considerable development through infancy. Several types of visual organisation that are found in early infancy are discussed here, under the headings, *Shape and size constancy*, *Form perception*, *Biomechanical motion*, and *Perception of objects*.

SHAPE AND SIZE CONSTANCY

As objects move they change in orientation, or slant, relative to an observer, and when they change in distance their retinal image size changes: an adult 12 feet away gives a retinal image that is half the size of that subtended by the same person at 6 feet from the observer. In order for the baby to make sense of these changes some degree of shape and size constancy—perception of objects' real shapes and sizes regardless of changes in orientation and retinal image size—needs to be present in visual perception.

Bower's early experiments

The first evidence for the presence of these constancies in early infancy was presented by Tom Bower (1966). He used conditioning procedures in which 2-month-old infants were conditioned to give a head-turn response in the presence of one stimulus (the conditioned stimulus), and they were then tested for their responses to stimuli that differed in their orientations, distances, and retinal and real sizes from the conditioned stimulus. The stimuli that elicited the most head-turn responses on these test trials should be those that appeared to the infants to be most like the conditioned stimulus. What he found was that the infants gave more responses to objects that were the same shape and size as the conditioned stimulus, even though their orientations and distances from the infants varied: that is, his 2-month-olds were responding to the objects' *real*, rather than retinal, shapes and sizes, and were therefore displaying shape and size constancy. Even this early an attainment, however, still leaves open the question of whether or not learning is involved: "even eight weeks gives a lot of opportunity for visual experience" (Gibson, 1970, p. 104). Recent findings argue for the presence of both of these constancies at birth, and these are discussed next.

Shape constancy and slant perception

Slater and Morison (1985) described two experiments on shape constancy and slant perception in the newborn baby. In the first, using a preferential looking procedure, newborns' preferences for one stimulus, an outline square, were found to change in a consistent manner with changes in slant, when it was shown paired with an outline trapezium that remained in the fronto-parallel plane relative to the infants: as the orientation of the square shifted progressively away from the frontal plane it became less and less preferred. This was a clear demonstration that changes to stimulus slant are detected by newborns, and that such changes can cause highly systematic changes to their looking behaviour.

In the second experiment newborns (an average of 2 days old) were desensitised to changes in slant during familiarisation trials, and during these trials each infant was shown either a square or a trapezium (see Fig. 2.1). On the test trials that followed, the square and the trapezium were paired together, the familiar shape being in a different slant than any shown earlier, and every one of the twelve newborns tested looked more at the novel shape. This indicates that the old shape was perceived as being old in spite of looking different, which suggests that newborn babies have shape constancy.

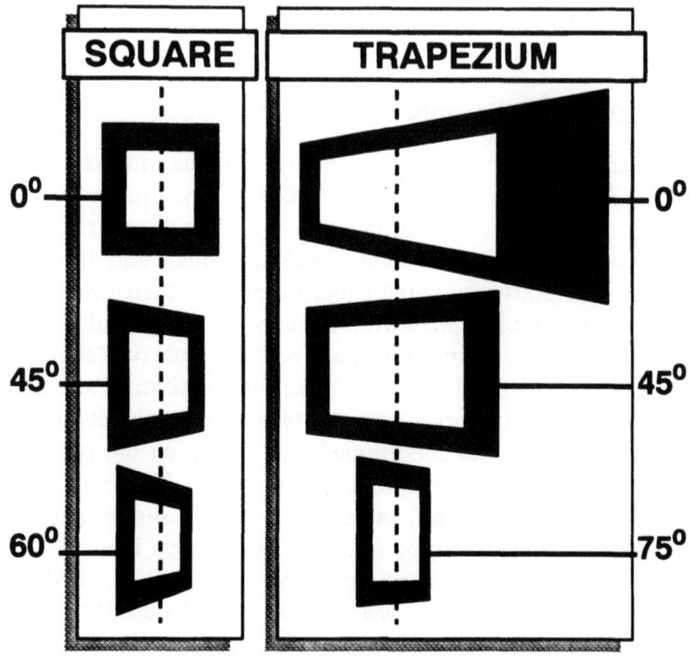

FIG. 2.1. The stimulus slants presented to newborn infants during familiarisation trials by Slater and Morison (1985). The familiarisation stimulus (for half the infants the square, for half the trapezium) was shown in six slants; the ones shown here and their mirror images.

Size constancy and response to retinal size

Figure 2.2 shows a newborn baby being tested in experiments on size constancy (Slater et al., 1990): the stimuli used in these experiments were cubes, one being half the size of the other. In the first (of two) experiments a preferential looking procedure was used and the infants were shown several pairings of cubes which varied in their sizes and distances from them. Highly consistent preferences were found, which could be described in terms of a simple rule: "Look longest at the stimulus which gives the largest retinal image size, regardless of its distance or real size." One pairing where neither cube was preferred was where the large cube was shown at twice the distance of the small one, and therefore their retinal sizes were identical (this pairing is shown in Fig. 2.2). These results are convincing evidence that newborns could base their responding on the basis of retinal size alone; indeed, when the different sized cubes' retinal sizes were the same, no preference was found. However, in the second experiment newborns were desensitised to changes in the distance (and hence retinal size) of a constant-sized cube during familiarisation trials, and subsequently they strongly preferred a different-sized cube to the familiar one.

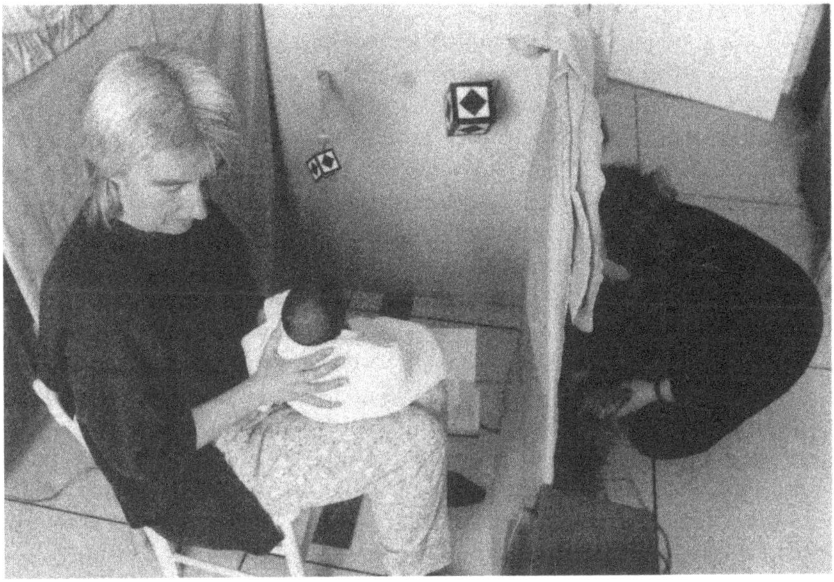

FIG. 2.2. A newborn baby being tested in a size constancy experiment

Overview

The findings from these studies demonstrate both a sensitivity to changes in slant and retinal size, and also the ability to perceive objective, real shape and size: that is, shape and size constancy are organising features of perception that are present at birth.

FORM PERCEPTION

The terms "figure", "pattern", "shape", and "form"' are often used interchangeably, and Zusne (1970, p. 1) commented that "Form, like love, is a many-splendored thing ... there is no agreement on what is meant by form, in spite of the tacit agreement that there is". Given this uncertainty it is worth mentioning that most theories of form perception have been concerned with static, achromatic, two- or three-dimensional figures that can stand as figures in a figure–ground relationship, and it is infants' detection of, and response to, these types of stimuli that are considered here.

Perception of simple shapes

It would be impossible for a functional visual system *not* to respond to at least some variations in stimulus shape, and we know that newborn babies make a variety of such discriminations (see Chapter 9 by Slater and Butterworth).

The findings from these studies are often not easy to interpret. The problem is the following: when a newborn baby discriminates between, say, a circle and a cross, it is possible that they might be making the discrimination on the basis of detecting the different orientations of the lines that make up the stimuli, rather than seeing the circle and cross as whole figures. An experiment by Cohen and Younger (1984) illustrates the problem. Six- and 14-week-old infants were habituated to a simple stimulus consisting of two lines which made either an acute (45°) or an obtuse (135°) angle. On subsequent test trials a clear age difference was found. The 6-week-olds dishabituated to a change in the *orientation* of the lines (where the angle remained unchanged) but not to a change in angle alone, while the 14-week-olds did the opposite in that they recovered attention to a change in *angle*, but not to a change in orientation (the test stimuli of Fig. 2.3 illustrate the sorts of stimuli used). This is a strong suggestion that shape perception in infants 6 weeks and younger may be dominated by attention to "low-order" variables of stimulation such as orientation, and that the rudiments of form perception emerge after this age.

The findings from a study by Slater, Mattock, Brown, and Bremner (1991a) questioned this conclusion. Newborn infants were shown either an acute or an obtuse angle which changed its orientation on each of six habituation or familiarisation trials (see Fig. 2.3). The purpose of these trials was to desensitise the infants to what would otherwise be the important cue of orientation—effectively asking the infants, "Can you detect the invariant cue of angle size?" On subsequent test trials all the infants looked more at the novel angle, suggesting that from birth infants *are* able to perceive angular relationships, which are possibly the basic elements or building blocks of form perception: certainly, they were responding to some invariant property of stimulation that was *not* orientation. However, Cohen (cited in Slater et al., 1991a) has suggested a "blob theory" of early visual perception that can perhaps account for these results without requiring any degree of form perception at birth. He argued that newborn visual acuity may be sufficiently poor that "their responses may have been based on the relative size of the blob at the apex of the angle rather than on the angular relationship between the two line segments." (p. 405).

The virtual impossibility of eliminating alternative, non- form interpretations of stimulus discriminations is the reason why an understanding of the origins of form perception has remained elusive. Other findings are perhaps more convincing in suggesting that form perception is present either at birth, or shortly after. These are considered next.

Stimulus compounds

All visual stimuli contain separate features that occur at the same spatial location, and which the mature perceiver "binds together" as a whole. With such an ability we see, for example, a red square or a green triangle, while

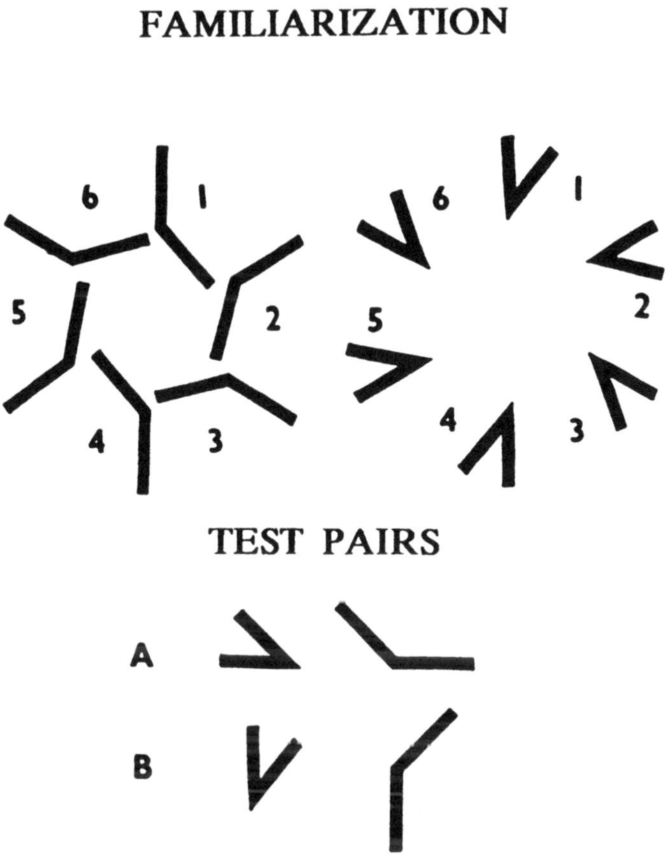

FIG. 2.3. Familiarisation and test stimuli used in an experiment on form perception. Half the infants were familiarised to the six variations of the obtuse angle (upper left), half to the six variations of the acute angle (upper right). On the test trials each infant was shown either pair A or pair B.

without it we would see redness, squareness, greenness and triangularity as separate, unrelated stimulus properties. Triesman (1985; 1986) has argued that different perceptual operations are required, (1) to analyse separate stimulus properties; and (2) to recombine them into wholes. She argued that in visual processing, "the early parsing of the visual field is mediated by separate properties, not by particular combinations of properties. That is, analysis of properties and parts precedes their synthesis." (1986, p. 117). Triesman's suggestion was not intended as a developmental theory, but it might well have such implications. For example, it has been argued that "the very early perception of two-dimensional stimuli must be regarded as the perception of parts rather than wholes" (Salapatek, 1975, p. 226). An understanding of the development of these abilities is critical to an understanding of form perception, since form perception can be said to be present only when the perceiver is able to synthesise parts of a stimulus into a whole.

An experiment that was designed to test whether newborn babies have the ability to process and remember stimulus compounds was reported by Slater et al. (1991b). An achromatic representation of the chromatic stimuli shown to the babies is given in Fig. 2.4. The babies were familiarised, on successive trials, to two separate stimuli. For half the infants these were a green diagonal (GD) stripe and a red vertical (RV) stripe: the other babies were familiarised to GV and RD. In the former case there are two novel compounds of these elements, RD and GV. On test trials the babies were shown one of the familiar compounds paired with one of the novel ones (Fig. 2.4 shows the four possible test pairings), and all of the 14 babies tested looked longest at the novel compound, the average novelty preferences being 76% of the looking time. Note that these novelty preferences could not have resulted if the infants had processed only the separate properties of the stimuli shown on the familiarisation trials, because the novel compounds consisted of stimulus properties (colour and orientation) that they had seen

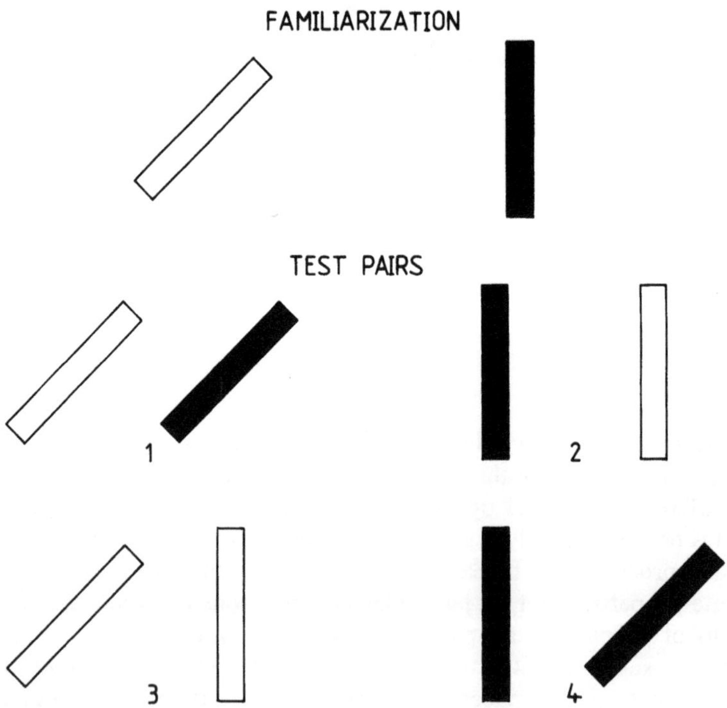

FIG. 2.4. Following familiarisation (above) to two stimuli which differ in colour and orientation, there are four possible test pairings of familiar and novel compounds (below).

before. Thus, the findings are clear evidence that newborn babies can process and remember simple stimulus compounds.

Subjective contours

Subjective contours are illusory contours that are perceived "in the absence of any physical gradient of change in the display" (Ghim, 1990; Kanizsa, 1979). An example of this illusion is pattern A in Fig. 2.5, and most adults

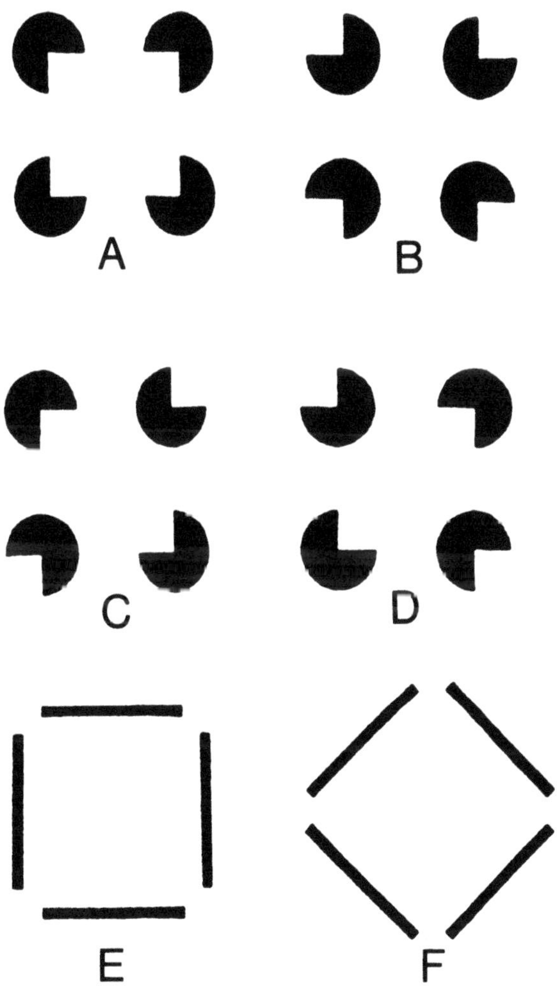

FIG. 2.5. Stimuli used by Ghim (1990). Pattern A (SC) produces subjective contours forming a square. Patterns B. C and D (NSC) do not produce subjective contours. The incomplete lines (E and F) were used in the test phase of an experiment following habituation to pattern A.

see the contours of a square, despite the fact that the contours are physically absent. Perception of subjective contours is dependent upon the alignment of the inducing elements, and when this alignment is altered the subjective contour of the square is not seen, as is apparent by looking at patterns B,C and D, in Fig. 2.5.

Convincing evidence that 3- and 4-month-olds perceive subjective contours was provided in a series of experiments by Ghim (1990), from whose work Fig. 2.5 is derived. In one experimental condition the infants were familiarised either to a pattern containing a subjective contour (SC, pattern A, Fig. 2.5) or to a non-subjective contour (NSC, one of patterns B,C or D). Following this, the infants in the SC group discriminated SC from the NSC pattern, but those in the NSC group did not discriminate between the familiarised pattern and a different NSC pattern. This leads to the conclusion that "the difference between patterns with and without subjective contours is greater than the differences between patterns without subjective contours" (Ghim, 1990, p. 225).

In Ghim's (1990) fourth experiment, infants were familiarised to the SC pattern, and on the test trials they were shown patterns E and F of Fig. 2.5, and they gave a strong novelty preference for the incomplete diamond pattern, indicating that the incomplete squarelike pattern (E, Fig. 2.5) was seen as being similar to the SC pattern. Note that this novelty preference could not have resulted if the infants had attended only to the corners in the SC pattern, since there are no corners in either of patterns E and F (Fig. 2.5). Ghim suggested that the results "support contentions that the infants filled in the gaps among the aligned elements in the SC pattern, and ... add to our belief that infants have knowledge of the complete form and its components after viewing patterns that produce forms with subjective contours" (pp. 243 & 244).

Categories and prototypes

In order to reduce, and make sense of, the infinite variety of our perceptions and experiences an essential human activity is categorisation: categorisation occurs whenever two or more perceptually discriminable stimuli or events are treated as being equivalent, and we allocate them to particular categories in terms of their possession (or absence) of invariant features that define the category. Infants, too, categorise their experiences, and two aspects of categorisation relevant to form perception are discussed here: orientation, and form prototypes.[1]

[1] The formation of face prototypes, and categorisation of faces in terms of gender and expressions, is discussed in Chapter 9 by Slater and Butterworth.

Bomba (1984) familiarised 4-month-olds to a number of striped patterns which differed in their orientations, but were all obliques (as opposed to being horizontal or vertical), and found that on test trials the infants generalised what they had seen to a differently oriented oblique (in the sense that they perceived a vertical pattern as novel and a new oblique as familiar). In a separate study he demonstrated that the infants could discriminate between the orientations of the different oblique patterns used, which suggests that in the former experiment the infants were treating the different obliques as members of the same category.

For many perceptual categories we can define a *prototype*, which is an ideal or average member, and the prototypical member is used both to organise and to define other members of the population and to select new members from incoming stimuli. An "ideal" prototype might be, for example, a perfect square, with equal length sides and right angles; the category "dog" does not have an ideal prototype, but something like a mongrel or cross-breed would be closer to an "average" prototypical member of the class than some of the more exotic sub-species. Categorisation and formation of prototypes go hand-in-hand: it is not possible to categorise stimuli unless one has some idea of what the defining characteristics of the category are.

Bomba and Siqueland (1983) investigated infants' categories based on form. In their experiments the stimuli used were prototypes of a square, a diamond, and a triangle, and various distortions of these figures (these are shown in Fig. 2.6). They found that 3- and 4-month-old infants discriminated between each prototype and its distorted versions, but treated the prototype as the "best" exemplar of the category: thus, when the babies were familiarised to a number of "distorted" exemplars of one of the categories, and later shown one of the distorted versions paired with the previously unseen prototype, they treated the prototype as the familiar stimulus. This was demonstrated by an apparently paradoxical novelty preference for the "old" (previously-seen) exemplar. Bomba and Siqueland call this a prototype effect, and their interpretation is this: the infants perceive the previously unseen prototype to be the best example of the recently acquired form category, and it is therefore more easily recognised (more familiar) than the distorted exemplar, although the latter had been seen earlier.

Overview

The evidence presented here suggests that form perception is present very early in infant perception. Newborn infants perceive stimulus compounds, which argues against a view that they respond to parts of stimuli separately. By 3 months of age (or maybe earlier since younger infants have not been

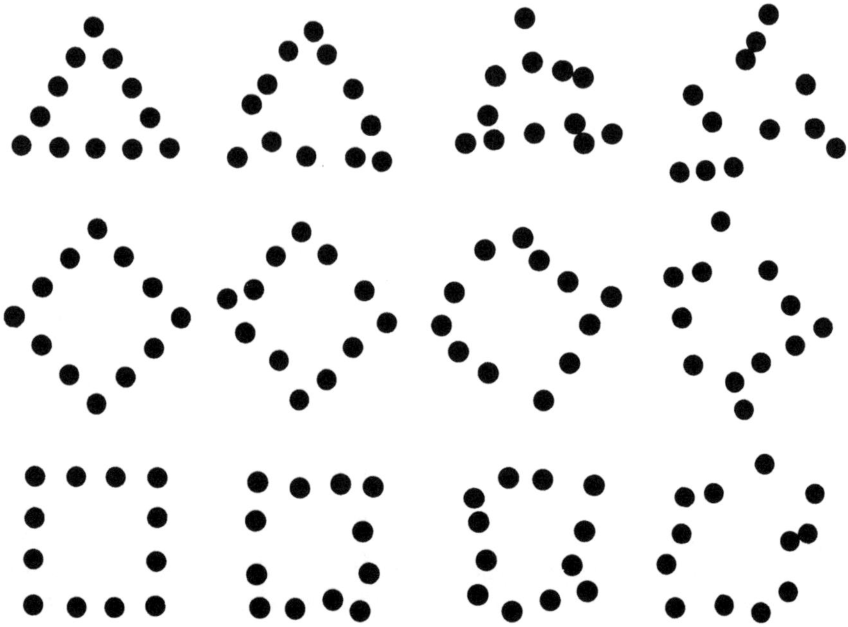

FIG. 2.6. Examples of the stimuli used by Bomba and Siqueland (1983). The prototypical triangle, diamond and square are on the left, and from left to right are distortions of each. Copyright Academic Press. Reprinted with permission.

tested) infants perceive subjective contours: this ability would not be possible without form perception since it requires the integration of perceptual information from two or more of the subjective contour's inducing elements. Also by 3 months infants have been shown to exhibit prototypicality effects, in the sense of extracting a form prototype from "distorted" exemplars of the form. As was discussed in the previous section, newborn babies detect the invariant (real) shapes of stimuli that vary in slant, and the real sizes of stimuli that vary in distance, and it is difficult to imagine how it would be possible to display shape and size constancy *without* having something like form perception.

BIOMECHANICAL MOTION

A great deal of the research on perceptual development (and much of that discussed earlier) has involved showing static two-dimensional stimuli to infants. However, in the real world outside the laboratory, the information that impinges upon the senses is constantly changing, and it can reasonably be argued that many organisational aspects of visual perception are best studied under conditions of change: "If the infant has any preadapted means for extracting information about the environment, it is reasonable to believe that the information to be extracted is an ecologically relevant one for the infant'" (von Hofsten, 1983, pp. 243-4).

One such aspect of organisation is the ability to detect the information contained in changing point-light displays. Biomechanical motions are the motions that correspond to the movements of a person (or other biological organism) when walking or displaying some other activity, and a point-light display to depict such motion is usually produced by filming a person in the dark who has points of light attached to their major joints (ankles, knees, hip, shoulder, elbows and wrists) and the head. Figure 2.7A shows such a display corresponding to a single, static frame, and observers shown such a picture are usually unaware that it represents a human form. However, if the displays are moving (as depicted in Fig. 2.7B) an impressive range of discriminations is easily made: adults perceive the human form, and from displays with durations as short as 200msec. can specify its actions (walking, running, dancing, press-ups, etc.); adults are also capable of recognising friends and detecting gender from such displays (Bertenthal, 1993).

A variety of evidence suggests that babies are sensitive to the biomechanical motions specified by the dynamic transitions of point-light

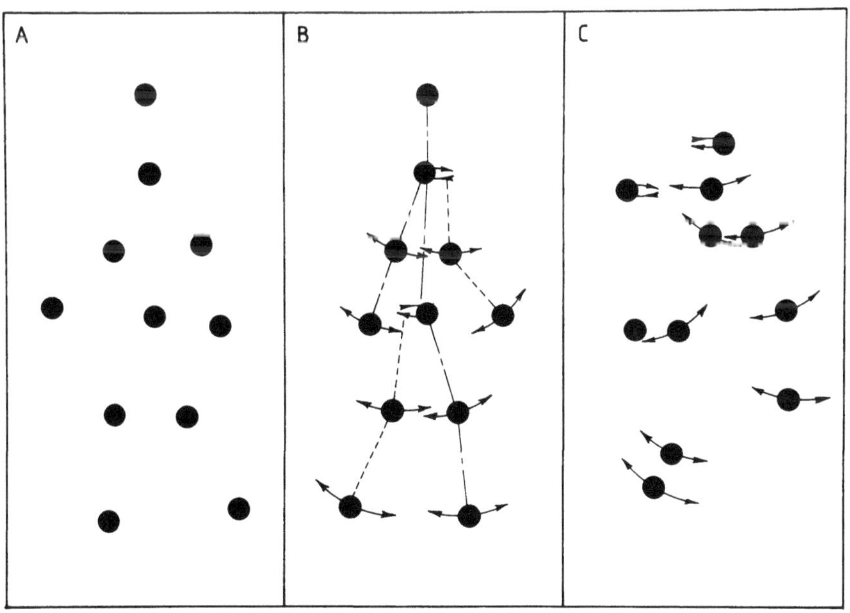

FIG. 2.7. Three possible point-light displays (derived from Bertenthal, 1993). (A) A static display is not usually seen as representing a human form. (B) When the display is in coherent motion, as depicted here, it is easily seen as a person walking. (C) If the point-light display moves in an incoherent or random motion perception tends to be of a swarm of bees.

displays. Displays have been produced in which the points of light depict an upright walker either with the lights at the major joints (a "coherent" display), or with the lights moving "off the joint", or randomly, or in a less coherent fashion than that of a real walker: random patterns (depicted in Fig. 2.7C) often suggest a moving swarm of bees. With these sorts of displays it has been found that infants as young as 3 months (younger ones have not been tested) choose to look at a coherent display in preference to a random one, and that they more readily encode "coherent" than "incoherent" displays, implying that they are detecting the organisational structure of the coherent one (Bertenthal, Proffitt, Spetner, & Thomas, 1985; Fox & McDaniels, 1982).

A number of processing constraints allow perception of biomechanical motions, as distinct from other forms of motion: for instance, the wrist can move back and forth and up and down relative to the position of the elbow, but it is always a fixed distance from the elbow. Bertenthal (1993) discusses infants' awareness of these constraints and suggests that "there is no clear lower-bound on the age at which they are first implemented. It is therefore quite reasonable to propose that these constraints are part of the intrinsic organization of the visual system." (p. 209).

There is an intriguing age change between 3 and 5 months in infants" responses to these displays. Babies of 3 months discriminate between an upright and an upside down point-light walker, as do older babies. However, 3-month-olds also discriminate between an upside down point-light walker and a random pattern of lights, but 5- and 7-month-olds do not (Bertenthal & Davis, 1988). Bertenthal and Davis's interpretation of this apparently paradoxical, age change is that by 5 months infants are responding to the perceived familiarity of the displays; that is, as a result of experience and accumulated knowledge they recognise the upright display as a human walker, while the inverted and random displays are perceived equivalently because they are both unfamiliar. By 5 months of age, therefore, infants respond to these sorts of displays at a higher level of processing: perception interacts with prior knowledge to affect what is perceived. A similar "inversion effect" emerges around 4 or 5 months in infants' perception of faces: "when upright faces were discriminated by 5- to 6-month-old infants, the same stimuli inverted 180° were not" (Fagan, 1979, p. 97; this "inversion effect" is discussed in more detail in Chapter 9). Adults also have difficulties with inverted point-light displays: an inverted display is often seen as several objects in motion, whereas the upright one is invariably seen as a moving person.

Bertenthal (1993) cites two additional studies in support of the claim that knowledge affects infants' perception of biomechanical motion. In the first, Fox and McDaniels (1982) found that 6-month-olds discriminated a point-light display of moving hands from an incoherent or perturbed display, but neither 2- nor 4-month-olds did so. Bertenthal points out that visually directed reaching appears around 5 months of age, so only the 6-month-olds would have had sufficient familiarity with the hands to allow the displays to be discriminated on the basis of familiarity. In the second study, Bertenthal (1993) showed 3- and 5-month-olds point-light displays of a person producing different types of walking (walking, marching, walking while waving arms above the head) and found that the older, but not the younger, infants generalised to a different display of the upright walker. This suggests that the 5-month-olds had extracted some *general* property of the human gait that was not specific to any individual display.

Thus, it seems that very young infants distinguish between biological and nonbiological motion on the basis of the *perceptual* information, or perceptual processing constraints, contained in the former, and that by 5 months of age, knowledge, or *conceptual* information, constrains the interpretation of the human gait, and by 6 months, movement of the hands. That is, as infants gain experience of the world they begin to respond to perceptual displays on the basis of their *meaning* in addition to (and sometimes in opposition to) their perceptual structure: there is "a change in the level of organization at which the representation is made accessible to cognitive processing" (Bertenthal, 1993, p. 210). These knowledge-based constraints will appear at different ages depending on the ways infants interact with and learn about their perceived world. As Bertenthal (1993, p. 210) puts it: "There is no reason to think that a particular age possesses some unique status. Some percepts will not interact with stored knowledge until later ages, whereas others might be constrained at earlier ages. The deciding factor is the relevance and accessibility of stored knowledge."

PERCEPTION OF OBJECTS

As is the case with most aspects of visual development, widely differing views have been expressed concerning infants' perception of objects. Piaget has been most influential in initiating research into object perception in infants, and he argued that infants' understanding of objects develops slowly over 6 stages of infancy, so that, for instance during the first 3 stages (until around 9 months) the expression "out of sight, out of mind" is literally close to the infant's understanding: they assume that objects cease to exist when they cease to visible, and exist again when they reappear. The main evidence Piaget used in drawing this conclusion was infants' failure to search manually for hidden objects. However, it has been suggested by several researchers that infants may have an early understanding of objects that is simply obscured by their difficulties in initiating manual search (see, for example, Bower, 1974; Baillargeon, Spelke, & Wasserman, 1985). Accordingly, in testing Piaget's and others' theories of object understanding, researchers have often used indices that do not depend on the production of actions. Two of these indices that are discussed here are infants' novelty preferences, and their surprise reactions to unexpected or impossible events.

A major focus of research into object perception has been infants' understanding of partly occluded, and of hidden objects. Kellman and his colleagues (Kellman & Spelke, 1983; Kellman, Spelke, & Short, 1986) investigated infants' perception of partly occluded objects using an habituation–dishabituation procedure. Four-month-old infants were habituated to a stimulus (usually a rod) which moved back and forth behind a central occluder, so that only the top and bottom of the rod was visible (as in the upper part of Fig. 2.8). On subsequent test trials the babies were shown two test displays without the occluder, one being a complete rod, the other being the top and bottom parts of the rod, with a gap where the occluder had been (the test trials, Fig. 2.8). Either of these test stimuli could have been the familiarised stimulus, and the question of interest was, what had the babies been seeing on the habituation trials? If they had seen the rod as being connected or complete behind the block, then the two-rod pieces would be the novel of the two test stimuli. If they had seen the rod as being in two separate parts, then the complete rod would be novel. Their results clearly supported the first of these possibilities: the babies spent more time looking at the two-rod pieces on the test trials.

Slater, Mattock, and Brown (1990) used the same stimulus arrangement, and replicated Kellman's findings with 4-month-olds. However, they obtained the opposite result with newborn infants, a looking preference for the *complete* rod. However, given the poor visual acuity of newborn infants, it seemed possible that their apparent limitations might have resulted from an inability to detect the depth relationship between the occluder and the rod: if they were not aware that the rod was *behind* the occluder, then perhaps there would be nothing to "fill in". Slater, Johnson, Kellman, and Spelke (1994) carried out a test of this possibility, by testing newborn babies with a large gap between the rod and occluder (a separation of 15cm), and the babies in this study gave the same novelty response as those in Slater et al. (1990); that is, following habituation to the occluded rod, the complete rod was novel, the two-rod pieces familiar.

Why do newborn infants perceive these displays differently from 4-month-olds? There are several sources of information that can be used to interpret occluded object displays. These include: (1) the common motion; (2) the perceptual similarity of the two rod pieces; (3) the clear depth relationship between the rod and occluder; and (4) the fact that two separate pieces are seen, never one. The first three of these cues specify completeness, whilst the fourth specifies two units, and it could be that at birth perception is dominated by that which is visible, not by that which can be inferred; that is, cue (4) predominates. We know that infants' ability to use these and other

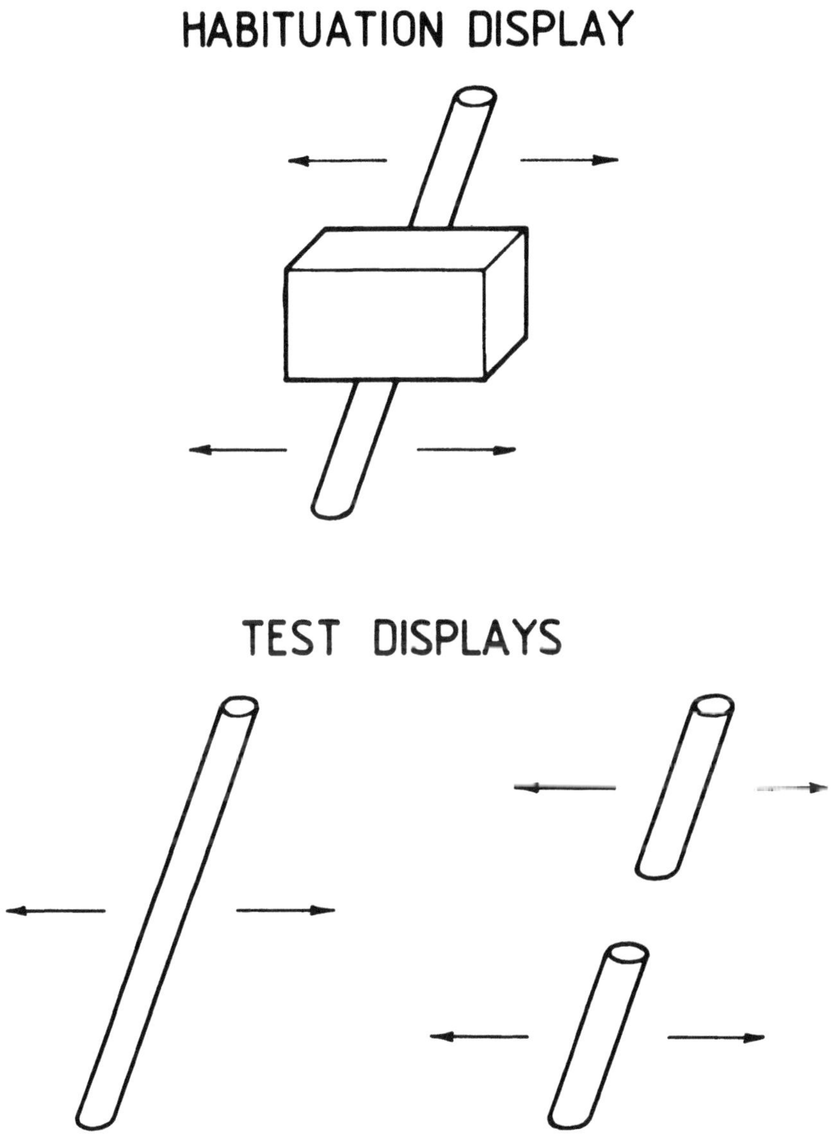

FIG. 2.8. Habituation and test displays in experiments on infants' perception of partly occluded objects. During habituation the rod moved back and forth behind the occluder.

cues changes in early infancy. One demonstration of this is by Johnson and Nanez (1995) who used a similar stimulus display and found that 2-month-olds looked equally at both test displays, suggesting that perhaps they were in a transitional period and were unsure as to whether there was one or two rods behind the occluder; but when Johnson and Aslin (1995) reduced the width of the occluder, so that more of the rod was visible, their 2-month-olds *did* show completion in that on the test trials they now looked more at the rod pieces.

In the studies described so far, the rod pieces were undergoing common motion behind the occluder on the habituation trials, and we know that this can be a powerful cue for object completion: if two perceptually dissimilar stimuli are seen undergoing common motion 4-month-olds expect them to be one complete stimulus (Kellman & Spelke, 1983). In recent studies, Amy Needham (1994, in collaboration with Renee Baillargeon) asked the question, "How do infants segregate *stationary* occluded objects?". She showed 4- and 4½-month-olds (the age difference turns out to be important!) two different displays (each infant saw only one of them): (1) an *identical condition* where the left and right sides of an object (or objects) were visible behind an occluder, and both sides were the same shape and colour; (2) a *nonidentical condition* where the left and right sides of an object (or objects) were again visible but this time the two sides were different shapes and sizes (see Fig. 2.9).

When adults are shown these displays they expect there to be *one* object in the identical condition, and two separate objects in the nonidentical condition. In order to find out what assumptions babies make about these displays, Needham first familiarised the babies to the stationary displays.

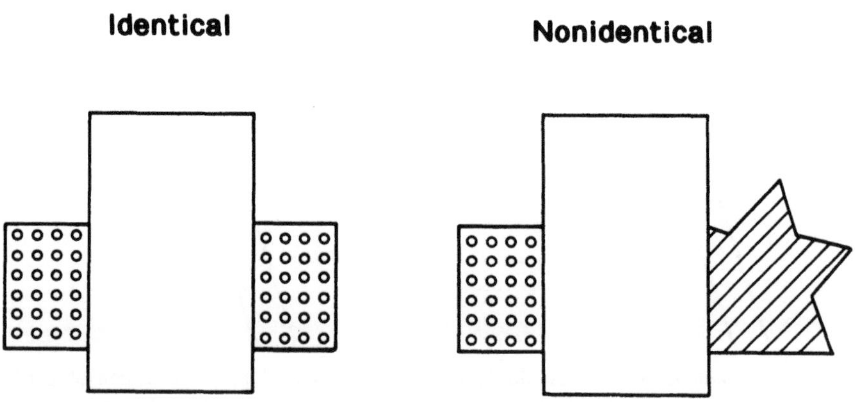

FIG. 2.9. When two object parts are seen behind an occluder, 4½-month-olds assume there to be one object if the parts are identical (left), and two if the parts are dissimilar (right). Derived from Needham, 1994.

Then a gloved hand reached into the compartment and grasped the right-hand portion of the occluded object(s), and the hand then caused the displays to move in one of two ways, either (a) *Move together*, in which both left and right sides moved simultaneously, or (b) *Move apart*, in which the right-hand portion moved but the left-hand portion remained where it was: this revealed to the babies that the display was composed of either one (move together) or two (move apart) objects. Needham measured the amount of time the babies spent looking at the new displays, reasoning that if they did *not* expect a particular outcome they would watch longer than if they *did* expect that outcome. Infants 4½-months old gave a clear finding: they looked longest at the move-apart event in the *identical* condition, and longest at the move-together in the *nonidentical* condition, indicating that, like adults, they expected one object in the former case and two in the latter. However, infants just two weeks younger (the 4-month-olds) gave a different response in the *identical* condition: they looked about equally at the move-apart and move-together events, suggesting that they were not sure whether the visible portions were one or two objects. There are several possible interpretations of this age difference that Needham considers: round about 4 months babies begin accurate visually directed reaching, and maybe their extra experience at reaching for and manipulating objects accounts for the difference; also around 4 months, or a little earlier, babies become more likely when holding a new object to hold it in front of their eyes for visual inspection, whereas younger infants are likely to bring the object to their mouths. These changes and possibly others could mean that in as short a space of time as one or two weeks "infants could be learning about the relative importance or reliability of different kinds of information" (Needham, 1994)

The story so far seems to be that newborn babies are aware of many of the cues, or types of information that tell the mature perceiver about objects' characteristics and properties, but they do not appear to understand which cues specify what. An early appearing cue is that of common motion, and by 2 months of age the common optical displacement of two visible object pieces behind an occluder specifies a unitary object. Common motion seems to be such a powerful cue in specifying object unity that Kellman (1993, p. 135) refers to it as a "primitive process" which is either innate or maturational in origin, rather than resulting from experience. By 4 months infants expect two stationary visible object portions, that are different in shape and size and seen either side of an occluder, to be two objects rather than one, but seem unsure about how to interpret two visible portions that are similar in shape and size. This uncertainty has been removed by 4½ months, by which age similarity specifies one object.

The studies described so far concern infants' understanding of partly occluded objects, and the sorts of information they use to infer that one or more objects are behind an occluder. When objects are *completely* occluded (that is, invisible!) an important question becomes, at what age can they infer or represent its existence? An experiment by Baillargeon et al (1985) suggests that they can do this long before 9 months of age (the age suggested by Piaget). They tested 5-month-old babies who were shown a solid block, which was hidden by a screen, but which should have prevented or blocked a moving drawbridge from travelling through a full 180° rotation. The babies spent more time looking at an "impossible" complete 180° rotation than at a "possible" 120° rotation, suggesting that they were aware not only of the block's continued existence behind the screen, but that they "knew" that its presence constituted an obstacle to the drawbridge's movement.

By 6 or 7 months infants can represent some of the properties of occluded objects. In several experiments Baillargeon and her colleagues (described by Baillargeon, 1993) have found that 6- and 7-month-olds understand: (1) that a moving toy car cannot pass through a solid object; (2) that a rotating screen will rotate through a shorter arc if there is a tall object behind the screen than if there is a small one (the screen should stop when it reaches the object); (3) that a rotating screen can compress a soft object (a ball of gauze), but not a hard one (a wooden box). In (1) the infants were first shown the object which was then occluded by a screen prior to rolling the car; and in (2) and (3) the rotating screen itself occluded the object as it reached the point of impact. Thus, the infants were representing the physical and spatial properties of *invisible* objects.

CONCLUSIONS

The newborn baby enters the world visually naïve but possessed of a number of means with which to make sense of the visual world. It is likely that rudimentary form perception is present at birth, in the sense that the infant perceives wholes rather than only separate elements, or parts, of two-dimensional visual stimuli. By 3 months of age, and possibly earlier, infants have been shown to perceive subjective contours, which is a clear indication of form perception, since such an ability requires the integration of two or more of the contour's inducing elements Newborns perceive stimulus compounds in that they "bind together" the components of a stimulus (such as colour and orientation) rather than processing these components or parts separately. Newborn infants also detect invariant information about shape and size across changes to slant or orientation, and retinal size, indicating that size and shape constancy are present at birth.

These processing abilities give some idea of the ways in which the young infant structures and organises perceptual information. While the newborn's world is not the "blooming, buzzing confusion" described by William James (1890, p. 488), it is clearly not the same as ours: "It must certainly lack associations, meaning and familiarity." (Gordon, 1989, p. 70). As we may expect, learning and experience soon have an effect on perceptual organisation. Even in the newborn period, infants learn about the visual stimuli they see, as indicated by a preference for novel stimulation after having been habituated to a now-familiar stimulus. Within hours from birth enough has been learned about the mother's face for it to be preferred to a stranger's. The prototypicality effects mentioned earlier result from experience with exemplars of the appropriate categories: since such prototypes can be formed very quickly in an experimental setting with 3-month-olds it may be that their formation is an innate biological predisposition of the visual system. Bertenthal (1993) has similarly argued that an awareness of the processing constraints that allow perception of biomechanical motions may be part of the intrinsic organisation of the visual system, but it is not until about 5 months that infants can recognise an appropriate display as being of a human walker.

Many types of visual organisation take time to develop, and this is particularly well illustrated with respect to infants' understanding of objects. It is clear that infants' awareness and use of the different sources of information that specify object properties undergoes change in the early months. This understanding develops without the lengthy period of manual exploration that Piaget (1954) emphasised, and those researchers who choose not to rely on infants' limited manual abilities are finding that from as early as 2 months infants become able to reason about the physical world. The picture that is developing is of "infants as budding intuitive physicists, capable of detecting, interpreting, and predicting physical outcomes", whose "physical world ... appears very similar to that of adults" (Baillargeon, 1993, p. 311).

ACKNOWLEDGEMENTS

The author's research was supported by the following grants from the Economic and Social Research Council: C00230028/ 2114/ 2278; RC00232466. Earlier versions of this chapter have been published in Walsh and Kulikowsi (eds), *Perceptual constancies: why things look as they do* (Cambridge University Press), and in Vital-Durand, Atkinson and Braddick (eds), *Infant vision* (Oxford University Press).

REFERENCES

Baillargeon, R., Spelke, E.S., & Wasserman, S. (1985). Object permanence in 5-month-old infants. *Cognition, 20*, 191–208.

Baillargeon, R. (1993). The object concept revisited: New directions in the investigation of infants' physical knowledge. In C. Granrud (ed.), *Visual perception and cognition in infancy*. Hillsdale, N.J.: Lawrence Erlbaum Associates Inc.

Bertenthal, B.I. (1993). Infants' perception of biomechanical motions: Intrinsic image and knowledge-based constraints. In C. Granrud (ed.), *Visual perception and cognition in infancy*. Hillsdale, N.J.: Lawrence Erlbaum Associates Inc.

Bertenthal, B.I. & Davis, P. (1988). *Dynamical pattern analysis predicts recognition and discrimination of biomechanical motions*. Paper presented at the annual meeting of the Psychonomic Society, Chicago, Illinois.

Bertenthal, B.I., Proffitt, D.R., Spetner, N.B., & Thomas, M.A. (1985). The development of infant sensitivity to biomechanical motions. *Child Development*, *56*, 531–543.

Bomba, P.C. (1984). The development of orientation categories between 2 and 4 months of age. *Journal of Experimental Child Psychology*, *37*, 609–636.

Bomba, P.C. & Siqueland, E.R. (1983). The nature and structure of infant form categories. *Journal of Experimental Child Psychology*, *35*, 294–328.

Bower, T.G.R. (1966). The visual world of infants. *Scientific American*, *215*(6), 80–92.

Bower, T.G.R. (1974). *Development in infancy*. San Francisco: Freeman.

Cohen, L.B. & Younger, B.A. (1984). Infant perception of angular relations. *Infant Behavior and Development*, *7*, 37–47.

Fagan, J.F. (1979). The origins of facial pattern recognition. In M.H. Bornstein & W. Kessen (eds), *Psychological development from infancy: image to intention*. Hillsdale, N.J.: Lawrence Erlbaum Associates Inc.

Fox, R. & McDaniels, C. (1982). The perception of biological motion by human infants. *Science*, *218*, 486–487.

Ghim, H-R. (1990). Evidence for perceptual organization in infants: Perception of subjective contours by young infants. *Infant Behavior and Development*, *13*, 221–248.

Gibson, E.J. (1970). The development of perception as an adaptive process. *American Scientist*, *58*, 98–107.

Gordon, I.E.G. (1989). *Theories of visual perception*. New York: Wiley.

Hebb, D.O. (1949). *The organization of behavior*. New York: Wiley.

James, W. (1890). *The principles of psychology*, Vol. 2. New York: Holt.

Johnson, S.P. & Aslin, R. (1995). Perception of object unity in 2-month-old infants. *Developmental Psychology*, 31, 739–745.

Johnson, S.P. & Nanez, J.E. (1995). Young infants' perception of object unity in two-dimensional displays. *Infant Behavior and Development*, 18, 133–143.

Kanizsa, G. (1979). *Organization in vision: essays on gestalt perception*. New York: Praeger.

Kellman, P.J. (1993). Kinematic foundations of infant visual perception. In C. Granrud (ed.), *Visual perception and cognition in infancy*. Hillsdale, N.J.: Lawrence Erlbaum Associates Inc.

Kellman, P.J. & Spelke, E.S. (1983). Perception of partly occluded objects in infancy. *Cognitive Psychology*, *15*, 483–524.

Kellman, P.J., Spelke, E.S., & Short, K.R. (1986). Infant perception of object unity from translatory motion in depth and vertical translation. *Child Development*, *57*, 72–86.

Needham, A. (1994). *Infants' use of perceptual similarity when segregating partly occluded objects during the fourth month of life*. Paper presented at the 9th International Conference on Infant Studies (ICIS), 2–5 June, Paris.

Piaget, J. (1953). *The origins of intelligence in the child*. London: Routledge and Kegan Paul.

Piaget, J. (1954). *The construction of reality in the child*. New York: Basic Books.

Salapatek, P. (1975). Pattern perception in infancy. In L.B. Cohen & P. Salapatek (eds), *Infant perception: from sensation to cognition*, Vol 1. New York: Academic Press.

Slater, A., Johnson, S.P., Kellman, P.J., & Spelke, E.S. (1994). The role of three-dimensional depth cues in infants' perception of partly occluded objects. *Early Development and Parenting*, *3*, 187–191.

Slater, A.M. & Morison, V. (1985). Shape constancy and slant perception at birth. *Perception*, *14*, 337–344.

Slater, A.M., Mattock, A., & Brown, E. (1990). Size constancy at birth: Newborn infants' responses to retinal and real size. *Journal of Experimental Child Psychology*, *49*, 314–322.

Slater, A.M., Mattock, A., Brown, E., & Bremner, J.G. (1991a). Form perception at birth:

Cohen and Younger (1984) revisited. *Journal of Experimental Child Psychology, 51*, 395–405.
Slater, A.M., Mattock, A., Brown, E., Burnham, D., & Young, A.W. (1991b). Visual processing of stimulus compounds in newborn babies. *Perception, 20*, 29–33.
Slater, A., Morison, V., Somers, M., Mattock, A., Brown, E., & Taylor, D. (1990). Newborn and older infants' perception of partly occluded objects. *Infant Behavior and Development, 13*, 33–49.
Triesman, A. (1985). Preattentive processing in vision. *Computer Vision, Graphics, and Image Processing, 31*, 156–177.
Triesman, A. (1986). Features and objects in visual processing. *Scientific American, 255* (5), 106–115.
von Hofsten, C. (1983). Foundations for perceptual development. In L.P. Lipsitt & C.K. Rovee-Collier (eds), *Advances in infancy research*, Vol. 2. Norwood, N.J.: Ablex.
Zusne, L. (1970). *Visual perception of form*. New York: Academic Press.

3 From Perception to Cognition

J. Gavin Bremner
Department of Psychology, University of Lancaster, UK.

Alan Slater's chapter in this section has presented evidence indicating that young infants are sophisticated perceivers of the world. And it is easy to read much of the evidence as indicating that in many important ways young infants perceive the world much in the same way as adults. Of course, some limitations of perception do exist. For instance, it is clear that very young infants have much poorer visual acuity than older ones. Also, current evidence suggests that it is some months before infants are capable of using binocular cues to depth. However, it seems that these basic limitations do not fundamentally change the nature of what is perceived. It appears that newborns are capable of using motion parallax as a dynamic cue to depth. And it is even possible that limited visual acuity early in life serves as a selective filter that directs the infant to the higher order properties of visual stimulation. A more important limitation in the neonatal period relates to perceptual completion. Whereas infants a few months old appear to "fill in" the occluded parts of an object (Kellman & Spelke, 1983), newborns apparently do not (Slater et al., 1990). In other words, newborn visual perception appears to be limited to what is visible at a particular time. This, in turn, is liable to create limitations in the infant's perception and knowledge of objects.

However, it is only a matter of a few months before most of these limitations are overcome, and the weight of evidence suggests that by 2 or 3 months, infants perceive the world objectively and possess quite advanced awareness of the principles governing the physical world. This raises important questions about the nature of cognitive development in infancy. Specifically, if the world is objectively perceived, is there any need to postulate the development of cognitive structures that conventional theory suggests are needed to interpret subjective sense data? It appears that this aspect of cognitivism is mistaken. On the other hand, however, a look at infants' activities in the everyday world reveals that much does develop. The primary problem for theories of infant development is to explain these developmental changes in the light of the evidence for perceptual sophistication in early infancy.

In this chapter, I shall begin by returning to some of the key evidence from Alan Slater's chapter that points to perceptual competence in early infancy, focusing in particular on evidence that seems to show that the Piagetian account of infant development is in error. However, I shall suggest that, given the nature of the response variables in studies of early perception, it is not clear what we should call the abilities that are revealed, since they generally do not appear in self-initiated behaviour. This will lead on to an investigation of possible developmental processes, a central point being that although infants appear perceptually competent at an early age, they do not display this competence in spontaneous purposive behaviour until some time later. I shall suggest that this delay cannot be explained simply as an issue of motor development, with infants gradually displaying more of their pre-existing competence as motor development proceeds. The psychologically exciting aspects of motor development are not so much the motor developments themselves, but the links that are formed between perceptual and motor activity to make action effective in the world. Thus, a central point about the argument will be that development in infancy is very much to do with the formation of links between pre-existing objective perception and emerging action, so that knowledge of the world implicit in perception eventually becomes explicit knowledge in the sense that it can be used to guide action. Expanding on this, I shall suggest that some aspects of this developmental process may be explained quite well through a marriage of *dynamic systems theory* and Gibsonian theory of *direct perception*, but I shall also suggest that there are some developmental phenomena that are not so clearly explained in these terms. The conclusion will be that there are multiple processes at work in the development of links between perception and action, and that further research may reveal that only some of these deserve to be thought of as cognitive processes in the conventional sense.

NEWBORNS AS OBJECTIVE PERCEIVERS

The development of a range of techniques based on habituation of looking has undoubtedly revolutionised our knowledge of the visual perceptual capabilities of young infants. Development of infant-controlled procedures has made it possible to use these techniques successfully with newborns. Additionally, the version generally referred to as the *familiarisation–novelty* technique has brought enormous power to this sort of investigation. This version involves presenting various exemplars of the same pattern, shape or object during habituation, and then testing for novelty preference between a novel exemplar of the habituated stimulus and a novel stimulus. For instance, various versions of a cross, varying in angular relationship, line thickness, etc., can be presented during habituation, followed by a test of novelty preference on a pairing of a novel version of the cross and a new shape, such as a triangle. This is basically the design used by Slater, Morison, and Rose (1983) with newborns, and the power of the technique lies in the fact that by suitable selection of habituation stimuli, the experimenter can effectively select the level of stimulus variable by holding it constant during habituation while varying lower levels of stimulus variable. If infants habituate to this stimulus variable and show a preference for a novel stimulus that differs on this variable, then we know that infants are capable of processing and discriminating between stimuli at the level chosen.

Use of this technique has revealed that newborn infants discriminate between shapes such as cross, circle and triangle (Slater et al., 1983), and that they are capable of processing shapes at least to the level of differences in angular relationships between elements (Slater, Mattock, Brown, & Bremner, 1991). More important for theories of cognitive development, however, are applications of the same technique to test for shape and size constancy.

Shape constancy describes our ability to see a shape as constant despite the fact that its retinal image changes with its tilt in the viewing plane. And size constancy is to do with the fact that we perceive the size of an object as constant despite changes in its retinal image size resulting from changes in distance. These are fundamental perceptual constancies, since, as the viewer or objects move in the world, the retinal image from a given object changes in size and form. However, conventional theories of perceptual development promoted the notion that perception was initially based on retinal images, and that it was only through development or learning that the perceptual constancies became established and the perceiver began to perceive objects rather than images.

Some time ago, using an operant conditioning technique, Bower (1966) obtained evidence suggesting that both shape and size constancy were present in early infancy. However, subsequent work using habituation techniques did not reveal evidence for shape constancy before around 6 months (McKenzie, Tootell, & Day, 1980). Subsequent work modified the story, however, Slater and Morison (1985) habituated newborns to one shape presented at different tilts and then presented the same shape in a new tilt (and hence presenting a novel retinal image) paired with a novel shape (that presented a retinal image that had been encountered during habituation). Newborns looked more at the novel shape, good evidence for shape constancy. Similarly, Slater, Mattock, and Brown (1990) habituated infants to a particular object presented at different distances and then tested for novelty preference between the same object at a new distance and a differently sized object. Again, newborns showed size constancy by looking more at the novel size object. It appears that earlier studies failed to obtain size constancy in young infants because they did not vary object distance during habituation, a procedure that led infants to work at the level of object distance or retinal image size rather than true size.

These findings constitute probably the strongest evidence that even newborns perceive an objective world, at least as far as the "here and now" is concerned. So where does this leave Piaget's (1954) account of *sensorimotor* development, according to which objective knowledge of the world develops only gradually through action in the infant's environment? To take the specific examples that we have been looking at already, according to Piaget, knowledge of the principles and size constancy only emerged late in the first year through processes of sensorimotor construction. On the face of it, the evidence that newborns apply both shape and size constancy would appear to show that Piaget was fundamentally wrong. However, there are at least two reasons why we should not jump to this conclusion too readily. Firstly, Piaget did not claim that young infants were capable of processing only retinal images: although the term "image" appears in translation, a better translation is probably "picture" (in other places he uses the term "tableau") and there is never a hint that he is referring to retinal images. Secondly, and connected to this, in his work on infancy, Piaget was not concerned with perception of the world. Instead, as with the primary thrust of most of his work, he was interested in how infants developed knowledge.

HABITUATION STUDIES AND PERCEIVING VERSUS KNOWING

If recent research on early infant ability are studies of perception while Piaget was studying knowledge, it is important to know what, if anything, lies at the root of this distinction. It is clear that Piaget set high criteria for knowing: he said that it is one thing to act in accordance with a particular principle (say size constancy) and quite another to know it as such. In the light of a statement like this, it is not at all clear what Piaget would have made of the results of habituation studies, although I think it is unlikely that he would have concluded that they revealed knowledge. We can certainly say that these studies reveal response in accordance with particular principles but, Piaget apart, there is a real issue of what we should call the "abilities" that are so revealed. In habituation procedures, the response measure is time looking at the stimulus, a response that is only arbitrarily related to the stimulus variables in question. This is true of much of the infant perception work (and also recent work on cognitive ability by Baillargeon, Spelke and their colleagues; see Chapter 6). So from this standpoint, the newborn evidence indicates perception of the cues to depth, but not that the infant can use these cues to guide action on the world. And even if evidence of the latter sort were detected, possibly this would *still* not satisfy Piaget that we were dealing with real knowledge, since this would still be a case of acting in accordance with particular principles, and he could well call for stronger evidence of knowing the world as a three-dimensional place. Later on in this chapter, I shall suggest that a distinction between perceiving and using perceptual information to guide action is crucial, and that Piaget's distinction between acting in accordance with particular principles and knowing them as such is doubtful and may instead be incorporated in a general developmental account by considering different processes through which perception and action become linked.

THE THEORY OF DIRECT PERCEPTION

Although not presented initially as a developmental theory, Gibson's (1979) theory of *direct perception* is seen by many as the antithesis of the principles upon which Piaget's account is based. A basic principle of the theory is that the structure of the world is available in perceptual information picked up by the individual, particularly in the flow of perceptual information that results as the individual actively explores the environment. Perception is fundamentally a dynamic process which is continuous over time; and Gibson stresses that it is never a matter of analysis of static retinal images. Information about the objective nature of the world, its three-dimensionality etc., is contained in the dynamic perceptual flow, and there is no need to construct three-dimensionality through interpretation of depth cues. At first, it might appear that this account does not really bear on Piagetian questions, since this is a perceptual theory while he was interested in the development of knowledge. However, from the Gibsonian perspective, in an important sense perceiving *is* knowing. And this knowing extends beyond perception of the structure of the world to perception of *affordances*, that is, what possibilities particular structures offer the individual in terms of action. So in this respect, Gibsonian theory questions the very basis of Piaget's account. And this approach has many adherents in infancy research, probably at least in part because such an account makes it less surprising to find that young infants possess impressive awareness of the world.

Many workers are, however, uneasy about the *direct perception* approach, since although it says much about the availability of environmental structures and their "pick-up" through dynamic perceptual processes, it says little or nothing about the structures of the mind that are necessary to support direct perception. So although the approach is enormously useful in reigning us back from invoking representational processes as necessary prerequisites for all infant abilities, it leaves us in the dark about the minimum but undoubtedly necessary structures of the mind that are needed to support objective perception.

DYNAMIC SYSTEMS THEORY

It could be said that while some theories, including Piaget's, laid stress on processes and structures in the individual at the expense of environmental structures, Gibsonian theory laid too much stress on the availability of environmental structure to a dynamic perceiver, saying too little about the internal structures or processes. From this point if view, what is needed is a theoretical framework which gets the balance between environmental and organismic factors right. Dynamic systems theory stresses the need to analyse behaviour as the outcome of the functioning of a complex system. And what makes it a promising candidate for getting the balance right is that this system need not be located within the individual, but can extend to the wider system of the organism and environment in interaction. Additionally, the approach is extremely flexible, being essentially "content free" and applicable to any problem or "content area" in which a complex system is involved. I should say that this flexibility should also be a cause for caution, since the approach is an explanatory tool rather than a psychological theory in its own right. We thus have to be careful to "plug in" the appropriate psychological or biological concepts in order to apply it successfully.

The approach is described in detail in Chapter 4 by Brian Hopkins and George Butterworth, so I shall merely summarise some of the main principles that reveal its applicability to the present problem. A basic premise is that complex systems are self-organising: they arrive at new states simply through their own functioning. Also, it is claimed that the behaviour of a system can be understood only in terms of a complex interaction between different factors that contribute to the functioning of the system. For instance, Thelen and Ulrich (1991) point out that those studying motor activity are mistaken in seeking to explain it purely in terms of some neural substrate, since the complexity of the activity is contributed to as much by the biodynamic properties of the limbs and muscles as by the functional characteristics of the motor cortex. For instance, much of the complexity involved in walking effectively "falls out of" bipedal dynamics, and there is no need to look for a neural control system that holds the key to it all. This is an important point when we compare this approach to more conventional cognitive approaches, since the implication is that the behaviour of the system cannot be explained by recourse to some single element (such as a representational structure). Instead, behaviour is an emergent property of a whole system composed of psychological, biological and physical components. Systems "prefer" particular states of equilibrium, but (and here is where development comes in) they tend to progress towards states of lower stability and eventually to new states of equilibrium, under the influence of particular forces acting from within or outside the individual. Part of the explanatory power of this approach lies in the claim that complex new states and their behavioural manifestations can be triggered by changes in quite simple parameters.

Proponents of this approach claim that it can be applied at any level, from physical systems through to systems composed of physical, biological and psychological factors; and an important point is that, when performing a psychological analysis, physical and biological factors or constraints must also be included as part of the system. Thus, if we were considering intention in reaching, it would be necessary to treat the infant's intent as just one component of a system that includes the physical dynamics of the arm and hand, and the way the muscles are controlled by motor regions of the brain. An outcome of this sort of analysis is that it often emerges that quite complex behaviours do not call for a conventional neurophysiological or psychological interpretation in terms of some mental or neural "copy" or template for the act. Sure enough, there is a form of representation of the act, but it is distributed within the system and cannot be identified as residing in a particular place such as the brain.

The commonest application of the dynamic systems approach in the area of infant development has been to issues in motor development. Here it is claimed that complex motor achievements such as crawling, walking and grasping can be explained as emergent properties of a system composed of physical and biological factors or constraints. According to Thelen and Smith (1994), this does away with the need to assume a cortical pattern generator supporting action. They identify immediate advantages in the removal of the need to explain aspects of a motor sequence at a cortical level, since much of the patterning can be explained in terms of the biomechanics of the limbs. And so, although hypothetical neural structures or psychological factors such as representational ability can in principle be included as part of any system, recourse to parsimony leads these workers to see how far it is possible to go in explaining infant behaviour without recourse to mentalistic concepts. Thus, in much of the theorising, there seems little place for psychological structures as constituents of the infant's mind. And to the extent that they do exist, they are much more fluid and more like propensities towards certain states than like rigid structures.

This approach, of course, has its own problems. Application of the detailed analysis that it demands leads to a preoccupation with minute aspects of action, and it is easy to form the view that this approach is in danger of being unable to see the psychological wood for the physical and biological trees. But then we can apply the same critical analysis to more conventional approaches to ask whether they invoke traditional psychological concepts, such as representation, reasoning and inference, too readily when studying early infancy. There are certainly grounds to question whether data gathered from habituation procedures can be taken as evidence for mental representation, or reasoning, and yet these terms are often used in interpreting data from infants under 6 months. The issue is really about the appropriate level of analysis, and hence the appropriate terminology to apply to the phenomena observed in early infancy. And I shall suggest that, although there is a need for more or less conventional psychological explanation, this need may be limited to specific phenomena and to phenomena emerging later in infancy.

DYNAMIC SYSTEMS AND DIRECT PERCEPTION

Although the major application of dynamic systems has been in the study of motor development in infancy, there is scope for applying the same analysis in a broader way so that it incorporates perceptual activities. Indeed, this is already happening in the analysis of visually guided action. And there is general potential for a link-up between this approach and Gibsonian theory. Both are essentially ecological systems theories; and the advantage of the dynamic systems approach is that, through putting together action systems and perceptual systems as components of an overall system, it may be possible to fill in the blanks on the organism side of the equation that some identify as shortcomings of the Gibsonian account. In other words, it is possible that a dynamic systems analysis will identify the minimum structures of the system that are required to permit objective perception. Where I think there is clear utility to a marriage between direct perception and dynamic systems is when it comes to the Gibsonian concept of *affordance*. The notion involved in this concept is that in addition to perceiving the world objectively, individuals directly perceive the connections between features of the world and their own actions. In other words, with no need for mediating cognitive structures, they perceive the implications of environmental features for particular actions. A good example here is affordances of surfaces for locomotion. The notion is that organisms directly perceive whether or not particular surfaces support locomotion, and the point is that the affordance is determined not just by the properties of the surface but by the characteristics of the organism, its weight, style of locomotion and so on. Thus, while water affords locomotion for certain insects, it does not afford locomotion for most other species (although for them it may afford swimming; or maybe drowning). More important, from a developmental perspective, in the case of the newly walking infant, only quite flat and stable surfaces support this new and rather precarious activity. And the interesting thing is that these young walkers are capable of perceiving the surfaces that afford locomotion, avoiding those that do not (Gibson et al., 1987).

At first sight, direct perception of affordances seems implausible. They are not, after all, features of the world available to be picked up, but rather relationships between perceived features and the habits of the individual. This might lead us to the view that development of affordances must be a constructional process, in which representations of the relationship between perceived features and actions are built up. And as I shall indicate later, I think cognitive processes of this sort mediate the development of many affordances that relate to complex activities such as problem solving. However, dynamic systems may provide a simpler solution in the case of affordances relating to the more "automatic" aspects of behaviour. Savelsbergh and van der Kamp (1993) have provided a developmental model for the progressive detection of affordances by marrying direct perception with dynamic systems analysis of behavioural development. Basically, the notion is that the dynamic systems analysis must encompass the factors involved in the action system, the perceptual system, and those environmental features providing perceptual structure. As new action systems emerge, these mesh or do not mesh with certain features in the perceptual world. The mesh is reached through action, not as mental construction, but as an emergent property of the perceptuomotor system. It is maybe inappropriate to call this direct perception of affordances, since that lays too much stress on perceptual activities. But certainly, the model would have it that in an "automatic" fashion, the link between the structure of the world and the structure of action is detected through action that includes, but is not limited to, perceptual activity.

A good example here would be the case of early object manipulation. Prior to the development of a controlled reach and grasp sequence, infants certainly should be able to perceive differences in object size, a crucial variable determining whether or not an object can be grasped. However the "graspability" of an object is determined by the relationship between object size and the maximum finger–thumb separation that will achieve a successful grasp. It is possible that detection of this affordance arises through the natural meshing of perceived object features and the characteristics of action.

It has already been widely recognised that Gibson's ecological approach and the dynamic systems approach have much in common and might profitably be combined (Reed, 1982; Turvey, 1990). And recent ecological accounts of the development of affordances use terminology that has much in common with dynamic systems. For instance, Adolph, Eppler, and Gibson (1993) write, "An adequate description of an affordance entails specification of how action is constrained by the fit between environmental properties and action capabilities." However, there appears to be a tendency for the link to stop at the level of common terminology, since the Gibsonian school tend to stick with rather vague generalities instead of specifying developmental processes with the mathematical precision available to dynamic systems. Thus we find it stated that development of perception of affordances occurs "... where observers notice and detect information for the animal–environment fit themselves through active exploration". This still leaves us very much in the dark about what sort of processes are involved in exploration, and what is involved in noticing and detecting. Is the information detected simply through the fact of mobility, or is there active spatial problem solving involved that might call upon cognitive processes? So what is left unsaid here is just what sort of psychological processes are involved in detection of affordances. The potential strength of the dynamic systems approach is that it tries to specify these processes quite precisely, and in doing so suggests that (at least within the limited scope of its present application) the processes involved can be quite low level.

THE IMPLICIT–EXPLICIT DISTINCTION

The main focus of this chapter is about the developmental implications of data on early perceptual competence. More specifically, my aim is to look at the sorts of developmental processes that are emerging as candidates for explaining infant development, both in the light of this body of evidence and the theoretical orientations that seem to come with it. The previous sections have filled in the background for this, and have even provided some tentative bases for developmental processes. In this section, my aim is to return to the linked issues of what we should call the abilities of young infants as revealed through current experimental techniques, how this "knowledge" changes during infancy, and what processes produce this change. And it is here that I want to bring in the *implicit–explicit* distinction as a basic descriptive principle.

Although this distinction has generated considerable interest recently, it appears to have almost as many interpretations as it has adherents. Some investigators apply the distinction in terms of knowledge revealed through action versus knowledge revealed through language. For instance, Gibson (1979, p. 260) defines explicit knowledge as information that can be linguistically expressed. Some define the distinction in a more general way. For instance, Karmiloff-Smith (1992) defines implicit knowledge or information as a form of representation not available to guide the mental activities of the individual, and proposes that this is transformed into explicit knowledge through a process of representational redescription. There is also a tendency to relate the distinction to conscious versus unconscious processes, with implicit learning conceptualised as the result of unconscious processing (Cleeremans, 1993), and *tacit knowledge* the outcome of such learning (Reber, 1993).

I would suggest that there is another sense in which the distinction may be usefully applied, particularly in early infancy, a way that is in keeping both with ecological psychology, with its reluctance to invoke cognitive processes, and with cognitive approaches. What we are faced with in early infancy is evidence that young infants perceive an objective and permanent world, but that they are far from being able to use this perception to guide action. My suggestion is that we consider these perceptual abilities implicit with respect to action, and that a major developmental process in early infancy involves the transformation of implicit (perceptual) knowledge into explicit knowledge that can be used to guide action. This definition need not be at variance with other definitions provided we are careful to define in particular instances the level of psychological activity to which we are applying the distinction. Thus, it becomes quite acceptable for a form of knowledge treated as explicit with respect to manual activity, to be redefined as implicit (procedural) knowledge with respect to linguistic activity. And it is even possible to subdivide knowledge used to guide manual activity in terms of the unconscious/conscious distinction, by distinguishing between automatic unconscious guidance of action and purposive conscious guidance of action (as in problem solving). The important point is that there are a set of levels at which knowledge becomes available to guide the activities of the individual; and this progression may be repeated during development on successively higher levels of psychological activity, or may jump levels through the operation of different processes. So defined, any form of knowledge is always implicit with respect to the higher level activity but explicit with respect to the lower level.

Linguistic activities enter the scene rather little during infancy; and, as we have already seen in this chapter, there is controversy over the degree to which it is appropriate to invoke mental processes in explaining early behaviour. However, there appears to be utility in a general distinction between implicit perceptual "knowledge" and explicit knowledge that can be used to guide action. I shall suggest that we need to subdivide this distinction further to recognise the difference between use of information for automatic guidance of action, and action under the control of purposive behaviour as seen in problem solving. This has much in common with the conscious–unconscious distinction, but while I would be happy to label automatic guidance of action as unconscious, I have qualms about labelling problem-solving in infancy as a conscious activity, since we do not have good measures of what is conscious and what is not during that period.

However, the distinction between automatic activities and purposive, problem solving activities appears fundamental, particularly in identifying the beginnings of what makes human psychology distinct, and it appears to me that it was the latter that Piaget was primarily concerned with. Furthermore, it makes sense to assume that knowledge judged explicit at the level of automatic action has to be transformed or supplemented before becoming explicit at the level of purposive flexible action typical of problem solving. It is here that Karmiloff-Smith identifies the need for representational redescription. But my account is very much about the processes occurring before that point, through which perception and action are first co-ordinated.

For present purposes, one clear advantage of the implicit–explicit conceptualisation is that, rather than portraying infants as progressing from a state of no or little knowledge to a state of mature knowledge, they are conceptualised as "knowledge rich" (or maybe, more appropriately, detectors of rich information) from the start; and development is treated as a set of changes in the way in which this knowledge or information is utilised. My suggestion is that the primary distinction between knowledge in early infancy and knowledge later is that early knowledge is implicit with respect to action, whereas, through one process or another, this knowledge becomes explicit in the sense that it is used to guide action. However, this transition rarely involves a simple translation of implicit to explicit: there is always something added that makes the explicit level more complex, or quite different.

DEVELOPMENTAL PROCESSES

On its own, the explicit–implicit distinction is developmentally descriptive, in the sense that, in itself, it does not illuminate the processes underlying development. However, earlier sections have laid the ground for us to consider the sorts of process that might explain developmental changes during infancy. For instance, Gibsonian theory generates some straightforward predictions, and dynamic systems analysis may in time provide a detailed account of some of the processes involved. The processes that emerge most clearly all relate in one way or another to the development of action; in particular, to the development of locomotion. For instance, although according to the theory of direct perception, perception is a matter of information pickup with no need for internal representation, perception is described as an active process. Thus one would assume that the effectiveness of perception would be closely related to motor development and, in particular, that the onset of locomotion would lead to more effective and extensive detection of information. This might well simply involve the pick-up of further perceptual information, or in current terms, further implicit knowledge.

In addition, important predictions emerge in relation to the concept of affordances. In the words of Adolph, Eppler, and Gibson (1993), "An affordance is the fit between an animal's capabilities and the environmental supports that enable a given action to be performed." And a given feature of the environment will hold one type of affordance for one species and a different one for another. For instance, water affords swimming for certain species but not for others. This has the important developmental parallel in the sense that the affordances detected will depend on the infant's ability to act. To say that a particular surface affords crawling makes sense only in relation to infants who can crawl. Thus as new motor achievements come on the scene, new affordances emerge. Since these affordances are essentially relationships between environmental structure and the structure of action, it is here that dynamic systems theory may help us to understand the process by which new affordances are picked up, through the meshing of the organismic and environmental sides of the overall system. And the current thrust of this approach is to describe the emergence of new affordances as taking place in an automatic manner through the natural functioning of the infant in his or her environment.

The development of affordances lends itself to analysis in terms of the implicit–explicit distinction. Prior to emergence of a new affordance, the relevant environmental feature was available to perception. Thus, the environmental information specifying the affordance was implicit in perception. But it is not until this information is meshed in as part of a system including both perception and the appropriate action that we can say that the affordance has been detected. And since an affordance is a relationship between perception and action which in itself may be sufficient to guide action, in terms of my earlier definition, it constitutes explicit knowledge.

In so far as current approaches appear to have been successful in analysing the developmental processes involved, it would appear that development just happens through the natural functioning of the perceptuo–motor system. Forgetting for the moment about changes in basic characteristics such as visual acuity (see Chapter 2), perception is to a large extent a constant, and is transformed into explicit knowledge at the level of action as it becomes meshed with new actions. This is something of an oversimplification, since it is clear that important perceptual developments do occur in the early months which may have direct implications for the infant's ability to act effectively. For instance, the emergence of stereopsis (binocular depth perception) at around 3 to 4 months (Granrud, 1986) provides more precise information about distance, and it may be no coincidence that accurate reaching for objects emerges around this time. But in this case, stereopsis probably does not so much provide new information about the world as provide the perceptual support needed for accurate action, and it is still the meshing of perception and action that leads to knowledge becoming explicit.

The claim of the dynamic systems approach is that there is no need to go beyond consideration of the environmental, mechanical and biological constraints in the system in order to reach an adequate developmental explanation. On the one hand, through its denial of the need to rely on mentalistic concepts, this approach has some clear advantages: reliance on mentalistic terminology (such as knowledge, understanding and reasoning) in explanations of infants' ability often seems inherently inappropriate. On the other hand, one cannot help asking if there is no more to infant development than the natural emergence of functions that link behaviour to the environment. In my view, although in time the dynamic systems approach may help to explain many of the basic activities of infants, activities which both emerge and are exercised at a relatively automatic unconscious level, this approach will have greater difficulties in dealing with the infant as an active problem solver engaged in means–ends analysis. In Chapter 5, Peter Willatts provides powerful arguments pointing to the need to treat the infant as an individual engaged in cognitive activities such as mental construction of means–ends solutions. Although in principle, the cognitive concepts that seem to be required in these cases can be incorporated within the systems analysis, it is hard to see how the resulting system can be analysed with the same rigour as in the case of simpler behaviours. (Indeed, this appear to be a general problem for the approach, since it appears to be applied most successfully to quite small fragments of behaviour.) Thus, at these higher levels, the systems approach is applied more as a metaphor, and it is not quite so clear that it has advantages beyond pointing out that multiple factors have to be taken into account in explaining development.

I would suggest that this distinction between automatic behaviours and the purposive ones seen in problem solving is crucial. Both forms are self-guided, but the latter are purposive in the sense that they involve deliberate manipulation and variation by the individual. It seems likely that this is not a rigid subdivision, since development may be partly a matter of behaviours becoming automatic after a period of achievement as a result of active problem solving. Thus, for instance, locomotion may become automatic, although its initial achievement may have been partly based on the infant trying out motor and postural variations. However, at a given point in development, there are some behaviours that appear automatic, while there are others that appear to involve problem solving under the control of a component of the system which we may want to call the mind, brain, or executive control system, depending on our theoretical preference.

It thus appears very likely that affordances are acquired in some cases as a result of purposive problem solving rather than just through automatic functioning. Any new motor achievement such as locomotion permits new scope for environmental exploration, but at the same time new problems are encountered, the solutions to which effectively constitute higher level affordances. In this respect, the global concept of learning through action that is encountered in the Gibsonian work needs to be unpacked, to investigate the different processes involved in learning through action. And, in addition to recognising that problem solving is dependent on information derived from perception, we have to recognise that problem solving itself (and particularly during infancy) is liable to determine perception. What seems to be called for here is a developmental model that is based on a complex interplay between perceptual information and the infant's current physical and mental activities.

It is possible to describe the product of development through these processes in terms of different forms of implicit-to-explicit shift. As already mentioned, in an important sense, detection of perceptual variables specifying an affordance make that affordance implicit in perception, but this cannot be called explicit knowledge until the infant can use it to guide action. What I am adding here is that there are two distinct processes through which perception comes to be used to guide action: firstly, at a relatively automatic level, such as when perceptual flow information is used to guide locomotion or update position; and secondly, at a level that seems much more cognitive, in which the infant is acting as a purposive problem solver, and discovers in the process certain ways in which perception and action fit together. Finally, it should be noted that this shift from implicit to explicit is not simply a matter of "plugging in" implicit knowledge to the action system. There is always something added that was not there before, in the sense that the connection involves the formation of an appropriate and often quite complex link-up between perception and action.

THE CASE OF LOCOMOTION

Thus far, the analysis has addressed relations between perception and action in a general way. This is a deliberate strategy, since the proposal is that all forms of developing action carry with them the need to acquire knowledge of how these actions relate to the perceptual world. However, it is worth ending the chapter by making the analysis more specific. It makes sense to select locomotion for this analysis, since there is already a substantial literature suggesting that the onset of locomotion has important implications for spatial cognition. Bertenthal and Campos (1990) review a range of studies showing that development of spatial behaviours such as visual cliff avoidance and spatial orientation bear important relationships to locomotor development. They argue that these changes in spatial behaviour that correlate with locomotor development do not reflect developments in spatial perception as such, but rather involve the use of pre-existing information, either for the first time, or in novel ways, to guide action. Additionally, the developments that are involved are quite specific, relating to self-produced bodily displacement. Thus, they are careful not to attribute all developments in visual control of action to the development of locomotion, and as a result, their account does not conflict with evidence that prelocomotor infants use visual information to maintain postural stability (Butterworth & Hicks, 1977). The point is that maintenance of the sitting posture and locomotion are very different activities, but development of both involves the use of visual information in new ways, to support a new activity. In both cases, pre-existing visual information is being used to guide action; and so, in terms of the previous definition, these constitute examples of the emergence of explicit knowledge at the level of action.

Extension of this analysis indicates a little of the true complexity of the problems that face us when we adopt any sort of systems approach. For, in addition to visual information being used to maintain the sitting posture, this new posture permits extended visual exploration of the environment, through rotational movement of head and trunk, and the specific visual flow that results may become crucial in the guidance of this activity. What is not yet clear, either in this case or in the case of locomotion, is whether we are dealing with development of visual guidance through a relatively low level calibration of perception and action (Rieser, 1989), or whether we are dealing with the development of new spatial reference systems required to maintain the stability of objects in space in the face of new visual transformations resulting from action (Bremner & Bryant, 1985). If the former is all that is involved, then these developments might fit well within the dynamic systems–Gibsonian framework. However, if we are dealing with the development of spatial reference systems, this pushes the account into the cognitive realm, since it can be argued that reference systems are not intrinsic to space but are mental constructions used to organise space.

Some further analysis reveals that there are quite a number of possible consequences of the onset of crawling. Accumulated evidence on visual cliff avoidance (Campos, Svejda, Campos, & Bertenthal, 1982) indicates that it is not perception but *wariness* of vertical drops that develops after crawling onset. This introduces an emotional dimension, and an immediate question arises about the origins of this wariness. Given the extent parents go to to protect their newly crawling offspring, it seems unlikely that infants learn to be wary through hard experience of falls. But it may be that parental anxiety when the infant approaches a drop is transmitted to the infant. This would be in keeping with the literature on social referencing, in which it is clear that infants use emotional cues from adults to guide their actions (Hornik & Gunnar, 1988), and Sorce, Emde, Campos, and Klinnert (1985) have shown that maternal emotional expression is an important determinant of whether or not infants cross the deep side of the visual cliff. Bertenthal and Campos point to another quite different way in which locomotion and emotion may be linked. Although visual and vestibular information are co-ordinated well before infants crawl, Bertenthal and Campos point out that prior to locomotion, disparities between visual and vestibular information are common. For instance, in cases where the infant is carried by an adult while looking at the adult's face, vision specifies stability while vestibular information specifies movement. However, during self-guided movement, attention is always directed to the stable world, and so the mobile infant becomes accustomed to visual–vestibular co-ordinations of the particular sort encountered during locomotion. The visual cliff presents an unusual visual–vestibular relationship, because the distant surface presents a slower rate of visual flow than the normal floor surface, and this leads to distress.

So here we have two quite different processes through which a plausible link between locomotion and emotion can be identified, one socially mediated and the other directly perceptual. The conventional next step would be to seek ways of identifying which of these alternatives best explains the link. However, Bertenthal and Campos suggest that both processes are operative; not just that, but that these are but two processes involved in an extended system of interacting component processes, all of which relate in some way or another to the onset of locomotion. Thus, they see the development of locomotion as having important implications for emotional development and social referencing, as well as the more obvious spatial behaviours such as visual orientation and attention. In doing this, they adopt a dynamic systems perspective, which extends the scope of the system under study to include the social environment. And they give a persuasive account of ways in which different different factors or constraints interact to produce new behaviours as emergent properties. However, it is interesting to note that the units within this system are very much the systems studied by others, and as a result the account becomes distant from the specific low level properties of dynamic systems, and more of a metaphor than a detailed explanation. This may be inevitable, and points to one of the problems of micro-analysis; namely, that it describes the components of behaviour well (as dynamic systems in their own right) but tends to feed them in as unanalysed components when analysing how they interact with each other. As Bertenthal and Campos point out, this is only a beginning for this type of analysis applied with appropriately broad scope, and it has to be said that others (for instance, van Geert, 1993) are already going much further to provide mathematically precise dynamic systems analyses of cognitive development.

This sort of approach is thus both exciting and challenging. But possibly the biggest challenge is provided by the proposition that we must include a social dimension in the system under analysis. If this is correct, then what is the status of conventional experimental investigation, in which it is assumed that the infant is the unit of analysis? If the system extends beyond the individual, do we not have to consider the whole experimental setting as the system from which the behaviour emerges? If so, we may have to conclude that any capacity detected through experimental techniques is not possessed solely by the infant. In a sense, we may be faced with an experimental version of Vygotsky's (1962) *intermental function*, in which the ability is possessed not by the individual but between child and adult in collaboration, and so another way in which early behaviours may reveal implicit knowledge is in the sense that the knowledge is not yet possessed by the infant as an individual.

This, in a sense, is just another way of restating the problem of interpreting the perceptual capacities of young infants. I have argued that these should not be interpreted as indicating explicit knowledge, since they are not yet used to guide the individual's actions. Another facet of this is that they emerge only in highly structured experimental settings designed to extract the best from infants. Some would argue that the emerging data are as much due to the structure or "scaffolding" provided by the social situation of the experiment as to the infant's own capabilities. And so whatever is possessed by the infant is implicit in the sense that it is expressed only through a form of strong social support. To my mind, this does nothing to reduce the importance of findings with young infants, but does indicate that we must take care over our interpretations. Also, if we accept this viewpoint, there is a need to supplement experimental investigations with more observational study of young infants in order to measure their capabilities in situations in which social structuring is reduced. Through this dual approach it may be possible to find out how the nascent abilities of young infants become transformed into competent self-determined action in the everyday world.

REFERENCES

Adolph, K.E., Eppler, M.A., & Gibson, E.J. (1993). Development of perception of affordances. In C. Rovee-Collier & L.P. Lipsitt (eds.), *Advances in infancy research*, Vol. 8, pp. 51–98. N.J.: Ablex.

Bertenthal, B.I. & Campos, J.J. (1990). A systems approach to the organising effects of self-produced locomotion during infancy. In C. Rovee-Collier & L.P. Lipsitt (eds), *Advances in infancy research*, Vol. 6, pp. 1–60. N.J.: Ablex.

Bower, T.G.R. (1966). The visual world of infants. *Scientific American, 215*, 80–92.

Bremner, J.G. & Bryant, P.E. (1985). Active movement and development of spatial abilities in infancy. In H. Wellman (ed.) *Children's searching: the development of search skill and spatial representation*. Hillsdale, N.J.: Lawrence Erlbaum Associates Inc.

Butterworth, G. & Hicks, L. (1977). Visual proprioception and postural stability in infancy: A developmental study. *Perception, 5*, 155–160.

Campos, J.J., Svejda, M.J., Campos, R.G., & Bertenthal, B. (1982). The emergence of self-produced locomotion: Its importance for psychological development in infancy. In D.

Bricker (ed.), *Intervention with at-risk and handicapped infants.* Baltimore, Md.: University Park Press.

Cleeremans, A. (1993). *Mechanisms of implicit learning: connectionist models of sequence processing.* Cambridge, Mass.: MIT Press.

Geert, P. van (1993). A dynamic systems model of cognitive growth: Competition and support under limited resource conditions. In L.B. Smith & E. Thelen (eds), *A dynamic systems approach to development: applications*, pp. 265–332. Cambridge, Mass.: MIT Press.

Gibson, J.J. (1979). *The ecological approach to visual perception.* Boston: Houghton Mifflin.

Gibson, E.J., Riccio, G., Schmuckler, M.A., Stoffregen, T.A., Rosenberg, D, & Taormina, J. (1987). Detection of the traversability of surfaces by crawling and walking infants. *Journal of Experimental Psychology: Human Perception & Performance, 13*, 533–544.

Granrud, C.E. (1986). Binocular vision and spatial perception in four- and five-month-old infants. *Journal of Experimental Psychology: Human Perception & Performance, 12*, 36–49.

Hornik, R. & Gunnar, M.R. (1988). A descriptive analysis of infant social referencing. *Child Development, 59*, 626–634.

Karmiloff-Smith, A. (1992). *Beyond modularity: a developmental perspective on cognitive science.* Cambridge, Mass.: MIT Press.

Kellman, P.J. & Spelke, E.R. (1983). Perception of partly occluded objects in infancy. *Cognitive Psychology, 15*, 483–524.

McKenzie, B.E.,Tootell, H.E., & Day, R.H. (1980). Development of visual size constancy during the first year of human infancy. *Developmental Psychology, 16*, 163–174.

Piaget, J. (1954). *The construction of reality in the child* (trans. M. Cook). N.Y.: Basic Books [originally published in French, 1936].

Reed, E.S. (1982). An outline of a theory of action systems. *Journal of Motor Behaviour, 14*, 98–134.

Reber, A.S. (1993). *Implicit learning and tacit knowledge: an essay on the cognitive unconscious.* Oxford: Oxford University Press.

Rieser, J.J. (1989). Development of perceptual-motor control while walking without vision: The calibration of perception and action. In H. Bloch & B.I. Bertenthal (eds), *Sensory-motor organizations and development in infancy and early childhood.* Dordrecht: Kluwer.

Savelsbergh, G.J.P. & van der Kamp, J. (1993). *A natural physical perspective on the development of infant eye–hand coordination: a search for the laws of control.* Annual report No. 16, Research & Clinical Center for Child Development, Hokkaido University, Sapporo.

Schwartz, A., Campos, J., & Baisel, E. (1973). The visual cliff: Cardiac and behavioural correlates on the deep and shallow sides at five and six months of age. *Journal of Experimental Child Psychology, 15*, 86–99.

Slater, A., Mattock, A., & Brown, E. (1990). Size constancy at birth: Newborn infants' responses to retinal and real sizes. *Journal of Experimental Child Psychology, 49*, 314–322.

Slater, A., Mattock, A., Brown, E., & Bremner , J.G. (1991). Form perception at birth: Cohen and Younger (1984) revisited. *Journal of Experimental Child Psychology, 51*, 395–406.

Slater, A. & Morison, V. (1985). Shape constancy and slant perception at birth. *Perception, 14*, 337–344.

Slater, A., Morison, V., & Rose, D. (1983). Perception of shape by the newborn baby. *British Journal of Developmental Psychology, 1*, 135–142.

Slater, A., Morison, V., Somers, M., Mattock, A., Brown, E., & Taylor, D. (1990). Newborn and older infants' perception of partly occluded objects. *Infant Behavior and Development, 13*, 33–49.

Sorce, J., Emde, R.N., Campos, J.J., & Klinnert, M. (1985). Maternal emotional signaling: Its effect on the visual cliff behavior of 1-year-olds. *Developmental Psychology, 21*, 195–200.

Thelen, E. & Smith, L.B. (1994). *A dynamic systems approach to the development of cognition and action.* Cambridge, Mass.: MIT Press.

Thelen, E. & Ulrich, B.D. (1991). Hidden skills: A dynamic systems analysis of treadmill stepping during the first year. *Monographs of the Society for Research in Child Development, 56* (whole No. 1).
Turvey, M.T. (1990). Coordination. *American Psychologist, 45*, 938–953.
Vygotsky, L.S. (1962). *Thought and language.* Cambridge, Mass.: MIT Press.

4 Dynamical Systems Approaches to the Development of Action

Brian Hopkins
Department of Psychology, University of Lancaster, UK.
George Butterworth
Division of Psychology, University of Sussex, Brighton, UK.

INTRODUCTION: THE LURE OF THE SNOWFLAKE

Johann Kepler's book, *The Six-Cornered Snowflake* (*De Nive Sexangula*), was published in 1611. Although Kepler (1571–1630) was better known for his laws of planetary motion, he also had an abiding interest in deriving laws that could explain qualitative changes in natural phenomena. He was the first to address scientifically the problem of morphogenesis, which may be defined as the spontaneous emergence of patterned forms in nature.

Kepler actually failed to find a lawful explanation for how snowflakes acquire a flat, hexagonal lattice structure. Yet, in some respects, he made an appropriate choice in casting the snowflake as a model for the development of form. We now know a lot more about snowflakes (Nittman & Stanley, 1986). They develop under conditions which do not contain any specific prescriptions for their ultimate structure and which amplify instabilities along the six axons leading to the corners of the ice crystal. The growth rate of the axons, as well as the spacing between their side branches (or dendrites), is extremely sensitive to small changes in the temperature and humidity of the vapour from which they are being formed. The lattice structure arises from the exchange of thermal energy with the surround, in a process of heat diffusion, to give the unique hexagonal shape

It is revealing that rather non-specific, quantitative, changes in thermal energy result in qualitative transitions in the growth of the whole snowflake. This dynamical process of energy exchange culminates in a structure that has been constrained to grow in six directions. Furthermore, while all snowflakes will develop a six-pronged structure, no two will be identical (see Nakaya, 1954, for a pictorial illustration of this point).

Explanations for the individual development of the snowflake have been offered in terms of theories of self-organisation. According to such "non-linear" or "dissipative systems" theories, patterns are the result of instabilities in energy exchanges with the environment. The general question is whether human development can be approached in this way, and if so what are the benefits? Living organisms, in contrast to snowflakes, also exchange information with the surround. Furthermore, they operate as irreversible systems, unlike the snowflake which ultimately reverts to its aqueous origins. These fundamental differences between animate and inanimate systems bring in their wake the "homunculus fallacy" by which the very process to be explained is often ascribed, circularly, to an identical internal device. An example of such circular reasoning would be to postulate an inner eye to scan the retinal image. The inner eye, in turn would itself require an inner eye in an infinite regress. The theory of self-organisation offers a way out of the homunculus trap and an escape from the problem of infinite regression.

Does a dynamical systems approach do more than merely generate a new set of developmental metaphors? We shall argue that motor development during infancy is particularly amenable to dynamical systems thinking and especially useful in proposing self-organisation as a basis for developmental theory. We shall also discuss perception because, in modern dynamical systems approaches, perception and action are not readily separated. We outline current developmental theories of the control and co-ordination of movement. Our examples are based on the acquisition of discrete behaviours such as reaching, and on rhythmical behaviours such as walking in infants. To conclude, we review the main strengths and weaknesses of the dynamical systems approach.

PUTTING THE MOTOR BACK INTO DEVELOPMENT

Movement enhances development

In recent years, there has been a growing realisation that movement can be an "engine" which drives developmental change, and this gives all the more reason for seeking an appropriate account of motor development. The modern view contrasts with the more prevalent assumption, dating back to Aristotle (384–322 BC) in his *De Anima*, that animal movements are the result of a primitive desire (*orektion*) rather than caused by rational thought (*logistikon*). This view was given scientific credibility by Descartes (1596–1650), whose mind–body dualism still finds some supporters in contemporary biology (e.g. Eccles, 1989).

One of the obdurate legacies of Cartesian dualism has been that perception and cognition have been studied separately from movement and action. At best, movement has been treated as a "marker" or "vehicle" (Zelaznik, 1993) for cognitive and other domains of development (as in Piaget, 1952), or as a medium for developmental assessment as in the motor milestones of infancy (Lockman & Thelen, 1993).

Many authors agree with Spelke (1990) that movements are essential for the development of fundamental cognitive abilities such as object permanence. In the same vein, Bushnell and Boudreau (1993) reinterpreted studies on the perceptual abilities of infants to suggest that motor development engenders "setting events" which promote the emergence of such abilities (see Bertenthal, Campos, & Barrett, 1984). For example, it is proposed that the development of haptic perception depends on infants using their hands as instruments of exploration, which in turn will reveal information about the tactile properties of objects. The emergence of reaching and grasping creates the circumstances for changes in the infant's looking behaviour during social interaction (van Beek, Hopkins, Hoeksma, & Samsom, 1994; Fogel, Dedo, & McEwen, 1992), and it provides a metric for absolute distance in depth perception (Yonas & Granrud, 1985).

Bipedal locomotion provides another illustration of movement as a setting event. With the onset of walking, the demands of maintaining balance generate new perceptual experiences that inform the infant about the properties of objects and surfaces relative to those of her own action system (Acredolo, 1978; Gustafson, 1984). Crawling demonstrates how a rhythmical movement (rocking) *interacts* with a discrete movement (reaching) to create a qualitative change in inter-limb coordination (Goldfield, 1989). Once acquired, crawling creates new perceptual experiences which in their turn afford further developmental change.

Motor development is an especially fruitful testing ground for the natural-physical approach of dynamical systems theory since growing muscles and limbs can be modelled as if they are springs and pendulums. Movements can be measured continuously using infra-red recording devices linked to computers, and parameters that potentially constrain motor development such as the centre of gravity, limb length or muscle mass can be subjected to rather precise measurements.

Ground versus air theories

According to Goldfield (1993), motor development has been subject to two opposing approaches which he calls air and ground theory. In air theory, mental structures continue to prescribe a movement even if the child is held in the air and thereby has no surface on which to act or react. Goldfield argues that air theories unwittingly rely on mind–body dualism and are divorced from the immediate environment of objects and surfaces. Such theories postulate that prescriptions for movement are stored in some central mechanism, such as a motor programme, and hence they fall into the homunculus trap. They offer a dual-state description, where the controller (mental structures) and that to be controlled (the body) are separated in an arbitrary fashion, and insurmountable theoretical obstacles arise (Shaw & Todd, 1980). Central devices, such as motor programmes, are fixed entities which cannot cope with the real variability of development.

Ground theories address actions, not just the disparate movements of traditional air theory. Actions are a set of relationships between properties defined across child and environment (Reed, 1982). For example, actions such as walking arise between reactive forces emanating from the environment, from muscles and according to how skilfully the child functions in performing a specific task. On this view, actions are "softly assembled", online, by marshalling the dynamical properties of the body relative to how a particular task is perceived. Soft assembly contrasts with air theory, where instructions are hard-wired into the central nervous system. In ground theory, actions (and the movements that go to make them up) are highly sensitive to variations in task demands. Such contextual constraints are referred to by dynamical systems theorists as context-conditioned variability (Turvey, Shaw, & Mace, 1978).

Thus, ground theories assume that, during development, movements become coalesced into increasingly refined actions through their interactions with various sources of perceptual information. As such, they avoid resorting to a homunculus, while stressing that perception and movement are mutually entailed components of a single developing system.

THE NATURAL-PHYSICAL APPROACH TO SELF-ORGANISATION

What is self-organisation?

Self-organisation refers to a process by which new (and more complex) structures emerge in open systems without specification from the environment. Prigogine is a major figure in understanding the mechanisms of self-organisation (Prigogine & Stengers, 1984). He found that at a critical value of energy being pumped into a chemical system, the system moves into a state of disequilibrium. In this marginal state, it is unusually sensitive to external perturbations which may trigger a sudden transition into a period of fluctuations from which a new stabilised order of greater complexity emerges (see Fig. 4.1) Once this new order is established, the system cannot return to its previous state . Prigogine called this "irreversible thermodynamics".

What is puzzling about self-organisation is that it takes place at all, given the Second Law of Thermodynamics which states that closed systems, which

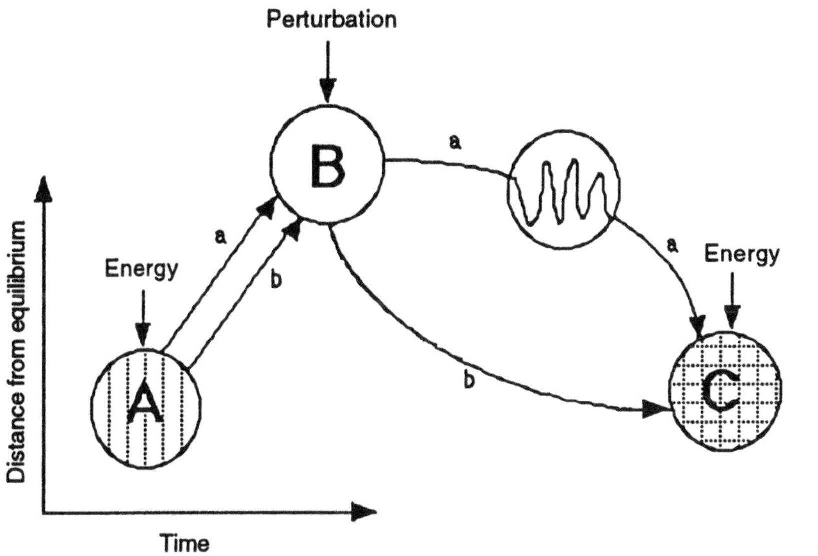

FIG 4.1. Displacing an initial thermodynamical state (A) to another (C) via a far-from-equilibrium state (B) and fluctuations arising from a perturbation. Note differences between paths (a) and (b). Path (a) makes an abrupt transition to a new (and more complex) thermodynamical state via a region of fluctuations, a typical (but not universal) feature of transitional behaviour in open, time-evolving systems.

interchange neither energy nor matter with their environments, evolve spontaneously to a state of maximum positive entropy or disorder. In such a disordered state, energy is distributed evenly throughout the system which, as a consequence, no longer displays any signs of structural differentiation. Clearly, living systems do not evolve to a state of disorder, but rather to states of increasing structural differentiation and complexity. How do they escape the end state of maximum disorder which the Second Law of Thermodynamics dictates?

Open systems actually have two contributions to their total entropy: positive entropy due to irreversible processes within the system and negative entropy (negentropy) due to energy exchange with the surroundings. When these are in balance, the system is stable. If positive entropy exceeds negentropy, then the system is irreversibly drawn to the equilibrium point of maximum entropy. With the infusion of more external energy, and thus negentropy, this process is temporarily perturbed and the system jumps suddenly to a new disequilibrium point which may then take over control of the dynamics. This reconciliation presents development as a continuous and irreversible process which does not need specific internal or external instructions. The emergence of new properties involves rearrangement of a system's existing elements into (temporarily) stable coalitions, as a result of energy exchanges with the environment. Figure 4.2 illustrates the general principles of self-organising systems.

The notion of self-organisation has proved to be a rich source for thinking about development in general and motor control in particular. Wolff (1986, p. 70) said:

> Simply labelling fetal or neonatal activity as the emergent property of "self-organizing systems" obviously achieves nothing more than to confuse an already complex issue with obscure jargon. Nevertheless, as a metaphor for guiding research, rather than as an explanatory concept, it leads to empirically testable hypotheses about early motor development that can be stated in a coherent theoretical framework. It calls attention to functional dynamics *among* component movements as one possible mechanism of developmental transformations that does not appeal to extrinsic executive agencies, motor programs or maturational timetables in order to "explain" development.

Motor control as a self-organising process

The natural–physical approach has as its main objective "to place the issues of movement control, coordination and development in complex systems on a theoretical substrate continuous with the natural sciences" (Hopkins,

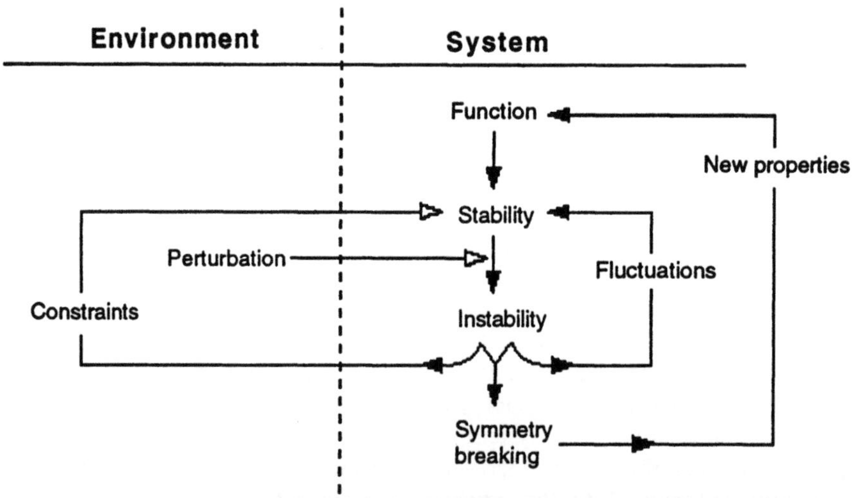

FIG. 4.2. Principles of self-organisation (the flow of time is not represented). A stable function becomes unstable through the lifting of constraints and susceptible to perturbations (which may be internal —► or external —▷). A particular perturbation may engender fluctuations in functioning which can eventually lead to symmetry breaking. Broken symmetry and a change in constraints may result in the emergence of new functional properties.

Beek, & Kalverboer, 1993, p.352). This objective does not imply reductionism in the naive sense that there is a single set of properties at a lower level of organisation which is sufficient to explain those at a higher one. Instead, it seeks to identify physical principles applicable across a variety of disciplines, scales and levels of observation. Adopting the terminology of D'Arcy Thompson (1917), who tried to understand morphogenesis using a similar strategy, it involves a search for a "community of essential similitudes". In devising models of motor control, self-organising principles go beyond mere metaphors.

An example of how movements are controlled by the physics of natural systems is given by the linear damped mass-spring model (Saltzman & Kelso, 1987; Feldman, 1966). In such a model, a limb is treated as a pendulum that oscillates under a local concentration of stored energy, in interaction with gravity and the restorative properties of the limb's muscles. The elasticity and stiffness of the musculature is generated during the active co-contraction of the agonist and antagonist muscles to define an equilibrium position. The limb moves through an abstract space defined by two axes—one connecting the initial and target positions of the limb and the other orthogonal to the first.

The advantage of treating muscles as if they are springs with a given mass is that the central nervous system does not have to specify in advance the moving limb's precise trajectory. Neural specification is restricted to setting the stiffness of the muscles and the equilibrium position of the underlying stretch reflex (Feldman, 1986). Once the thresholds have been specified and relayed to the motor neuron pool, the movement trajectory emerges from the mechanical properties of the activated muscles. Thus, in keeping with a cardinal principle of self-organisation, movements are controlled without reference to a central, prescriptive controller. Control is distributed across the dynamics of the nervous system and the limb, thereby avoiding the need for homunculus-like feedback mechanisms. (Note, however, that mass-spring models have been criticised for their neurophysiological assumptions; see, for example, van Ingen Schenau, 1989).

Mass-spring models taken alone, however, do not address the greatest theoretical challenge faced by the dynamical systems approach: namely, how information arising from interaction with the environment guides coordinated movements to achieve particular goals. Only living organisms are intentional systems with goal-directed actions. They are regulated and guided by perceptual information, whereas mechanical systems depend only on forces (Skarda & Freeman, 1987). Needless to say the introduction of the problem of intentionality presents serious challenges yet to be fully overcome.

THE DYNAMICAL SYSTEMS APPROACH

Background and scope

All types of dynamical systems theory take as their origin Poincaré's (1854–1912) qualitative dynamics. He succeeded in extracting qualitative information from quantitative measures to describe the sequence of instantaneous states of a system. These are plotted as trajectories over time in "circle" or "return" maps to provide a means to visualise the dynamics of physical systems.

The dynamical systems approach serves as an umbrella for a variety of compatible theoretical perspectives, which include catastrophe theory (Thom, 1976), chaos theory (McCauley, 1993), logistic growth models (May, 1975), irreversible non-equilibrium thermodynamics (Nicolis & Prigogine, 1977), synergetics (Haken, 1977), and topological dynamics (Bhatias & Szego, 1970). Given that these theories originally arose as answers to questions in mathematics, physics, chemistry and biology, the dynamical approach can be characterised as truly interdisciplinary. Not surprisingly, therefore, it aims to discover physical principles that are applicable across a variety of disciplines and scales of observation.

The scientific problem is to describe and explain how relationships at the microlevel of organisation dealing with energy, matter and information can give rise to qualitatively new properties at macrolevels (Alexander, Giesen, Muench, & Smelser, 1987). In connecting these levels of a system it is not to be expected that surface complexity arises from a deeper simplicity. Rather the opposite is true, with surface simplicity (e.g. of control and co-ordination) emanating from deeper complexity (Yates, 1987).

Linear versus non-linear dynamics

Dynamics is the study of the ways in which systems change over time. There are, generally speaking, two sorts of dynamics: linear and non-linear. Linear dynamics is based on the classical mechanics defined by Newton's laws of motion (Newton lived from 1643–1727). His third law (for every action, there is an opposite and equal reaction) is interesting because it acknowledges that a system's interactions with its environment involve both being (known as symmetry preservation) and becoming (symmetry breaking). Linear systems make proportional adjustments to any external disturbances, and consequently any change is performed in a smooth, continuous way.

In contrast, the systems addressed by non-linear dynamics change suddenly, when perturbed in disequilibrium. In this state, these systems display intermittent dynamics: a mixture of steady and fluctuating behaviour in which the system is maintained in a marginal state between being static (ordered) and being dynamic (disordered). Intermittent regimes provide stability and a degree of flexibility to switch between modes of co-ordination, which enable the system to adjust to environmental changes.

Mathematicians have shown that a linear system can be transformed into a non-linear one by including a threshold function in the equations describing motion. For example, a thermostat is a linear system made non-linear at a given set-point which, when attained, triggers heating or cooling. It certainly shows an abrupt change, but it does not qualify as a dynamical system since it fails to demonstrate one of the necessary hallmarks. Dynamical systems undergo qualitative change via intermittent (fluctuating) dynamics, whereas room temperature just goes up or down as a consequence of the set-point being attained. Moreover, feedback in thermostatic systems falls foul of the homunculus trap in that a thermostat contains an a priori prescription (the set-point) indicating the action it must take. Consequently, such closed-loop systems do not display self-organisation even though they behave in a seemingly non-linear manner. For these reasons simple feedback devices do not fall under the dynamical systems approach to movement control and co-ordination.

Determinism versus stochasticity

Development has been portrayed in strongly deterministic terms both in psychology (e.g. Werner, 1948) and biology (e.g. Waddington, 1975). There are important distinctions to be made within the dynamical approach about determinism in development (see Hopkins & Butterworth, 1990).

Theories contributing to the dynamical approach differ in whether the agent of change is only deterministic (i.e. it uniquely specifies past and future states, and their initial conditions are known precisely) or whether it includes a stochastic term. The word stochastic stems from the Greek *stochastikas* meaning "skill in aiming", thus implying the creative use of chance to achieve a particular goal. As a result, they can be classified as fully deterministic (e.g. topological dynamics), primarily stochastic (e.g. irreversible thermodynamics), or both deterministic and stochastic (e.g. chaos theory). Catastrophe theory is a special case in that it was originally conceived as being fully deterministic (Thom, 1975), but has since been reformulated to include random processes—the so-called stochastical catastrophe theory (Cobb & Zacks, 1985).

It is known that there is stochastic competition for a limited number of target sites, resulting in irreversible neural events such as selective cell death and axonal retraction in the development of the brain (Stent, 1981). Analogous findings have been reported for movements: namely, that stochastic processes are crucially involved in bringing about transitions in modes of co-ordination (Kelso, Scholz, & Schöner,1986). The point is that development involves an interplay between determinism (necessity) and stochasticity (constrained chance). This leads to a further distinction, between order and control parameters, which lies at the heart of the dynamical systems approach.

Order and control parameters

As the name suggests, an order parameter is a single entity that describes the orderly macroscopic behaviour of a system in a stable state. The dynamics of order parameters enslave (or literally give orders to) processes at the microlevels so that they co-operate in performing task-specific functions (Haken, 1977; Wunderlin, 1987). Order parameters have also been treated as "informators" in that they provide an informational field that assists in harnessing the system's components to link perception with motor dynamics (Haken, Kelso, Fuchs, & Pandya, 1990).

Recent experiments suggest that the relative phase of movement may be an important order parameter in the development of walking (Clark, Whitall, & Phillips, 1988; Forrester, Phillips, & Clark, 1993). Walking involves moving the limbs in separate relative phases of intralimb and interlimb co-ordination The relative phase can be defined as the angular difference between the motions of two limbs. For interlimb co-ordination, with relative phase defined as the percentage of one leg's cycle at which the other leg begins its own movement, infants and adults were indistinguishable. Both had on average a 50% phase difference between limb cycles. However, infants with less than 3 months of walking experience had significantly higher variability in the relative phase of movement. Comparable findings have been obtained for intralimb co-ordination, where the relative phase consisted of angular differences between phases of thigh and shank motions. These findings suggest that walking experience of 3 months marks an important transition in the development of bipedal locomotion.

Other recent studies have addressed relative phase as an "informator" that may be involved in perceiving biological systems in motion. A technique using point-light displays has been devised in which infants are presented with computer displays showing moving points of light at the major joints of stick figures. Infants and adults perceive these moving points of light as if they are real people walking (Bertenthal & Pinto, 1993). This brings us back to the point that perception and movement may share the same dynamical information during development. It also offers a way of linking information obtained through perception to goal-directed action, and eventually may allow psychologists to address how intentionality enters into the dynamics of living systems.

A control parameter is a boundary condition that acts as a constraint on the dynamics of the order parameter. For biological systems, three general classes of constraints have been identified (Newell, 1986): organismic (e.g.

neural or morphological); environmental (e.g. properties of objects); and task-specific constraints (e.g. instructions or the goal of a task). When a control parameter is increased beyond some critical value, it can transiently lose its constraining influence on the order parameter, which may then manifest stochastic or even chaotic behaviour before making a sudden transition to a different state. Control parameters do not prescribe variations in the patterning of the order parameter in a strictly deterministic fashion. Rather, they control only in leading unspecifically through regions of instabilities or in keeping the system within a stable operating range.

In a developmental context, control parameters may be rate-limiting constraints on the emergence of new behavioural organisation (Soll, 1979). Potential rate-limiting factors in the development of reaching include changes in muscle torque which counter the postural imbalance induced by unimanual reaching (Thelen et al., 1993; Zernicke & Schneider, 1993). Another important rate-limiting control parameter is gaining postural stability over head and trunk (Savelsbergh & van der Kamp, 1993). In fact, a behavioural transition may actually be under the control of the slowest constituent developmental process within the system. This may be a biomechanical constraint, such as gaining sufficient strength in the legs for walking, or the control parameter may be cognitive, hormonal or neural. The psychologist has to look beyond the psychological level of explanation to fully comprehend the development of movement control

BERNSTEIN'S PROBLEM AND A SOLUTION

The degrees of freedom problem

Reaching to grasp an object involves 3 joints in the arm and another 14 in the hand. The upper arm can move along 3 axes and the lower arm and hand along 2. Initiating the movement involves more than 20 muscles in the arm and many more in the hand when adjusting the fingers to the object's properties. Walking is even more complex, involving as it does 3 joints and over 50 muscles in each leg (plus all the other joints and muscles from other body parts incorporated into the action). These are just "selections" from a musculo-skeletal system (MSS) that consists of nearly 800 muscles, about 200 bones and more than 100 joints, each of which can be characterised by two parameters of position and velocity. Furthermore, the MSS must be linked to the nervous system where the potential variability is enormous, with 10^{14} neurons in 10^3 different varieties of nerve cells that might be involved.

In theory, the vast number of neuromuscular elements involved in a movement can be combined in an almost infinite number of ways. In practice, they are not, as reaching and walking show. Nevertheless, they still involve many mechanical degrees of freedom along which the system can vary independently. How then do the redundant degrees-of-freedom become constrained? This question, known as Bernstein's problem, is associated with the problem of context-conditioned variability or how movements are controlled and co-ordinated, given the continuously changing properties of muscles, limbs and environment (Turvey, Shaw, & Mace, 1978). These issues raise deep problems for all developmentalists.

One of Bernstein's (1967) great insights was to realise that a central executive, such as a motor programme, could not master the many redundant degrees of freedom nor the indeterminacy involved in the control of movement. There are simply too many components for all possible contingencies to be stored in the central nervous system. Bernstein's solution was to propose that the central nervous system controls the motor system by forming movement synergies that are also known as co-ordinative structures (Easton,1972). A co-ordinative structure can be defined as a temporary marshalling of many degrees of freedom into a task-specific functional unit (Turvey, Shaw, & Mace, 1978). At the level of the muscular skeletal system, a synergy is a collection of muscles, often spanning several joints, which are constrained to act co-operatively in achieving a particular goal.

Bernstein proposed a three-step process in the acquisition of a new co-ordinative structure. This process cannot begin before the learner can "freeze" linkages in limb and torso segments so as to reduce the number of degrees of freedom at the periphery. The next step involves freeing-up or decoupling these linkages so that all possible degrees of freedom arising from reactive forces and motion-dependent torques can be incorporated into the emerging mode of co-ordination. During the third step, which involves reassembling the original linkages, the reactive forces are exploited to generate more differentiated, energy-efficient movements. In fact, this step not only involves exploiting peripheral sources of information, but is also increasingly attuned to information about environmental properties that can assist in a specific task.

The development of spontaneous kicking movements in babies provides a concrete illustration of this process (Thelen, 1985). Initially, the movements of the three joints of the leg are tightly coupled, reflecting freezing of potential degrees of freedom. Between 1 and 5 months, the coupling becomes much looser and there is increasing joint differentiation. By about 6 months, when crawling soon emerges, the tight coupling between all pairs of joints is resumed. A similar sequence of changes in movement co-ordination has also been reported for the development of reaching in human infants (von Hofsten, 1984) and for grooming in young mice (Golani & Fentress, 1985).

Motor equivalence and equifinality

Although the redundant degrees of freedom have been presented as a problem here, they are actually a necessity if biological systems are to adjust flexibly to changing environmental circumstances. This point is important for motor equivalence, which depends on the motor system having many degrees of freedom, so that a variety of movements and their different muscle contractions and joint rotations can produce the same outcome (Hebb, 1949). Conversely, of course, the same movement can lead to different outcomes, but such examples are usually restricted to culturally determined social behaviour (e.g. side-to-side movements signify "no" in northern Europe, while in some southern European countries they can mean "yes').

Perhaps the first description of motor equivalence in development was given by Trettien (1900). In a longitudinal study, he found that infants took different developmental pathways to independent walking. Some progressed from sitting to walking via crawling, while others omitted this phase and began to walk after standing up from sitting. These differences may either be hereditary (Robson, 1970) or a reflection of culture-specific child-rearing practices, or a function of both factors (Hopkins & Westra, 1988). Another example comes from a study on the co-ordination of kicking movements in 3-month-old infants (Schneider, Zernicke, Ulrich, & Jensen, 1990) who were placed in both supine and (supported) sitting positions. The infants differentially adjusted muscle torques so as to produce the same pattern of kicking in both positions. Clearly, motor equivalence is a potent means of resolving the problem of peripheral indeterminacy and for exploring the intrinsic dynamics of the body relative to particular environmental tasks.

TRANSITIONS AND ATTRACTORS

Development as changes between attractor states

As we have pointed out, non-linear dynamical functions in development may involve sudden transitions from one state of organisation of the system to another. A transition is any change accompanied by a marked alteration in a system's properties (i.e. in an order parameter). There are various kinds of transitions, including the pitchfork bifurcation shown in Fig. 4.3 where the system subdivides into two sub-systems, which themselves are not structurally stable.

An important point about such topologies of change is that they do not necessarily stop at the first transition (the primary bifurcation). They may go on to display bifurcation cascades that lead to secondary, tertiary and more branches, in some cases, eventuating in a bifurcation to chaos. In fact, such a scenario may very well typify early development. Once a system completes a transition, it typically settles into a new stable state, as if attracted to that particular form.

An attractor can be defined as an area in the system's state space towards which the system converges over time (Thompson & Stewart, 1986). The attractor constrains the dynamics of a system into a region known as the basin of attraction. Four basic types of attractors have been identified (see

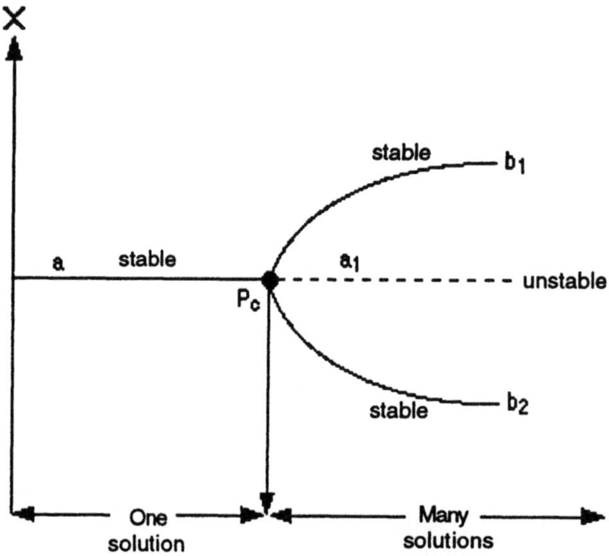

FIG. 4.3. A pitchfork bifurcation illustrating the relationship between order and control parameters in the realisation of phase transitions. The bifurcation diagram shows an order parameter (X) changes through a linear scaling of a control parameter. A thermodynamical branch (a) loses its stability at a critical value of the control parameter (Pc). At this value, fluctuations or perturbations are no longer damped. If fluctuations do not destroy the system, their random motion transports it to a bifurcation point (•) where it irreversibly abandons the stable branch for one of the two pitchfork-shaped developmental paths (b_1, b_2), which suddenly become available. Which path is "chosen" depends on the dynamics of fluctuations (i.e. on chance).

Fig. 4.4): fixed point, limit cycle or periodic, quasi-periodic and chaotic or strange attractors. The general advantage of an attractor is that it simplifies complexity into a two-dimensional spatial map (in the cases of point and limit cycle attractors) or three-dimensional spatial images (for quasi-periodic, and chaotic attractors). Inspection of these maps may supply the first clues about the organisational principles responsible for the system's behaviour. In performing complex actions such as walking, appropriate attractor regimes offer a degree of resistance to perturbations, in energy-efficient ways, relative to task constraints (Hoyt & Taylor, 1993).

Figure 4.4 illustrates the basic types of attractor regimes with examples from motor development to which they may apply.

Development can be depicted as a process of discovering those attractor regimes that allow the "soft-assembly" of task-specific actions (Bingham, 1988). Posture has recently been modelled as a fixed point attractor governed by the same intrinsic dynamics as rhythmical movements

TYPE	CHARACTERISTICS	DIMENSION	EXAMPLES
	All trajectories in phase space attracted to a stable equilibrium point regardless of initial positions. Resistant to perturbations in achieving point.	0	a. Damped linear mass- spring system. b. Reaching and grasping (Thelen et al., 1993)
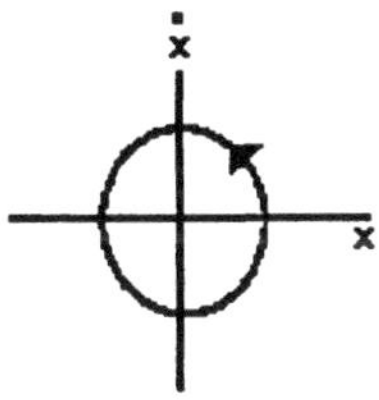	All trajectories in phase space attracted to a stable oscillation with fixed amplitude and frequency, which is function of system's parameters, not initial conditions. Oscillation can resist strong perturbations.	1	a. Damped non-linear mass spring system. b. Locomotion (Clark et al., 1990)
	Two or more limit cycles weakly interact to produce a qualitatively different pattern. Trajectory of limit cycle with higher frequency enveloping slower one giving rise to a stable 3-D torus attractor shaped like a doughnut	2	a. Weakly coupled non- linear oscillatiors. b. Non-nutritive sucking in newborn (Wolff, 1991)
	Trajectories stretch in a fan like structure and then fold back to local area of phase space as they are under two antagonistic influences (attraction vs. divergence). Due to stretching and folding, trajectories never cross the same path twice making them unpredictable in local areas. Nevertheless trajectories arise from deterministic interactions within system, thus distinguishing chaos from random noise. Unlike other attractors have sensitive dependence on initial conditions: nearby trajectories diverge at exponential rates tending to amplification of very small perturbations.	Fractal, non-integer with at least 2 positive Lyapounov exponents	a. Two or more strongly coupled non- linear oscillations. b. Cyclical movements (Robertson et al., 1993)

FIG. 4.4. Four basic types of attractors. Top-to-bottom: fixed point attractor, limit-cycle or periodic attractor, quasiperiodic or torus attractor and chaotic (Lorenz) or strange attractor. A fixed point attractor can be represented by straight lines terminating at a point (as depicted here) or by a trajectory spiralling inwards to a point depending on the nature of the intrinsic dynamics. f^1 and f^2 are the frequencies of the two of the oscillators of the torus attractor. The higher frequency can envelop the trajectory of the slower one when two or more limit-cycle oscillators become phase-locked. The dimension of an attractor gives a lower limit to the number of order parameters needed to model the dynamics of a system. A fractal dimension is a fractional number between 1 (a line) and 2 (a surface). The fractal dimension of a snowflake curve is 1.26. A Lyapounov exponent is a non-metrical measure of the exponential rates of divergence (positive exponents) or convergence (negative exponents) of trajectories in an attractor. It can be used to distinguish chaos from noise.

(Schöner, 1990). This leads to the far-reaching proposal that posture, rhythmical and discrete movements could all emerge as different solutions of the same mass-spring dynamics. Developmentally, this implies that infants will search for the dynamics that enable them to bring posture into the service of movements, with posture specifically providing bodily stability as a pre-requisite for corrective adjustments to actions.

Development has been portrayed as a series of attractors that provide preferred, but not obligatory stable states of a self-organising action system (Fogel & Thelen, 1987). The main difficulties in pushing the attractor concept beyond metaphorical applications revolve around issues concerning data length and sampling frequency. Estimating how many dimensions constitute an attractor requires long time series of data, particularly if a chaotic attractor is to be identified. For example, to be able to distinguish chaos from noise reliably, data length in the order of 10^6 points are required and 500 data points are considered to be an absolute minimum. Some relief from these problems is on the way in the form of methods for deriving (rather simple) chaotic dynamics from relatively short time series with as few as 100 data points (Albano, Mees, de Guzman, & Rapp, 1987).

EXAMPLES OF APPLYING THE ATTRACTOR CONCEPT TO MOTOR DEVELOPMENT

Spontaneous movements in newborns

Despite these problems, attractor dynamics during infancy have been investigated using non-linear dynamic modelling techniques During the neonatal period, fluctuations in spontaneous movements or cyclical motility (CM) may be generated by intrinsic dynamics that are weakly linked to other systems (Robertson, Cohen, & Mayer-Kress, 1993). By 2 months, the intrusion of chaos into the system invokes a strong coupling between CMs during wakefulness and visual attention, in which the CMs drive the attention system.

Changes in CM were investigated longitudinally in 30 infants from 1 to 4 months of age (Robertson, 1993). Movements were detected by sensors mounted on an infant seat and recordings lasted from 1 to about 5 hours. Behavioural state criteria were registered to distinguish sleep and waking states. It was found that the dynamics of CM changed at 2 months during wakefulness. There was a significant drop in the predictability of CM for short intervals, together with an increase in rapid fluctuations. These changes signal the onset of chaotic organisation of wakefulness The result is the emergence of a new ability to explore the local environment and to maximise the extraction of relevant sources of information (Robertson et al., 1993).

Reaching and walking infants

Developmental change in reaching has been described using the attractor concept. An intensive longitudinal study of 4 infants from 3 weeks to 1 year, suggested that reaching emerges via a Hopf bifurcation (Thelen et al.,1993). The Hopf bifurcations are the most elementary, structurally stable transitions in a non-linear system in that they require changes in only one control parameter. This finding was based on data showing that rotation-like movements of the arms (interpreted as a limit cycle attractor) give way to goal-directed unimanual reaching (point attractor). It was further concluded, that limit cycle dynamics are transformed into a point attractor by stiffening the arms as a result of co-activating the appropriate muscles, thus negatively damping oscillations of the reaching arm.

The development of walking has also been offered as an example of a Hopf bifurcation (Zanone, Kelso, & Jeka, 1993). The stepping movements of the newborn drop out of the repertoire about 2 months after birth and there follows a period of some 6 months in which alternating leg movements in the upright position are no longer displayed (Touwen, 1976). This period of quiescence can be regarded as a fixed point attractor and the subsequent appearance of the true walking movements as an attractor to a limit cycle (Clark, Truly, & Phillips, 1990; 1993; Clark & Phillips, 1993). The intralimb co-ordination of newly walking infants corresponds to coupled, non-linear limit cycle oscillations, but the shank and thigh showed trajectories that were more variable than for adults. Taking the knee as the point of coupling between the two segments, phase plane plots of its angular velocity against displacement during walking cycles were made (Clark et al., 1993). The resultant trajectories formed a torus-like shape for adults suggesting the coupling between segments derives from a quasi-periodic attractor (see Fig. 4.4). The newly-walking infant did not achieve a torus-like orbit until there had been 2 months of walking experience.

These demonstrations support a developmental scenario in which the limb segments enter cyclical regimes which, when stabilised through experience, become coupled in the form of a quasi-periodic attractor. The burning question from a dynamical systems perspective is what leads to the transition to independent walking? Findings from pre-walking infants implicate balance (Clark, Whitall, & Phillips, 1988) and extensor strength for single leg support (Thelen, 1986) as the rate-limiting control parameters on the transition to independent walking.

As for the transition from neonatal stepping to the quiescent period, Thelen's experiments point to a constraint relating fat deposition to muscle power in the legs (Thelen, Fisher, & Ridley-Johnson, 1984). That this transition depends on such a non-specific control parameter is not immediately obvious, but nevertheless is supported by measurements which show that fat increases more rapidly than muscle tissue in the limbs of babies between the ages of 2 and 6 months (Maresh, 1984).

CONCLUSIONS

This brief overview of dynamical systems thinking has attempted to show how transformations in the control and co-ordination of movement and posture are decisive agents of developmental change, particularly during infancy. In addition, it stresses that change in biological systems is not only deterministic, but also driven by random processes. Some of the main points that the dynamical approach emphasises can be summarised as follows:

1. Development is not due to single causes. It is a process of self-organisation resulting from interactions between many processes relative to the demands of particular tasks.
2. Developmental change emerges from an interplay between deterministic and stochastic (random) processes. The random element enables the creative assembly of new actions, relative to specific task demands, and determinism ensures the achievement of species-characteristic end states for behaviour.
3. Development is subject to internal and external constraints which prevent certain actions but permit others. Within the boundaries of these constraints, permissible actions are assembled opportunistically into stable task-specific devices.
4. When constraints imposed by the intrinsic dynamics of the body are overcome, fluctuations in behaviour are eventually followed by new forms of action that emerge in a discontinuous fashion.
5. Action systems develop asynchronously, such that one system may act as a rate-limiting factor on the emergence of new behaviours.

These and other insights into development are by no means new. For example, Gesell & Amatruda, (1945) already had a dynamical approach to development (Hopkins et al., 1993). What is new is the array of mathematical tools provided by the approach that can be used to model distinctions between stabilities (continuity) and instabilities (discontinuity) in development. Development is both complicated and noisy that makes it difficult to distinguish relevant processes from the "sea of noise" that typifies living systems (Morrison, 1991). In theory, the dynamical approach can make such distinctions. In practice, to go beyond metaphorical application, dynamical systems thinking may require psychologists to attend closely to the mathematical foundations of the natural–physical approach to living systems (see Robertson et al., 1993).

Following this brief overview, it should be made explicit that the primary task of the dynamical approach is to describe *organisational principles* (rather than *mechanisms*) that capture qualitative change at the global level of behaviour. An important contribution of the dynamical approach is its (re-)emphasis on how self-organising transformations in the control and co-ordination of movement and posture are decisive agents of developmental change, especially during infancy. The challenge now is to build a theory that will enable us to pose new and testable questions about the principles and mechanisms of developmental change. In turn, this will require the use of available mathematical models (to validate the principles) and the experimental manipulation of age-appropriate control parameters (to tease out the mechanisms).

GLOSSARY

Attractor: region in state space to which the behaviour of a system is attracted and where it will eventually settle down. It serves to organise the temporal flow of events in a dynamical system which can be captured by a number of geometrical forms that are two-dimensional (fixed-point and limit cycle attractors) or three-dimensional (quasiperiodic or chaotic attractors).

Chaotic attractor: an infinite collection of unstable periodic behaviours that tend to visit certain regions in the attractor more frequently than others. The behaviours never cross the same path twice and they are unpredictable in the long term. The hallmark of a chaotic attractor is a sensitive dependence on initial conditions which means that very small perturbations can result in almost any kind of regular behaviour. Even though its behaviour has a random-like appearance, a chaotic attractor is fully deterministic and generated by fixed rules that do not involve any elements of chance.

Constraint: a condition that preserves the symmetry of a system and restricts its degrees of freedom. When perturbed may lead to symmetry breaking. Applied to movement co-ordination, a constraint is a boundary condition that eliminates or restrains certain configurations of action while permitting or enabling others. There are two general classes of constraints: holonomic or law-governed constraints which restrict without having any material embodiment in the system (e.g. the laws of motion) and non-holonomic or rule-governed constraints that are physically embodied in the system (e.g. a schema) and which serve as prescriptions for action.

Control parameter: is not a specific ordering principle, but guides the system through its respective collective states in unspecific ways. Close to the critical value of a control parameter, systems with any degrees of freedom may be captured by descriptions of the low dimensional dynamics of the order parameter.

Co-ordinative structure: a functional grouping of muscles spanning a number of joints that is flexibly assembled to achieve a specific goal. Also referred to as a synergy or functional generator. It is seen as a solution to the degrees-of-freedom problem in that muscles are not controlled as separate units but as functional groupings.

Degrees of freedom problem: in engineering, the degrees of freedom of a system are the minimum number of independent co-ordinates that are needed to specify uniquely the state or configuration of the system without violating how its parts are interrelated. The arm has seven degrees of freedom: 3 at the shoulder (flexion–extension; abduction–adduction; rotation about its own axis), 1 at the elbow (flexion-extension), 1 at the radio-ulnar joint and 2 at the wrist. At the level of muscles, the arm has 26 degrees of freedom in that there are 10 muscles at the shoulder, 6 at the elbow, 4 at the radio-ulnar joint and 6 at the wrist. Thus, the problem of controlling the movements of the arm would be reduced if the basic units to be controlled by the brain were joints rather than individual muscles (or motor units). Bernstein's (1967) solution to the problem was to propose that the brain controls are functional groupings of muscles or what are termed co-ordinative structures.

Determinism: the doctrine of linear causality which holds that the state of a system at one moment determines its states at all subsequent moments. While they are in some sense deterministic, nonlinear systems do not show such (long-term) predictability in that their initial conditions do not dictate their subsequent behaviour in the same way. Chaos is a form of determinism without predictability.

Dissipative systems: nonlinear dynamical systems that are capable of assimilating large reserves of energy from the environment and converting them into increasing structural complexity. Such thermodynamically open systems exist in a far-from-equilibrium state such that spontaneous internal fluctuations can be amplified to the point that they change the system's behaviour.

Dynamical systems: any system that changes over time. Change can be continuous or discontinuous, and an important contribution of the dynamical systems approach is the provision of criteria for distinguishing between these two types of change. The dynamics involved do not refer to mechanical forces and masses as in Newtonian mechanics, but to the most simple and abstract description of how the global behaviour of a system evolves over time.

Fixed point attractor: the simplest form of an attractor involving a stable steady state in which there is an absence of change and a tendency to return to the same state after small perturbations. A simple example of a fixed point attractor is a linear damped mass-spring system in which all the trajectories converge to a state of equilibrium.

Homunculus fallacy: proposing anticipatory or prescriptive mechanisms such as plans, programmes, representations or schemes for the control of action. The application of these internal devices to development raises the further problem of infinite regression: where do they come from and what controls them?

Irreversible thermodynamics: extension of classical thermodynamics to nonlinear systems and far-from-equilibrium situations in which self-organisation may occur. Shows how new forms of order may emerge via state transitions when energy flows exceed the dissipating capacity of an existing structure. The process by which this is achieved is irreversible (i.e. once a new structure emerges, the system cannot return to its initial reference state).

Limit cycle attractor: a stable oscillation with a fixed frequency and amplitude making the behaviour of the system very repetitive. When in a limit cycle attractor, the system requires strong perturbations to shift it to another attractor. Captures the trajectories of a variety of rhythmical movements as a closed ring in the state space.

Linear v. nonlinear dynamics: linear dynamics can account only for the behaviour of systems that are fully prescribed by their initial conditions. In contrast, nonlinear dynamics deals with systems whose behaviour is not predictable over long periods of time either from their initial conditions or from their history of inputs. The equations of motion for such systems include threshold values which when breached result in sudden discontinuous changes to qualitatively different states.

Macrolevel v. microlevel: two different ways of describing the organisation of a system that originated in classical thermodynamics. The macrolevel describes the global state of the system using the smallest number of variables. Order parameters are operationalised at this level of description. Description at the microlevel consists of accounting for all the possible number of elements making up a system. Control parameters are sought at this level. This distinction raises a very fundamental problem in all sciences: namely, how changes in the interrelationships between elements at the microlevel of organisation can give rise to qualitatively new properties at the more macroscopical level.

Mass spring systems: a spring attached to some surface at one end and to a mass at the other end. When a spring of a given length and stiffness is released after being stretched or compressed it begins to oscillate. Over time, the amplitude of its oscillation decreases until the spring reaches equilibrium or its resting length. Thus, its movement characteristics, such as displacement and velocity, emerge from its inherent dynamical properties which include not only stiffness but also damping. The behaviour of this linear damped mass-spring system corresponds to a point attractor and thus has been used to model discrete movements such as reaching. When such a system is periodically driven by an external force, it results in a stable oscillatory movement which corresponds to a limit-cycle oscillator. The system can be made nonlinear by the inclusion of a nonlinear damping term. If fed by a constant source of energy, it may demonstrate oscillatory movements autonomously. When such a system is forced at different frequencies and amplitudes, it can make a transition to more complex behaviour that corresponds to quasiperiodic or even chaotic attractors. The attraction of mass-spring systems for the natural–physical approach is that motor control can be modelled with minimal recourse to some internal mechanism of regulation: no error-correction device is required as the system adjusts itself automatically.

Motor equivalence: based on the more general notion of equifinality or the tendency of a system to converge on an equilibrium state regardless of its initial conditions. In movement terms, stresses that a variety of different muscle contractions and joint rotations can produce the same outcome. This many-to-one transformation between all possible initial states and a single final state is a defining characteristic of nonlinear dynamical systems. Linear systems have only one-to-one transformations.

Natural–physical approach: derived from the physics of self-organising systems and Gibson's (1979) direct realist theory of perception. An interdisciplinary field of study concerned with pattern formation in complex, open systems of action. Its main theoretical stance is to minimise the role of prescriptive mechanisms through the pursuit of natural laws that link the dynamics of behaviour to its sources of information.

Order parameter: low-dimensional collective variables that express co-operative relationships between many degrees of freedom found in complex systems and simplify this description for an external observer. Order parameters are determined by and created from the co-operation of microscopical quantities while at the same time they govern the qualitative behaviour of the whole system in a form of circular causality.

Quasiperiodic attractor: while similar to a periodic attractor, it differs in that its behaviour is not strictly periodic. Thus, its behaviour does not repeatedly visit the same values in the state space. When the behaviour of a system is made of two or more independent oscillators that are weakly coupled, then it becomes quasiperiodic. With increases in the strength of the couplings, the behaviour may become periodic.

Self-organisation: process by which new structures emerge without specification from outside. Thus these new spatial and temporal patterns arise as a result of some internal regulation in response to changing external conditions that do not specify what should be changed, and not through the external imposition of a particular organisation. The simplest form of self-organisation is a phase transition.

Soft assembly: intended to convey the idea that movements are not hard-wired in the nervous system, but arise from nonlinear interactions between many sources of determination such as neural activity, the anatomical properties of muscles, bones and joints, the passive and mechanical forces acting on the body and the energy delivered to the moving limbs. Thus, movements are assembled on-line relative to the physical properties of the body while at the same time taking account of the intentions and perceptions of the task to be performed.

State (phase) space: an abstract space which visualises the temporal evolution of a dynamical system. The co-ordinates of the space are formed by variables that are relevant to the system being studied. In a two-dimensional state space designed, for example, to capture the dynamics of leg movements during walking, these variables would be velocity and displacement. The resultant trajectories in the space constitute a phase portrait. The advantage of these portraits is that provide a relatively simple means of revealing the nature of the underlying dynamics of a complex system.

Stochasticity: refers to any process in which there is a random variable or element of probability in its structure that depends on some parameter which may be discrete or continuous. In a stochastic process consisting of a sequence of discrete events, the outcome of one event has no bearing on the outcome of any other.

Symmetry breaking v. symmetry preservation: the concept of symmetry in physics refers to the set of invariances of a system that are preserved when some operation is performed on the system. For example, a square rotated by 90° is indistinguishable from the original and thus has symmetry under rotation by 90°. Symmetry breaking occurs when the features of a system are no longer invariant under transformation. The constraints preserving the invariances in the system are broken and there follows the spontaneous emergence of a state of lower symmetry. Symmetry breaking is thus synonymous with the appearance of new properties. Symmetry preservation refers to the maintenance of equilibrium between the constituents of a system (i.e. to the maintenance of a particular invariance under all possible changes). Gibson (1979), for example, assumes the preservation of perceptual symmetries under changing perspectives as one of the cardinal features of direct perception.

Transition: a quantitative or qualitative change in the state of a well-defined system. The time taken to change should be markedly shorter than that spent in prior and subsequent states. A quantitative transition involves a change in the number of attractors and a qualitative transition a change between different sorts of attractors. Nonlinear dynamics provides the mathematical tools for distinguishing between these two types of transition.

REFERENCES

Acredolo, L.P. (1978). Development of spatial orientation in infancy. *Developmental Psychology, 14*, 224–234.

Albano, A.M., Mees, A.I., de Guzman, G.C., & Rapp, P.E. (1987). Data requirements for reliable estimation of correlation dimensions. In H. Degn, A.V. Holden, & L.F. Olsen (eds), *Chaos in biological systems*, pp. 207–220. New York: Plenum Press.

Alexander, J.C., Giesen, B., Muench, R., & Smelser, N.J. (eds) (1987). *The micro-macro link*. Berkeley, Calif.: University of California Press.

Beek, Y. van, Hopkins, B., Hoeksma, J.B., & Samsom, J.F. (1994). Prematurity, posture and the development of looking behaviour during early communication. *Journal of Child Psychiatry and Psychology, 35*, 1093–1107.

Bernstein, N.A. (1967). *The coordination and regulation of movements*. Oxford: Pergamon Press.

Bertenthal, B.I., Campos, J.J., & Barrett, K.C. (1984). Self-produced locomotion: An organizer of emotional, cognitive and social development in infancy. In R. Emde, & R. Harmon, (eds), *Continuities and discontinuities in development*, pp. 175–210. New York: Plenum Press

Bertenthal, B.I., & Pinto, J. (1993). Complementary processes in the perception and production of human movements. In L.B. Smith & E. Thelen (eds), *A dynamic systems approach to development: applications*, pp. 209 239. Cambridge, Mass.: MIT Press.

Bhatias, N.P. & Szego, G.P. (1970). *Stability theory of dynamical systems*. New York: Pergamon.

Bingham, G.P. (1988). Task-specific devices and the perceptual bottleneck. *Human Movement Science, 7*, 225–264.

Bushnell, E.W. & Boudreau, J.P. (1993). Motor development and the mind: The potential role of motor abilities as a determinant of aspects of perceptual development. *Child Development, 64*, 1005–1021.

Clark, J.E. & Phillips, S.J. (1993). A longitudinal study of intralimb coordination in the first year of independent walking: A dynamical systems approach. *Child Development, 64*, 1143–1157.

Clark, J.E., Truly, T.L., & Phillips, S.J. (1990). A dynamical systems approach to understanding the development of lower limb coordination in locomotion. In H. Bloch, & B.I. Bertenthal, (eds), *Sensory-motor organizations and development in infancy and early childhood*, pp. 363–378. Dordrecht: Kluwer.

Clark, J.E., Truly, T.L., & Phillips, S.J. (1993). On the development of walking as a limit-cycle system. In L.B. Smith, & E. Thelen (eds), *A dynamic systems approach to development: applications*, pp. 71–93. Cambridge, Mass.: MIT Press.

Clark, J.E., Whitall, J., & Phillips, S.J. (1988). Human interlimb coordination: The first six months of independent walking. *Developmental Psychobiology, 21*, 445–456.

Cobb, L. & Zacks, S. (1985). Applications of catastrophe theory for statistical modeling in the biosciences. *Journal of the American Statistical Association, 80*, 793–802.

Easton, T.A. (1972). On the normal use of reflexes. *American Scientist, 60*, 591–599.
Eccles, J.C. (1989). *Evolution of the brain: creation of the self.* London: Routledge.
Feldman, A.G. (1966). Functional tuning of the nervous system with control of movement and maintenance of a steady posture, III: Mechanographic analysis of execution by man of the simplest motor tasks. *Biophysics, 11*, 766–775.
Feldman, A.G. (1986). Once more the equilibrium point hypothesis (model) for motor control. *Journal of Motor Behavior, 18*, 17–54.
Fogel, A., Dedo, J.Y., & McEwen, I. (1992). Effect of postural position on the duration of gaze at mother during face-to-face interaction in 3-to-6-month-old infants. *Infant Behaviour and Development, 15*, 231–244.
Fogel, A. & Thelen, E. (1987). Development of early expressive and communicative action: Reinterpreting evidence from a dynamic systems perspective. *Developmental Psychology, 23*, 747–761.
Forrester, L.W., Phillips, S.J., & Clark, J.E. (1993). Locomotor coordination in infancy: The transition from walking to running. In G.J.P. Savelsbergh (ed.), *The development of coordination in infancy*, pp. 359–393. Amsterdam: North-Holland.
Gesell, A. & Amatruda, C.S. (1945). *The embryology of behavior.* New York: Harper.
Gibson, J.J. (1979). *The ecological approach to visual perception.* Boston: Houghton-Mifflin.
Golani, I. & Fentress, J.C. (1985). Early ontogeny of face grooming in mice. *Developmental Psychobiology, 18*, 529–544.
Goldfield, E.C. (1989). Transition from rocking to crawling: Postural constraints on infant movement. *Developmental Psychology, 25*, 913–919.
Goldfield, E.C. (1993). Dynamical systems in development: Action systems. In L.B. Smith & E. Thelen (eds), *A dynamic systems approach to development*, pp. 51–71. Cambridge Mass.: MIT Press.
Gustafson, G.E. (1984). Effects of the ability to locomote on infants' social and exploratory behaviors: An experimental study. *Developmental Psychology, 20*, 397–405.
Haken, H. (1977). *Synergetics: an introduction.* Berlin: Springer.
Haken, H., Kelso, J.A.S. Fuchs, A., & Pandya, A. (1990). Dynamic pattern recognition of coordinated biological motion. *Neural Networks, 3*, 395–401.
Haken, H.H., Kelso, J.A.S., & Bunz, H. (1985). A theoretical model of phase transitions in human hand movements. *Biological Cybernetics, 51*, 347–356.
Hebb, D. O. (1949). *The organization of behavior: a neurophysiological theory.* New York: Wiley.
Hofsten, C. von (1984). Developmental changes in the organization of prereaching movements. *Developmental Psychology, 20*, 378–388.
Hopkins, B., Beek, P.J., & Kalverboer, A.F. (1993). Theoretical issues in the longitudinal study of motor development. In A.F. Kalverboer, B. Hopkins & R. Geuze (eds) *Motor development in early and later childhood: longitudinal approaches*, pp. 343–371. Cambridge: Cambridge University Press.
Hopkins, B. & Butterworth, G. (1990). Concepts of causality in explanations of development. In G. Butterworth & P.E. Bryant (eds), *Causes of development: interdisciplinary perspectives*, pp. 3–32. Brighton: Harvester Press.
Hopkins, B. & Westra, T. (1988). Maternal handling and motor development: An intracultural study. *Genetic, Social and General Psychology Monographs, 114*, 377–408.
Hoyt, D.F. & Taylor, C.R. (1981). Gait and the energetics of locomotion in horses. *Nature, 292*, 239–240.
Ingen Schenau, G.J. van (1989). From rotation to translation: Constraints on multi-joint movements and the unique action of bi-articular muscles. *Human Movement Science, 8*, 301–337.
Kelso, J.A.S., Scholz, J., & Schöner, G. (1986). Nonequilibrium phase transitions in coordinated biological motion: Critical fluctuations. *Physics Letters A, 118*, 279–284.

Lockman. J.J. & Thelen, E. (1993). Developmental biodynamics: Brain, body, behavior connections. *Child Development, 64*, 953–959.

Maresh, M.M. (1984). Bone, muscle and fat measurements: Longitudinal measurements of bone, muscle and fat widths from roentograms of the extremities during first six years of life. *Pediatrics, 61*, 971–984

May, R.M. (1976). Simple mathematical models with very complicated dynamics. *Nature, 261*, 459–467.

McCauley, J.L. (1993). *Chaos, dynamics and fractals: an algorithmic approach to deterministic chaos.* Cambridge: Cambridge University Press.

Morrison, F. (1991). *The art of modeling dynamic systems.* New York: Wiley.

Nakaya, U. (1954). *Snow crystals.* Cambridge, Mass.: Harvard University Press.

Newell, K.M. (1986). Constraints on the development of coordination. In M.G. Wade & H.T.A. Whiting (eds), *Motor development in children: aspects of coordination and control*, pp. 341–360. Dordrecht: Martinus Nijhoff.

Nicolis, G. & Prigogine, I. (1977). *Self-organization in nonequilibrium systems: from dissipative structures to order through fluctuations.* New York: Wiley.

Nittman, J. & Stanley, H.E. (1986). Tip splitting without interfacial tension and dendritic growth patterns arising from molecular anisotropy. *Nature, 321*, 663–668.

Piaget, J. (1952). *The origins of intelligence in children.* New York: Norton.

Prigogine, I. & Stengers, I. (1984). *Order out of chaos: man's new dialogue with nature.* New York: Bantam Books.

Reed, E.S. (1982). Outline of a theory of action systems. *Journal of Motor Behavior, 14*, 98–134.

Robertson, S.S. (1993). Oscillations and complexity in early infant behavior. *Child Development, 64*, 1022–1035.

Robertson, S.S., Cohen, A.H., & Mayer-Kress, G. (1993). Behavioral chaos: Beyond the metaphor. In L.B. Smith & E. Thelen (eds), *A dynamic systems theory approach to development: applications*, pp. 119–150. Cambridge, Mass.: MIT Press.

Robson, P. (1970). Shuffling, hitching, scooting or sliding: Some observations in 30 otherwise normal children. *Developmental and Child Neurology, 12*, 608–617.

Saltzman, E.L. & Kelso, J.A.S. (1987). Skilled actions: A task-dynamic approach. *Psychological Review, 94*, 84–106.

Savelsbergh, G.J.P. & Kamp, J. van der (1993). The coordination of infant's reaching, grasping, catching and posture: A natural-physical approach. In G.J.P. Savelsbergh (ed), *The development of coordination in infancy*, pp. 289–317. Amsterdam: North-Holland.

Schneider, K., Zernicke, R.F., Ulrich, B.D., & Jensen, J.L. (1990). Understanding movement control in infants through the analysis of limb intersegmental dynamics. *Journal of Motor Behavior, 22*, 493–520.

Scholz, J., Kelso, J.A.S., & Schöner, G. (1987). Nonequilibrium phase transitions in coordinated biological motion: Critical slowing down and switching time. *Physics Letters A, 123*, 390–394.

Schöner, G. (1990). A dynamic theory of discrete movement. *Biological Cybernetics, 63*, 257–270.

Shaw, R.E. & Todd, J. (1980). Abstract machine theory and direct perception. *Behavioral and Brain Sciences, 3*, 400–401.

Skarda, C.A. & Freeman, W.J. (1987). How brains make chaos in order to make sense of the world. *Behavioral and Brain Sciences, 10*, 161–195.

Soll, D.R. (1979). Timers in developing systems. *Science, 203*, 841–849.

Spelke, E.S. (1990). Origins of visual knowledge. In D.N. Osherson, S.M. Kosslyn, & J.M. Hollerbach (eds), *Visual cognition and action*, Vol. 2, pp. 99–127. Cambridge, Mass.: MIT Press.

Stent, G.S. (1981). Strength and weaknesses of the genetic approach to development of the nervous system. *Annual Review of Neurosciences, 4*, 163–194.

Thelen, E. (1985). Developmental origins of motor coordination: Leg movements in human infants. *Developmental Psychobiology*, *18*, 1–22.

Thelen, E. (1986). Treadmill-elicited stepping in seven-month-old infants. *Child Development*, *57*, 1497–1506.

Thelen, E., Corbetta, D., Kamm, K., Spencer, J.P., Schneider, K., & Zernicke, R.F. (1993). The transition to reaching: Mapping intention and intrinsic dynamics. *Child Development*, *64*, 1058–1098.

Thelen, E., Fisher, D.M., & Ridley-Johnson, R. (1984). The relationship between physical growth and a newborn reflex. *Infant Behavior and Development*, *7*, 479–493.

Thom, R. (1975). *Structural stability and morphogenesis: an outline of a general theory of models*. (trans. D.H. Fowler). Reading, Mass.: Benjamin.

Thompson, D.W. (1917). *On growth and form*. Cambridge: Cambridge University Press.

Thompson, J.M.T. & Stewart, H.B. (1986). *Nonlinear dynamics and chaos: geometrical methods for engineers and scientists*. Chichester: Wiley.

Trettien, A. (1900). Creeping and crawling. *American Journal of Psychology*, *12*, 1–57.

Touwen, B.C.L. (1976). *Neurological development in infancy*. London: Heinemann.

Turvey, M.T., Shaw, R.E., & Mace, W. (1978). Issues in theory of action: Degrees of freedom, coordinative structures and coalitions. In J. Requin (ed.), *Attention and performance*, *VII* pp. 557–595. Hillsdale, N.J.: Lawrence Erlbaum Associates Inc.

Waddington, C. (1975). *Evolution of an evolutionist*. Edinburgh: Edinburgh University Press.

Werner, H. (1948). *Comparative psychology of mental development*. New York: International University Press.

Wolff, P. H. (1986). The maturation and development of fetal motor patterns. In M.G. Wade & H.T.A. Whiting (eds), *Motor development in children: aspects of coordination and control*, pp. 65–74. Dordrecht: Martinus Nijhoff.

Wolff, P.H. (1991). Endogenous motor rhythms in young infants. In J. Fagard & P.H. Wolff (eds), *The development of timing control and temporal organization in coordinated action*, pp. 119–133. Amsterdam: North-Holland.

Wunderlin, A. (1987). On the slaving principle. *Springer Proceedings in Physics*, *19*, 140–147.

Yates, E.F. (1987). General introduction. In E.F. Yates (ed.). *Self-organizing systems: the emergence of order*, pp. 1–14. New York: Plenum Press.

Yonas, A. & Granrud, C.E. (1985). Reaching as a measure of infants' spatial perception. In G. Gottlieb & N. Krasnegor (eds), *Measurement of audition and vision in the first year of life: a methodological overview*, pp. 301–322. Norwood, N.J.: Ablex.

Zanone, P.G., Kelso, J.A.S., & Jeka, J.J. (1993). Concepts and methods for a dynamical approach to behavioral coordination and change. In G.J.P. Savelsbergh (ed.), *The development of coordination in infancy*, pp. 89–135. Amsterdam: North-Holland.

Zelaznik, H.N. (1993). The role of motor development in infancy. In G.J.P. Savelsbergh (ed.), *The development of coordination in infancy*, pp. 79–88. Amsterdam: North-Holland.

Zernicke, R.F. & Schneider, K. (1993). Biomechanics and developmental neuromotor control. *Child Development*, *64*, 982–1004.

2 COGNITIVE DEVELOPMENT

Cognitive Development: Introduction

For many years, ideas about cognitive development were dominated by Piaget's theory of sensori-motor development, according to which early knowledge of the world is constructed through action on the world. And much of the literature in this area stemmed from Piaget's account of the development of concepts of objects and space, according to which objective awareness of the world arises relatively late in infancy through construction of an objective representational world from subjective sense data.

As we have seen from the preceding section, this Piagetian viewpoint is seen by many as no longer viable. The Gibsonian theory of direct perception is based on the principle of objective perception; that is, that information of about the world is available in perceptual stimulation in objective form. And the consequence is that there is no need to propose cognitive structures whose purpose is to represent the perceived world in objective form. Certainly, there is growing evidence for objective perception in very early infancy, right back at birth in fact, and such evidence sits more comfortably in a Gibsonian framework than in a Piagetian one.

But it is not only the evidence on perceptual competence of young infants that presents a challenge to the Piagetian account. There is now a large body of work, much of it carried out by Renee Baillargeon and Elizabeth Spelke, which indicates that the young infant's understanding of physical reality is much more advanced than Piaget recognised. This evidence is based on variants of the habituation-novelty technique, with longer looking times at events that violate the rules of reality taken as evidence of the infant's awareness of how the world should operate; and the results are certainly compelling enough. However, we are left with the problem of explaining why, if infants possess such advanced knowledge, they fail to reveal it in their purposive behaviour until so much later. In the penultimate chapter of the previous section, Bremner suggested that these habituation-style tasks reveal a form of knowledge that is not yet explicit in the sense of being available to guide action. In the first chapter of this section, Willatts tackles the Baillargeon evidence more directly, claiming that such work treats the infant as a "couch potato", an individual who observes the world but does not act. Of course, there are perfectly good reasons why these studies are as they are: it is precisely because infants might act in a very limited way that other means of extracting their level of knowledge are adopted. But there are potential important limitations to what these methods can extract. As Willatts points out, while young infants may be able to recognise that a hidden object cannot be retrieved unless the cover is first removed, this does not mean that they are capable of selecting precisely the right action to affect object retrieval on their own. And from his point of view, cognitive development in infancy is in large part to do with with means-ends problem solving through which the knowledgeable observer-infant becomes a competent actor on the basis of prior knowledge.

There is another aspect of this that may be worth considering. It is apparent from the work of Baillargeon and colleagues that quite young infants are well tuned to detect violations of normal event sequences carried out by others. One wonders whether this aptitude is geared to a social process in cognitive development. Although young infants cannot solve means-ends problems through their own efforts, maybe a necessary (but not sufficient) source of information about effective action on the world is gained through watching others act on objects.

In the second chapter, Rutkowska takes a broader perspective on cognitive development, looking at the degree to which current approaches in Cognitive Science relate both to Piaget's theory and to more recent conceptualisations of infant development. She points out how there is now general dissatisfaction with the Piagetian notion of representation as an internal model of reality, but also notes that there the primary opponent theory—ecological psychology—has problems in having little to say about action. Part of this problem may be avoided by ecological approaches adopting dynamic systems theory (see Chapter 4). But Rutkowska suggests that representation is still a valid concept when it is used to describe the correspondences that are established between environmental features and action, and presents Karmiloff-Smith's model of representational redescription as a possible developmental account of cognitive development in the face of early perceptual competence. There is much in common between Rutkowska's theoretical analysis and proposals arising in the chapters by

Willatts (Chapter 5) and by Bremner (Chapter 3, in Part 1). Again the general message is that to understand cognitive development, we need to look at the relationships between infants' knowledge of the world as observers and their action capabilities. It appears that it is in development of relationships between "observer knowledge" and action that representation has its part to play, and it is largely development of these relationships that constitute cognitive development.

In the third chapter, Mandler addresses another central issue in infant cognition, the development of categorisation. This is another case in which although young infants appear to have to be perceptually sophisticated, there is a good deal of development to occur at a cognitive level. Mandler points out that although young infants are capable of perceptual categorisation, this is really very far from the ability to form true conceptual categories. Although perceptual categorisation is probably very useful in relation to perceptual recognition, it is only conceptual categories that contain meaning. And Mandler develops an account of the way conceptual categories are constructed out of perceptual categories through a process of active perceptual analysis. One can wonder to what extent there is a link here with the development of affordances, since an affordance could be seen as a functional category that contains meaning in terms of the infant's action. However, Mandler's data provide striking evidence that this is not all there is to it: infants are capable of categorising objects as animate versus inanimate, and even categorise correctly in cases when perpetual similarity is high; as, for example, in the case of aeroplanes versus birds. There is little case for this sort of category knowledge deriving from affordances or even conceptual knowledge of the relationship between perception and action.

These capabilities are made doubly impressive when we remember that they are not based on the real objects concerned, most of the research in this area being based on categorisation of toy objects and photographs or even line drawings of objects. The investigator coming from research involving infants' understanding of the everyday environment may be surprised that infants can perform at all with such artifacts of reality. But maybe this gives us a hint as to where to look for developmental mechanisms. Even before infants begin to use words, parents spend much time with them in play with toy objects and picture books, and it is very likely that these activities provide part of the basis for the formation of categories. Maybe the perceptual analysis that Mandler sees at the roots of conceptual category formation is strongly facilitated by the social structuring supplied by parents.

It is interesting to note that, despite differences in the orientation of these first three chapters, there is a common theme running throughout them: namely, that young infants show considerable competence at a basic or perceptual level and that cognitive development involves transforming perceptual "knowledge" or using it in a new way, in order to serve the infant's needs for action. Whether the process involved in this transformation is problem-solving, representational redescription, or perceptual analysis, the general theme is the same: infants come into the world well equipped to perceive it, but still have a long way to go before they can analyse the world at a cognitive level, whether this be in order to apply conceptual analysis to the world, or to guide action appropriately.

Development implies change, and the previous chapters in this section, and indeed the other chapters in the book, are concerned to describe and to account for some of the changes that occur in various domains of infant development. However, in Chapter 8 Bornstein et al. point out that developmental psychology is as much interested in stability as it is in change. Stability here refers to consistency in the relative rank ordering of individuals over time: we might expect that the bright and capable infant will become the bright and capable child, and conversely, that the infant who is slow to develop might become the child who struggles at school. Research intended to explore this proposed stability or consistency in development has been with us for many years, and a major focus has been on continuity in intellectual development from infancy to early (or late) childhood. This research usually takes the form of measuring infants' capabilities at one point in time and measuring their abilities on standardised tests of intelligence, language or other cognitive abilities months or years later.

Bornstein et al. suggest that there have been three "waves" of this research. The first wave has been to demonstrate that performance on standardised tests of infant development, tests that have been available for over 50 years, does not correlate with these children's later performance on tests of cognitive abilities. However, from about the end of the 1970s it began to be argued that the so-called "mental scales" on the tests of infant development were primarily measuring motor and perceptual development rather than mental development . The search was then on for valid measures of cognitive abilities in infancy which might be potential predictors of later development, and the "second wave" of this research demonstrated that measures of habituation to visual stimuli in infancy *do* predict later development, albeit to a moderate degree. As infants habituate (show a decline in visual attention) to a repeatedly-presented stimulus, this probably reflects a growing cognitive familiarity with the stimulus, and it has been argued that rapid habituators are rapid processors of information.

The third, and most recent, "wave" is to find tasks, other than habituation, that are genuinely measuring cognitive abilities in infants and which are potential, or proven, predictors of later development. This area of research has strong theoretical implications since it is changing our conceptions of the nature of intelligence in infancy. It is also of considerable practical importance in that it will ultimately lead to tests of infant cognitive development that will allow us to detect infants "at risk" for cognitive delay with a view to introducing measures to remediate or reduce the delay at a very early age.

5 Beyond the "Couch Potato" Infant: How Infants Use Their Knowledge to Regulate Action, Solve Problems, and Achieve Goals

Peter Willatts
Department of Psychology, University of Dundee, UK.

The last 10 years have been an exciting period for researchers studying the development of infant cognition. New work has established that young infants appear to possess a core of knowledge about the basic principles of the physical world, such as solidity, causality, trajectory, and number (see Baillargeon, 1993; Leslie, 1988; Mandler, 1992; Meltzoff, 1990; Spelke, Breinlinger, Macomber, & Jacobson, 1992 for reviews). This core of knowledge allows infants to interpret and anticipate the immediate outcome of physical events. Infants appear to know that solid objects should not pass through each other, should not hang in mid-air without a visible means of support, and that objects moving on a trajectory follow a continuous path and do not jump mysteriously from one place to another. There is also abundant evidence that young infants can represent the existence of hidden objects, and that their representations specify not only the continued existence of an object, but also include information about position, size, physical properties such as rigidity and flexibility, and even number.

A second claim arising from this new work is that young infants are able to reason with their representations and can generate new information about an event, even when that event has not been perceived directly. For example, Baillargeon (1986) habituated 6-month-old infants to a sequence in which the middle section of a track was screened, a toy truck was released at one side, ran down the track, disappeared behind the screen and reappeared on the other side. On subsequent test events, infants first saw a solid block placed either behind the track (the possible event) or on the track (the impossible event). The block was screened, the truck released, and it was seen to emerge at the far side in both events. Although on the surface the appearance of the test events was the same, infants looked reliably longer at the impossible event. Baillargeon concluded that infants: (1) represented the continued existence of the hidden block and the truck; (2) included information about the position of the block in their representation; (3) understood that one solid object should not pass through another; and (4) anticipated the outcome of each event by making an inference about the constraint that the block would impose on the movement of the truck. Infants were more interested when the outcome of the impossible event did not accord with their reasoning, and this heightened interest resulted in their longer looking time. Thus, not only do infants possess a core of physical knowledge, but they also make use of active representations to reason with this knowledge (Spelke et al., 1992).

These *core knowledge* and *active representations* hypotheses of infancy stand in stark contrast to Piaget's (1953; 1954) views on the nature of sensory-motor knowledge and intelligence. Piaget claimed that infants have no innate physical knowledge and can discover the properties and characteristics of objects only by observing the effects of their actions. For example, he described several observations which were interpreted as showing how his own children acquired concepts of size and shape constancy by observing the effects of moving objects towards or away from themselves (Piaget, 1954, obs. 86–91).

Piaget also denied that infants had any innate capacity for thinking and reasoning, and one source of evidence for this claim comes from his observations of problem solving. According to Piaget, the one problem-solving strategy available to infants is trial-and-error where they first try out a potential solution, evaluate the outcome, and determine what to do next on the basis of feedback. It is only in the final stage of the sensory-motor period that infants begin to solve problems by mentally generating and evaluating possible solutions, and this capacity to plan solutions arises from the internalisation of previously successful actions that were originally co-ordinated by trial-and-error (Willatts, 1989).

For Piaget, exploration of the world through perception and action is the route by which infants develop processes for thinking and reasoning and the capacity to use symbolic representations. This means that cognitive development in infancy depends primarily on the infant's growing abilities at examining, manipulating, and exploring objects. Thus, Piaget emphasised the importance of the development of motor skills such as reaching and crawling for the development of concepts such as object permanence and spatial knowledge. For example, following the onset of reaching and grasping, the subsequent development of a variety of object-directed actions such as shaking, mouthing, and striking provide the components from which simple means–end behaviours become co-ordinated. At around 7 or 8 months, infants begin to deliberately remove a cover to search for a hidden object (Willatts, 1984a), or pull a support to retrieve an object that is resting on it (Willatts, 1984b; 1996). This means–end behaviour is clearly intentional because the first action is performed in order that a second, future action can be carried out.

Although Piaget regarded intentional means–end behaviour as among the first genuine acts of intelligence, he did not see any need to interpret it as showing an early capacity for representation and reasoning. Piaget denied that the infant needs to represent a hidden object in order to remove a cover and search for it. Instead, he argued that infants simply treat the cover as a visible index for the presence of the hidden object: "searching for an object under a screen when the subject has seen it disappear there (Stages IV and V) does not necessarily presuppose that the subject 'imagines' the object under the screen, but simply that he has understood the relation of the two objects at the moment he perceived it (at the moment when the object was covered) and that he therefore interprets the screen as a sign of the actual presence of the object." (Piaget, 1954, p. 84). As evidence for such a severe limitation on infants' understanding, Piaget described the occurrence of what is now known as the A not–B search error where the infant returns to the original place of hiding (place A) to search for an object which has subsequently been hidden at a new place (placc B). Piaget interpreted these search errors as showing that young infants do not have a representation of an object as a substantial thing which is independent of action, but instead regard objects as tied to specific actions at a specific place. In Piaget's view, search that is guided by a representation of the hidden object develops in the final stage of infancy (after 18 months) when infants first show a capacity for symbolic representation.

The core knowledge and active representations hypotheses offer a very different account of the development of infant intelligence. In many recent studies, infants have been too young and immature to show the motor skills that Piaget felt were critical for cognitive development. The fact that these young infants are able to reason about the outcomes of events that are nor directly observable shows that the ability to think and reason does not need to emerge through the gradual internalisation of action. Similarly, the fact that young infants' reasoning is in accord with physical principles shows that at least some physical knowledge is not acquired through the gradual exploration of the world. However, there is one puzzling feature of young infants'' behaviour that does not fit easily with these hypotheses. If infants display such a range of sophisticated knowledge when they observe events, why do they display such a degree of ignorance when they begin to act on objects and try to solve problems for themselves?

There appears to be a striking difference between the ability of young infants to reason with physical knowledge when interpreting events, and their ability to reason with this knowledge to solve means–end problems. For example, infants can detect when a physically impossible event involving a hidden object has occurred, but are unable to search for a hidden object themselves. If infants as young as 3 months possess a concept of object permanence, why do they apparently fail to use this knowledge immediately on simple means–end tasks such as search or pulling a support, and only produce solutions several months later (Willatts, 1984a; 1994; 1996)?

There is a similar apparent dissociation between knowledge and performance on the A not–B search task. Eight-month-old infants will search for a hidden object, and we know from work by Baillargeon and her colleagues (Baillargeon & Graber, 1988; Baillargeon, DeVos, & Graber, 1989) that they can also remember the correct location of an object that was hidden behind one of two covers for an interval as long as 70 seconds. However, when the object is hidden at a new place on the B trials, 8-month-old infants will persistently reach to the incorrect location after a much shorter interval (Bremner, 1978; Butterworth, 1977; Gratch et al., 1974).

THE INFANT AS A "COUCH POTATO"

One possible explanation for these apparent failures of infants to apply their knowledge when attempting to solve problems is that the methods used for studying young infants are inadequate for revealing all of the knowledge and mental processes that are necessary for problem solving. Studies of young infants have generally made use of a single paradigm based on visual observation. Infants observe events that are either physically possible or impossible but which on the surface appear to look the same. Infants typically look longer at events that are physically impossible, from which it can be concluded that they must have interpreted what should have happened, anticipated the outcome, and were more interested when the observed outcome failed to match with their expectation. This visual observation paradigm has proved to be enormously successful in revealing both the existence of an impressive core of physical knowledge in young infants, and ability to use this knowledge in conjunction with representations to interpret a wide range of events. However, the paradigm offers a relatively limited view of infants who are really nothing more than "couch potatoes" in these experiments. The infant merely has to sit and watch the events unfold, but never has an opportunity to act on objects and make the events happen for themselves. Of course, young infants who have not yet developed sufficient manual skills would be unable to manipulate objects, but what of infants who have achieved a sufficient level of skill? Is it possible that the "couch potato" paradigm has shown only that infants possess a core of physical knowledge and processes for reasoning about observed events, but has failed to show that infants also possess a core of processes for thinking and for solving problems?

Surprisingly, we know relatively little about infants' problem solving, and this is a serious deficiency in our understanding of infant intelligence. Problem solving involves considerably more than concepts, memories, and perception of environmental invariants which a couch potato infant can use to interpret events. In addition, problem solving also involves co-ordinating, guiding, monitoring, and evaluating a sequence of goal-directed actions, and can be especially powerful because the sequence of actions can be predetermined at the level of symbol manipulation or thought. Thus, the study of problem solving in infancy offers a means of studying the origin and development of mental processes as they come to guide goal-directed action (Fabricius & Willatts, 1995; Willatts & Fabricius, 1996). The worry is that in reducing the role of infants in our studies to that of a couch potato, we may have ignored the development of several fundamental mental processes.

Researchers have been aware of this issue for some time and there have been a number of attempts to explain why infants have such difficulty applying their knowledge when solving problems. In general, these explanations are based on the assumption that infants do possess sufficient knowledge and processes for reasoning to solve problems, but that performance often breaks down because of inadequate executive control. For example, one current interpretation of the A not–B search error is that it arises from immature control of inhibitory processes that are mediated by prefrontal cortex, rather than a lack of conceptual knowledge (Diamond, 1991). By arguing that failures at problem solving reflect difficulties in regulating behaviour, researchers have sought to defend the claim that infant intelligence is based on a core of knowledge and active representations that are not constructed by experience. In the remainder of this chapter, I shall consider how successful these explanations are at defending this claim.

DEVELOPMENT OF MEANS–END BEHAVIOUR

One approach has been to argue that infants as young as 3 months understand that hidden objects continue to exist, and their understanding of occlusion events is essentially the same as that of an adult (Baillargeon, 1993). This approach denies there is any substantial change in infants' knowledge, and we must therefore look for other reasons to explain their failure to search. A simple explanation is that young infants lack sufficient motor skill to conduct a search, but this proves not to be the case. Willatts (1984a) showed that 6-month-olds could readily pick up both a screen and a toy, although their "search" occurred as a sequence of independent actions in which the infant first picked up the screen, played with it, then noticed the toy, and picked it up as well. This type of search at 6 months was not intentional and directed towards the goal of retrieving the hidden toy, because infants' behaviour with the screen was exactly the same on trials when a toy had been hidden as on trials when no toy had been hidden. In contrast, the same infants searched intentionally when tested again at 7 and 8 months, and showed this by deliberately picking up the screen and setting it aside more often when the toy was hidden.

An alternative suggestion for failure to search intentionally is that co-ordination of the necessary skilled behaviour overloads the infant's limited attentional capacity. Essentially, the infant knows the hidden object continues to exist, intends to remove the cover in order to find it, but the attentional demands of reaching interfere with the infant's ability to keep the original goal in mind. For example, Bushnell (1985) argued that reaching between 5 and 8 months is visually guided, and the demands of executing an accurate, visually-guided reach would naturally interfere with the encoding of a means–end sequence. Because attention may be completely taken up by monitoring the relation between the seen target and the seen hand, the infant is unable to think beyond the initial step of retrieving the screen to reaching for the hidden object. Only when reaching becomes practised and automatic at around 8 or 9 months will attention be released so that infants can think ahead to achieving the final goal.

Although this is a plausible explanation for the relatively late appearance of intentional search and other means–end behaviour, there is a good reason for rejecting this account. One of the strongest pieces of evidence that Bushnell offers in support of her claim that reaching is visually guided comes from a study of perceptual adaptation by McDonnell and Abraham (1979). Infants' reaching for visual targets was observed while they were wearing prism glasses that displaced the visual field laterally. If reaching is visually guided, such a displacement should have minimal effects because the seen hand and the seen target are not displaced relative to each other and the reach can still be guided successfully. Additionally, there should also be minimal evidence of any after-effect on displacement of reaching when the prisms are removed. Although McDonnell and Abraham did record such after-effects, they found that their magnitude decreased markedly at 7 months, but increased by 9 months.

Their interpretation of this finding was that control of reaching becomes increasingly visually guided at 7 months, but changes to a more ballistic, visually elicited form at 9 months. However, this *increase* in visual guidance at 7 months coincides exactly with the *first* appearance of intentional search reported by Willatts (1984a), and also with the first appearance of another early means–end behaviour—pulling a support to retrieve a toy. In a longitudinal study, Willatts (1996) reported a significant increase between 6 and 7 months in the occurrence of behaviour that suggested infants were intentionally pulling a cloth to retrieve a toy resting on the far end. At 6 months, infants generally picked up the cloth support in order to play with it or examine it. In the course of this activity, the toy was dragged nearer, and when it eventually came within reach, infants would often retrieve it. Their behaviour with the cloth when it was presented without a toy resting on it was exactly the same as when there was a toy, further suggesting that infants were acting on the cloth for its own sake and were not attempting to use it to retrieve the toy. In contrast, infants at 7 months were far more likely just to pull the cloth without any play, and did so more often when there was a toy on the cloth than they did when they were simply offered a cloth without a toy. It is therefore difficult to maintain that the attentional demands of visually-guided reaching interfere with the occurrence of intentional means–end behaviour when in fact the two occur together.

An altogether different explanation for the failure of young infants to search for hidden objects has been offered by Baillargeon, Graber, DeVos, and Black (1990) who suggest that infants may have difficulty planning the sequence of means–end actions required to solve a search problem. They point out that a state-space analysis of means–end problems such as search identifies several important components that are necessary to achieve a solution (Nilsson, 1971). In a state-space analysis, the problem is defined as a set of states which describe different situations that can be reached by the problem solver (the problem space). Of these, the initial state is the initial situation which confronts the problem solver, and the goal state is the final state that the problem solver is trying to achieve. The solution path is a set of intermediate states that connect the initial state to the goal state. Action operators are the actions or procedures which transform one state into another. For example, the two action operators that transform the initial state on a search task (object behind screen) into the goal state (object in infant's hand) are first, picking up the screen, and second, picking up the object.

Baillargeon et al. suggest that infants would fail to search if they have a different goal state from that of retrieving the hidden toy, or are unable to represent the initial state. However, they reject both of these possibilities. Infants as young as 5 months are clearly interested in retrieving the goal, and will persist in reaching directly for it even when it has disappeared from view by the simple method of turning the room lights out (Clifton, Rochat, Litovsky, & Perris, 1991; Hood & Willatts, 1986). Infants do not lose interest in an object simply because it has gone out of sight, and do not ignore an object that was hidden because they do eventually pick it up, even though they are unable to search (Willatts, 1984a). The goal object is usually a highly attractive toy which is clearly preferred to the cover or screen, and in an unpublished study I found that both 5- and 6-month-old infants reached for a toy significantly more often than either a cover or a support cloth when both objects were visible and presented alongside each other. It is also unlikely that infants are unable to represent the initial state of a search problem, given that infants will reach for objects in the dark, and can detect the occurrence of "impossible" events that require a representation of the existence and location of objects that are hidden from view (Baillargeon, 1993).

If infants do represent both the initial and goal states of a means–end problem, then their failure to solve the problem intentionally may be due to a lack of knowledge about the relevant action operator. For example, infants may be unaware that one consequence of picking up a cover will be to render the hidden object accessible, and this would be a serious limitation on their problem solving because they would not understand how their actions on objects could produce a specific and desired outcome.

An ingenious experiment by Baillargeon et al. (1990) used the visual observation paradigm to try to examine this issue. In this study, 5-month-old infants were shown object retrieval events to determine whether they understood that a toy placed under a cover could be retrieved only after the cover had been removed. Infants were shown two different covers that stood beside each other, with both at the left side of the display. The cover at the far left was an inverted, transparent cup, and the cover next to it (slightly to the right of the cup) was an inverted cage. A toy bear was clearly visible under one of these covers. A person reaching across from the right of the display would have to use different procedures to retrieve the bear, depending on which cover it was under. When the bear was under the cage, the cage would have to be removed first before the bear could be retrieved. When the bear was under the cup, the cage would have to be removed first in order to reach the cup, and then the cup would have to be removed in order to retrieve the bear.

The entire display was hidden from view with a screen, and infants viewed a sequence of events in which first the cage and then the bear were withdrawn from behind the screen. In the possible event, the bear had originally been positioned under the cage. A hand moved across from the right, went behind the screen, appeared with the cage, set it down, then reached back, and reappeared with the bear. In the impossible event, the bear had originally been positioned under the cup, but the sequence of events was exactly the same: first the cage appeared and then the bear. However, this was an impossible event because the bear was apparently retrieved without first removing the cup under which it had been placed.

Even though both these events had exactly the same surface appearance, infants looked significantly longer at the impossible event. Baillargeon et al. concluded that infants must have represented the initial location of the bear under the cover, understood the cover had to be removed before the bear could be grasped, and were therefore surprised to see the bear without first seeing the cover. This conclusion was reinforced by the findings of a control experiment in which the inverted cup at the left was replaced by a low dish, again with the cage beside it. The bear was positioned either beneath the cage or in the dish. Because the bear was not covered when it was in the dish, it could be retrieved directly in both situations after the cage had been removed. Once the display was screened, infants saw the same sequence of events as before. In contrast to the previous experiment, infants looked for the same amount of time at these two events, presumably because both were physically possible.

A second unpublished study (Baillargeon, DeVos, & Black, 1992, cited in Baillargeon, 1993) showed that 6-month-old infants may also be able to identify the correct sequence of actions for retrieving an object by pulling a support. Infants were shown a possible and an impossible event in which they first viewed a long, rigid platform. In the possible event, a toy bear was placed on the far end of the platform. In the impossible event, the bear was placed next to the end of the platform, but was not resting on it. A screen was then moved across to conceal both the platform and the bear. The upper right-hand corner of this screen had been removed to make a small window. Infants next saw a hand which reached behind the screen, grasped the end of the platform and pulled it until the bear's head appeared in the window. The hand then grasped the bear and removed it from the platform. Again, infants looked longer at the impossible than the possible event, suggesting that they had represented the position of the bear relative to the platform, understood that the bear should move with the platform only if it was standing on it, and were more interested in the event that produced an outcome which should not have occurred.

Both these studies show that infants looked longer when the outcome of either a search or support event was inconsistent with the spatial information provided at the outset. Baillargeon interpreted these findings as evidence that young infants do have the relevant operators to solve means–end problems. To detect the impossible events, infants must have encoded the relevant spatial relations between the objects and understood their implications for object retrieval. If infants do represent initial and goal states and possess the relevant operators, then there must be some other explanation for their failure to solve means–end problems.

Baillargeon's suggestion is that infants fail to carry out an appropriate evaluation of the relevant operator for achieving the subgoal on these means–end tasks. Infants do not choose to remove covers or pull supports because they perceive these intermediaries as being in conflict with their original goal. If this goal is to grasp an attractive toy, grasping the cover or support is rejected as an appropriate method because these are unattractive objects that the infant does not want. However, there are two main problems with this conflict hypothesis. First, it does not explain why infants ever manage to solve means–end problems at all. If an intermediary perceived as unattractive is avoided at 6 months, it should still be perceived as unattractive and avoided at 8 months. Clearly it is not; and Baillargeon's explanation fails to account for the rapid improvement that occurs within the space of two months. Second, it is based on the mistaken assumption that infants who fail to solve means–end problems ignore the intermediaries. In fact, young infants invariably do the opposite and show too much interest in the cover or support for their behaviour to be rated as intentional, even when they do manage to retrieve the goal object (Willatts, 1984a; 1996).

One attempt to investigate this conflict hypothesis was reported by Kolstad (1993) who tested 6-month-old infants on two different versions of a support task. In one version, infants were initially presented with a cloth and a toy that was visibly separate. The cloth was positioned in front of the infant, and the toy was then set down on the far end of the cloth. In the second version, the toy was initially fastened to the cloth to produce a single cloth–toy object, and both were set down together. Kolstad reported that infants were far more successful at retrieving the toy when it was fastened to the cloth than they were when the two had originally been seen as separate. She argued that infants avoided the cloth when it was separate from the toy because it was the toy they wanted, not the cloth. In contrast, they did approach the cloth when it was joined to the toy because it was seen to be part of the desired object and did not provoke a conflict.

However, in a more recent study I have been unable to replicate this finding (Willatts, 1996, experiment 2). Six-month-old infants were no more successful at solving a support task when the toy was attached to the cloth than they were when the toy and cloth were separate, and their behaviour with the cloth was exactly the same regardless of whether the toy was attached, separate, or even when there was no toy present at all. Performance improved considerably at 7 months with evidence that infants could produce intentional solutions, but again there was no difference between the toy-separate and toy-attached tasks.

One possible explanation for the difference between these studies could be the measures that were recorded to identify intentional behaviour. Kolstad recorded how often infants retrieved the toy, while Willatts recorded the behaviours that occurred and rated them for intention to achieve the goal (e.g. playing with the cloth suggests no intention, but pulling the cloth suggests intentional behaviour). When the infant picks up the cloth to play with it, the toy occasionally falls off and cannot be retrieved, but of course this could never occur when it is attached to the cloth. Although 6-month-old infants in my own study were rather more successful at retrieving the toy when it was attached to the cloth, this was not a significant effect. However,

Kolstad used a much larger toy that would have been easier to dislodge in this way, and perhaps this was the reason for their lower rate of toy retrieval. Whatever the explanation, the difference between these studies highlights the need to consider the method infants use to achieve a goal, rather than simply whether the goal is achieved or not. Development of means–end behaviour does not involve a shift from ignoring the intermediaries to using them effectively; instead, it involves a shift in how they are used and whether their use is intentional and aimed at achieving a future goal.

This shift in the method used to solve means–end problems suggests that young infants do not have the relevant operators but begin to acquire them between 6 and 8 months. But if this is the case, how can we explain the findings of Baillargeon et al.? The answer is that infants do not need means–end operators to interpret the events in these visual observation studies. Instead, infants' interpretations could be based on more general information that does not specify exactly how to achieve means–end solutions. Infants clearly must represent the spatial information in the original display because they distinguish the outcomes even though the events are hidden from view. To achieve this, all they need do is keep track of the steps and update their representation as the event unfolds. For example, if an empty hand moves behind the screen and re-appears with the cover, the infant deletes the cover from its representation. When the hand next retrieves the object, the infant can interpret this as a possible event by referring to its updated representation. If the cover was not removed, the infant has to imagine the hand and object passing through the cover, which is impossible.

Although this is evidence for an impressive capacity for constructing and updating symbolic representations which must include spatial information, it does not mean that infants can use this information to direct their own actions to solve problems. The reason is that when infants interpret these concealed events they never have to consider the *specific* action that is required for solving the problem. In the case of search, the action of uncovering is hidden from view. All the infant needs to do is notice the outcome and update its representation of the initial state. In contrast, action operators for problem solving relate spatial information to outcomes through very specific actions. In the case of search, this specific action is removal of the cover, which involves picking it up and setting it aside. Although the study of Baillargeon et al. shows that infants do know a covered object can be retrieved only if the cover is no longer in place, it does not show that they understand exactly how this should be accomplished.

The same interpretation can be applied to the study with the platform support. Differential looking at the possible and impossible events shows that infants understand that objects in contact will move together when the support is pulled, but this does not mean that they have the relevant operator for solving the problem. This operator requires the specific knowledge that pulling the support towards the infant will bring the object within reach. When the infant sees the hand pull the platform, she can work out how the object will move. However, when trying to solve the problem herself, the infant must first select the appropriate action from a variety of alternatives such as pulling, pushing, lifting, shaking, and rotating, and this is what young infants appear unable to do.

This state of affairs is not at all uncommon. For instance, I know that the front panel of my dishwasher must first be removed before I can gain access to a broken switch in order to replace it, but I have no idea how to remove the panel. Although I lack the specific action operator to solve the problem, I do have sufficient knowledge to decide whether a technician has carried out the repair correctly. Knowledge of the physical constraint that one object imposes on the movements of another is necessary to evaluate whether a sequence of actions has been performed correctly, but is not sufficient to enable performance of the sequence.

Baillargeon's studies show that young infants do have knowledge which allows them to interpret a variety of actions and events. They know that moving a cover makes an object accessible and pulling a support will move an object resting on it. However, young infants may be unable to solve means–end problems because their knowledge does not specify the precise action sequence to achieve a goal. It will, therefore, be important to specify the exact nature of this difference in knowledge in order to understand exactly what is meant by the claim that young infants have a core of physical knowledge (Munakata, McClelland, Johnson, & Siegler, 1994). One possibility is that infants have to learn about the specific actions that will produce a desired outcome, and the period between 6 and 8 months may be when infants acquire the necessary operators for means–end problem solving through play and exploratory behaviour.

There is another possible explanation for infants' difficulties with means–end problem solving. Young infants may be unable to plan the correct sequence of actions because they are unable to conduct a means–end analysis. Means–end analysis is the best known example of the general class of problem-solving strategies known as problem reduction or subgoaling (Newell & Simon, 1972). In a means–end analysis, the problem solver first determines that the goal cannot be achieved directly, and then sets a subgoal to remove an obstacle or reduce a difference between the problem solver's current position and the goal state. More often than not, the subgoal itself cannot be achieved directly, in which case the problem solver repeats the means–end analysis procedure, this time focusing on achieving the subgoal. This continues until a recursive sequence of steps is constructed, each consisting of an action to achieve a subgoal, the last of which can be achieved directly. If young infants lack this capacity for subgoaling, they may be unable to solve means–end problems.

Baillargeon (1993) suggests that young infants do have a subgoaling capacity because there are many observations which show they produce a sequence of actions to achieve a goal. As an example, she cites an observation made by Piaget of his son who at 3 months discovered how to pull a chain and jiggle a rattle that was attached to it (Piaget, 1953, p. 163). While this behaviour was probably intentional (see Willatts, 1989, for a discussion of this observation and more recent work), it does not reveal an early capacity for subgoaling. Pulling the chain is the method (operator) by which the goal of moving the rattle is achieved; it is not the method by which a subgoal of overcoming an obstacle to moving the rattle is accomplished. Since the baby has no other method of moving the rattle, pulling the chain does not achieve any subgoal. Behaviours may be sequenced in many different ways, not all of which entail subgoal–goal relations (Willatts, 1990).

In fact, it is possible that early means–end behaviour does not require a capacity for subgoaling, even though the structure of simple means–end problems such as search and use of a support can be described in terms of a subgoal–goal relation. Infants' first successes at means–end problem solving may simply be the result of extending their initial core of physical and spatial knowledge. This will be a gradual process as infants discover the consequences of specific actions on objects in particular spatial configurations. Although such problem solving is planful in the sense that actions are directed towards a future goal, it may not be necessary for infants to think through and mentally plan a solution each time a new problem is encountered. Instead, infants may simply notice the relevant spatial information when an object is hidden or placed on a support, and that information activates a plan that has already been constructed and is available for use. Thus, infants may learn how to remove covers and pull supports through their everyday encounters with objects, and subsequently come to use these procedures in an automatic way, just as they come to reach directly and automatically for objects.

Evidence that means–end planning and a capacity for subgoaling may be a later development comes from a study by Willatts and Rosie (1996). Infants were tested on their ability to mentally construct a new plan and solve a 2-step means–end problem. A toy was placed on the end of a support and covered with a cloth. To solve this problem, infants had first to pull the support, retrieve the cover, and search under it for the toy. Infants were also tested on a control task on which they were presented with the same arrangement of the support and cover but with no hidden toy. As a warm-up, all infants were tested on the component 1-step tasks (search for a hidden toy and use of a support). The study had a longitudinal design with infants tested on all tasks at monthly intervals between 6 and 10 months.

Trials on which infants solved these 2-step tasks were identified by rating each of 5 key behaviours for evidence of intention to retrieve the toy. To count as a solution, the infant had to show intention on all of these behaviours. An example of a solution would be a trial on which the infant pulled the cloth without any play, maintained fixation on the cover, retrieved the cover, removed the cover without play, and looked for the hidden toy. Although some solutions appeared at 8 months, they occurred with equal frequency on the planning and control tasks, suggesting that occasionally infants were merely retrieving the visible objects and had not planned to retrieve the hidden toy. However, a clear difference emerged at 9 months with infants producing many more solutions when the toy could be recovered. Practice at the task over the preceding months can be ruled out as the reason for the appearance of these solutions because a different group of 9-month-old infants, who were tested for the first time on the same 2-step problem, showed exactly the same level of performance (DiModugno & Willatts, 1993).

Two pieces of evidence suggested that solutions of this 2-step problem were tapping different abilities from solutions of the simpler 1-step problems. First, it was possible to estimate the number of expected 2-step solutions from infants' 1-step performance. For example, an infant who solved each of the 1-step search and support problems 50% of the time would be expected to solve the 2-step problem only 25% of the time. At 8 months, infants produced significantly fewer 2-step solutions than would be expected from their 1-step performance, suggesting that merely having the relevant operators for solving each of the 1-step problems was not sufficient to solve the 2-step problem. Infants had to conduct a means–end analysis to arrive at the sequence of actions for retrieving the hidden toy, and were unable to do this. At 9 months, performance on the 2-step task was exactly at the level expected from 1-step performance, and showed that infants could conduct a means–end analysis and were able reason about the sequence of actions that would lead to the goal.

The same children were seen again at 3 years and given IQ and vocabulary tests (Willatts & Slater, 1996). Significant positive correlations were found between their 2-step planning scores at 8 and 9 months and measures of IQ and vocabulary, but there were no correlations between the 1-step scores at any age and the 3-year-old measures. This finding suggests that individual differences on 2-step problem solving reflect more stable, central processes which are involved in the development of intelligence, but that differences on 1-step problem solving are transitory and more superficial. This contrast supports the claim that 1-step and 2-step problem solving may have different origins (and the discussion of the implicit–explicit distinction by Bremner in Chapter 3 is also relevant to this contrast). If 1-step means–end problem solving is the product of experience rather than thinking, it is hardly surprising that performance shows no relation with IQ at 3 years. However, if 2-step problem solving derives from the operation of more central processes of intelligent thinking, it is possible that there are relatively stable individual differences in these central processes, and the relation with IQ at 3 years is evidence for such stability.

The argument I am making is that development of early means–end behaviour is likely to depend heavily on learning about the effects of different actions on objects. The 6-month-old infant who sees a toy being hidden knows it is under the cover, but does not know how to move the cover to get the toy. Instead, he has to settle for retrieving the cover which is the only object he can see, but once this is accomplished, the toy becomes accessible. Over the next few weeks, repeated opportunities to manipulate objects will provide the infant with a rich source of information about the specific effects of different actions. Not only will this lead to the acquisition of means–end operators, but operators that are appropriate to different situations. For example, a cloth cover can be pulled horizontally to reveal the hidden object, but a rigid cup must be lifted vertically to avoid dragging the object along with it. Although there has been no systematic investigation of how specific types of action operators develop, studies have found that success at search is related to the type of cover and the method needed to remove it (Dunst, Brooks, & Doxsey, 1982; Rader, Spiro, & Firestone, 1979; Willatts, 1984a). It is therefore likely that ability to search in different situations is related to the infant's experience at manipulating a variety of covers.

If lack of an appropriate action operator accounts for infants' failure to search, it should be possible to show that infants who have the remove-cover operator are able to search. If infants still fail, we shall have to look for another explanation. In order to test this hypothesis we need an independent assessment of infants' means–end ability. In the case of search, one possible method is to present the object under a transparent cover. Although infants as young as 5 months can retrieve an object from under a transparent cover (Bower & Wishart, 1972), it is unclear whether this demonstrates a genuine means–end ability. Infants may simply ignore the transparent cover and instead knock it over while attempting to reach directly for the object.

A different approach was used by Munakata et al. (1994). Seven-month-old infants were tested on a task where they had to pull a towel to retrieve a toy. As a control, infants were presented with the towel but no toy. Both toy and no-toy tasks were run in two conditions in which either a transparent or an opaque screen was placed between the infant and the toy. The dependent measure was the number of retrieval responses where a retrieval response was defined as a pull that brought the entire towel from behind the screen. Infants produced more retrieval responses, on the toy task than the no-toy task when the screen was transparent; but the number of retrievals was lower and did not differ on the two tasks when the screen was opaque. This result suggests that 7-month-old infants have sufficient means–end ability to retrieve a visible toy, and that their failure to retrieve the hidden toy in the opaque-screen condition reflects some difficulty other than means–end ability.

However, Munakata et al. offered an objection to this interpretation. It is possible that young infants may need visual feedback to monitor the movement of the toy when pulling the towel in order to know when it has come within reach. When attempting to solve the opaque-screen tasks, infants may have set out with the intention of retrieving the toy, pulled the towel once, but gave up because they did not pull it enough to bring the toy from behind the screen. Given that the towel was relatively long and infants at this age are less efficient at pulling a long towel to retrieve a toy (Willatts, 1996, experiment 3), it is possible that the opaque screen interfered with means–end performance.

Munakata et al., therefore, conducted a further study that was designed to overcome this problem. Infants were first trained on a completely new task on which they learned to push a button to make a hinged ledge drop. When this training was successfully completed, they were given a demonstration of how to retrieve a toy with the apparatus. A toy was placed on the ledge, the infant's parent pushed the button to release it, and this allowed the toy to slide down a ramp to a position where the parent could pick it up. These demonstrations were given with the toy behind both a transparent and opaque screen on alternate trials. Infants were then tested on this apparatus either with or without a toy in each of two conditions where the ledge was screened with a transparent or opaque screen. The pattern of results was the same as for the towel-pulling study. Infants pushed the button more on the toy task than the no-toy task when the screen was transparent, but produced fewer button pushes on the opaque-screen condition and, instead, pushed at the same rate on the toy and no-toy tasks. Since infants had originally learned to push the button without seeing a toy, their lower level success in the opaque-screen condition could not be due to the lack of visual feedback.

Munakata et al. argue that, even though infants had sufficient means–end ability to push the button and retrieve the visible toy, they were unable to apply this ability when the toy was hidden from view. They suggest the reason for this failure in the opaque-screen condition was that infants had to represent the hidden toy, and this representation lacked sufficient strength to direct and regulate the action of reaching to the button and pushing it. Extending this interpretation to search behaviour, they also suggest that the reason why young infants fail to search is because their representation of the hidden toy lacks sufficient strength to direct the reaching system. Why then are infants able to recall the existence of a hidden object when they are required only to observe an event? Munakata et al. have an ingenious answer. They propose that a concept of object permanence is not an "all-or-none-affair" such that infants either have the concept or do not. Instead, knowledge of object permanence may develop over time with representations of hidden objects gradually becoming stronger and capable of driving a greater range of behaviours. Young infants will be able to detect the occurrence of physically impossible events when tested as couch potatoes because their relatively weak and underdeveloped knowledge is sufficient to direct simple behaviour such as looking. However, these infants will be unable to solve problems when tested as active participants until their knowledge representations have developed further.

This *graded representation* hypothesis offers a distinctive explanation for why the competent couch potato infant is incompetent as an active participant. The proposal that infants' knowledge representations undergo considerable development is by no means new (e.g. Piaget, 1953; 1954), but it does challenge current claims that the content of early infant knowledge is similar to that of adults (e.g. Baillargeon, 1993). However, neither the core knowledge nor the active representations hypothesis rules out the possibility that innate knowledge can be enriched and extended.

Although the graded representation hypothesis offers a novel explanation for infants' failure to apply their knowledge to solve means–end problems, there are several points that still need to be addressed. First, it will be important to provide a more detailed account of how a representation increases in strength, and how a stronger representation comes to direct reaching as well as looking. As it currently stands, this assertion appears somewhat arbitrary. In the context of a parallel distributed processing model of object permanence development which Munakata et al. have developed, differential control of looking and reaching by the representation of the occluded object is achieved by simply applying two different activation thresholds, with a higher threshold for reaching. However, the PDP model does not explain why reaching would require a higher threshold. In addition, this claim appears to contradict the finding that infants as young as 5 months will reach accurately for an object they cannot see but do remember (Hood & Willatts, 1986).

Second, the interpretation of the button-push experiment depends entirely on the assumption that infants did demonstrate intentional means–end behaviour when they pushed the button and retrieved the visible toy. If this was not intentional means–end behaviour, then the lower rate of success in the opaque-screen condition may be due to lack of means–end ability rather than a lack of representational ability. The task was unfamiliar to infants and there was no visible mechanism to suggest the connection between the button and the ledge. Infants first had to be taught to push the button to release the ledge, and during training they had no opportunity to see how the apparatus could be used for retrieving a toy—the only time they observed this was during the demonstrations by the parent. It seems reasonable to conclude that infants probably had only a rudimentary understanding of how to operate the apparatus to retrieve the toy. Under these circumstances, how did they manage to get the toy in the transparent-screen condition? While they may have engaged in intentional means–end behaviour, it is also possible that the toy merely drew their attention to the ledge which in turn reminded them of the button. If this is what happened, then infants may have pushed the button just to release the ledge and without any intention of retrieving the toy. In the remaining conditions infants would be less likely to push the button, either because there was no visible toy to direct their attention to the ledge, or because the ledge itself was hidden behind the opaque screen. Clearly, this important experiment needs to be repeated with appropriate control tasks that can test for this alternative means–end deficit explanation.

Finally, although the graded representation hypothesis can explain why young infants fail to search for a hidden object, it does not explain why infants at the same age also fail to retrieve an object resting on a support (Willatts, 1996). In this situation the object is visible and the infant does not need a representation to direct reaching. Instead, I have argued that infants must first acquire specific action operators before they can solve this type of means–end problem, and this will also be necessary in the case of search.

The visual observation paradigm can reveal important information about infants' knowledge and reasoning when interpreting events, but when infants are allowed to be only couch potatoes, all we can assess is their knowledge for interpreting events. The paradigm is inadequate for showing whether infants also possess the relevant knowledge for solving problems themselves. Infants may detect when the correct sequence of actions has been performed on a means–end task, but may be unable to produce that sequence until they have gained specific experience with the effects of their actions. In addition, it is also possible that early means–end behaviour, although planful, does not reveal a capacity for means–end planning and reasoning about sequences of operators. Instead, the study of infant problem solving suggests that the use of a strategy of means–end analysis develops much later than the ability to reason about events that are simply observed.

INHIBITORY PROCESSES AND THE PRODUCTION OF A NOT–B SEARCH ERRORS

When infants eventually can search for an object by the age of 8 or 9 months, why do they return to the original place of hiding when the object is hidden at a new place? Different explanations for the occurrence of the A not–B search error have been the focus of numerous studies, but one current interpretation is that these errors reflect a difficulty with inhibiting interfering information, rather than some other conceptual deficit (Diamond, 1991). In one early study, Diamond (1985) showed that infants consistently searched accurately when the object was hidden at a new place if the delay between hiding the object and searching was kept below a critical duration. However, if the delay was increased by as little as 2 seconds beyond this critical duration, infants would consistently make errors and search instead at the previously correct location. Across the period of 7 to 12 months, the duration of the critical delay increased steadily from about 1 second at 7 months to 10 seconds at 12 months. In subsequent studies, this finding has been replicated using a delayed response task in which the hiding location is varied randomly across trials (Diamond, 1990; Diamond & Doar, 1989).

Diamond has argued cogently that the occurrence of these errors is mediated by prefrontal cortex, and the improvement with age reflects maturation of this region of the brain. Adult rhesus monkeys with lesions to prefrontal cortex make the same pattern of errors after short delays on these tasks, but monkeys with lesions to other areas such as the hippocampus are successful and show impairment only after much longer delays (see Diamond, 1990 for a detailed review). In addition, there is some direct evidence that maturation of prefrontal cortex is associated with improved performance on A not–B in human infants. Bell and Fox (1992) found that increased power in the EEG recordings from the prefrontal cortex of infants was associated with ability to produce accurate search after longer delays in 12-month-old infants.

Diamond proposes that prefrontal cortex is involved in two important processes that are necessary for successful performance on any search task where the location of hiding changes from trial to trial. First, the infant must inhibit reaching back to the place that was correct just a moment ago. On the first trial there is no previous response to inhibit and therefore search is always accurate. However, on subsequent trials where the object is hidden at a different place, the infant must inhibit repeating a previously successful response and reach to the new location. Second, the infant must maintain a representation of the object at the new location, and must use this representation to direct his or her search. The difficulty arises when infants must use their representation for the new location of the object to inhibit reaching back to the previous location. This difficulty increases over longer delays, and eventually infants are unable to exert the necessary inhibitory control. Diamond (1991) suggests that growth in the neural connections between prefrontal cortex and the supplementary motor area during the first year may account for the increased ability of infants to maintain this inhibitory control over longer delays.

It is important to understand that Diamond is not claiming that infants simply forget the location of the hidden object when the delay increases. If this was the only reason for search errors, then infants should make an equal number of errors on A trials and B trials because the delay between hiding and searching is the same. Baillargeon et al. (1989) have also used a visual observation task to show that 8-month-old infants can remember the correct location of a hidden object for up to 70 seconds, so inadequate memory is not the reason for errors. Instead, Diamond claims it is failure to maintain inhibitory control of reaching that is the primary reason for their occurrence. Thus, search errors are really nothing more than slips of action and do not indicate any deep lack of knowledge on the part of the infant. They occur because the infant's experience of successfully retrieving the object has more of an influence on behaviour than the sight of where the object has just been hidden.

There are several reasons why this account can be challenged, and it can be argued that infants do make errors because their knowledge of how to search is less than adequate. Diamond's explanation carries one important implication. If infants are able to remember where the object is hidden but simply reach back because they cannot maintain inhibition of a previously successful and prepotent response, then they should be aware they are making an error. In fact, infants do occasionally look at the correct cover while reaching for the incorrect one (Diamond, 1988; Hofstadter & Reznick, 1996). Hofstadter and Reznick (1996) tested infants on a delayed response task and reported that when the direction of looking and reaching differed, looking was more often correct. In addition, Hofstadter and Reznick compared infants' performance on two versions of the task: they could either reach for a cover, or they could only look but were prevented from reaching. They found that infants' first looks were directed more often at the correct location than their reaches, and looking showed less evidence of perseveration than reaching. Although greater accuracy in looking than reaching is consistent with the claim that infants really do know where the object is but fail to control their reaching, this finding is inconclusive because it may show nothing more than interest in the last place where the object was seen. Being interested in a place is not at all the same as knowing that an object is concealed there.

Establishing that infants do know when they are making an error and do not expect to find the object when they search at the wrong place requires more than just a couch potato assessment of their looking. Instead, we need evidence of infants' intentions when they search and make errors; and this evidence will provide a key test of Diamond's hypothesis. As far as I am aware, there has been no study to examine this prediction, but such evidence should be quite easy to obtain. Suppose we test infants on a task where they are allowed to find the hidden object on A trials, but on later B trials the object is secretly removed after it is hidden. If infants really do remember where the object is hidden, we should see from their behaviour after searching whether they did or did not expect to find it. For example, infants who pick up the incorrect cover should not look under it for the object, but instead should correct their mistake and reach across to the second cover. Infants who do pick up the correct cover and expect to find the object should look for it, and, when they fail to see it, they should be far less likely to reach across to the incorrect cover. Such observations of infants' behaviour after searching in these situations should establish whether errors are merely slips of action or the result of some deeper confusion. If it turns out that infants do expect to find the object at A, then Diamond's account will need some drastic revision.

A more serious problem for Diamond's account comes from studies which show that infants continue to make errors when the object is visible beneath a transparent cover (Butterworth, 1977; Willatts, 1985), or even when there is no cover at place B (Bremner & Knowles, 1984). If the object can still be seen and its location does not need to be remembered, why should the infant search incorrectly? Diamond's answer is that two abilities are required on A not–B: memory and inhibition. Errors occur maximally when both are taxed (opaque covers); but errors still occur, though at a lower rate, when there is no memory load (transparent covers) and only inhibition is taxed (Diamond, 1991).

Butterworth (1977) offered a very different explanation for infants' difficulty with transparent covers. His study showed that infants made errors on B trials when the covers were either transparent or opaque, but made very few when there were no covers and they could reach directly for the object. Butterworth argued that errors occur because infants have difficulty adjusting and co-ordinating spatial codes for the positions of the cover and object. Because both the cover and the object occupy the same location, there is a potential confusion which may be overcome by using different spatial codes. When searching, infants may use a self-referent code to identify the position of the cover, but a landmark-based code for the position of the object, and a landmark-based code would be easier to update. On the initial trials at place A, both codes specify the same location for search, and errors would not occur. However, when the object is hidden at place B, the self-referent code would indicate the previous cover as the correct location, while the updated landmark-based code would specify the new location. Because these codes are in conflict when the place of hiding changes, infants choose either one or the other and make errors when they select the self-referent code. Failure to inhibit a previously successful response is not the reason for errors because infants do inhibit their previous response when they choose the landmark-based code. This code-conflict hypothesis can also explain why infants make errors with transparent covers because there is still the same difficulty with co-ordinating two spatial codes.

However, two later studies suggest that the code-conflict hypothesis may need some modification, and both propose that errors may occur because infants' understanding of the properties and functions of containers and occluders is deficient. Bremner and Knowles (1984) tested infants on a modified task in which there was a cover at A and an object that was visible and uncovered at B. Even though infants could retrieve the object directly and there was no simultaneous coding problem because it was uncovered, they still made errors and reached back for the original cover. Bremner and Knowles offered two explanations for this result. First, it is possible that infants may have used dual coding for the positions of the cover and object on the A trials, but did not understand they should give up this strategy in favour of a single code on the B trials. Second, infants may have searched at the original place because it had acquired the function of containment. Bremner (1985; 1994) has suggested that infants may have much to learn about how objects can function as containers or screens. The object may be hidden behind a screen, beneath a cover, or within a box, in fact, in a multitude of different ways that have only one feature in common—the object is hidden from view. If infants have to learn how to manipulate different objects in order to acquire the appropriate operators for solving means–end problems, they may also have to learn about the specific ways that different objects can function as containers or hiding places. For example, Bremner (1994) speculates that infants' experience at finding objects without previously seeing them hidden may be far more extensive than their experience at searching after a hiding event because parents frequently tidy up toys after the infant has gone away. If one consequence of such experience is that infants sometimes believe that a toy may be found in a container without having seen it hidden there, then it would not be surprising that they are tempted into searching at previously correct location.

In another study, Willatts (1985) tested infants on a modified A not–B task in which they were presented with an object that was placed on one of two cloths. Infants were very successful at pulling the correct cloth to retrieve the object on A trials, and continued at the same level of success when the object was placed on the second cloth on the B trials. Even though this task clearly involved a means–end co-ordination which had to be adapted from place A to place B, there was no evidence that infants failed to inhibit a previously successful response. In contrast, two other groups of infants did make errors and pulled the previously correct cloth on B trials when there were either transparent or opaque covers at the ends of the cloths.

One possible reason for infants' success when the object was visible and uncovered could be that the object and support cloth were not perceived as occupying the same location. The object was some distance from the infant, but the edge of the cloth was within reach so that a single spatial code could be used for both and there would be no conflict. However, when the object was covered in the other tasks, there would be code conflict and consequent errors. A second possible reason for the difference in performance on these tasks could be that infants' knowledge of how to use supports is more advanced than their knowledge of how to manipulate covers. Pulling a cloth provides a great deal of information about how one support works and another does not because the critical relation "object-on-cloth" persists right up to the moment the object is picked up and the goal is achieved. However, retrieving an object from under a cover provides less information because the critical relation "object-under-cover" is available for a shorter time and is destroyed before the goal is achieved. This difference in the availability of the object-intermediary relation may mean it takes longer for infants to notice the relevant information that is necessary to gain a complete understanding of how to deal with a choice of covers. One consequence of their incomplete understanding of covers might be that infants are less certain about when to switch from acting at one place to another.

Finally, there is evidence that infants continue to make search errors even when they have not been allowed to reach for the cover at place A. Butterworth (1974) reported a study using opaque covers in which infants merely watched while an object was hidden at A, but were prevented from searching. Nevertheless, these infants made errors when they were allowed to search on the B trials. It is difficult to see how these errors can be explained as failure to inhibit a previously rewarded response when there was no such response to inhibit. However, both the code conflict and incomplete knowledge explanations can account for this striking result.

Although these alternative explanations address different issues, they have in common the view that infants' knowledge of search is imperfect and errors occur because infants are uncertain about the reasons for switching to a new place to find the object. Although infants can search intentionally for a hidden object by 7 or 8 months, the A not–B problem introduces a new factor which requires more than a basic ability to search. This new factor is choice of where to search, and it is infants' attempts to cope with this choice that exposes their limitations. These limitations include difficulty with co-ordinating and updating spatial codes, understanding the function of covers and containers, and attending to relevant information.

I do not wish to rule out the claim that inefficient inhibition of previous, prepotent responses contributes to errors, but the evidence does not support inefficient inhibition as the sole explanation. Inhibitory processes clearly do have a role, but researchers have failed to give a complete account of how these processes come to regulate behaviour. Infants do need to inhibit previous responses, and lack of ability to inhibit would certainly produce errors. However, infants also need to know *when* they should inhibit previous responses, and this is where knowledge about how to search plays a part. Success on A not–B involves much more than simply preventing a reach to cover A from occurring. It requires keeping track of where the object has moved, coding for its position, evaluating the covers as potential obstacles to retrieval of the object, and choosing between them. Thus, infants need an adequate knowledge base to be able to carry out a task analysis which will tell them why reaching to A will fail, and why reaching to B will succeed. Only when this analysis has been completed will they be in a position to inhibit a reach to A and initiate a reach to B. Improvement on tasks such as A not–B will therefore depend on the development of knowledge, ability to use that knowledge for conducting a task analysis, and ability to inhibit behaviour. Deficiencies in any of these components will lead to problems, and even children of 2 years or older who have achieved a sufficient degree of inhibitory control to solve invisible displacement problems continue to make search errors on tasks where their knowledge is limited and the mechanics are imperfectly understood (Hood, 1995).

CONCLUSION

The core knowledge and active representations hypotheses offer a radically new account of infant intelligence, but much of the work on which these hypotheses are based has employed the visual observation paradigm. Although this paradigm can tell us a good deal about the cognitive abilities of very young infants, it can supply only part of the story, and it is important that we are aware of this limitation.

The visual observation paradigm treats the infant as a couch potato who merely sits, watches, and offers an opinion (by showing varying degrees of interest). What this methodology is able to do is show whether infants have the knowledge to evaluate the content of an event. However, researchers have often assumed that this knowledge is the same as the knowledge required to produce the event. It is this assumption that I believe to be mistaken, because, as all sports fans know, being a couch potato is not necessarily a qualification for being a member of the team. Infants may be able to evaluate the sequence of actions that solved a problem, but generating the sequence involves other processes and different knowledge. For this reason, the visual inspection paradigm is inappropriate as the sole method for studying the origin and development of mental processes as they come to guide goal-directed action. Instead, I have advocated an approach that allows infants to be active participants by letting them solve problems. Both these approaches in conjunction will provide a more complete account of the development of infant intelligence. Similarly, I have argued that an account which attempts to explain the development of cognition in terms of increasing ability at inhibitory control will also provide only part of the story. Inhibitory processes are undoubtedly important, but development will also depend on infants increasing their knowledge of the circumstances in which it is necessary both to inhibit a previous behaviour and initiate a new behaviour.

Throughout this chapter I have argued that infants continue to gain knowledge about the effects of their actions, and this knowledge in turn contributes to new achievements such as means–end problem solving. However, this is not a re-statement of Piaget's view that thought is the by-product of sensory-motor skill and that the co-ordination of actions through overt trial-and-error leads to the ability to mentally co-ordinate actions and to think how to generate solutions. The core knowledge and active representations hypotheses and the results of studies of early problem solving challenge the Piagetian account and lead to a quite different conclusion. The finding that young infants are able to plan means–end solutions expands our view of infant cognition to include the ability to construct solutions that require appropriate use of knowledge and flexible representations. If the evidence continues to accumulate for thinking and intelligent, planned problem solving in infancy, this will mean that infants can think much more than we thought was possible, and would show the existence of a rich and complex form of intelligence.

ACKNOWLEDGEMENT

The author's work reported in this chapter was supported by grants R000231772 and R000233894 from the Economic and Social Research Council (UK).

REFERENCES

Baillargeon, R. (1986). Representing the existence and the location of hidden objects: Object permanence in 6- and 8-month-old infants. *Cognition*, *23*, 21–41

Baillargeon, R. (1993). The object concept revisited. New directions in the investigation of infants' physical knowledge. In C.E. Granrud (ed.), *Visual perception and cognition in infancy*, pp. 265–315. Hillsdale, N.J.: Lawrence Erlbaum Associates Inc.

Baillargeon, R., DeVos, J., & Graber, M. (1989). Location memory in 8-month-old infants in a non-search AB Task: Further evidence. *Cognitive Development*, *4*, 345–367.

Baillargeon, R. & Graber, M. (1988). Evidence of location memory in 8-month-old infants. *Cognition*, *20*, 191–208.

Baillargeon, R., Graber, M., DeVos, J., & Black, J. (1990). Why do young infants fail to search for hidden objects? *Cognition*, *36*, 255–284.

Baillargeon, R., DeVos, J., & Black, J. (1992). *Young infants' reasoning about the use of supports to bring objects within reach.* Unpublished manuscript.

Bell, M.A. & Fox, N.A. (1992). The relations between frontal brain electrical activity and cognitive development during infancy. *Child Development*, *63*, 1142–1163.

Bower, T.G.R. & Wishart, J.G. (1972). The effects of motor skill on object permanence. *Cognition*, *1*, 165–172.

Bremner, J.G. (1978). Spatial errors made by infants: Inadequate spatial cues or evidence for egocentrism? *British Journal of Psychology*, *69*, 77–84.

Bremner, J.G. (1985). Object tracking and search in infancy: A review of data and a theoretical evaluation. *Developmental Review*, *5*, 371–396.

Bremner, J.G. (1994). *Infancy*, 2nd edn. Oxford: Blackwell.
Bremner, J.G. & Knowles, L.S. (1984). Piagetian stage IV search errors with an object that is directly accessible both visually and manually. *Perception, 13*, 307–314.
Bushnell, E.W. (1985). The decline of visually guided reaching in infancy. *Infant Behavior and Development, 8*, 139–155.
Butterworth, G. (1974). *The development of the object concept in human infants*. Unpublished D. Phil thesis, University of Oxford.
Butterworth (1977). Object disappearance and error in Piaget's stage IV task. *Journal of Experimental Child Psychology, 23*, 391–401.
Clifton, R.K., Rochat, P., Litovsky, R.Y., & Perris, E.E. (1991). Object representation guides infants' reaching in the dark. *Journal of Experimental Psychology: Human Perception and Performance, 17*, 323–219.
Diamond, A. (1985). Development of the ability to use recall to guide action, as indicated by infants' performance on AB. *Child Development, 55*, 868–883.
Diamond, A. (1988). Differences between adult and infant cognition: Is the crucial variable presence of absence of language? In L. Weiskrantz (ed.), *Thought without language* (pp. 337–370). Oxford: Clarendon Press.
Diamond, A. (1990). The development and neural bases of memory functions as indexed by the AB and delayed response tasks in human infants and infant monkeys. *Annals of the New York Academy of Sciences, 608*, 267–317.
Diamond, A. (1991). Neuropsychological insights into the meaning of object concept development. In S. Carey & R. Gelman (eds), *The epigenesis of mind: essays on biology and cognition*, pp. 67–110. Hillsdale, N.J.: Lawrence Erlbaum Associates Inc.
Diamond, A. & Doar, B. (1989). The performance of human infants on a measure of frontal cortex function: The delayed response task. *Developmental Psychobiology, 22*, 271–294.
Dimodugno, M.K. & Willatts, P. (1993). *"Examining" aspects of infant attention.* British Psychological Society Developmental Section Annual Conference, Birmingham, England, September 1993.
Dunst, C.J., Brooks, P.H., & Doxsey, P.A. (1982). Characteristics of hiding places and the transition to stage IV performance on object permanence tasks. *Developmental Psychology, 18*, 671–681.
Fabricius, W.F. & Willatts, P. (1995). *Towels of Hanoi: Strategy monitoring and choice in 18-month-olds.* Paper presented at the 103rd Convention of the American Psychological Association, New York, August.
Gratch, G., Appel, K.J., Evans, W.F., LeCompte, G.K., & Wright, N.A. (1974). Piaget's stage IV object concept error: Evidence of forgetting or object conception? *Child Development, 45*, 71–77.
Hofstadter, M. & Reznick, J.S. (1996). Response modality affects human infant delayed-response performance. *Child Development, 67*, 646–658.
Hood, B.M. (1995). Gravity rules for 2–4 year-olds? *Cognitive Development, 10*, 577–598.
Hood, B.M. & Willatts, P. (1986). Reaching in the dark to an object's remembered position: Evidence for object permanence in 5-month-old infants. *British Journal of Developmental Psychology, 4*, 57–65.
Kolstad, V. (1993). *The development of infants' understanding of pulling tools.* Poster presented at the 60th meeting of the Society for Research in Child Development, New Orleans, March, 1993.
Leslie, A. (1988). The necessity of illusion. In L. Weiskrantz (ed.), *Thought without language*, pp. 185–210. Oxford: Clarendon Press.
McDonnell, P.M. & Abraham, W.C. (1979). Adaptation to displacing prisms in human infants. *Perception, 8*, 175–185.
Mandler, J.M. (1992). How to build a baby: II Conceptual primitives. *Psychological Review, 99*, 587–604.

Meltzoff, A.N. (1990). Towards a developmental cognitive science: The implications of cross-modal matching and imitation for the development of representation and memory in infancy. *Annals of the New York Academy of Sciences, 608*, 1–37.

Munakata, Y., McClelland, J.L., Johnson, M.H., & Siegler, R.S. (1994). *Now you see it, now you don't: A gradualistic framework for understanding infants' successes and failures in object permanence tasks*. Technical report PDP.CNS.94.2, Department of Psychology, Carnegie Mellon University.

Newell, A. & Simon, H.A. (1972). *Human problem solving*. Englewood-Cliffs, N.J.: Prentice-Hall.

Nilsson, N.J. (1971). *Problem-solving methods in artificial intelligence*. London: McGraw-Hill.

Piaget, J. (1953). *The origin of intelligence in the child.* London: Routledge & Kegan Paul.

Piaget, J. (1954). *The construction of reality in the child.* London: Routledge & Kegan Paul.

Rader, N., Spiro, D.J., & Firestone, P.B. (1979). Performance on a stage IV object-permanence task with standard and non-standard covers. *Child Development, 50*, 908–910.

Spelke, E.S., Breinlinger, K., Macomber, J., & Jacobson, K. (1992). Origins of knowledge. *Psychological Review, 99*, 605–632.

Willatts, P. (1984a). Stages in the development of intentional search by young infants. *Developmental Psychology, 20*, 389–396.

Willatts, P. (1984b). The stage-IV infant's solution of problems requiring the use of supports. *Infant Behavior and Development, 7*, 125–134.

Willatts, P. (1985). Adjustment of means–ends coordination and the representation of spatial relations in the production of search errors by infants. *British Journal of Developmental Psychology, 3*, 259–272.

Willatts, P. (1989). Development of problem solving in infancy. In A. Slater & J.G. Bremner (eds), *Infant development*, pp. 143–182. London: Lawrence Erlbaum Associates Ltd.

Willatts, P. (1990). The goal-directed nature of early sensory-motor coordinations. In H. Bloch & B.I. Bertenthal (eds), *Sensory-motor organizations and development in infancy and early childhood*, pp. 179–186. London: Kluwer Academic.

Willatts, P. (1994). *The role of spatial knowledge in means–end problem solving*. Paper presented at the 9th International Conference on Infant Studies, Paris, June.

Willatts, P. (1996). *Development of means–end behavior in young infants: Pulling a support to retrieve a distant object*. Manuscript submitted for publication.

Willatts, P. & Fabricius, W.F. (1996) *The Towels of Hanoi: The origin of forward search planning in infancy*. Manuscript submitted for publication.

Willatts, P. & Rosie, K. (1996). *Development of means–end planning in young infants*. Manuscript submitted for publication.

Willatts, P. & Slater, A. (1996). *Prediction of intelligence at 3 years from assessment of infant means–end planning ability*. Manuscript in preparation.

6 Reassessing Piaget's Theory of Sensorimotor Intelligence: A Perspective from Cognitive Science

Julie C. Rutkowska
School of Cognitive and Computing Sciences, University of Sussex, Brighton, UK.

PERSISTENT ISSUES

Whether endorsed or (more likely, nowadays) disputed, Piaget's (1953; 1955) theory of the role that sensorimotor intelligence plays in the development of the mind has been the most significant single influence on the way infancy researchers pose questions and interpret data. This chapter offers a contemporary evaluation of Piaget's ideas by locating infancy research within the broader context of theoretical advances in cognitive science. Two questions provide the background to this analysis: What is the current status of sensorimotor functioning in explanations of ability? And what, then, might be its significance for our understanding of development? The picture that emerges has implications for the three main components of Piaget's perspective on infant development.

First is the issue of the infant's initial state. We need to characterise early mechanisms so that they are "open to development" in an appropriate way (Piaget, 1953). How does Piaget's approach to action-based mechanisms fare, and his commitment to progressive co-ordination of sensory and motor schemes as the key to development? Currently influential interpretations of infancy data generally attribute something more by way of preadaptation to the infant. However, they lack consensus as to what this "more" is—from ecological psychology's preattuned realist infant, directly perceiving environmental affordances, to the nativist cognitivist infant, operating *ab initio* with concepts and representations.

Next is Piaget's characterisation of the outcome of development in terms of conceptual and representational mechanisms that support superior understanding of the world by overcoming (what he considers) the limitations of perception and action within it. Piaget makes very traditional assumptions about the nature of intentionality, identifying the infant's transformation from a biological subject to a conscious psychological one with evidence for conceptual-representational functioning, such as anticipatory "cognizance" (Piaget, 1976; 1978) of a goal of action as evidenced by means–end co-ordinations towards the end of the first year. So deeply rooted are such traditional views that it is difficult to entertain alternatives to Piaget's core assumption that pragmatic knowledge is qualitatively different from, and inferior to, the kinds of conceptual and representational abilities that he believes develop through a radical reconstruction of sensorimotor mechanisms during the course of infancy. Nevertheless, it is important for our appreciation of Piaget's theory, and of infancy in general, to take account of other options, over and above alternatives that merely attribute precocious concepts and representations to ever younger infants.

Finally the general form of development remains an issue. Several related aspects of Piaget's constructivism are at stake. In view of current evidence for infant preadaptations, many find it increasingly hard to concur with Piaget's claim that our knowledge of the world is not in large measure predetermined. The apparent domain specificity of such preadaptations also seems to question the need for, or at least the power of, any general-purpose developmental process along the lines of Piaget's notorious equilibration. What, then, of his commitment to epigenesis, wherein the structure of knowledge is a mutual product of the environment and the subject's activity within it, prefigured in neither the world nor the centralised mind (Piaget, 1971)? If the subject's activities are a necessary component of coming to know the world, how might they affect the nature of that knowledge?

THREE PARADIGMS FOR COGNITION

A useful starting place from which to assess the current status of the sensorimotor is Varela's cartography of ideas in cognitive science, which aims to integrate European and American traditions of cognitive inquiry (Varela, 1988; 1993; cf. Varela, Thompson, & Rosch, 1991). Cognitive science's attempt to understand intelligence is undergoing a number of significant changes, and Varela identifies three major paradigms, marking shifts that follow a historical progression as far as mainstream cognitive science, with its allegiance to computational explanation, is concerned. In Fig. 6.1, these developments in cognitive science are schematised in terms of cumulative, concentric circles of activity, that are used to locate contributors' names that appear in this chapter and/or that are likely to be familiar to readers.

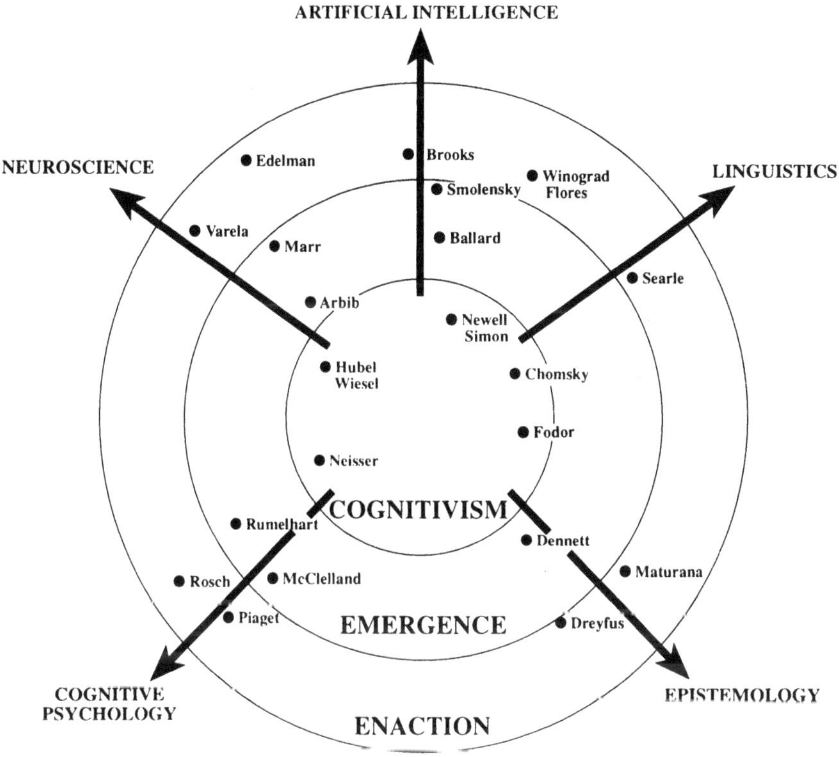

FIG. 6.1. Contributors to three paradigms for cognition (after Varela, 1988).

For infancy purposes, it is important to note that it is the most recent cognitive interpretations of infant abilities that mesh closely with assumptions of the longest standing inner circle of "cognitivism". By way of contrast, Varela locates Piaget's seminal sensorimotor perspective at the forefront of the newly emerging outer circle of "enaction".

Traditional cognitivism

Approaches committed to the most traditional *cognitivism* are dominated by a "between the ears", centralised and disembodied focus on the mind. They locate the abilities of intelligent systems primarily with internal representations, which model things in the world. In the computational discipline of artificial intelligence (hereafter, AI), this world-view sees representations as internal symbol structures that make explicit information about objects, their properties and their location with regard to one another and to the subject (Newell & Simon, 1976). The more exhaustive and explicit the representation, the greater should the subject's knowledge be. Rule-governed manipulation of such structures (i.e. computation) underlies the reasoning processes that use them to formulate goals and plan behaviour.

Traditional AI systems built along these lines are notoriously brittle—a system may be good at a game like chess, but will be stopped in its tracks by encountering even another game environment. It seems virtually impossible to get into a single system all the knowledge and program rules for deploying it that seem necessary for flexible, adaptive behaviour (cf. Dreyfus, 1981). This kind of *domain specificity* of knowledge may be a drawback for AI implementations, but some cognitivist positions consider it is actually an important property of the mind's structure. For example, Chomsky's (1980) view of language as a human-specific, circumscribed "mental organ" falls within the inner circle of traditional cognitivism. So too does Fodor's (1980; 1983) view of mental processes as formal computations, with its influential distinction between input systems (e.g. low-level vision and speech perception) and central systems (e.g. thought and problem solving). The former are assumed to be modular, hard-wired, data-driven, informationally encapsulated computational reflexes; the latter to be voluntary and flexible, with unrestricted access to the subject's beliefs and knowledge.

Some of the most notable current ideas about the infant mind fit closely with this perspective. A similar perception–cognition distinction is at the heart of Spelke's (1988; 1990; 1991) interpretation of a range of impressive data on young infants' understanding of the physical world. This proposes that a visual input system delivers an unsegmented array of surface points, which is then carved up into "unitary objects" by a central conceptual system that employs unchanging principles such as cohesion, boundedness and rigidity. Related views include Baillargeon's (1986) ideas of conceptually based belief in object permanence. Such proposals for preadapted, domain-specific knowledge of the physical world are matched by attribution to young infants of conceptually rather than perceptually grounded social understanding of persons (e.g. Legerstee, 1992).

This style of "conceptual" explanation is compatible with some aspects of Piaget's traditional, centralised view of higher mental functioning. It differs from it in considering such mechanisms as the starting point not the outcome of infancy. And its domain-specific assumptions are incompatible with Piaget's more general-purpose notion of intelligence, in which the infant's developing physical and social understanding are served by the same mechanisms, and language acquisition is firmly rooted in broader cognitive-symbolic developments. Detailed evaluation is available elsewhere (e.g. Rutkowska, 1991; 1993; Willatts, this volume, Chapter 5), but two points about this new nativism are relevant here. One is that it downplays the nature and possible import of output systems; hence, having nothing significant to say about action. The function of central processes is simply rationalistic: producing beliefs about the world that can be expressed in terms of propositions that are true or false. The behavioural aspect of action is treated as, at best, an index of such central beliefs and knowledge; and any environmental contribution to adaptive functioning is minimised. This turns out to make it hard to say anything substantive about epigenetic development, a point that will be taken up later. Notably, related cognitivist positions set little store by the idea of "development", constructivist or otherwise. For Fodor (1975), the language of thought in which innate concepts are represented renders implausible the possibility of acquiring truly novel concepts. For Chomsky (1980, p. 1), natural development is considered more like growth than like development or even learning, as in "the growth of rich and highly articulated structures along an intrinsically determined course under the triggering and partially shaping effect of experience, which fixes parameters in an intricate system of predetermined form".

Emergence

Varela sees the first major advance in computational ideas about cognition in the notion of *emergence* that is central to recent work in parallel distributed processing or connectionism. This purports to characterise cognition at a subsymbolic level, in terms of multiple, interconnected simple units operating in parallel (cf. neurons, though how appropriately is debatable). Rather than relying on fixed, sequential programmed rules, computation generally involves statistical inference; the whole network settles into a stable pattern of activation by trying simultaneously to satisfy many soft or weak constraints that are meaningful only if considered collectively.

Rule-like behaviour that traditionalists attributed to an explicit program is assumed to emerge from patterns of activity recurring within the network (e.g. Rumelhart & McClelland, 1986). Furthermore, individual units are unlike molar classical symbols, which too often tended to be equivalent to linguistically meaningful whole concepts. Ideally they operate as subsymbols or microfeatures that support dimension-shifted representation (Clark & Lutz, 1992). For example, no single unit would correspond to something like "dog" or a "cat". Instead, units might code properties such as legs, fur, barking, tail, purring and so forth. The overall pattern of activation of these units would determine discrimination and recognition of an input as a dog, cat or neither. Varela's notion of emergence is compatible with viewing symbolic processes of a classical variety as an emergent global property of the local functioning of such networks; that is, as a rough approximation to the operation of a connectionist system (Smolensky, 1988).

Compared with traditional computational systems, on some tasks, connectionist networks can achieve relative flexibility under noisy or variable circumstances by settling into the most likely of a range of related solutions. Pattern discrimination or categorisation has been one of the great implementational successes of self-organising connectionist systems (though explanatory theories of how they work remain contentious). This illustrates a continuing link with infancy concerns through Hebb's (1949) "old connectionism", which was a significant influence on 60s and 70s attempts to explore Piagetian issues by developing notions of model/schema formation in infant cognition (Rutkowska, 1990). More recently, psychologists suggest that such systems may bridge the gap between cognitivist accounts of perception and the theory of direct perception's notion of unmediated pick-up of invariants from the optic array (e.g. Humphreys & Riddoch, 1986; Marr, 1982). In particular, connectionist systems often claim to provide roles for both environmental information and the subject's information processing; operate without the extra-perceptual concepts, memory or knowledge of mysterious origin that are anathema to the direct perception theorist; and imply that their (purported) biological plausibility makes them a strong contender for evolutionarily determined preadapted organisation.

This might make emergence seem a promising paradigm for infancy, and one concurring with positions that take direct perception to offer a more plausible account of early infant perception than is possible for Piaget's strongly constructivist style of cognitivism (e.g. Butterworth, 1989; Gibson, 1987). Motor/output processes might be encompassed too, since this style of parallel computation can be fitted to ecological psychologists' ideas of how groups of muscles may be organised to operate collectively in "coordinative structures" (Kugler, Kelso, & Turvey, 1982).

Ecological psychology, which aims to extend the theory of direct perception to a theory of direct action, offers a radical alternative to psychologies that take conceptual-representational abilities as the starting point for infant development (Gibson, 1979). In relation to perceiving, making sense of the world is seen as a question of pragmatic knowledge—acting in the environment, not formulating more or less accurate central beliefs about it (Shaw & Turvey, 1980). This appears to endorse Piaget's preoccupation with action, but the perspectives diverge considerably on assumptions about action-based abilities. Contra Piaget, ecological psychology considers that genetic preattunement enables infants, from the outset, to see at least some of what things are "for"—their "affordances" for activity; and to generate potential purposive acts or "effectivities" that complement those environmental affordances (Gibson, 1979; Jones, Spelke, & Alley, 1985). For example, anything that exhibits an invariant combination of properties including solidity, boundedness and being about infant hand size affords grasping for an infant. This goes against the grain of Piaget's insistence on reciprocal assimilation, whereby all "looking in order to act" is a developmental outcome of the infant's initially unconnected sensory and motor exchanges with the environment, and better fits contemporary evidence for pre-experience functional links between sensory and motor processes.

Piaget and ecological psychology diverge also in their characterisation of mechanisms for action, yet converge in presenting pictures of limited power for tackling developmental issues. Piaget's notion that sensorimotor schemes underlie the subject's voluntary activity is opaque, not least because he speaks of these underlying mechanisms almost exclusively in terms of behavioural processes. For example, discussion of the initial organisation and development of vision primarily features movements involved in "looking" or "directing the glance" (Piaget, 1953). How sensory processes might work and what they might be doing, key topics of contemporary inquiry, remain unexplored. Piaget regularly emphasises abstract structures into which he assumes schemes become co-ordinated, a precursor of the structure of operational schemes underlying environment-independent thought, at the expense of clarifying what mechanisms the infant requires to co-ordinate sensory *and* motor components of purposive activity.

Ecological psychology's treatment of action is likewise problematic, undercutting its challenge to Piaget. At its psychological grain of analysis, seemingly familiar notions like "intention" and "attention" are introduced as alternatives to Piaget's mysterious schemes, in order to account for the subject's contribution to control of action. These appear too molar to work as psychological primitives. For example, "intention to grasp" is said to be part of the effectivity of grasping (Michaels & Carello, 1981). But, is it useful to assume that the neonate's reaching and grasping reveals an underlying intention equivalent to that of the nine-month-old? A finer-grained way of discussing infants' psychological mechanisms seems necessary in view of the kinds of developmental restructuring that are typical even of everyday activities like prehension; for example, infants' progressive ability to adjust grasping to the weight of an object prior to contact (of which more later). Certainly, neither Piaget's schemes nor his version of representational development offer much help here.

Ecological psychology's insistence on subject–environment mutuality, which is illustrated in "effectivity–affordance" and "intention–goal object" relations, marks an important theoretical advance. But just how mutual *is* this perspective's style of explanation, given its (over)commitment to direct realism? Insistence on locating information, including affordances, objectively in the environment (e.g. Gibson, 1979; Turvey, Shaw, Reed, & Mace, 1981) appears at odds with Gibson's (1979) argument that, strictly speaking, affordances are *neither* objective nor subjective. It seems more straightforward to see them as *both*: the functionality of things in the environment emerging in their use for action by a perceiving and behaving subject.

In the past, direct perception and Piagetian frameworks have been used to support unprofitable debates about whether early infant abilities offer more support for perception *or* for behaviour (often inappropriately equated with action) as the basis of early knowledge. However, recent theorising is marked by spreading acknowledgement that there is no real dichotomy here; perception and behaviour are of equal significance to adaptive action, and both Piaget and Gibson, despite apparently different emphases, held action to be central to development (e.g. Bertenthall & Pinto, 1993; Costall, 1994; Rutkowska, 1993).

Enaction

Action and subject–environment mutuality are central to Varela's advocacy of a constructivist final paradigm: *enaction*. Connectionist systems associated with emergence do not go far enough in this direction. Despite pleas to biological plausibility, they remain far from modelling real-life development and deployment of mental processes. Their sensory interfaces with environmental inputs rarely consist of intensity arrays, tending to involve experimenter selection and hand-coding to a degree that questions the label "self-organising"; and networks generally model or simulate only isolated subsystems, rather than being part of a whole system that is embedded in a real environment. Furthermore, they persist with "recovery" or "discovery" metaphors for the subject's relationship to information.

Varela describes information as the phlogiston of cognitive science, in so far as the notion is constantly overexploited to explain regularities in the way we know the world. From a biological perspective, he contends, there is no pre-given order outside the subject's activities. At many levels of biological structure, from the cell upwards, significance and information emerge from processes that establish domains of interaction between a "self" and its environment. The central nervous system's sensorimotor neurons and interneurons are but one specialist adaptation for achieving closure, a reflexive interlinking of subject and environment processes that supports construction of a coherent unity, in this case, neurocognitive identity. For this epigenetic perspective, evolutionary, cultural and developmental history determine the world that is "enacted" or "brought forth" in perceiving and behaving; hence, Piaget's allocation to the nascent enaction paradigm:

> The basic notion then is that cognitive capacities are inextricably linked to a history that is lived, much like a path that does not exist but is laid down in walking. Consequently the view of cognition is not that of solving problems through representations, but as a creative bringing forth of a world where *the only required condition is that it is effective action*: it permits the continued integrity of the system involved. (Varela, 1988, pp. 59–60; italics added)

The in-principle aims of Piaget's "neither nativist nor empiricist" constructivism clearly justify this placement. However, some differences between the perspectives prove relevant to comparing their developmental implications. In particular, Piaget's ideas appear to end up more realist at heart than Varela's commitment to a fully co-relative perspective on subject and known world. Certainly, Piaget's idea of knowledge is one involving acting on the world, not simply copying it. Yet it remains consistent with action giving rise to representations that *model* selected aspects of an objective reality, with the relation between knowledge structures and reality being one of "isomorphic models among which experience can enable us to choose" (Piaget, 1970, p. 15).

Recent computational directions that Varela considers relevant to elaborating the notion of enaction focus on attempting to build and understand *autonomous systems*, a new route to phrasing questions about the flexible, general knowledge that eluded traditional AI systems. Two lines of research converge on this aim. *Artificial life* (or "A-Life") concerns itself with how complex-seeming self-organisation in many types of system, from chemical through to social, may emerge from the interplay of fundamentally simple processes (for a popular introduction, see Levy, 1992; and see Varela & Bourgine, 1992, for examples of more technical papers). *Animat* research labels an interdisciplinary attempt to use insights about how animals work to build simulated animals or real robots that can exhibit adaptive behaviour in order to survive in a constantly changing, often unpredictable environment (for reviews, see Meyer & Guillot, 1991; 1994). Contributing to both of these directions is computational work in behaviour-based robotics (for an important collection of papers, see Maes, 1990a).

In keeping with Piaget, this work takes sensorimotor intelligence seriously. Perceptual and motor skills are viewed as the hard problems solved by intelligent systems, and solutions to them as imposing important constraints on remaining components of natural intelligence. Trying to understand intelligence by working incrementally from the (evolutionary) bottom up is a favoured strategy, reflected in slogans like "insects first, people later" (cf. Cliff, 1991). Contra Piaget's thinking, there is little enthusiasm for the explanatory power of concepts or of representations that model the world. Ecological psychology's commitment to direct perception and action is often cited as a source of inspiration, illustrated by the assumption that the best model of the world is the world itself. This should not, however, be taken to mean that researchers in this vein do or must agree to advocate the type of methodological realism that is central to ecological psychology. Bersini (1992) argues, rightly in my view, that some animat researchers' attempts to distance themselves from over-centralised models of the mind have resulted in them promoting too exclusively the environment's role in accounts of their systems' activities. This is not necessitated by either of the animat movement's key concerns: "behaviour rather than excessive rationality" and "autonomy rather than programmer dependence". Bersini proposes the term *syntactic subjectivism* to label approaches, including Varela's enaction, which more appropriately highlight mutual constraints between subject and environment, taking on board the experiential and the ecological.

A prominent feature of much of this new work is commitment to grounding intelligence in *situated action*, viewed as a mechanism alternative to more traditional abstract cognitivist models (e.g. see *Cognitive Science*, 1993). This contrasts with Piaget's treatment of sensorimotor intelligence in some important respects, founded on the assumption that the irrevocably subjective situatedness that arises from an embodied system's physical embedding in an environment can support rather than hinder intelligent functioning.

SITUATED ACTION IN BEHAVIOUR-BASED ROBOTICS

Piaget treats action predominantly as a stepping-stone to purportedly more valid and objective knowledge that is freed from environmental constraints. This leads him to offer a deficit account of infant action, working backwards from abilities he believes the young infant lacks until the end of the Sensorimotor Period, rather than forwards from a focus on the early mechanisms that are possessed. "Forwards" is the direction favoured by "bottom-up" behaviour-based robotics, and its ideas about action prove more compatible with Varela's positive perspective on the effective action that emerges from an ongoing co-relative subject–environment relationship. Looking at typical models, and at their implications for notions of representation, helps to clarify this contrast.

Emergent functionality

Recent computational work that endorses a situated approach to the mind adopts *emergent functionality* as a key organisational principle (Rutkowska, 1994a; 1994c). This assumes that the complex abilities of situated systems can emerge indirectly from the operation of independent, seemingly simple components, without the hierarchical control and planning that is typical of traditional AI systems. Central to the functionality of these components is their interplay with the environment (e.g. Maes, 1990b; Steels, 1991).

How a system organised along these lines can work is illustrated by the architecture of Brooks's (1986; 1990; 1991) artificial Creatures. This decomposes a situated system into a number of simple task-achieving behaviours, each of which links specific sensory and motor capacities so that it can (ideally) interact independently and reactively with properties of the environment in which it is embedded. The robot's contribution to interaction between individual task-achieving behaviours bypasses traditional selection and ordering controlled by explicit goal-directed planning. Instead, layered control is achieved by building first the lowest level task-achieving behaviour, debugging its operation, then building another on this foundation and so on. For example, a robot for real-world exploration can be built by starting with Level 0: "do not come into contact with other objects". Adding Level 1: "wander aimlessly" will produce moving around without hitting things. With the addition of Level 2: "visit interesting places" (e.g. corridors of free space detected by sensors), the robot's behaviour comes to look like exploring, without any goal or plan directed at that function.

Brooks sees such systems' organisation as carving up vertically rather than horizontally, with no traditional decomposition into a sequence of processing components between sensors and actuators, devoted to perception, then modelling, then planning, and finally task execution and motor control. Nor is there a central place where an exhaustive, general-purpose description of *the* world is delivered as a preliminary to planning what behaviour(s) to execute. Brooks's (1990) classic title, "Elephants don't play chess", clearly marks disaffection for the rationalistic notions of explicit central representations, goals and plans that characterised the explanations of traditional cognitivism—and towards which the Piagetian infant's development can be seen to be heading.

Such systems have important implications for our understanding of sensorimotor intelligence and of Piaget's position on it. By demonstrating the sufficiency of novel architectures for behavioural control, they begin to suggest alternatives to traditional notions that have been exploited by Piaget and in subsequent theorising about infancy. For example, Bruner's (e.g. 1968; 1973) explanations of infants' early competence on a range of activities drew on then prevailing ideas that featured goals and feedback in the control of "skilled action". Disputing Piaget's chronology for the infant's developmental path, he concluded that the serial ordering of component behaviours must be governed by a controlling intention from the outset. In early prehension, for example, behaviours such as bringing hands together at the midline and mouth opening were interpreted as revealing precocious anticipation of the behavioural goal towards which as yet unsuccessful selection and sequencing of preadapted components was aiming (fine motor manipulation in the first case, oral exploration in the second). There are, however, a range of problems with clarifying the functional significance of infant hands' "proximal midline activity"; and systematic longitudinal observations of infants before they attain top-level reaching suggest that mouth opening regularly follows rather than proceeds the infant making contact with an object (Rutkowska, 1992; 1994a; 1994b). It is possible that early prehension may be controlled along the lines of exploration in Brooks's Creature. Preadapted sensorimotor pairings, say between vision and reaching or between manual contact and retrieval to the mouth, may be interacting independently with the infant's experience of the environment to generate an *illusion* of hierarchically controlled sequencing and goal-directedness.

Just what kind of explanation best captures this kind of control is a hotly disputed issue. Psychology in general has difficulty in formulating "spanning concepts" to discuss structures and processes that emerge from mutual interplay of subject and environment, and this may be one reason for the rising appeal of dynamic systems theory as an anti-cognitive contender (e.g. Beer & Gallagher, 1992; for infancy applications, see Hopkins & Butterworth, Chapter 4, this volume and Thelen & Smith, 1994). Brooks often discusses mechanisms in purely physical and engineering terms, provocatively laying emphasis on special-purpose wires and denying the relevance to his work of computational notions, whether of classical or connectionist varieties (e.g. Brooks, 1991). However, the workings of the *subsumption architecture* that supports layered control appear compatible with classical computational concepts involving programs and symbol manipulation, provided these are used to define architectures that have a high degree of (inter)dependence with the environment. Thus, there are many parallels with a computational model of the infant that rejects conceptual central processes in favour of multiple "action programs", whose co-ordination of sensory and motor processes drive and are driven by ongoing transactions with the environment rather than by an internal model of it. (Rutkowska, 1993; 1994a; 1994c, Cf. Vera & Simon's, 1993, argument that situated action is "thoroughly symbolic").

Implications for representation

These new approaches to action diverge from Piaget's perspective on the developmental import of sensorimotor intelligence as far as *representation* and the reasoning that it supports are concerned. Work in behaviour-based robotics often claims that it has no need for representations. It is, however, quite compatible with viewing representation in terms of mechanisms that establish *selective correspondence* with the environment, rather than as internal models that substitute for things in the world in the overplayed traditional sense of representation that is favoured by Piaget. Such action-based mechanisms need not be considered trivially representational as Piaget might contend. They map clearly onto Dretske's (1988) analysis of (unconventional) natural systems of representation, whose expressive elements neither mean anything in isolation nor have their meanings assigned to them by any external source. The meanings of their elements are intrinsic to the system and arise from the way they evolve, develop or are designed to play a role in its perceiving and behaving in its environment.

In infants, for example, low-level directionally selective visual elements can be considered to have acquired the function of indicating an approaching object on a hit course from the way they are used by an action program to invoke effective (avoidance) behaviours in our environment of evolutionary adaptedness. Animat design simulates this kind of evolutionary adaptedness. Thus, a sonar pattern associated with free space does not indicate or mean anything in isolation to one of Brooks's Creatures, but it acquires the function of indicating a place to visit from the way it is wired into a task-achieving behaviour that effectively embeds the animat in the environment for which it is designed.

Such ideas are also compatible with Israel's (1988) behaviour-based notion of the need for "information and control states" to explain a system's attunement to constraints in its world. Coming from the linguistic situation semantics framework, this illustrates how such views of representation may encompass human activities that are uncontroversially seen as representational. In general, the quest for an increasingly objective model of the world, which drives Piaget's view of the direction of development, may be supplanted by a notion of representation as a vehicle for controlling our subjective interventions, movements and actions in the environment (Clark, 1994).

Contemporary work on situated systems also changes the focus on Piaget's assumption that sensorimotor schemes are the developmental precursors of thought operations. For Piaget, the logic inherent in co-ordinations of action is said to be reconstructed at the level of internal thought, ultimately enabling objective logico-mathematical knowledge. This view equates the development of reasoning with proficiency in formal inference. However, an alternative to this pervasive traditional view is offered by the notion of *situated inference*. The validity of formal inference depends on a central system applying the right abstract rules, irrespective of what they are applied to, as in Fodor's version of a computational theory of mind or Piaget's vision of mature thought. Piaget sees the infant as moving in this direction by the end of the Sensorimotor Period, with overt actions giving way to internal actions on "an image of absent objects and their displacements" (Piaget, 1955, p. 4).

By way of contrast, situated inference depends on the subject's embedding circumstances (Barwise, 1987). A basic kind of situated inference exploits constant environmental features. If those conditions break down, such inference will cease to be valid, even if identical computational steps have been followed. Along these lines, infants can be seen as employing situated inference when "deciding" that it is appropriate to generate avoidance behaviour. The soundness of such processing depends upon the reliability of the infant's action-based representation, which in turn depends on the continuation of natural environmental conditions. In the face of unnatural conditions such as a laboratory shadow-caster, the infant may inappropriately attempt to avoid an expanding shadow, revealing that their action-based understanding is capable of a key property of conventional systems of representation: misrepresentation (Dretske, 1988). From this perspective, development may not involve increasingly abstract thought so much as a widening appreciation of constraints on action. The infant's increasingly insightful behaviour may not require "mental combination" based on images, as Piaget contends, so much as action-based representation of preconditions for successful behaviour (Rutkowska, 1993; Willatts, 1989).

These examples illustrate how Piaget's ideas about the relation between sensorimotor mechanisms and representation are interestingly different from those that are coming to characterise work on situated robotic systems. However, a potentially significant area of *rapprochement* merits attention. This comes from recent computational work that is informed by the role that visual behaviours play in the adaptive functioning of real-life creatures: the *animate vision* paradigm.

Earlier, it was suggested that Piaget's ideas about the psychological mechanisms underlying action are too motor-fixated to be of much use for clarifying how sensorimotor processes contribute to intelligent functioning. Taken in conjunction with the numerous recent findings that point to pre-adapted perceptual organisation in infancy, it is difficult to take seriously Piaget's (e.g. 1953) claims that behavioural exchanges with the environment are central to the development of such organisation. It seems superfluous to propose a process of motor construction, involving a looking scheme that develops from looking for its own sake (functional or reproductive assimilation) to differentiate into more specific schemes that deal, say, with stationary versus moving objects, (generalising and recognitory assimilation). Looking behaviour may affect what sensory processing outcomes are sought and when, but not processing itself, even if the information value and meaning of the patterns that it generates are ultimately determined by their usefulness for action.

Ballard's (1989; 1993) work suggests that this conclusion will prove to be wrong: perceptual and behavioural aspects of action are inextricably intertwined in ways that are just starting to become clear. The way that eye movements, especially gaze control, work for embodied animals is enabling the design of robots whose information processing and real-time action control are more successful than those that rely more exclusively on traditional central processing.

Piaget's idea of behavioural-motor involvement in visual processing is supported by Ballard's (1989, p. 1639) argument that "the visuo-motor system is best thought of as a very large amount of distinct special-purpose algorithms where the results of a computation can only be interpreted if the behavioral state is known." Taking the behavioural state of the system into account can constrain the interpretation of input data in ways that are unavailable to a static imaging device, often simplifying the processing problem. For example, when a stationary point is being fixated, it is possible to interpret optical flow as a depth map; when a moving target is being pursued, this interpretation ceases to be valid. To the extent that humans exploit such mechanisms, it must be noted that these ideas of a motor-constructive contribution to information processing do not necessarily entail the kind of developmental construction that Piaget proposes. They might be prewired through evolution. It would, however, be premature to reject the possibility of a role for individual experience.

The developmental potential of this research direction becomes clearer if we look at proposals for the role of visual behaviours in the control of action, though these turn out to be less compatible with Piaget's theory. Contemporary infancy research continues Piaget's interest in relationships between infants' understanding of objects, space and their own activities (for reviews, see Bremner, 1989; Harris, 1989). This work makes an important distinction between egocentric and allocentric strategies for coding object position. Subjective egocentric codes are centred on the subject's body (e.g. "It's on my right."), whereas objective allocentric codes relate position to the surrounding spatial framework (e.g. "It's at a specific landmark."), and a developmental shift between them has been considered a significant advance in infants' spatial and object understanding. An interesting alternative to either of these familiar ideas is suggested by animate vision, in the form of a frame of reference centred on the subject's fixation point.

This superficially simple idea illustrates the kind of *deictic representation* that is being formulated in studies of situated action—instead of representing things by trying to match them to a comprehensive general purpose internal world model, they are actively represented in terms of their relation to the subject and their function in the subject's changing engagement with a task (e.g. Agre & Chapman, 1990). In the case of eye-hand coordination, for example, adopting position co-ordinates relative to a fixation point frame of reference supports a "do-it-where-I'm-looking" hand movement strategy that does not require precise information about the three-dimensional layout and relative position of objects in the environment.

An egocentric code, as infancy researchers are well aware, is of limited value even for activities as straightforward as reaching for an object, let alone for remembering its position; it can effectively support ballistic (open loop) control of behaviour in a stable world, but any change in position of subject or of object will render it out of date and invalid. A deictic position code based on a fixation point frame of reference, such as "the-block-I'm-fixating", does not suffer from this limitation. Because its referent constantly alters with the subject's activity, it is automatically updated and offers a form of invariant position code that can support feedback-governed (closed loop) control strategies, achieved by directing the hand to the centre of the retinal co-ordinate system while simultaneously moving it in depth relative to the plane of fixation. Thus, this kind of active position code is viewer-oriented without being viewer-centred in the limiting way that static egocentric codes are, and it is object-centred without requiring an objective description of the features or location of the object involved.

Ballard makes suggestions for extending these basic ideas about visual behaviours to search and identification tasks; learning eye-hand co-ordination problems such as block manipulation; and spatial position memory. In search, for example, neither uniform image sampling nor a comprehensive model of what is being looked for are biologically plausible, but strategies such as looking for a characteristic property like colour are (e.g. to locate a box of film, redirect gaze until Kodak yellow is encountered). Further details of the range of mechanisms proposed are beyond the scope of this chapter. However, what all the examples share is commitment to the view that gaze control and fixation are not just a way of getting high-resolution images for visual processing: they are task-dependent strategies for problem solving. The subjective viewpoint inherent in vision is not a problem to be overcome, in evolution or in development, but an adaptive way for a real-world system to deploy its resources.

As far as the infant's appreciation of objects and of space goes, details of animate vision mechanisms may prove relevant to clarifying the outcome of development. They appear compatible, for example, with Bremner's (1989) view that the egocentric–allocentric dichotomy may not capture how infants are changing. Increasing use of landmarks to guide search for objects does not appear to involve abandonment of self-referent coding in place of a supposedly more objective spatial code. Instead, landmarks may support updating of what remains a self-referential code, by aiding fixation during the infant's movements. What animate vision work already makes clear is just how complex are the workings of a seemingly basic behaviour like fixation. What is also clear is how little these ideas match up with Piaget's assumption that action-based coding of objects is superseded by an appreciation of space as a container in which the self and other objects are located, ultimately yielding an objective representation of the world in which the self and its activity have no privileged place.

EQUILIBRATION REVISITED

So far, some advances in cognitive science have been outlined that suggest new ways of looking at the mechanisms infants (and adults) may exploit in interacting with the world, and their implications for the Piagetian view of sensorimotor functioning and the direction of development have been considered. But do these new ideas have a distinctive story to tell about *developmental processes*? At an explicit level, the answer is "not yet". The robotics work of the preceding section involved only systems whose processes exhibit stable organisation, not changing organisation over time. Most consistency in ideas about changing mechanisms is to be found in research on genetic algorithms. Though there are many genetic algorithms, all are informed by evolutionary principles of change. Essentially, they explore phylogenetic acquisition of the genetic basis for solutions to problems such as locomotion, by simulating mutation and crossing-over in populations of chromosomes, fitness–reproduction relations and so forth. Some animat constructors suggest that the hand-design approach favoured by Brooks and others is simply too difficult to be feasible at any but a toy scale. Instead, they propose using genetic algorithms to guide robots' acquisition of their own control architectures through interaction of initially random "neural" networks and an environment (e.g. Cliff, Husbands, & Harvey, 1992). As far as individual learning is concerned, very diverse methods and questions are being investigated, and general principles are not yet forthcoming. Of clear import for developmental psychology, however, is this area's avowed aim of ultimately providing generalisations about adaptive behaviour in terms of a principled typology of environments, problems tackled and proposed solutions (Meyer & Guillot, 1994). This prompts the question of what might be said about the general form of infant development. Reservations have been expressed about Piaget's assumption of a general shift from reliance on action mechanisms to model-like internal representations. So what might development with the focus on situated action begin to look like?

Emergent functionality in development

In the preceding section, some parallels were drawn between the notion of emergent functionality and the possible organisation of early infant action. Of special relevance to understanding sensorimotor processes in development, emergent functionality is said to serve a system well "when there is a lot of dependence on the environment and it is difficult to foresee all possible circumstances in advance" (Steels, 1991, p. 459), a condition that applies *par excellence* to the young infant.

Organisation of infants' early sensorimotor co-ordinations along the lines of an emergent functionality architecture would confer a clear developmental advantage: preadaptation without rigid predetermination (Rutkowska, 1994a; 1994b). An apparent paradox of everyday infant activities is that their development often appears predetermined, yet permits considerable flexibility. Whatever mechanisms underwrite "normal" development are also capable of generating more unusual or exotic variants (e.g. locomotion by scooting in place of walking, Dennis, 1960). They would be severely (over)restricted if based on predetermined "goal-seeking". Emergent functionality would allow sensorimotor co-ordinations that had proven useful in the course of evolution, or sequences of such co-ordinations, to be "tuned in" if their viability is confirmed through interaction with the particular environment encountered. In the face of altered environmental conditions and/or properties of the infant (e.g. physical-motor disabilities) novel co-ordinations could be established.

This view of emergent functionality connects in interesting ways with developmentalists' interest in social *scaffolding* of infants' construction of activity (e.g. Rogoff, Malkin, & Gilbride, 1984; Valsiner, 1987). In contrast with the Piagetian infant, who is essentially a monadic creature, concern here is with social constraints on the developmental space within which infants' learning can operate. Scaffolding can usefully be thought of as temporarily engineered emergence of function that has the potential to become permanent adaptive change. One of its key characteristics involves adults manipulating the relationship between infants' sensory and motor capacities and the environment, so that the infant repeatedly experiences an outcome that they would neither spontaneously attempt, nor be able to attain, without support. The infant experiences reaching a "goal" that is in the adult's mind, not his or her own, through activity that is controlled more by the adult than by the infant. As far as infant mechanisms are concerned, the alignment of the sensory and motor processes involved, and their operation's outcome, are purely serendipitous—accidental and unplanned but fortunate; nothing at the level of an action program or a task-achieving behaviour co-ordinates them. Such scaffolded functionality has the potential, however, to become stable adaptive change. For this to work, development needs a process that will fix viable patterns of activity as permanent adaptive changes to processing potential.

Representational redescription in infancy

Karmiloff-Smith's (1992) computationally informed theory of *representational redescription* currently presents the widest-ranging evidence for a general-purpose endogenous process in cognitive development. It promises to clarify Piaget's (1976; 1978) important questions of how practical success relates to theoretical understanding of how and why things work, without resorting to his less satisfactory solution in terms of equilibration. Comparing Piaget's cognitivism with more contemporary varieties, Karmiloff-Smith notes the significance of early preadaptations, unforeseen by Piaget, which give the infant a step up on the developmental path. However, she questions cognitivist positions such as Fodor's which see early abilities as evidence for modular, domain-specific knowledge. The integration of knowledge that characterises domain-specific systems is better considered an outcome of interactive experience. Evidence of recurrent qualitative change over many domains, ages and forms of representation show that the new nativism proposed by Chomsky, Spelke and others does not tell the whole story. As suggested earlier, understanding the general form of change entails including output systems in any account of cognitive development, so as to incorporate Piaget's apposite focus on action.

What is shared by the many developmental data that support representational redescription is evidence that local reactions, in which every problem is represented and handled independently, are transformed to general anticipation, with connections between tasks being explicitly acknowledged. Thus, children may master the ability to use a word correctly for two purposes, but only subsequently come to represent it as a single word with two functions. Domains of integrated knowledge are being constructed through an internal process that operates in conjunction with the subject's activities. Karmiloff-Smith characterises the general form of this process as *knowledge explicitation*, a form of abstraction whereby knowledge that is implicit *in* the system's functioning (Level I representations) becomes explicit knowledge *for* the system (Level E representations). In the current context, we need to ask whether representational redescription operates within infancy. If early abilities are assumed to involve conceptual mechanisms, as Spelke and others propose, this mapping proves difficult to make (Rutkowska, 1994d).

Relating levels of representational explicitation to the kind of abstraction that characterises concepts is far from straightforward. Philosophers generally suppose concepts to support interrelated and flexible knowledge through the way they explicitly represent invariances as properties of things (e.g. concepts allow you to represent that a range of things share a property, and to entertain the notion that other, arbitrary things might possess that property too). In the representational redescription model, Level I representations are assumed to mediate rigid and context bound input–output relations that characterise the first phase of behavioural mastery. So, if infant abilities are conceptual in nature, they might be expected to require at least Level E1 representations, whose flexibility is attributed to them having extracted components of representations for use outside their original input–output context. However, Karmiloff-Smith doubts this is the case for infancy. She suggests, for example, that Spelke's unchanging principles are most likely at Level I, embedded in response to environmental stimuli. Rather than the notion of representational redescription in infancy being awry, this may mean that young infants operate without concepts as philosophers characterise them (cf. Hobson, 1991).

Developmentally, if infants' early object understanding is grounded in a Fodorean central system, it is hard to see how the underlying representations could be redescribed at a qualitatively new knowledge level. Only change such as enrichment of core principles, as suggested by Spelke (1991), would be straightforward. In fact, many of the habituation phenomena that support attribution of central concepts to infants may be amenable to explanation in terms of "input" computations of low-level vision (Rutkowska, 1991; 1993); their significance may be quite different from studies that investigate infants' use of sensory inputs in activity (cf. Costall, 1994; Willatts, Chapter 5, this volume).

Representational redescription's place in infancy becomes clearer if we assume that infant abilities lie in action mechanisms, and see the infant as a developing situated agent. Then, central processing is concerned with coordinating action, not with building propositional beliefs, and redescription can operate to alter this level's selective use of sensory and motor processes; hence, the infant's contribution to control of action. This offers a good fit between phases of representational redescription and empirical data on infants' changing levels of control in domains such as prehension. Thus, three distinct levels are found in infants' appreciation of object size-weight covariation as indexed by grasping and lifting a series of objects (Mounoud & Hauert, 1982). At 6- to 8-months, infants presented with an inappropriately light trick object will treat it like a normal object with proportional size and weight, persisting with a local, one-off adjustment to the current task. Around 9- to 10-months, lifting will be disrupted—for example, by rapid upward arm movement—and affective responses suggest that an anomaly has been detected. By 14- to 16-months, the two preceding responses are integrated, with quick compensation following initial disruption.

Such examples of anticipatory development in the second half of the first year converge with the representational redescription framework in a number of important ways. Notably, there is reorganisation of what appears to be already successful functioning (cf. the centrality in scaffolding of fostering "success"). In keeping with a focus on situated action, information in recurring patterns of sensory and motor activity becomes explicit in the infant's action-based representation, supporting anticipatory rather than reactive functioning. At the computational level of action program control, this can be viewed as abstraction of novel perceptual and motor variables from a range of local problem solutions; and more generally as a process of making explicit, or becoming attuned to, novel constraints on action (cf. Clark's, 1994, view that concepts may turn out to be abstractions of control-related features). Like representational redescription, this process is conservative; initial mechanisms are supplemented but not replaced by the development of anticipatory mechanisms, as the final level infant's ability to integrate them shows.

The success-based nature of this form of change is in clear disagreement with Piaget's (1953; 1976; 1978) long-standing assumption that disadaptation ("disturbance") is the fundamental trigger for the equilibration-governed development that results in cognizance of how and why action works. There are, however, important agreements too. Notably, the process is endogenous and general-purpose across ages and domains of activity—it is not so much constrained by domains of knowledge as serving to construct them. The notion of construction is significant here, for this kind of change is genuinely *epigenetic* in both process and product. Inputs to the process by which novel representations are abstracted are determined equally by the subject's activities and by the environment in which they occur. And those novel representations are not internal models of an outside world, but distributed representations that govern the operation of future perceptual and behavioural processes in novel action.

CONCLUSIONS

The past 25 years of infancy research have seen an ascendance of cognitive theories that often proposed their central mental processes as redressing the balance of Piagetian action's apparent preoccupation with "peripheral" sensorimotor aspects of infant ability. The main conclusion of looking at recent theoretical advances in cognitive science is that behaviour is back, with a vengeance, but embedded in ideas about action that often diverge significantly from those of Piaget.

As far as infants' initial mechanisms are concerned, the "something more" than Piaget's proposals that needs attributing to the infant by way of preadaptation can increasingly be viewed in terms of more innovational accounts of action than were available to Piaget. It may be appropriate to talk from the outset of infants' perceptual–behavioural action, rather than purely sensorimotor activity. While this conclusion appears to favour ecological psychology over cognitivist accounts of the mind, recent views of action prove compatible with work from computational cognitivist directions. A clear focus on perceiving and behaving playing equal roles *within* action supersedes conflicting interpretations of the theories of Gibson (meaning is in perception) and Piaget (perception is misleading until supplemented by behaviour).

Early representation remains a key issue, but focussing on action-based representation should lead to greater concern with how adaptive functioning and meaning depend on the subject's situatedness in the environment, not on disembodied internal models of it. These directions should enrich our understanding of non-conceptual action as the core of infant intelligence (Hobson, 1991; Reddy, Hay, Murray & Trevarthen, in Chapter 10 of this volume; Rutkowska, 1993).

Ideas about representation and reasoning that emerge from exploring situated action question Piaget's assumptions of the inferiority of subjective, action-based understanding, and his traditional view that things are improved through shifting to purportedly objective conceptual mechanisms. This is not to say that there are no qualitative shifts in the way that infants' knowledge is organised, but anticipatory developments may owe more to changing control of action than to acquisition of concepts and representational ability. While this view of where infant development goes to questions Piaget, ideas about how it gets there continue to support some of his general ideas. In particular, preadaptations need not imply predetermination of domain-specific knowledge; and proposals for epigenetic change through a general-purpose endogenous process need to be taken seriously. The overall conclusion, however, is subtly but significantly different from Piaget: both the developmental process and its outcome are grounded in *effective action*.

REFERENCES

Agre, P.E. & Chapman, D. (1990). What are plans for? In P. Maes (ed.), *Designing autonomous agents*. Cambridge, Mass.: MIT Press/Bradford Books.

Baillargeon, R. (1986). Representing the existence and the location of hidden objects: Object permanence in 6- and 8-month-old infants. *Cognition, 23*, 21–41.

Ballard, D.H. (1989). Reference frames for animate vision. In N.S. Sridharan (ed.), *Proceedings of the eleventh international joint conference on artificial intelligence*. San Mateo, Calif.: Morgan Kaufmann.

Ballard, D.H. (1993). Sub-symbolic modelling of hand-eye coordination. In D.E. Broadbent (ed.), *The simulation of human intelligence*. Oxford: Blackwell.

Barwise, J. (1987). Unburdening the language of thought. *Mind and Language, 2*, 82–96.

Beer, R. & Gallagher, J.C. (1992). Evolving dynamical adaptive networks for adaptive behavior. *Adaptive Behavior, 1*, 91–122.

Bersini, H. (1992). Animat's I. In F.J. Varela & P. Bourgine (eds), *Towards a practice of autonomous systems: proceedings of the first European conference on artificial life*. Cambridge, Mass.: MIT Press/Bradford Books.

Bertenthal, B.I. & Pinto, J. (1993). Complementary processes in the perception and production of human movements. In L.B. Smith & E. Thelen (eds), *A dynamic systems approach to development: applications*. Cambridge, Mass.: MIT Press/Bradford Books.

Bremner, J.G. (1989). Development of spatial awareness in infancy. In A. Slater & J.G. Bremner (eds), *Infant development*. Hove & London: Lawrence Erlbaum Associates Ltd.

Brooks, R. (1986). A robust layered control system for a mobile robot. *IEEE Journal of Robotics and Automation, RA 2*, 14–23.

Brooks, R. (1990). Elephants don't play chess. In P. Maes (ed.), *Designing autonomous agents*. Cambridge, Mass.: MIT Press/Bradford Books.

Brooks, R. (1991). Intelligence without representation. *Artificial Intelligence, 47*, 139–160.

Bruner, J.S. (1968). *Processes in cognitive growth: infancy*. Barre, Mass.: Clark University Press.

Bruner, J.S. (1973). Organization of early skilled action. *Child Development, 44*, 1–11.

Butterworth, G.E. (1989). Events and encounters in infant perception. In A. Slater & J.G. Bremner (eds), *Infant development*. Hove & London: Lawrence Erlbaum Associates Ltd.

Chomsky, N. (1980). Rules and representations. *Behavioral and Brain Sciences, 3*, 1–61.

Clark, A. (1994). *Representationalism refreshed?* Talk presented at the University of Sussex, Brighton, 14 June (paper under review).

Clark, A. & Lutz, R. (eds) (1992). *Connectionism in context*. London: Springer-Verlag.
Cliff, D. (1991). The computational hoverfly. In J.-A. Meyer & S.W. Wilson (eds), *From animals to animats: proceedings of the first international conference on the simulation of adaptive behavior*. Cambridge, Mass.: MIT Press/Bradford Books.
Cliff, D., Husbands, P., & Harvey, I. (1992). Issues in evolutionary robotics. In J.-A. Meyer, H.L. Roitblatt, & S.W. Wilson (eds) *From animals to animats 2: proceedings of the second international conference on simulation of adaptive behavior*. Cambridge, Mass.: MIT Press/ Bradford Books.
Cognitive Science. (1993). Special Issue: *Situated Action. 17(1)*.
Costall, A. (1994). On neonatal competence: Sleepless nights for representational theorists? In P. van Geert & L.P. Mos (eds), *Annals of Theoretical psychology*, Vol. 7. New York: Plenum.
Dennis, W. (1960). Causes of retardation among institutional children: Iran. *Journal of Genetic Psychology*, *96*, 47–59.
Dreyfus, H.L. (1981). From micro-worlds to knowledge representation. In J. Haugeland (ed.), *Mind design: Philosophy, psychology, artificial intelligence*. Cambridge, Mass.: MIT Press/ Bradford Books.
Dretske F.I. (1988). *Explaining behaviour: Reasons in a world of causes*. Cambridge, Mass.: MIT Press/Bradford Books.
Fodor, J.A. (1975). *The language of thought*. New York: Cromwell.
Fodor, J.A. (1980). Methodological solipsism considered as a research strategy in cognitive science. *Behavioral and Brain Sciences*, *3*, 63–110.
Fodor, J.A. (1983). *The modularity of mind*. Cambridge, Mass.: MIT Press/Bradford Books.
Gibson, E.J. (1987). Introductory essay: What does infant perception tell us about theories of perception? *Journal of Experimental Psychology: Human Perception and Performance*, *13*, 512–523.
Gibson, J.J. (1979). *The ecological approach to visual perception*. Boston, Mass.: Houghton-Mifflin.
Harris, P.L. (1989). Object permanence in infancy. In A. Slater & J.G. Bremner (eds), *Infant development*. Hove & London: Lawrence Erlbaum Associates Ltd.
Hebb, D.O. (1949). *The organization of behaviour*. New York: Wiley.
Hobson, P. (1991). Against the theory of "Theory of Mind". *British Journal of Developmental Psychology*, *9*, 33–53.
Humphreys, G.W. & Riddoch, J. (1986). Information processing systems which embody computational rules: The connectionist approach. *Mind and Language*, *1*, 201–212.
Israel, D. (1988). Bogdan on information. *Mind and Language*, *3*, 123–140.
Jones, R. Spelke, E.S. & Alley, T. (1985). Work group on perceptual development. In W.H. Warren & R.E. Shaw (eds), *Persistence and change: proceedings of the first international conference on event perception*. Hillsdale, N.J.: Lawrence Erlbaum Associates Inc.
Karmiloff-Smith, A. (1992). *Beyond modularity: a developmental perspective on cognitive science*. Cambridge, Mass.: MIT Press/Bradford Books.
Kugler, P.N., Kelso, J.A.S., & Turvey, M.T. (1982). On the control and coordination of naturally developing systems. In J.A.S. Kelso & J.E. Clark (eds) *The development of movement control and coordination*. Chichester: Wiley.
Legerstee, M. (1992). A review of the animate–inanimate distinction in infancy: Implications for models of social and cognitive knowing. *Early Development and Parenting*, *1*, 59–67.
Levy, S. (1992). *Artificial life: the quest for a new creation*. London: Jonathan Cape.
Maes, P. (ed.) (1990a). *Designing autonomous agents*. Cambridge, Mass.: MIT Press/Bradford Books.
Maes, P. (1990b). Situated agents can have goals. In P. Maes (ed.), *Designing autonomous agents*. Cambridge, Mass.: MIT Press/Bradford Books.
Marr, D. (1982). *Vision*. San Francisco: Freeman.

Meyer, J.-A. & Guillot, A. (1991). Simulation of adaptive behaviour in animats: Review and prospect. In J.-A. Meyer & S.W. Wilson (eds), *From animals to animats: proceedings of the first international conference on the simulation of adaptive behavior.* Cambridge, Mass.: MIT Press/Bradford Books.

Meyer, J.-A. & Guillot, A. (1994). From SAB90 to SAB94: Four years of animat research. In D. Cliff, P. Husbands, J.-A. Meyer, & S.W. Wilson (eds.), *From animals to animats 3: proceedings of the third international conference on simulation of adaptive behavior.* Cambridge, Mass.: MIT Press/Bradford Books.

Michaels, C.F. & Carello, C. (1981). *Direct perception.* New York: Prentice Hall.

Mounoud, P. & Hauert, C.A. (1982). Development of sensorimotor organization in young children: Grasping and lifting objects. In G.E. Forman (ed.), *Action and thought: from sensorimotor schemes to thought operations.* New York: Academic Press.

Newell, A. & Simon, H.A. (1976). Computer science as empirical inquiry: Symbols and search. *Communications of the ACM, 19,* 113–126.

Piaget, J. (1953). *The origin of intelligence in the child.* London: Routledge & Kegan Paul.

Piaget, J. (1955). *The child's construction of reality.* London: Routledge & Kegan Paul.

Piaget, J. (1970). *Genetic epistemology.* New York & London: Columbia University Press.

Piaget, J. (1971). *Biology and knowledge.* Edinburgh: Edinburgh University Press.

Piaget, J. (1976). *The grasp of consciousness.* London: Routledge & Kegan Paul.

Piaget, J. (1978). *Success and understanding.* London: Routledge & Kegan Paul.

Rogoff, B., Malkin, C., & Gilbride, K. (1984). Interaction with babies as guidance in development. In B. Rogoff & J.V. Wertsh (eds), *Children's learning in the zone of proximal development.* San Francisco: Jossey-Bass.

Rumelhart, D.E. & McClelland, J.L. (1986). PDP models and general issues in cognitive science. In D.E. Rumelhart & J.L. McClelland (eds), *Parallel distributed processing,* Vol. 1. Cambridge, Mass.: MIT Press/Bradford Books.

Rutkowska, J.C. (1990). Action, connectionism and enaction: A developmental perspective. *AI & Society, 4,* 96–114.

Rutkowska, J.C. (1991). Looking for "constraints" in infants' perceptual-cognitive development. *Mind and Language, 6,* 215–238.

Rutkowska, J.C. (1992). *Early prehension intention.* Paper presented at the BPS Developmental Section Annual Conference. Edinburgh, 5–8 September.

Rutkowska, J.C. (1993). *The computational infant: looking for developmental cognitive science.* Hemel Hempstead: Harvester Wheatsheaf.

Rutkowska, J.C. (1994a). Emergent functionality in human infants. In D. Cliff, P. Husbands, J.-A. Meyer, & S.W. Wilson (eds), *From animals to animats 3: proceedings of the third international conference on simulation of adaptive behavior.* Cambridge, Mass.: MIT Press/ Bradford Books.

Rutkowska, J.C. (1994b). *Prehension intention from 12 to 22 weeks.* Poster presented at the 9th International Conference on Infant Studies. Paris, 2–5 June.

Rutkowska, J.C. (1994c). Scaling up sensorimotor systems: Constraints from human infancy. *Adaptive Behavior, 2,* 349–373.

Rutkowska, J.C. (1994d). Situating representational redescription in infants' pragmatic knowledge. *Behavioral and Brain Sciences, 17,* 726–7.

Shaw, R.E. & Turvey, M.T. (1980). Methodological realism. Behavioral. *Behavioral and Brain Sciences, 3,* 94–7.

Smolensky, P. (1988). On the proper treatment of connectionism. *Behavioral and Brain Sciences, 11,* 1–23.

Spelke, E.S. (1988). Where perceiving ends and thinking begins: The apprehension of objects in infancy. In A. Yonas (ed.), *Perceptual development in infancy: the Minnesota symposium on child psychology,* Vol. 20. Hillsdale, N.J.: Lawrence Erlbaum Associates Inc.

Spelke, E.S. (1990). Principles of object perception. *Cognitive Science, 14*, 29–56.

Spelke, E.S. (1991). Physical knowledge in infancy: Reflections on Piaget's theory. In S. Carey & R. Gelman (eds), *The epigenesis of mind: essays on biology and cognition.* Hillsdale, N.J.: Lawrence Erlbaum Associates Inc.

Steels, L. (1991). Towards a theory of emergent functionality. In J.-A. Meyer & S.W. Wilson (eds), *From animals to animats: proceedings of the first international conference on the simulation of adaptive behavior.* Cambridge, Mass.: MIT Press/Bradford Books.

Turvey, M.T., Shaw, R.S., Reed, E.S., & Mace, W.M. (1981). Ecological laws of perceiving and acting. *Cognition, 9*, 237-304.

Thelen, E. & Smith, L.B. (1994). *A dynamic systems approach to the development of cognition and action.* Cambridge, Mass.: MIT Press/Bradford Books.

Valsiner, J. (1987). *Culture and the development of children's action.* Chichester: Wiley.

Varela, F.J. (1988). *Cognitive science: a cartography of current ideas.* Author's unpublished translation of F.J. Varela (1989). *Connaitre – Les sciences cognitives: tendances et perspectives.* Paris: Editions du Seuil.

Varela, F.J. (1993). *Organism: A meshwork of selfless selves.* Keynote address delivered at the Second European Conference on Artificial Life. Brussels, 24–26 May.

Varela, F.J. & Bourgine, P. (eds) (1992). *Towards a practice of autonomous systems: Proceedings of the first European conference on artificial life.* Cambridge, Mass.: MIT Press/Bradford Books.

Varela, F.J., Thompson, E., & Rosch, E. (1991). *The embodied mind: cognitive science and human experience.* Cambridge, Mass.: MIT Press/Bradford Books.

Vera, A.H. & Simon, H.A. (1993). Situated action: A symbolic interpretation. *Cognitive Science, 17*, 7–48.

Willatts, P. (1989). Development of problem solving in infancy. In A. Slater & J.G. Bremner (eds), *Infant development.* Hove: Lawrence Erlbaum Associates Ltd.

Wood, D., Bruner, J.S., & Ross, G. (1976). The role of tutoring in problem solving. *Journal of Child Psychology and Psychiatry*, 17, 89–100.

7 Development of Categorisation: Perceptual and Conceptual Categories

Jean M. Mandler
University of California, San Diego, USA; and
MRC Cognitive Development Unit, University College, London, UK.

INTRODUCTION

The field of infant categorisation has been bedevilled by the use of the same terms to mean different things. I hesitate to add to an already overexuberant terminology, but it is obviously crucial for us to define our terms carefully. First, there is the distinction between *concept* and *category*. I shall use the term concept to refer to a summary representation that forms the core meaning or the intension of a notion. It answers the question: what kind of thing is it? The concept of tiger consists of the sort of thing we think a tiger is. The term category, on the other hand, emphasises the extension of a concept; it answers the question: which things are tigers? The distinction is obviously only heuristic, and in addition is appropriately applied only to conceptual categories.

We can see that we are already in terminological trouble because I have had to modify the term category with the term conceptual. Given the definitions I have just laid out, what other kinds of categories could there be? Unfortunately, the same term, category, has also been used to refer to something that might better be called a perceptual schema. Perceptual categories or schemas are summary representations of what things look like, which is importantly not the same thing as a summary representation of what something is. A perceptual category does not have an intension. A perceptual category or perceptual schema of tigers is some kind of prototypical representation of what tigers look like. At least some of this knowledge is also part of the concept of "tiger" (for example, has stripes), but it doesn't work the other way around. My notion of a tiger as a wild jungle animal, which is part of my concept, is *not* part of my perceptual prototype of what tigers look like.

It is a pity we have used the same term for two such different kinds of representations. As Nelson (1985) has pointed out, conceptual categories are part of our explicit knowledge system; they are accessible to conscious thought. We can think about tigers, list their attributes, and argue over which of these are defining and which characteristic. We have much less access to our perceptual categories. Perceptual categories are often highly sophisticated and detailed, and allow us to use subtle distinctions in recognition decisions, yet much of this information is procedural and inaccessible. The difference in accessibility of the two kinds of knowledge can be illustrated by considering knowledge about faces. We have extensive, detailed, and abstract information about the proportions of the human face that we have used since infancy to categorise faces as male or female, or old or young (Fagan & Singer, 1979). In spite of having used this information to recognise people all our lives, we do not know what it is, in the sense that we cannot bring it to awareness and express it to ourselves or others. It requires artistic training or attentive perceptual analysis to conceptualise this kind of perceptual information.

Forming a perceptual category, although often making use of sophisticated information (as in the subtle differences in proportion of male and female faces), is not one of the higher cognitive processes. The perceptual systems of all organisms are designed to categorise. The process may work in a connectionist fashion (e.g. McClelland & Rumelhart, 1985); perceptual patterns get built up on top of each other, resulting in a summary representation or prototype that coexists comfortably with individual exemplar patterns. In this view perceptual categorisation is part and parcel of the perceptual system itself. It is the sort of thing one can build into an industrial vision machine. Such a machine can learn to discriminate nuts from bolts as they come down the assembly line, but we would not want to say that it has a concept of what a nut or a bolt is. Thus, there are differences between perceptual and conceptual categories in the type of information they summarise; whether or not the information is accessible; and also in the amount of information they contain. There are also differences in the course of acquisition.

Babies begin to form perceptual categories from birth (and in the case of auditory categorisation perhaps even earlier). It is highly unlikely that these very early perceptual categories have any conceptual content; that is, any particular meaning. For example, if 3-month-olds are shown a series of pictures of horses, within a few trials they will form a perceptual category of horses that excludes zebras and various other animals (Eimas & Quinn, 1994). Similarly, if shown a series of pictures of cats, they will form a perceptual category of cats that excludes lions and dogs (Quinn, Eimas, & Rosenkrantz, 1993). Do we want to say that these young infants have acquired a basic-level concept of horses or cats? If these are treated merely as visual patterns with no other meaning, it does not seem correct to talk about concept formation. Later, of course, this will change; meanings will become associated with horse-patterns and cat-patterns. But perceptual categorisation begins in the absence of conceptual meaning and may continue with little or no conceptual content for the first few months of life.

The development of conceptual categories seems to proceed in an altogether different way from learning to recognise a particular kind of shape. Conceptual categorisation has to do with forming meanings and is only secondarily concerned with what things look like. We have collected data showing that a good deal of conceptual categorisation proceeds from the top down (Mandler, Bauer, & McDonough, 1991; Mandler & McDonough, 1993). For example, we found that on an object-manipulation task (also called the sequential-touching task) 18-month-olds have no difficulty differentiating animals and vehicles as global classes, but within these domains rarely differentiate one basic-level class from another. For example, they treat any animal as different from any vehicle but they treat dogs and rabbits or dogs and horses as if they were the same kind of thing. Thus, babies appear to form concepts such as animal before they form concepts of horses or dogs or cats. Similar data were also found for the categories of plants, furniture, and kitchen utensils (Mandler et al., 1991). Concept development appears to consist in large part of differentiating broad, global concepts into finer and finer subgroups. This raises a number of interesting questions. How do perceptual and conceptual categories become organised together? Very young babies form perceptual categories such as horse and cat. Do they also form a perceptual category of animals? And does not perceptual categorisation also proceed by a process of differentiation, as Gibson (1969) suggested many years ago?

SOME DIFFICULTIES WITH THE NOTION OF BASIC-LEVEL CATEGORIES

The horses, dogs, and cats used in these experiments are usually called basic-level categories. I have already noted that for young babies these categories seem to be purely perceptual and without conceptual content. However, the term "basic level" is usually meant to refer to a conceptual category (e.g. Mervis & Rosch, 1981). Thus, there is potential for confusion. Unfortunately, "basic level" has never been given an adequate definition, so it is difficult to know what to do with it. For example, it is sometimes defined as an objectively determined level of categorisation that, among other things, reflects similarity in the shapes of exemplars (e.g. Mervis & Crisafi, 1982), and at other times as a knowledge-based form of categorisation determined by culture and/or expertise (e.g. Mervis & Mervis, 1982).

Rosch and Mervis (1975) originally defined basic-level categories as the level of abstraction at which objects are most naturally divided into categories. They proposed that both artifacts and biological objects consist of information-rich bundles of attributes that form natural discontinuities in the correlational structure of the environment. Wings, feathers, and beaks are not distributed randomly across animals but instead form a cluster associated with birds. Basic-level cuts were said to be made at these points of discontinuity, forming a level of abstraction that carries the most information and possesses the highest cue validity. Cue validity in turn was defined as the extent to which a cue (attribute) predicts a given category, for example, the extent to which the attribute wings predicts that an object is a bird. Rosch et al. (1976) tested these notions with a series of experiments designed to draw out the consequences of there being a particular level of abstraction in object taxonomies that is the most informative. For example, in a study of the nonbiological categories of musical instruments, fruit, tools, clothing, furniture, and vehicles and the biological categories of trees, fishes and birds, they found that for the nonbiological categories, subjects listed the most attributes at the subordinate level (e.g. folk-guitar), slightly fewer attributes at the basic level (guitar) and many fewer attributes at the superordinate level (musical instruments). However, attribute naming did not significantly differ across levels for the biological taxonomies.

Similar results were found for listing the movements that are typically made when interacting with these objects (e.g. petting animals, sitting on furniture); differences were found among levels of categorisation for the nonbiological domains, but not for biological ones. Other experiments showed that the basic and subordinate levels for artifacts had more overlap in the shapes of various exemplars than did superordinate categories.[1] Experiments on nonbiological categories indicated that people may not be able to form an image higher than the basic level,[2] and they identify objects faster when given basic-level names than when given superordinate names.

[1] In this case the same result was found for animals, except that Rosch et al. (1976) reclassified animals on the basis of the previous results, so that what had been the life-form level (fish) was now called the basic level. This point is discussed further later.

[2] This oft-cited conclusion seems dubious. Rosch et al. (1976) measured imagery only indirectly. Subjectively, it is often very difficult to form an image even at the basic level. For example, when I imagine a chair, it is sketchy and devoid of detail, but is either a straightbacked chair or an overstuffed chair or a rocking chair, not a summary form of these subclasses. Although I can switch rapidly back and forth among subordinate images, it seems I must choose one of them as a representative of the larger class.

Overall, these experiments found few if any significant differences between subordinate- and basic-level classes, but on most measures these categories differed significantly from superordinate categories.

Unfortunately, the measure of cue validity that was originally proposed as the objective criterion for determining the basic level turns out to be incorrect: cue validity is always greatest for the superordinate level, not the basic level (Murphy, 1983).[3] Various other measures of cue validity have been attempted and also found wanting (Medin, 1982). Instead, the best measure that could be found was that the basic level is the highest level at which a few characteristics, such as number of attributes or commonality of shape, appear (Rosch et al., 1976). However, without an adequate specification of what that level is, the truth of this proposition is difficult to judge. We have no guarantee that the highest level at which certain characteristics are found in, say, the domain of animals, will predict the highest level at which the same characteristics are found in the domain of musical instruments. As mentioned above, in most of the tests Rosch et al. (1976) conducted, no significant differences were found between subordinate-level classes and basic-level classes. So we are faced with nonsignificant differences in our quest to determine characteristics that will uniquely determine the basic level.

This difficulty is illustrated by the fact that Rosch's own data showed that her hypotheses as to what was basic level in both the animal and plant domains were incorrect. The principles that govern categorisation at the basic and superordinate levels proposed by Rosch et al. (1976), such as speed of identification and being able to list many attributes, worked in the expected way only for some artifacts; they did not work for biological categories. In addition, there are many natural categories, such as bodies of water and rocks, for which we have no information or criteria to help us determine what is basic. Even for artifacts, most categories such as buildings, reading materials, and so forth, have never been tested. In some cases, more recent work has disconfirmed the status Rosch et al. (1976) proposed for artifacts such as musical instruments. Rosch, et al. proposed that the basic level in musical instruments consisted of concepts such as guitar, clarinet, and trumpet. But using their criterion of number of attributes listed and ease of identification, it appears that the basic level is at the level of strings, woodwinds, and brass (Palmer et al., 1989).

---

[3] To illustrate this point, consider that a feature such as eyes uniquely predicts the superordinate animal class but does not differentiate most kinds of animals at the basic level. Similarly, the feature wings uniquely predicts flying animals but does not differentiate birds from other flying animals. This difficulty with the criterion of cue validity was already signalled in Rosch et al. (1976).

Rosch's theory was derived from folk taxonomies of animals and plants and not from artifact domains (for which there are no folk taxonomies). Rosch assumed that the generic level of folk taxonomies (see Berlin, Breedlove, & Raven, 1973) had the special status she termed the basic level. The generic level is the level at which we name robins and maples. Yet it did not work out that way in the data. Rosch et al. (1976) found that Americans were not very familiar with the posited generic level for animals and plants but were more familiar with the life-form level instead. American adults apparently know birds, fish, and trees but not robins, sea bass, and maples. But bird is a life-form (like mammal), whereas robin is generic or basic level; fish is a life-form, sea bass is generic or basic level; tree is a life-form, maple is generic or basic level. So, the theory that the basic level matched the generic level of folk taxonomies was incorrect. In spite of this, the notion that there is something special about the basic level has been so widely accepted that it is now sometimes said to be a universal human characteristic that is merely underused in certain cultures (Berlin, cited by Lakoff, 1987), or that children have a natural affinity for the basic level that may possibly be innate (Medin & Barsalou, 1987).

There has never been a satisfactory definition of the basic level, only data that sometimes fit some of our intuitive notions. Our intuitions, in turn, seem to be based on what is important in our cultural experience and our language. Therefore, they are the concepts that infants must *learn* as being "basic" or important, not something that is objectively given in the environment, which Mervis and Rosch (1981) have also acknowledged. But if it is cultural experience that teaches children basic-level concepts, then it is difficult to understand what role the natural discontinuities in the environment are playing or how the basic level could be developmentally special, even if it does eventually come to dominate our conceptual system in some way.

Nevertheless, Mervis and Rosch (1981) suggested that basic-level categories are primary or foundational in the sense that they are more fundamental psychologically than categories at other levels and are the first kinds of categories that children acquire. Although Inhelder and Piaget's (1964) work on classification had suggested that superordinate categorisation was a late development, at the time Rosch first proposed her theory there was still little developmental data specifically contrasting basic-level and superordinate categorisation, and virtually none on very young children. Rosch et al. (1976) themselves conducted only two developmental experiments, and these did not constitute adequate tests of the hypothesis (Rosch, et al., 1976, experiments 8 & 9). First and foremost, the youngest children in these experiments were 3 years of age, which is too old to assess the nature of the earliest concepts, since these begin considerably earlier than 3 years.

One study used a sorting task (a free classification task) in which children were asked to sort items into either basic-level or superordinate categories of clothing, furniture, and vehicles. The results indicated that even in the first grade children had great difficulty doing superordinate classification, in spite of the fact that the items used were very common ones. There are at least two reasons why children were better at basic-level classification in this experiment. First, the criterion used was unduly strict: sorting was considered incorrect if a superordinate class was subdivided. For example, if a child put shoes and socks in one pile and shirt and pants in another pile, they were scored as incorrect, even though the instructions did not tell the children how many piles to use. Second, the task used a confounded design (see Mandler, et al., 1991). If one wants to test whether basic-level classification is easier than superordinate classification, it is not correct to use sorting of shirts, chairs, and cars as the basic-level classification, and contrast it with sorting of clothing, furniture, and vehicles. Shirts, chairs, and cars represent both basic-level *and* superordinate contrasts, and if children do well on such a task one can't tell whether that is due to their using the basic-level or the superordinate information that is provided by the contrasts, or more likely both. To test the basic level one must contrast shirts, pants, and shoes, or cars, trucks, and motorcycles. However, this confounding of basic-level and superordinate information has characterised all the sorting tests in the literature (e.g. Saxby & Anglin, 1983).

It is not obvious that children would do well on a true basic-level task; indeed, in our work with very young children they do not (Mandler, et al., 1991). Using the object-manipulation (sequential-touching) task, which is a version of the sorting task designed for younger children, we found excellent categorisation of animals and vehicles at the superordinate level in 1½- to 2½-year-olds. But when we eliminated the confounding between basic-level and superordinate information and tested true basic-level classes by contrasting, for example, dogs with rabbits, or cars with motorcycles, instead of dogs with cars, we found very little basic-level categorisation at 1½ years, and consistent basic-level performance only by 2½ years. Only when we used a confounded design such as Rosch et al. (1976) used, contrasting dogs with cars, for example, did we find basic-level categorisation on this task in the second year (Mandler & Bauer, 1988).

The other developmental experiment that Rosch et al. (1976) reported was a match-to-sample test with 3- and 4-year-olds, again studying superordinate v. basic-level contrasts, this time in the animal and vehicle domains. Although performance was at ceiling by 4 years, the 3-year-olds were roughly at chance on the difference between animals and vehicles. Although I do not know exactly why this result occurred, it is certainly at variance with data that Bauer and I collected, using a match-to-sample task but with much younger children. We found a high rate of superordinate matching-to-sample (87% correct) in 1½- to 2½-year-old children (Bauer & Mandler, 1989), suggesting that whatever the reason for the poor performance that

Rosch et al. found, it was not due to lack of the relevant knowledge. It seems likely that the poor performance of Rosch et al.'s 3-year-olds was due either to lack of precise understanding of the verbal instructions or to the type of pretraining procedure that was used. Matching-to-sample tests often use pretraining that emphasises the importance of perceptual similarity (e.g. Daehler, Lonardo, & Bukatko, 1979), which, of course, de-emphasises superordinate category membership.

The other developmental tests that have been used consist of various linguistic measures, primarily having to do with the greater frequency of basic-level than superordinate terms in both children's and adults' language (Anglin, 1977; Rosch et al., 1976). Indeed, the only clear evidence for a privileged level of concepts is lexical in nature. Basic-level names *are* used more frequently than superordinates in daily speech and in speech to children. This is the main reason, of course, why they are the first names children learn, since they can learn only the language they hear. As Brown (1958) noted long ago, however, the fact that basic-level names are the first to be learned tells us nothing at all about the underlying conceptual system onto which they are mapped. He, in fact, suggested that it was likely that this underlying conceptual system was more global in nature than the vocabulary being learned to refer to it.

Rosch was sensitive to the difficulties I have outlined in giving a developmental interpretation to her data, because she later noted that the principles of categorisation she espoused had to do with explaining categories coded by the language of a given culture, and did not constitute a theory of development (Rosch, 1978). Yet both Mervis and Rosch (1981) and Mervis and Mervis (1982) have explicitly claimed that basic-level categories are the first to be acquired, and by this they do not mean culturally or developmentally variable concepts, but rather, a specific kind of concept, such as chair or bird (i.e. objects that have overall similar shapes, elicit similar motor patterns, and so forth). This is also the interpretation that has come to be the dominant view in developmental psychology. The position is often modified by the qualification that children's basic-level categories may differ from adult basic-level categories (Mervis & Mervis, 1982), but this only complicates the issue because then there are no criteria to delimit the term. In any case, the tension remains between Rosch's claim that the theory has to do with linguistically coded categorisation and the view that it speaks to the foundations of concept formation itself. Obviously, if children begin to form concepts before language begins, then some kind of conceptual categorisation is prior to linguistic categorization. Indeed, it is widely accepted that language could not be learned without a conceptual base onto which it can be mapped (Bowerman, 1980; Cromer, 1991; Maratsos, 1983). If one is going to claim that basic-level concepts are the first to be formed, then one must examine the nature of prelinguistic categories.

As soon as prelinguistic categorisation is studied the ambiguity about the conceptual status of basic-level categories becomes obvious. If basic-level categories are the first to be formed, are they perceptual or conceptual in nature? Do babies first learn about what things look like or about what they are? Rosch and her colleagues meant basic-level to refer to concepts (Mervis & Rosch, 1981), but because they did not make any distinction between conceptual and perceptual categories, they could and did use primarily perceptual tasks to test their theory. Perhaps what they uncovered was some *important level of perceptual categorisation*; for example, some level of abstraction at which it is easiest to form a perceptual prototype or schema. However, this possibility has not been addressed. To date we have no information as to whether infants form perceptual categories such as collies that are differentiated from dachshunds as easily as they form perceptual categories such as dogs that are differentiated from cats (Quinn et al., 1993).

Clarifying this issue is not helped by the fact that most theories of adult categorisation also make no distinction between perceptual and conceptual categories. At least since Bruner's (1957) proposal that both types of categorisation proceed by similar rules, there has been a tendency to assume a common set of processes whether categorising random dot patterns (Posner & Keele, 1968), geometric forms (Medin & Schaffer, 1978), disease symptoms (Nosofsky, Kruschke, & McKinley, 1992) or natural kinds and artifacts (Smith & Osherson, 1988). In this view, whether the stimuli are meaningless perceptual patterns, instances of a natural domain such as animals, or abstract concepts like diseases makes no difference; categorisation is categorisation is categorisation. There have been too few tests of this notion (e.g. Reed & Friedman, 1973) to know whether it is correct or not, but it strikes me as a risky assumption. We have no guarantee that learning to categorise a set of random dot patterns or a series of pictures of horses will proceed in the same way as learning the concept of animal, let alone more abstract concepts, such as diseases or professions.

THE RELATION BETWEEN PERCEPTUAL AND CONCEPTUAL CATEGORISATION

How to construct conceptual categories out of perceptual information has been a conundrum since psychology started. The standard view has been expressed by Quinn and Eimas (1986, p. 356), thus:

> The categories of infants ... are sensory in nature, whereas the categories and concepts of adults are often far removed from the world of sensory data ... Nor can it be readily envisioned how the attributes of adult concepts can be constructed from the attributes innately available to infants. Nevertheless, a commonly, if often tacitly, held view is that the nontransducible attributes of

adult concepts are somehow derived from the sensory primitives available to infants. Adequate (that is, testable) descriptions of the developmental process remain to be offered, however.

No distinction is being made here between categories and concepts, which is part of what creates the classic dilemma: How does one get to attributes like "used to sit on" or "has babies" or "domesticated" from sensory attributes like "red", "square", and "rough textured"? Piaget (1952) tried to solve it by a stage theory that posited a transition from one kind of categorisation to the other around age 1½. He was aware that babies form perceptual categories, since these are simply one type of sensorimotor learning. But he was unable to provide a satisfactory account of how perceptual categories (and other sensorimotor schemas) are transformed into the conceptual categories that are used for thought. Thus, he joined a long line of theorists who could not figure out how to get from there to here. His theory stated only that over the course of the sensorimotor period, schemas gradually become freed from their sensorimotor limitations, speeded up, and eventually become interiorised in the form of images. In this view, images constitute the first non-sensorimotor, conceptual form of representation. Imagery allows infants to re-present objects and events to themselves, and so provides the foundation for the beginning of thought. It is not clear, however, how it is that forming images conceptualises the perceptual displays that are being processed, or how it expresses abstract or functional properties, so we still have no theory of how this process produces adult-like concepts.

Other proposals for the transition from perceptual to conceptual categories have been related to language. For instance, a common assumption is that babies form basic-level categories such as dogs and cats on perceptual grounds, and these perceptual prototypes become conceptualised by having information become associated with them. As Eimas (1994) puts it, when perceptual categories become sufficiently enriched by new perceptual information they begin to take on the characteristics of concepts. In most such accounts this process includes learning a name; the name solidifies an otherwise rather hazy notion. Thus, an infant might first learn to recognise dogs, then learn certain facts about dogs, such as that they bark and chew on bones, and that they are called "dogs". What is not clear about this account is how the attributes of barking and chewing on bones are themselves represented. Are these images? Is "chew on bones" a perceptual attribute? As with Piaget's account we have to ask how an image becomes a meaning. It is also not clear which of these attributes form the intension; that is, the definitional core or central idea of what a dog is. Presumably there can be no reference to *animal*, since that is a superordinate concept that will be a later, and primarily linguistic, acquisition.

The dilemma that this view faces is how to reconcile an empirical account of concept formation (empirical in the sense that information must be learned from experiencing the environment rather than built-in in the form of innate ideas) with the constraint that we experience the world via our senses. There is no conceptual sense organ; concepts must be created. So we must find a way to construct concepts out of perceptual data, not just to add associative links between one sight and another.

CONCEPT FORMATION BY PERCEPTUAL ANALYSIS

I have proposed an alternative account to Piaget's notion that concept formation is a late development in infancy. I have suggested that the conceptual system is formed simultaneously and in parallel with the the sensorimotor system, and that *perceptual analysis* is the mechanism by which the conceptual system is created (Mandler, 1988; 1992). Perceptual analysis is a process in which a given perceptual array is attentively analysed and a new kind of information abstracted. The information is new in the sense that a piece of perceptual information is recoded into a nonperceptual form that represents a meaning. The process is different from the usual perceptual processing, which occurs automatically and is typically not under the attentive control of the perceiver. Most of the perceptual information normally encoded is neither consciously noticed nor accessible at a later time for purposes of thought. Perceptual analysis, on the other hand, involves the active recoding of a subset of incoming perceptual information into meanings that form the basis of accessible concepts.

Perceptual analysis is a version of what Karmiloff-Smith (1986) calls redescription of procedural information. Information gets recoded into a different format, and in the process some of the original information is lost. What we consciously attend to and store in a form that we can potentially think about involves a reduction and redescription of the huge amount of information provided by our sensory receptors; and that is used to form perceptual categories. As discussed earlier, a great deal of the perceptual information that we process, from faces for example, is stored in procedural form, as illustrated by the fact that we readily learn such complex perceptual categories, but cannot state what the information is that we use. To form an explicit knowledge system requires a different format—what we might call a vocabulary of meanings. The process of redescribing perceptual information forms such a vocabulary. These meanings are not themselves accessible, but they form the basis of concepts that *are* accessible.

I assume that the capacity to engage in perceptual analysis is innate. However, it seems likely that before such analysis can begin there must have developed some stable perceptual schemas, or perceptual categories. Many of these are formed by 3 months of age; for example, categories such as the horses and cats investigated by Eimas and Quinn (1994) and Quinn et al. (1993). It is about the same time that the first indications of perceptual analysis appear. The measures are necessarily indirect, but are implicated in many accounts in terms of increasing alertness and the analytical nature of perceptual activity after the first few months of life (Fox, Kagan, & Weiskopf, 1979; Ruff, 1986; Werner & Kaplan, 1963). Perceptual analysis can also be inferred from Piaget's (1951) account of early imitation, in which he describes his children as young as 3 to 4 months displaying intense concentration on the models he provided.

I shall use the concept of animate thing or animal to illustrate how perceptual analysis can produce a vocabulary of meanings that form a primitive definition of what an animal is. There is an excellent source in perception to deliver part of the information needed for this concept, namely, the perceptual categorisation of motion. Infants perceptually differentiate the motion of people from similar but biologically incorrect motion as early as 3 months of age (Bertenthal, 1992). It is not yet known whether the perceptual system can also make the more abstract categorisation of animate v. inanimate (mechanical) motion in general. I have made the assumption that it can, and that perceptual analysis can then be applied to the resulting perceptual categories (but it could be applied instead to smaller, perceptually more similar categories, such as legged or winged animals). What perceptual analysis does is to abstract and characterise some of the properties that accompany these types of movements. For example, the infant can characterise those things that move in one way as starting up on their own and sometimes responding to the infant from a distance, and those things that move in another way as not starting up on their own and never responding from a distance to what the infant does. A conjunction of a few of these simple meanings would be sufficient to constitute an early concept of animal.

Although these meanings are derived from perception, they differ in several ways from perceptual features themselves. They are more abstract and less detailed than perceptual features; they may even be inaccurate, in the sense that they use a simplified prototypical version of some feature to represent a highly varied class.[4] For example, self-motion varies a great deal in its physical details, depending on whether it is legs, fins, torso, or wings that carry the motion. The idea of starting up on one's own is a generalisation or construction at a more abstract level of something common to all the various motions. It is that more abstract level that I am calling a

[4] An example of the distortion that can come with simplified meanings is the tendency of infants in our object-handling experiments to make dogs, fish, and elephants all move by means of a hopping motion.

meaning, a meaning that lets us treat elephants, birds, fish, and snakes as functionally alike.

What is needed to further this account is to specify the format in which these meanings are represented. There is not space here to describe the work done on this topic. A detailed account is provided in Mandler (1992). Here I will only mention that the format of the earliest meanings is thought to be that of the image-schema. I have suggested that perceptual analysis involves a redescription of perceptual inputs into schematic conceptualisations of space. The resulting image-schemas are abstracted from the same type of information used to perceive, but they eliminate most details of the spatial array that are processed during ordinary perception. Image-schemas are not the same as images, but form the spatial underpinnings of images; at the same time they constitute the primitive meaning elements such as self-motion and contingent motion that I have discussed here, as well as other relations such as agency, containment, and support.

This discussion should make it clear why there is no guarantee that the processing that takes place in creating perceptual categories should be the same as that which takes place in creating concepts. One of the most important differences is that the attention-based perceptual analyses leading to concept formation (and imagery) are selective. So far as we know, the perceptual schematisation used to form a perceptual category is not selective; indeed, there is reason to believe that it registers a reasonably accurate account of the information in the environment. Selective attention, on the other hand, works only on a subset of the information that is being processed.

HOW DO WE TELL PERCEPTUAL AND CONCEPTUAL CATEGORIES APART?

How can we determine if an infant has formed a prototype of a perceptual pattern or has conceptualised some pattern as a meaningful thing? Although we can't answer this question yet in a systematic way, McDonough and I (Mandler & McDonough, 1993) collected data that serendipitously differentiated perceptual and conceptual categorisation. In conjunction with the data of Quinn and Eimas discussed earlier (Eimas & Quinn, 1994; Quinn et al., 1993), we found a double dissociation between performance on basic-level and superordinate categories of animals, depending on the nature of the task that was used. Such double dissociations have classically been used to infer that different kinds of processes and/or representations are being used. The data suggested some experimental ways to differentiate perceptual and conceptual functioning in babies.

Two kinds of tasks are involved in this dissociation; they are basically the same task, but use different stimulus presentation. One is the standard familiarisation-preferential looking task, using realistic pictures of objects (either photos or elaborate line drawings). Six or eight familiarisation trials of varied members of a given category are presented two at a time, followed by a preferential looking test. For this test, paired comparisons of a new within-category member and a contrasting-category member are used. The dependent measure is looking time. The other task is based on Ruff's (1986) object-examination task (see also Oakes, Madole, & Cohen, 1991). It is also a familiarisation-preferential looking task, but it uses little models of objects instead of pictures. It uses the same type of familiarisation and test trials, but the objects are handed to the infant one at a time. The dependent measure is examination time. An illustration of an infant engaged in examining an object in this task is shown in Fig. 7.1. The question is under what circumstances do young infants show perceptual categorisation of animals or vehicles at either the basic level (e.g. differentiating dogs from horses) or the superordinate or domain-level (e.g. differentiating animals from vehicles)? It turns out you get very different answers depending on which familiarisation test you use.

To begin, let me return to the results discussed earlier on the pattern of successes and failures that 18-month-old children show on another task using objects rather than pictures; namely, the sequential-touching task (Mandler et al., 1991). We examined categorical responses to both basic-level and superordinate classes using this task in the age range from 18 to 30 months. We found that on this task 18-month-olds were responsive to superordinate (global) categories, distinguishing clearly between animals and vehicles, no matter how varied the animal exemplars were, but they did not react to most basic-level animal distinctions. They made distinctions only between land animals and water animals and air animals; they did not differentiate among mammals. Similar findings were obtained for vehicles and their subclasses.

We claimed that the global categorisation of animals and vehicles had to be conceptual on two grounds:

1. Domain-level global contrasts involve too much within-class perceptual variability to be categorised by the perceptual system alone. This argument says that the perceptual dissimilarity of the items is too great to enable categorisation on the basis of perceptual features. The shapes of elephants, birds, and fish vary too much to form a purely perceptual category. Therefore, if infants are sensitive to the category of animals, it has to be based on some kind of conceptual meaning.

2. The second argument is that the perceptual system alone cannot determine choice of responses in any kind of complex self-instructing task. In the case of the sequential-touching task the infant must choose which of a number of toys to play with, which depends on voluntary control over

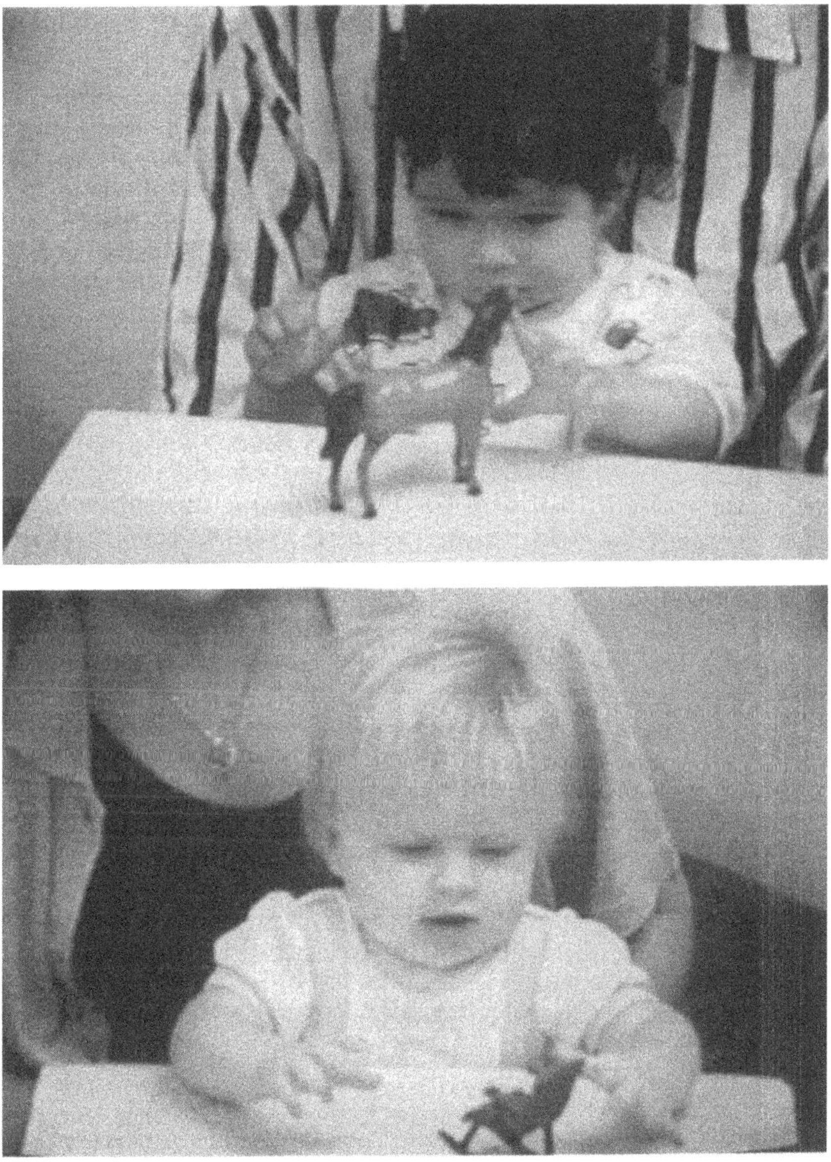

FIG. 7.1. Two 9-month-old infants, each examining an object in the object-examination task.

attention more than a visual looking task need do. Object examination activates the motivational, conceptual system, and is not an automatic attentional shift to something perceptually new, which might be what is going on in the preferential looking task with young infants.

Because 18-month-olds did make a tripartite division of the animal domain into land-, air-, and water-animals, we wanted to test younger infants to see if initially there is no division of the domain of animals. Unfortunately, we were not able to use the sequential-touching task because placing a large number of objects in front of 7- or 9-month-olds seems to overwhelm them. So we switched reluctantly to the object-examination task described earlier. We were reluctant because we wanted to study basic-level contrasts as well as global ones. We thought we would not have a problem with global contrasts, because of the first argument above: the shapes of global category members differ too much to account for categorisation by perceptual factors alone. But for the basic level, exemplars look a lot alike and the object-examination task is just another familiarisation-preferential looking task. So we expected that it would give the same kind of data, and the second argument would no longer hold: perceptual similarity alone might determine the looking response and so we would not know if the infants had a conceptual category or not.

To our surprise, however, we found that in the animal domain 7- to 11-month-old infants on the object-examination task showed categorisation only at the global level, and *not* at the basic level (Mandler & McDonough, 1993). Specifically, the infants did not differentiate dogs from fish or dogs from rabbits, although they did differentiate animals from vehicles and most impressively birds from airplanes (where all the items looked quite similar). Thus, although the usual view is that basic-level categorisation should be easier than superordinate categorisation for infants, we found sub-categorisation approximating the basic level only for vehicles, and no evidence for subcategorisation of animals.[5] To illustrate the lack of effect of similarity of physical appearance on categorization, Figs 7.2 to 7.4 show examples of the various stimuli used in our experiments. Figure 7.2 shows examples of the animals and vehicles the infants successfully categorised; it illustrates the considerable within-class variation (especially for the animals

---

[5] Our southern California infants spend much of their time in cars and many of them have travelled by plane as well. Linda Smith (personal communication) has conducted similar tests to ours with infants who reside in Indiana, a more rural culture. She finds global categorisation just as we do, but earlier differentiation of the animal domain than of the vehicle domain. The models she uses are less realistic and emphasise heads and facial features more than do ours, which may account for the difference. However, it may also be that the rate at which the domains of animals and vehicles become differentiated is determined by the amount of experience with these two classes in the first year of life.

FIG. 7.2. A superordinate or global contrast: examples of the animals and vehicles that infants successfully categorise in the object-examination task in spite of extensive within-class perceptual differences. From Mandler and McDonough (1993). Reproduced with the permission of ABLEX Publishing Corporation.

in this particular set) and also the between-class variation in shape (and to some extent in texture) that these stimuli provide. Figure 7.3 shows the birds and aeroplanes that the infants also successfully categorised; here a high degree of both within- and between class similarity can be seen. Finally, Fig. 7.4 shows the dogs and fish the infants failed to categorise, in spite of high within-class similarity and between-class dissimilarity.

In more recent work on this issue McDonough and I are currently finding that 9-month-olds can differentiate birds and land animals. Thus, there may be an initial distinction between birds (or air creatures) and other animals. More research is needed, but if we ignore the lack of differentiation between dogs and fish, our data suggest that the *smallest* categories of animals that babies conceptualise are the life-form categories of mammals and birds. Needless to say, it would be unsatisfactory to call this level of conceptualisation a child-basic category, in so far as that implies partaking of whatever benefits accrue to the much smaller basic-level categories of adults. In addition, of course, these data do not easily fit those of Eimas and Quinn (1994) and Quinn et al. (1993), discussed earlier, showing that even 3- to 6-month-olds *can* categorise animals at the basic level. Using the standard picture-looking task, they found that 3-month-olds categorised horses as different from cats, zebras, and giraffes. They also categorised cats as dif-

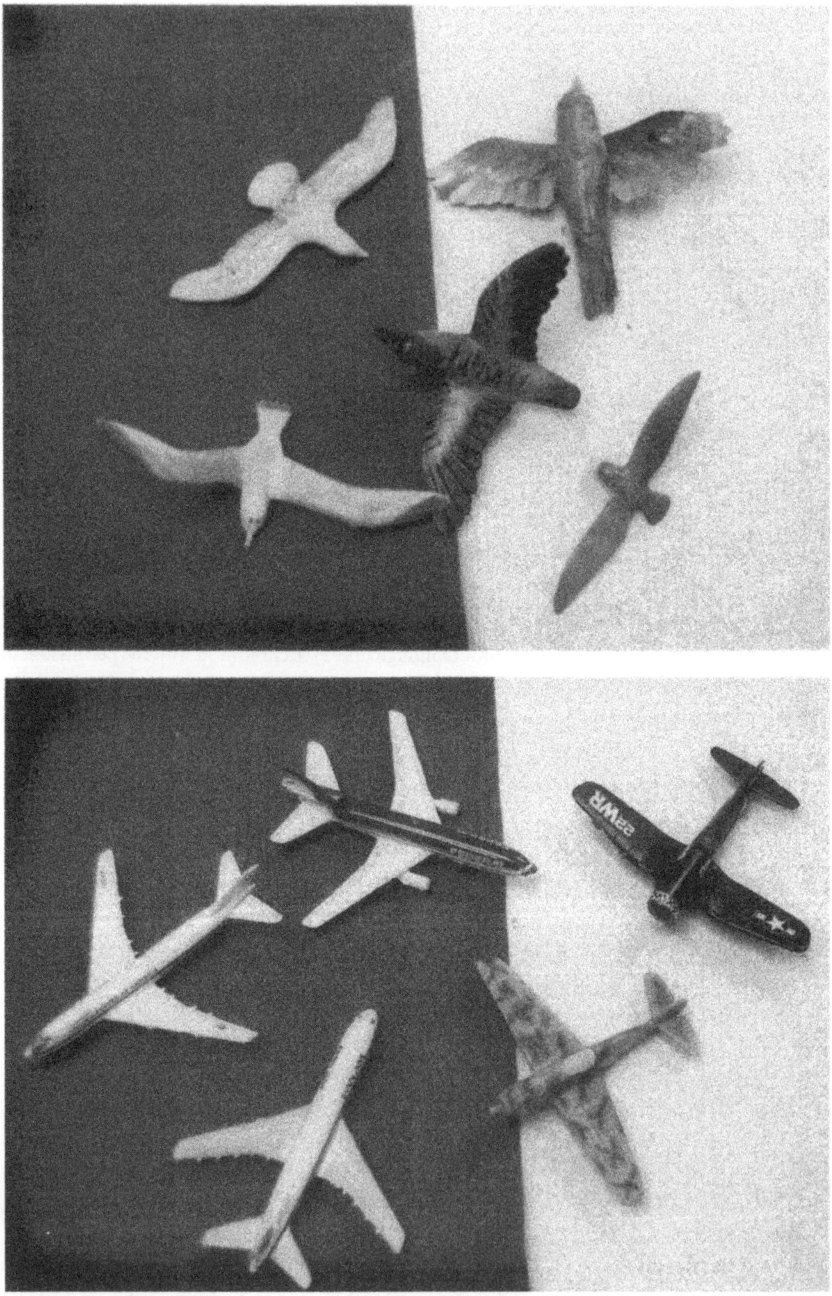

FIG. 7.3. A cross-domain contrast: examples of the birds and aeroplanes that infants successfully categorise in spite of their perceptual similarity.

FIG. 7.4. A basic-level contrast: examples of the dogs and fish that infants fail to categorise in spite of within-class perceptual similarity and between-class perceptual differences.

ferent from lions, horses, and dogs. We all assume these achievements represent a purely perceptual operation.

If infants subcategorise animals on the standard picture- looking task, why do they not do so on ours? This question led us to think again about looking-time data we collected when we first began to study global categorisation in infants less than a year old. We had studied 11-month-olds but had never published the data because they were negative. They showed a *failure* to categorise at the superordinate (global) level, using the standard picture-looking task. We used two kinds of global contrasts: animals v. vehicles and furniture v. clothes. The pictures were detailed, realistic line drawings of exemplars of these categories. On these tasks we used the same procedure as Eimas and Quinn (1994), except that we gave eight familiarisation trials instead of six. We showed a pair of stimuli from a category side by side on each trial; after four pairs were seen, they were repeated, again two at a time, but with different pairings. Then we gave paired preferential-looking tests, using a new item from the familiarisation category and an item from the other category. For these test pairs, the overall shape of the items was made as similar as possible, given that they come from such different categories. Birds and airplanes were easy to make look alike (as can be seen in Fig. 7.3); a sock was made to look remarkably like an overstuffed chair (as long as meaning is ignored). Even a pair of overalls and a high chair were made to have almost identical outline shapes. These tests were all miserable failures; 11-month-olds showed no preferential looking at exemplars of new categories.

In addition to these data, Roberts and Cuff (1989) also had difficulty showing responsivity to the superordinate category of animals in 9- to 15-month-olds, again using realistic picture stimuli, whereas Roberts (1988) had no difficulty showing responsivity to a basic-level category in 9-month-olds using the same technique. We also had more difficulty showing sensitivity to a category of bathroom things (a contextual category in which there is no perceptual similarity among the exemplars), using picture stimuli and 14-month-olds as subjects, than we did when we used the sequential-touching task (Mandler, Fivush, & Reznick, 1987). In addition, it may be noted that two prior studies with infants that have showed the presence of the domain-level (superordinate) category of animals also used objects (Golinkoff & Halperin, 1983; Ross, 1980), although Ross's subjects were not allowed to interact with the objects.

So we find what appears to be a double dissociation on categorisation of animals in data collected from several labs that contrast picture-looking and object-handling tasks. Infants as young as 7 months respond to the superordinate contrast of animals and vehicles when objects are examined, but not when looking at pictures. The same infants tend not to respond to basic-level animal categories when objects are examined, but do respond to basic-level contrasts when pictures are used.

Because of the sketchy nature of the existing data, and the fact that they come from several labs all using somewhat different techniques, these conclusions are still tentative. Among other things, we need to discover what perceptual cues infants are using to identify our little objects as animals or vehicles. Even if it is conceptual class membership that is controlling examination time in the object-examination task, there must be a perceptual basis for determining that a given item is a member of a class. It might be textural cues (e.g. natural v. machine-made texture) or subtle differences in the outlines of natural and artifactual objects, or indeed, any of a number of bases. Whatever the features are that are being used by 7-month-olds to recognise that something is an animal or a vehicle, if the features are highlighted, they may be sufficient to allow global perceptual categorisation even by infants as young as 3 months.

It should also be noted that most of the existing data come from the domain of animals. There are few data on responses to basic-level categories in other domains in preverbal infants. In one of the few such tests, we did find basic-level categorisation of vehicles in our object-examination task (although not when using the sequential-touching task; Mandler et al., 1991).[6] Our previous data had indicated similarity in the development of conceptual categorisation in the domains of animals, vehicles, plants, furniture, and kitchen utensils; in all these cases it appeared to consist of differentiation from broader to finer classes. However, the data base is simply too small at present to be confident that concept formation (or for that matter, perceptual categorisation) follows the same developmental course for all types of objects.

In spite of these caveats, the data we have to date on animals suggests that object-manipulation tasks may be measuring something different from the standard habituation–dishabituation or preferential-looking tests so commonly used in infant research. It may be that the habituation–dishabituation tests are lower level than we have tended to think, reflecting automatic attention shifts to differences in perceptual categories, not necessarily conceptualisation of what it is that is being looked at. Another indication of difference between the tasks is that in looking-time experiments subject loss is often high. The task is not motivating by itself. If you let infants suck on a bottle to make them willing to participate, then what part of the attentional system is directed toward the looking-time task itself? Subject loss in object-handling experiments is nil. Infants appear to be devoting their entire attention to the objects. Eventually, of course, the data from the two kinds of test must converge, since at some point in develop-

[6] As discussed earlier, the sequential-touching task seems less likely than the object-examination task to rely on perceptual categorisation.

ment pictures of superordinate category exemplars will activate the conceptual notion of animals.

There is another difference between the perceptual and conceptual categories formed in the first year that is important to understanding their functions, and needs to be mentioned at least briefly. We are currently investigating how one-year-olds make inductive generalisations about the conceptual categories they have developed (Mandler & McDonough, 1996). We find that when 14-month-olds learn a property about a given animal or vehicle, such as that a dog eats or a car is opened with a key, they generalise these properties across the entire domain of animals or vehicles, without regard to the perceptual similarity of the exemplars. They rarely cross these domain boundaries in their generalisations. Thus, the infants do not confine their inductive inferences to the basic-level classes they have observed, but instead use larger, conceptually demarcated categories to constrain their inferences. There are many interesting ramifications of this finding, but I mention it here primarily to indicate that the global concepts of one-year-olds are not just some form of preconcept (e.g. Piaget, 1951), but are genuine conceptual categories that serve the same inferential functions as they do for older children and adults. Indeed, one might use the fact of inductive generalisation as one of the criteria for accepting that the global categories we have uncovered are conceptual in nature.

HOW PERCEPTUAL AND CONCEPTUAL CATEGORIES CONVERGE

We have seen that there are a number of differences between perceptual and conceptual categorisation in infancy. It appears that perceptual categories may conform to at least some of the principles described for basic-level categories (Rosch et al., 1976). These perceptual categories are formed very early, at a time when meaning lags behind, in the sense that nothing differentiates one category from another but physical appearance. At this point in development, conceptual categorisation is either nonexistent or still very crude.

However, when concepts or conceptual categories are considered, a different picture emerges. Here we see that far from being basic-level, the earliest categories are broad and global in nature. The data from the object-handling tasks give us a clue as to the primitive nature of this early meaning system. Infants, who can clearly see the differences between objects representing dogs, fish, and rabbits, do not behave toward them in a differential fashion. At the same time, they do treat birds and aeroplanes differentially, in spite of their great similarity in perceptual appearance. As discussed earlier, one of the earliest meanings on which the concept of animal is based may be something like "moves by itself". Dogs, fish, and rabbits all equally fit the notion of animals as things that move by themselves. If the initial concept of animal is such a simple one, there may be no basis other than physical appearance to distinguish one of these subcategories from the other.

This simple concept of animal, however, can account for the patterns of property generalisation we have observed (Mandler & McDonough, 1996). It can also account for why infants do not differentiate dogs, rabbits, and fish in our experiments, even though they look quite different, but do differentiate birds and aeroplanes, even though they look quite similar. Although both bird and aeroplane wings are characterised by abrupt changes in contour at the point where the wing is attached to the body, there are small perceptual differences in the two cases. If infants have conceptualised one class of objects as self-starters and another class of objects as non-self-starters, these meanings could direct their attention to the differences in the relevant parts. So they might notice small differences in bird wings and aeroplane wings. On the other hand, even though dog legs, fish fins, and bird wings all look quite different, if they carry the same meaning of self-motion for the infant, there is no particular reason to pay attention to these "unimportant" perceptual differences. According to data we are currently collecting, the first differentiation among self-movers that occurs is between birds and other animals. That could be due to the salience of the perceptual differences, but it could also be due to the meaning system having directed the infants' attention to this motion-relevant feature. If so, this is an indication that conceptual processes are beginning to influence perceptual ones.

When do these two kinds of categorisation converge? Surprisingly, the convergence is still far from complete at 18 months (Mandler et al., 1991). However, some convergence begins during the first year. Recall that Quinn et al. (1993) found that 3-month-olds can perceptually categorise dogs and cats. These two categories of mammals must be among the most frequently experienced by infants in our culture during the first year. To see if this familiarity might improve performance on discrimination among mammals on the object-examination task, McDonough and I have been studying the course of development of these two conceptual categories. Consonant with our other object-handling data, we find that 7-month-olds do not distinguish between them. By 9 months, however, there begins to be some differentiation between these two categories, and by 11 months infants are distinguishing them quite well. If one ignores the differences in looking and handling tasks, these data sets describe a U-shaped function: categorisation at 3 months, lack of categorisation at 7 months, and categorisation again at 11 months. If, however, one considers the two kinds of tasks to represent different forms of categorisation, then, first, purely perceptual categorisation is taking place, followed by conceptual categorisation, and finally by an amalgam that takes into account both perceptual appearance and meaning. The seeming U-shaped development of a single process disappears and in its place a straightforward development of two different processes occurs.

Around a year to 18 months, language presumably begins to become important in this amalgamation. A good deal of what parents teach young children by the way they name things is to carve up domains such as animals into smaller conceptual packages. As we have seen, children have the preverbal meaning of animal, and they can also see the perceptual difference between dogs and cats. Now their parents take out the picture books and also tell them that this-shaped animal (dog) has a different label from that-shaped animal (cat), and perhaps also that a dog barks and a cat meows. All this must suggest to children that the difference between cats and dogs may matter. Now the concept of animal can begin to be subdivided into something approximating basic-level concepts. Dogs are *animals* that are called "dogs" and that bark. It is interesting in this regard that in the initial stages of noun learning, children do not particularly rely on shape. But as basic-level labels begin to be learned, they increasingly rely on shape to determine the reference of new nouns (Jones & Smith, 1993). Such a finding suggests that they are making the connection between nouns and the perceptual-shape categories they have learned over the course of the first two years.

By the time children are around two years of age, their concepts may begin to take on the functions and characteristics described by researchers who have studied basic-level concepts. But we see that a long and complex history has preceded this development. If we are considering concepts, then basic-level concepts are not primary, but rather are a considerable developmental achievement. This achievement involves the differentiation of very broad categories that are closer to superordinate categories than to basic-level ones. This differentiation seems to involve both individual perceptual analysis and cultural and linguistic influences. On the other hand, if we are considering perceptual categories, the basic level is early and may be the first to be acquired. It must be stressed, however, that this has not yet been determined. There is no experimental evidence as to exactly where the first perceptual categorical cuts take place. They make take place at the subordinate level as easily as at the basic level. Answering this question will be an important endeavour in the coming decade.

ACKNOWLEDGEMENTS

Preparation of this chapter was supported in part by NSF research grant DBS-9221867. Thanks to Dan Gruen for taking the photographs for Figs 7.1 and 7.4.

REFERENCES

Anglin, J.M. (1977). *Word, object, and conceptual development*. New York: Norton.

Bauer, P.J. & Mandler, J.M. (1989). Taxonomies and triads: Conceptual organization in one- to two-year olds. *Cognitive Psychology, 21*, 156–184.

Berlin, B., Breedlove, D.E., & Raven, P.H. (1973). General principles of classification and nomenclature in folk biology. *American Anthropologist, 75*, 214–242.

Bertenthal, B. (1992). Infants' perception of biomechanical motions: Intrinsic image and knowledge-based constraints. In C. Granrud (ed.), *Visual perception and cognition in infancy*. Hillsdale, N.J.: Lawrence Erlbaum Associates Inc.

Bowerman, M. (1980). The structure and origin of semantic categories in the language-learning child. In M.L. Foster & S. Brandes (eds), *Symbol as sense*. New York: Academic Press.

Brown, R. (1958). How shall a thing be called? *Psychological Review, 65*, 14–21.

Bruner, J.S. (1957). On perceptual readiness. *Psychological Review, 64*, 331–350.

Cromer, R.F. (1991). *Language and thought in normal and handicapped children*. Oxford: Blackwell.

Daehler, M.W., Lonardo, R., & Bukatko, D. (1979). Matching and equivalence judgments in very young children. *Child Development, 50*, 170–179.

Eimas, P.D. (1994). Categorization in early infancy and the continuity of development. *Cognition, 50*, 83–93.

Eimas, P.D. & Quinn, P.C. (1994). Studies on the formation of perceptually based basic-level categories in young infants. *Child Development, 65*, 903–917.

Fagan, J.F., III & Singer, L.T. (1979). The role of simple feature differences in infant recognition of faces. *Infant Behavior and Development, 2*, 39–46.

Fox, N., Kagan, J. & Weiskopf, S. (1979). The growth of memory during infancy. *Genetic Psychology Monographs, 99*, 91–130.

Gibson, E.J. (1969). *Principles of perceptual learning and development*. New York: Appleton-Century-Crofts.

Golinkoff, R.M. & Halperin, M.S. (1983). The concept of animal: One infant's view. *Infant Behavior and Development, 6*, 229–233.

Inhelder, B. & Piaget, J. (1964). *The early growth of logic in the child*. London: Routledge & Kegan Paul.

Jones, S.S. & Smith, L.B. (1993). The place of perception in children's concepts. *Cognitive Development, 8*, 113–139.

Karmiloff-Smith, A. (1986). From meta-processes to conscious access: Evidence from children's metalinguistic and repair data. *Cognition, 23*, 95–147.

Lakoff, G. (1987). *Women, fire, and dangerous things*. Chicago, Ill.: University of Chicago Press.

Mandler, J.M. (1988). How to build a baby: On the development of an accessible representational system. *Cognitive Development, 3*, 113–136.

Mandler, J.M. (1992). How to build a baby II: Conceptual primitives. *Psychological Review, 99*, 587–604.

Mandler, J.M. & Bauer, P.J. (1988). The cradle of categorization: Is the basic level basic? *Cognitive Development, 3*, 247–264.

Mandler, J.M., Bauer, P.J., & McDonough, L. (1991). Separating the sheep from the goats: Differentiating global categories. *Cognitive Psychology, 23*, 263–298.

Mandler, J.M., Fivush, R., & Reznick, J.S. (1987). The development of contextual categories. *Cognitive Development, 2*, 339–354.

Mandler, J.M. & McDonough, L. (1993). Concept formation in infancy. *Cognitive Development, 8*, 291–318.

Mandler, J.M. & McDonough, L. (1996). Drinking and driving don't mix: Inductive generalization in infancy. *Cognition, 59*, 307–335.

Maratsos, M. (1983). Some current issues in the study of the acquisition of grammar. In J.H. Flavell & E.M. Markman (eds), *Cognitive development*: Vol. 3 of P. H. Mussen (Series ed.), *Handbook of child psychology*. New York: Wiley.

McClelland, J.L. & Rumelhart, D.E. (1985). Distributed memory and the representation of general and specific information. *Journal of Experimental Psychology: General, 114*, 159–188.

Medin, D.L. (1983). Cue validity. Structural principles of categorization. In T. Tighe & B. Shepp (eds), *Perception, Cognition, and Development: International Analyses*. Hillsdale, N.J.: Lawrence Erlbaum Associates Inc.

Medin, D.L. & Barsalou, L.W. (1987). Categorization processes and categorical perception. In S. Harnad (ed.), *Categorical perception*. New York: Cambridge University Press.

Medin, D.L. & Schaffer, M.M. (1978). Context theory of classification learning. *Psychological Review, 85*, 207–238.

Mervis, C.B. & Crisafi, M.A. (1982). Order of acquisition of subordinate-, basic-, and superordinate-level categories. *Child Development, 53*, 258–266.

Mervis, C.B. & Mervis, C.A. (1982). Leopards are kitty-cats: Object labeling by mothers for their thirteen-month-olds. *Child Development, 53*, 267–273.

Mervis, C.B. & Rosch, E. (1981). Categorization of natural objects. *Annual Review of Psychology, 32*, 89–115.

Murphy, G.L. (1982). Cue validity and levels of categorization. *Psychological Bulletin, 91*, 174–177.

Nelson, K. (1985). *Making sense: the acquisition of shared meaning*. Orlando, Fla.: Academic Press.

Nosofsky, R.M., Kruschke, J.K., & McKinley, S.C. (1992). Combining exemplar-based category representations and connectionist learning rules. *Journal of Experimental Psychology: Learning, Memory, and Cognition, 18*, 211–233.

Oakes, L.M., Madole, K.L., & Cohen, L.B. (1991). Infants' object examining: Habituation and categorization. *Cognitive Development, 6*, 377–392.

Palmer, C.F., Jones, R.K., Hennessy, B.L., Unze, M.G., & Pick. A.D. (1989). How is a trumpet known? The "basic object level" concept and perception of musical instruments. *American Journal of Psychology, 102*, 17–37.

Piaget, J. (1951). *Play, dreams, and imitation in childhood*. London: Heinemann.

Piaget, J. (1952). *The origins of intelligence in children*. London: Routledge & Kegan Paul.

Posner, M.I. & Keele, S.W. (1968). On the genesis of abstract ideas. *Journal of Experimental Psychology, 77*. 353–362.

Quinn, P.C., Eimas, P.D., & Rosenkrantz, S.L. (1993). Evidence for representations of perceptual similar natural categories by 3-month-old and 4-month-old infants. *Perception, 22*, 463–475.

Quinn, P.C. & Eimas, P.D. (1986). On categorization in early infancy. *Merrill-Palmer Quarterly, 32*, 331–363.

Reed, S.K. & Friedman, M.P. (1973). Perceptual vs conceptual categorization. *Memory and Cognition, 1*, 157–163.

Roberts, K. (1988). Retrieval of a basic-level category in prelinguistic infants. *Developmental Psychology, 24*, 21–27.

Roberts, K. & Cuff, M.D. (1989). Categorization studies of 9- to 15-month-old infants: Evidence for superordinate categorization? *Infant Behavior and Development, 12*, 265–288.

Rosch, E. (1978). Principles of categorization. In E. Rosch & B. Lloyd (eds), *Cognition and categorization*. Hillsdale, N.J.: Lawrence Erlbaum Associates Inc.

Rosch, E. & Mervis, C.B. (1975). Family resemblances: Studies in the internal structure of categories. *Cognitive Psychology, 7*, 573–605.

Rosch, E., Mervis, C.B., Gray, W., Johnson, D., & Boyes-Bream, P. (1976). Basic objects in natural categories. *Cognitive Psychology*, *3*, 382–439.

Ross, G.S. (1980). Categorization in 1- to 2-year-olds. *Developmental Psychology*, *16*, 391–396.

Ruff, H. (1986). Components of attention during infants' manipulative exploration. *Child Development*, *57*, 105–114.

Saxby, L. & Anglin, J.M. (1983). Children's sorting of objects from categories of differing levels of generality. *Journal of Genetic Psychology*, *143*, 382–439.

Smith, E.E. & Osherson, D.N. (1988). Conceptual combination with prototype concepts. In A. Collins & E.E. Smith (eds), *Readings in Cognitive Science*. San Mateo, Calif.: Morgan Kaufmann.

Werner, H. & Kaplan, B. (1963). *Symbol formation*. New York: Wiley.

8 Stability of Mental Development from Infancy to Later Childhood: Three "Waves" of Research

Marc H. Bornstein
Child and Family Research, National Institute of Child Health and Human Development, Bethesda, USA.
Alan Slater, Elizabeth Brown, Elizabeth Roberts, and Jacqueline Barrett
Department of Psychology, Washington Singer Laboratories, University of Exeter, UK.

INTRODUCTION

> *Some things are sacred.*
> *For developmental psychology, predicting later behavior from early behavior is sacred... And so the search for early predictors of later IQ continues.*
> —McCall (1981, p. 141)

This telling observation about developmental study reflects two noteworthy points. The first is that developmental psychology is as much interested in stability as it is in change in human ontogenesis: whilst most of the chapters in this book are about changes in development, this one is about stability. Stability describes consistency in the relative rank ordering of individuals with respect to the expression of some ability over time. For example, a stable infant ability would be one that some infants draw upon to perform relatively well when they are very young, and again to perform well when they are older; conversely, infants who perform poorly when very young will also perform poorly when older. The second point deriving from McCall's observation is that, in the last half of the 20th century, developmental psychologists have been searching for examples of abilities, systems, or domains that show stability (in the sense described above) as well as ones that show change, and intelligence has become a prime object of that search.

In what we could call the "first wave" of prediction research, it was demonstrated on innumerable occasions that infant performance on most standardised scales of development—the best known being the Griffiths, Bayley, Cattell, and Gesell—did not correlate with children's later performance on more traditional psychometric assessments of intelligence. With the exception of extreme cases such as severe subnormality, "the findings of these early studies of mental growth of infants have been repeated sufficiently often so that it is now well established that test scores earned in the first year or two have relatively little predictive validity, in contrast to tests at school age or later" (Bayley, 1970, p. 1174). This conclusion was echoed by many others; for example, "Prediction of later intellectual functioning from infant intelligence tests really becomes possible at 24 months of age" (Lewis & Brooks-Gunn, 1981, p. 136).

The failure of infant test scores to predict later intelligence led to theoretical views that emphasised instability or discontinuity in mental development from infancy to childhood, with the accompanying implication that infant intelligence (if it existed) may be different in kind from intelligence in the post-infancy childhood years (McCall, 1979).

The Latin word *infans*, from which the word "infant" derives, means "unable to speak"; traditionally, the beginnings of language signal the end of infancy. Children produce their first meaningful words in the second year of life, and it is not until around 18 to 24 months that language acquisition enters a period of rapid development: speech becomes more symbolic (rather than being closely linked to sensorimotor actions); language becomes the major form of communication, the "vocabulary explosion" commences; and multiword utterances are more common. On this basis it has been plausible to argue that the cognitive abilities of childhood, such as language, numeracy, thinking, problem solving, and reasoning—those capacities that will be so critical at school and later—simply have not made their appearance in infancy, and so there is no basis in infant performance for their prediction. As Clarke (1978, p. 256) put it:

> The rather poor long-term predictions of individual development which ... characterize our science do not primarily rest upon inadequacies in the methods of measurement... They lie in development itself. No science can predict accurately qualities which have not yet made any appearance in the development of the pre-school child, whether these be genetically programmed or dependent upon future transactions between constitution and environment.

From about the end of the 1970s, however, researchers began to question the nature and validity of the infant tests on which both the predictive data and such deductions about intelligence at large were made. It began to be argued that the "mental scales" on infant assessments primarily measure perceptual and motor development, which is different in kind from the information processing, cognitive, and intellectual abilities it was hoped to predict in childhood. For example, in the revised second edition of the

Bayley Scales of Infant Development (BSID; Bayley 1993) many items on the Mental Scales appear to measure perceptual-motor development: At 4 months, items include:

#36 "eyes follow rod",
#44 "uses eye-hand coordination in reaching",
#45 "picks up cube".

And at 12 months, items include:

#73 "turns pages of book",
#79 "fingers holes in pegboard",
#97 "builds tower of three cubes".

By 2 years of age, such seemingly perceptual-motor items are fewer in number, and they have been replaced with a preponderance of items that would generally be considered more "cognitive": many are to do with verbal comprehension, recall of geometric forms, and comparison of masses. At this point in development, predictive validity of the BSID increases (Bayley, 1949).

There is little reason to expect measures of perceptual-motor abilities in infancy to predict later IQ. Accordingly, the search began in a "second wave" of prediction investigation for information-processing or other cognitive measures of infant performance that might more reasonably tap abilities which are similar to, and could therefore predict, abilities measured by childhood intelligence tests. The last 15 years or so has witnessed a burgeoning of such research activity: it is now becoming clear that there may be several possible predictors; and it appears that a moderate degree of predictability in intellectual development from infancy to adolescence exists. In the light of recent findings, our understanding of intelligence in infancy and of the course of cognitive growth in human beings is changing.

In this chapter, we first review samples of this stability research, under the headings *Visual information processing* and *Understanding causal relations*. Some of these measures are now themselves aging, some are newer. Next, we discuss briefly some possible antecedents of these abilities in infancy and then some possible mechanisms underlying stability. Finally, we consider some compelling questions left still unanswered in this developmental work and implications of these findings for theories and models of intellectual development.

VISUAL INFORMATION PROCESSING

In earlier reviews of this area, Bornstein (Bornstein 1985a; 1989; Bornstein & Sigman, 1986) made the point that attention and information processing have traditionally been conceived of as being central to mature cognitive functioning. Thus, the focus of much of the second wave of prediction research fell on infants' attention to and processing of visual stimuli, usually when tested in an habituation paradigm. Habituation is an aspect of learning in which repeated applications of a stimulus result in decreased responsiveness that cannot be accounted for in terms of simple change in state, or response fatigue, or sensory adaptation (Bertenthal, Haith, & Campos, 1983; Bornstein, 1985a), but more probably index growing cognitive familiarity with the stimulus. In a typical habituation test, an infant is placed in an otherwise homogeneous environment and shown a visual stimulus (Fig. 8.1). This stimulus will initially attract the infant's attention, but as time passes the baby's attention will usually wane. Habituation, therefore, refers to the decrement of visual response to the repeated stimulus; and dependent measures taken from visual attention, as it declines and reaches a criterion of habituation, reflect infants' processing of information. Visual attention is likely to recover if the infant, having habituated to the now "familiar" stimulus, is shown a new or novel stimulus; the recovery of attention is called "novelty preference" or dishabituation.

Visual recognition memory (VRM) is a related process and refers to the degree of preference the infant shows for novelty (compared with familiarity) after the infant has looked at the "familiar" stimulus for a fixed period of time ("study time"). In this design, the study time is usually so brief that no decrement of attention will have occurred.

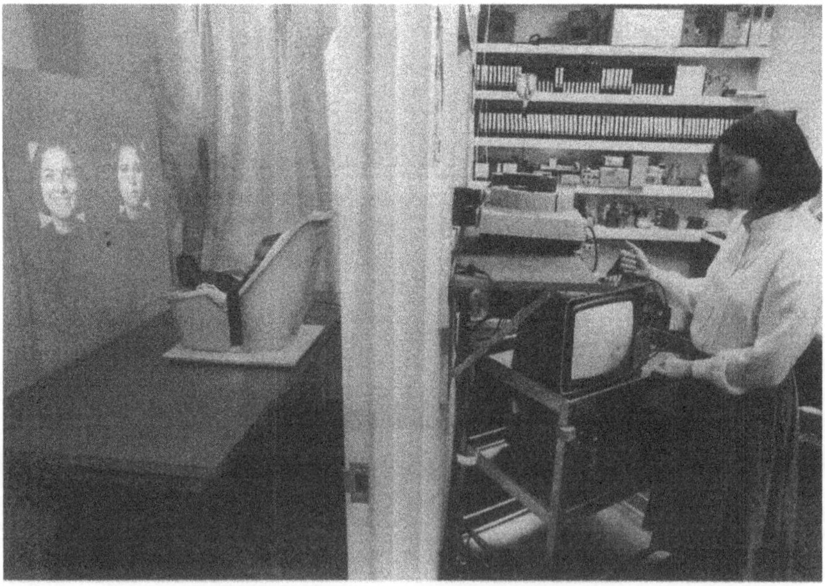

FIG. 8.1 Laboratory arrangement to study visual perception in infants: the experimental room is on the left, and the control room is on the right.

McCall (1994, Table 8.1) provides a task analysis of the habituation and recognition memory paradigms. Presumably, these kinds of information processing on the part of the infant include encoding, storing, retrieving, and comparing new and familiar stimulation. The decrement of visual attention and the recovery of attention to novel stimulation tell us that infants can discriminate between familiar and novel stimuli. Habituation/dishabituation/VRM have been used on innumerable occasions to study different aspects of perceptual and cognitive development. With this usage in mind, some 25 years ago Kessen, Haith, and Salapatek (1970, p. 346) wrote: "Few behavioral phenomena rival habituation in usefulness as a measure of the infant's sensitivity and few have as many implications for theories of psychological development." Their remarks are applicable to prediction studies; as mentioned earlier, infant performance in this procedure tells us that during habituation infants presumably acquire information about and form a memory of the now-familiar stimulus. For several reasons measures of habituation have been seen as potential predictors of later intellectual functioning:

1. Habituation to visual stimuli is thought to involve information processing, attention, and memory, all of which are implicated in intelligence (e.g. Bornstein, 1985a; McCall, 1994).
2. Habituation is characterised by inter-age differences with older infants taking less time to reach the same criterion of habituation than younger ones (e.g. Bornstein Pêcheux, & Lécuyer, 1988; Slater & Morison, 1985).
3. Infants habituated to one stimulus later distinguish a novel stimulus in comparison with their internal representation of the familiar stimulus (e.g. Bornstein, 1985a; Slater, Morison, & Rose, 1983).
4. Infants who habituate in shorter times ("short lookers") process stimuli more rapidly than infants who take longer to habituate ("long lookers"),(e.g. Colombo, 1993; Colombo, Mitchell, Coldren, & Freeseman, 1991).
5. Simpler stimuli provoke more rapid habituation than do more complex stimuli in infants of a given age (e.g. Bornstein, 1981; Caron & Caron, 1969).
6. Infants "at risk" for cognitive delay or handicap habituate less efficiently than "normal" age-matched controls (e.g. Cohen, 1981; Friedman, 1975; Lester, 1975).

In short, habituation and VRM have been widely interpreted in terms of speed and rate or accuracy, efficiency, and completeness of information processing (Bornstein & Sigman, 1986; Fagan & McGrath, 1981; McCall & Carriger, 1993; O'Connor, Cohen, & Parmelee, 1984; Rose, Slater, & Perry, 1986; Sigman et al., 1991).

Psychometric Considerations

There are many different habituation procedures, and many different dependent measures that can be drawn from them. An important enterprise is to establish the psychometric adequacy of these measures, particularly by examining their test–retest reliabilities. Normally, those measures that give reasonable test–retest reliabilities may stand as better predictors, because if a measure does not correlate with itself it is unlikely to correlate well with other concurrent or future measures (Bornstein & Benasich, 1986; Colombo et al., 1987a; 1987b; Slater, 1995).

Several groups of researchers have assessed the short- and long-term reliability of various measures of habituation in infants in the first year of life (e.g., Bornstein & Benasich, 1986; Bornstein et al., 1988; Colombo et al., 1987a; 1987b; Pêcheux & Lécuyer, 1983; 1989; Rose et al., 1986). The findings from these studies are both encouraging and discouraging (Bornstein, 1988, provides a summary). What is encouraging is that quantitative measurements at points close in time (day-to-day and week-to-week assessments) tend to yield psychometrically adequate test–retest reliability estimates (*r*s in the range of 0.40 to 0.60), but what is discouraging is that measurements at points more distant in time (month-to-month assessments) tend to yield lower stability estimates (*r*s around 0.20, and often close to zero if the measurements are separated by months or more). Thus, habituation shows some degree of short-term reliability in infancy, but the size of the correlation is considerably influenced by the duration of the test–retest interval. Reliability will be affected by many factors, including the procedure used, the infants' ages, and the stimuli shown. Although the infant measures have consistently low short-term reliability, McCall and Carriger (1993) showed that it is statistically possible for a low-reliability measure (such as the infant assessment) to predict an outcome measure (such as IQ) so long as the reliability of the outcome measure is high (discussed later in *Some interim conclusions*).

Predictive Validity of Visual Information Processing

Typical predictive studies of information-processing measures in infancy were described by Bornstein (1985b; Tamis-LeMonda & Bornstein, 1989); by Slater (Rose et al., 1986; Slater et al., 1989; Slater, 1995); and by Sigman (Sigman et al., 1991). In a long-term observation extending from 4 months to 4 years, we saw mother–child dyads at three points (Bornstein, 1985b): at 4 months, infant habituation in the laboratory was assessed; at 1 year, toddler productive vocabulary size was assessed; and at 4 years, children's intelligence was assessed using the Wechsler series. At 4 months and at 1 year, mothers' didactics were also evaluated on the basis of home obser-

FIG. 8.2. A 4½-year-old being given an intelligence test.

vations; didactics included mothers' pointing, labelling, showing, demonstrating, and the like. Path analysis determined direct and unique longitudinal effects of independent variables on dependent variables. Maternal didactic efforts in infancy contributed to both the 1-year and 4-year child cognitive outcomes. However, infant habituation showed strong predictive links both to toddler productive vocabulary size at 1 year and childhood intelligence test performance at 4 years, independent of maternal early and late didactic contributions.

Infants between 6 weeks and 6 months of age were tested and habituated on three separate occasions by Slater and his colleagues, each testing session separated by a minimum of 24 hours (Rose et al., 1986; Slater et al., 1989). At an average age of 4½ years, subjects were retested (see Fig. 8.2) using the *British Ability Scales* (BAS) and the *Wechsler Preschool and Primary Scales of Intelligence* (WPPSI). A number of statistically significant correlations between performances at the two ages were obtained. They were specific to (1) measures derived from the habituation or familiarisation phase of the infant testing, rather than from subsequent dishabituation or novelty test phase, and (2) verbal, rather than performance, components of the intelligence test scores. Pertinent psychometric findings from this study were that the predictive infant measures were only those that minimally satisfied two criteria: (1) there were consistent changes with age, and (2) there was significant test–retest reliability of the measures. In order to investigate the long-term predictive validity of the infancy measures, a subsample of the infants was retested at an average age of 8 years. The results from this testing, expressed as a correlation matrix showing the relations between the infant measures and children's intelligence test scores at 8 years, are given in Table 1. The negative correlations in the table indicate that the infants with the quicker habituation times (the "short lookers") have higher IQs when they become older children.

In the longest-term study to date, Sigman et al. (1991) collected habituation data from preterm infants and tested the same children on various information-processing measures at 12 years of age. Sigman et al. presented the preterms with a 2 × 2 black-and-white checkerboard at 40 weeks postconception, measuring visual attention (including first fixation, fixation of the first stimulus presentation, and total fixation across all presentations). At 12 years, these investigators measured information processing, sustained attention, use of novelty, as well as IQ. The strongest predictions obtained between habituation and IQ, $r = -0.38$.

Several studies have correlated infant visual recognition memory scores with later measures of cognitive functioning (e.g. DiLalla et al., 1990; Fagan & McGrath, 1981; Rose et al., 1988; 1991; 1992). For infants tested in the age range of 4 to 7 months, the average correlation with child cognitive

TABLE 8.1
Correlations Between Infant Habituation Measures and the Scores of 8½-year-old Children

Infant Measures	*Child Scores*			
	WISC-R full	*WISC-R verbal*	*WISC-R performance*	*British Ability Scales*
TFT	-0.576^{a}	-0.746^{d}	-0.282	-0.347
DFL	-0.694^{c}	-0.680^{b}	-0.604^{b}	-0.717^{d}
ALD	-0.613^{b}	-0.640^{b}	-0.499	-0.679^{b}
	$p<0.05^{a}$			
	$p<0.025^{b}$			
	$p<0.01^{c}$			
	$p<0.005^{d}$			

NOTES:
TFT = total fixation time accumulated to reach a criterion of habituation; DFL = duration of the first look at a visual stimulus; ALD = average duration of all looks at the habituated stimulus.

The stimuli shown to the 6 week- to 6-month-old infants were complex coloured slides.

ability (IQ, vocabulary and language, reading, and form discrimination) is 0.42. Thus, a substantial body of research now documents that infants who show efficient habituation or VRM in the first 6 months of life, later, between 2 and 12 years of age, perform better on traditional assessments of cognitive competence, including standardised psychometric tests of intelligence as well as measures of representational ability (e.g. language and play).

Bornstein and Sigman (1986) found the median predictive correlation to be 0.47; and they confirmed that the predictive validity of habituation is not associated with one laboratory, one particular infant response measure, or a sampling characteristic of the infants tested. More recently, McCall and Carriger (1993) analysed the research evaluated by Bornstein and Sigman, together with research published later, in a meta-analysis of 31 samples from 23 studies that assessed habituation (among other related measures) in infancy, and IQ, vocabulary, or memory tests between 1 and 8 years of age. They found a raw median correlation between the infant and the later child measures of 0.45. By contrast, McCall (1983) reported correlations of 0.12 and 0.26 between the standardised infant tests (such as the Bayley Scales) administered between 0 and 6 months of age and 7 to 12 months of age, respectively, with childhood intelligence tests spanning the age range 8 to 18 years. Thus, the amount of variance accounted for by the new information-processing procedures represents as much as a 20-fold increase over that for earlier infant tests. The "second wave" of infancy research unearthed stability where the "first wave" had not.

UNDERSTANDING CAUSAL RELATIONS

Today a "third wave" of predictive studies is cresting, using infancy measures other than those derived from tests of visual information processing *per se*. Ones we discuss here derive from two approaches to infants' understanding of causal relations. Causal relations are to be found in many behavioural contexts: they can vary from short- to long-term, and they can have concrete or abstract goals. An example of a long-term causal relation with an abstract goal would be when we work for a period of time in order to get paid at the end of that time; a short-term relation with a concrete goal would be to open a match box in order to take out a match. Infants' understanding of causality has usually been investigated with respect to concrete relations, and the two experimental tasks discussed here are called "means–ends problem solving" and "enabling relations" (see also Chapter 5 by Peter Willatts). Successful solution in both these tasks requires the ability to co-ordinate actions into a temporal sequence and understanding of cause–effect associations. As we describe below, infant performance on these two tasks is showing modest predictive validity.

Means–Ends Problem Solving

The development of means–ends problem solving, where one or more behaviours serve as the means in order to attain a desired end goal, was first described by Piaget (1953). According to Piaget, planful means–ends behaviour first appears in Stage IV of sensori-motor development ("The coordination of secondary schemes and their application to new situations"), beginning approximately at 8 months.

Willatts (1992) used a two-step means–ends task in which the infant is shown an attractive toy which is placed out of reach on a cloth, and the toy is then covered. In order to retrieve the toy, the infant has to pull the cloth towards himself or herself to bring the cover within reach, lift the cover (these are the two steps, the means), and pick up the toy (the end). Babies only 6 months or so cannot do this. They possess the requisite motor skills but cannot solve the problem (Willatts, 1989). This was demonstrated by Baillargeon (1993) who reported that, with a one-step task (visible toy out of reach on a cloth), if infants thought the toy and the cloth were one object (i.e. joined together in some way), they would pull the cloth and obtain the toy, but if they had previously seen the cloth and toy separately they would not, although they showed interest in the toy. It seems that 6-month-olds simply cannot combine separate behaviours to solve a means–ends problem. An 8-month-old at work on this task is shown in Fig. 8.3.

Performance on the two-step task gradually appears from about 7 months; and in order to demonstrate this Willatts tested the same infants at five ages, including 6, 7, 8, 9, and 10 months. Babies who solve the problem usually do so quickly, with few if any irrelevant behaviours and with clear intention. Thus, it is possible to obtain an "intention score" as a measure of an infant's success. It is this infant score that Willatts used in predictions of children's 3-year performance on the *British Picture Vocabulary Scale* (BPVS, the British version of the American *Peabody*, PPVT) and their IQ as measured by the *British Ability Scales* (BAS). Across-age correlations for the number of intentional behaviours were, in general, low and non-significant (range of $rs = -0.02$ to 0.37) with the exception of 8 to 9 months ($r = 0.71$). The correlations between the infants' means–ends intentional behaviours at 6, 7, and 10 months, and 3-year assessments were also low. However, infants' intention scores at 8 and 9 months significantly predicted their 3-year vocabulary and IQ measures (range of $rs = 0.42$ to 0.64).

Enabling Relations

Enabling relations exist when, for a given outcome or goal, one behaviour in a sequence must be performed before another. For example, in order to make a telephone call the receiver or handset is lifted, the number dialled,

FIG 8.3. An 8-month-old is presented with an out-of-reach toy on a cloth (top), and pulls the cloth in a single uninterrupted movement (bottom) to retrieve the toy (photograph by Peter Willatts).

and then one speaks to the person who answers the phone: in any other order these behaviours would not achieve the desired outcome. Enabling relations can be distinguished from *arbitrary relations*: an example of the latter would be when we need to put on an overcoat, a hat, and boots in order to go out in cold weather, but the order in which these items are donned is not critical.

Infants' understanding of enabling relations has been investigated by Bauer (1992) and by Mandler and McDonough (1995) (see also McDonough & Mandler, 1994). Some of the simple enabling relations tasks they have used include the following: *make a rattle:* the infant is shown a button, and a transparent box with a slot in the top, and after seeing the actions modelled by the experimenter the infant has to put the button in the box and then shake the "rattle"; *make a rocking horse:* the infant is shown a toy horse and a stand that is curved on one side (the rocker), and after seeing the actions modelled has to place the horse on top of the stand (the horse is held in place by magnets) and then press the stand to make it rock. Some of the simple arbitrary relations they have used are the following: *put a ring on a bear's arm and brush its head*; *lace a hat on the bunny and feed it a carrot*. These titles give a clear indication of the tasks; and the experimenter models the actions with toy bears/rabbits, and encourages the infant to imitate the actions.

Using these and other tasks, a consistent set of developmental findings has emerged. Notably, (1) infants are good at imitating both sorts of tasks, but are much less likely to carry out the actions for arbitrary tasks in the order in which they were modelled; and (2) The two types of task are differentially affected by forgetting: 11-month-olds remember both tasks after a 24-hour delay, but when they are tested after a 3-month delay (when 14 months old) they have forgotten the arbitrary sequences, but still give clear evidence of remembering the enabling relations. Remarkably, when the same infants were tested after a one-year delay (when they were 23 months old), they also gave evidence of remembering the enabling relations tasks.

It is reasonable to suppose that enabling events are more meaningful than arbitrary ones, and the difference in memory for the two types of event is a clear indication that, from a very early age, more meaningful events are more memorable. The finding that the actions for the enabling events are remembered in the correct order, even after a year's delay, suggests that infants represent and remember some information in an organised and structured, rather than piecemeal, fashion and that some part of this organisation includes temporal information. It then seems reasonable to suppose that differences among infants in their ability to understand and to imitate enabling relations could constitute a measure of their cognitive maturity, and hence potentially predict later cognitive ability. This turns out to be the case, and in some of our recent findings measures of infants' performance on enabling relations tasks at 12, 15, and 18 months show both between- and across-age intercorrelations (*r*s in the range of 0.30 to 0.68). Significantly, these measures also predict language ability (production and comprehension) at 18 months, with *r*s in the range of 0.30 to 0.50.

In summary, measures of information processing in infancy have some value as predictors of later childhood cognitive abilities, and it is becoming increasingly clear that other measures of cognitive ability in infancy, such as an understanding of causal events and relations, also predict later mental ability. As research continues, we can expect the number and variety of predictors to increase. Other infancy tasks that might also predict childhood intelligence include cross-modal transfer (recognising an object in one modality that has been experienced in another) and performance on visual expectation tasks (the ability to predict the appearance of stimuli that appear in a regular order). In the next two sections, we discuss the possible origins of these abilities and speculate about some processes that might underlie them. In the final section, we draw some interim conclusions about the usefulness of measures of infant information processing and causal understanding as predictors of childhood cognitive functioning.

ORIGINS AND MECHANISMS

Origins

By about the middle of the first postnatal year, infants vary in their ability to process information; and individual differences in information processing in infancy are adequately reliable and moderately predictive of later childhood cognitive performance. These findings from middle infancy raise the question of what the earliest origins of infant cognitive skills might be.

In the view of some (e.g. McCall, 1977; see Hoff-Ginsberg & Tardif, 1995), distal and global variables like socioeconomic status (SES) may play a significant or even determinative role. For others (e.g. Bouchard et al., 1990; Plomin, 1986; 1989; Thompson, Fagan, & Fulker, 1991), genetic factors embodied in measures such as maternal IQ may express themselves in individual differences in children. Stability findings from early life often steer infancy researchers toward thinking in terms of endogenous processes. It would be premature to characterise stability of any infant measure as reflecting processes in the infant, however, without first considering the potential roles of experience.

Experience manifestly influences perception as well as its development (Bornstein, 1992). Clearly, many factors contribute to mental development in the child. In order to know how and why development is proceeding in the individual, it is necessary to understand potential contributions of experience as well as inborn characteristics. Stability could be mediated by early, contemporaneous, or cumulative (early *and* contemporaneous) experience: the child is never alone in development. To pin stability on the infant and to differentiate among competing experience models, one needs to measure infant performance as well as relevant early and late experiences.

Experiments show that some stability appears to lie in the child, above the contribution of the environment, and that contribution is not simply or solely dependent on exploratory activity or motivation in the child. To determine the antecedents of some cognitive skills in 5-month-olds, Bornstein and Tamis-LeMonda (1994) obtained several sets of data in the context of a short-term prospective longitudinal design. They studied a variety of naturalistically occurring maternal behaviours at home at 2 and at 5 months. In addition, at 2 months, infant visual discrimination ability was measured in the laboratory; and at 5 months, infant habituation and VRM were measured. Maternal IQ was evaluated separately. Laboratory and home sessions were conducted by different observers to minimise observer knowledge about infant and mother performance at other times. Infant habituation performance at 5 months shared unique variance with maternal responsiveness in the home at 5 months, and was uniquely predicted by infant visual discriminative capacity at 2 months. Infant VRM at 5 months was not accounted for by any prior infant or maternal variables. So, there is some unique stability in very early infant functioning, and infant information-processing performance is also sensitive to concurrent experience of maternal behavior. Other predictive infant tasks, such as understanding causal relations, need to be submitted to equivalent multimeasure longitudinal analysis.

Mechanisms

The work on origins suggests that some stability lies in the infant. What of the predictive research? Habituation and other measures in infancy, and cognitive performance in childhood, could be mutually supported by one or more consistent and effective features of the cognitive environment. Studies exist, however, that address and undermine major alternative environmental, interactional, or maternal factors that may carry the predictive relation. Experience certainly contributes to child cognitive growth; but some stability appears to exist in the child, independent of environmental contributions.

For example, maternal education is not systematically related to any common habituation variable in infants (Mayes & Bornstein, 1995). We have also investigated contributions of maternal behaviour and IQ. In one study, infant habituation at 5 months was measured in relation to two cognitive outcomes—language comprehension and play sophistication—in the same children at 13 months (Tamis-LeMonda & Bornstein, 1989). Mothers' didactic activities (measured during naturalistic observations in the home) were also assessed at the two ages. Structural equation modelling was then used to examine the unique contributions of maternal interaction and infant habituation to toddler cognitive abilities. Figure 8.4 shows that maternal behaviours are predictively consequential. However, habituation at 5 months predicted 13-month play sophistication, language comprehension, and representational competence (a latent variable constructed of the two indicator variables), and, as shown by the italicised correlation, habituation predicted these outcomes after the influences of both 5- and 13-month maternal didactics were partialled. In a follow-up study, we examined infant habituation at 5 months, infant vocal and exploratory activities and mothers' didactic stimulation of infants at 5 months, as well as mothers' IQ, all in relation to 13-month-olds' symbolic play and attention span (Tamis-LeMonda & Bornstein, 1993). Again, maternal IQ proved predictive, but infant habituation predicted toddler attention span and symbolic play as well as exploratory competence (a latent variable constructed of the two indicator variables). Again, habituation predicted these outcome measures independent of other infant activities, as well as maternal didactics and maternal IQ.

Family influences, both genetic and experiential, clearly affect child cognitive growth. Taken together, however, findings from these studies confirm some direct and unique stability between infant habituation and childhood cognitive performance, after controlling for environmental experiences, including maternal education and didactic stimulation, and other influences external to the infant, like maternal IQ. Habituation in infancy appears to predict cognitive status in childhood in at least moderate

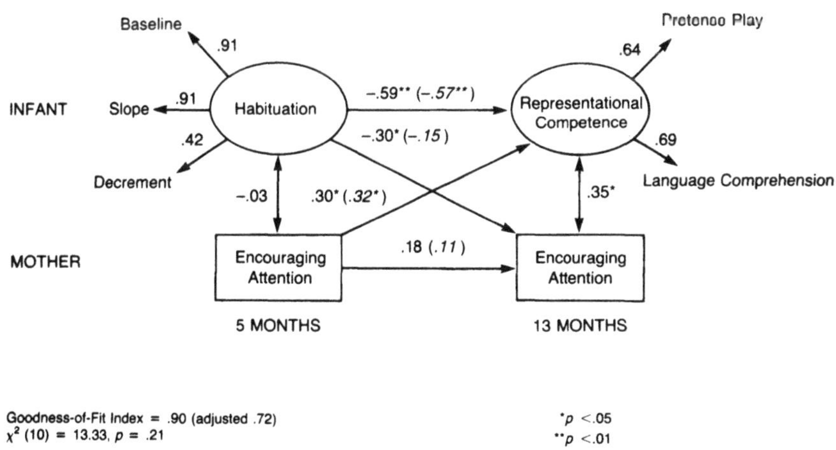

FIG. 8.4. Infant habituation and maternal encouragement of attention at 5 months in relation to maternal encouragement of attention and toddler representational competence at 13 months.

degree, and some "stability" in mental performance appears to reside *in* individual children.

What mechanisms or processes might underlie this stability in infant-to-child cognitive performance? Several possibilities have now been proposed. We have discussed the possible role of experience, and here we discuss three further possibilities: first, speed or efficiency of *Information processing*; second, *Memory abilities*; and third, *Inhibition of attention*.

Information processing. Although habituation has been interpreted in terms of classical (e.g. Rescorla & Wagner, 1972) as well as operant conditioning (e.g. Malcuit, Pomerleau, & Lamarre, 1988), and certainly habituation represents an elementary kind of learning (e.g. Thompson & Spencer, 1966), the primary interpretation is in terms of speed or efficiency of *information processing*. Many of the infant procedures as well as child (and adult) IQ tests turn on performance processes, at least one of which is speed or efficiency of information processing. That is, IQ presumably reflects efficiency of information processing (Campione, Brown, & Ferrara, 1982; Cooper & Regan, 1986; Deary, 1992) and mental representation skills (Hunt, 1983), among other important characteristics (Zigler, Abelson, & Seitz, 1973). Moreover, there is evidence that information processing correlates with adult IQ in the range of $r = -0.30$ to -0.50 (Eysenck, 1987; Jensen, 1982; Vernon, 1987; see also, Lehrl & Fischer, 1990.) Thus, some infants process information in the habituation paradigm more quickly (reaching habituation criterion more efficiently), and those same children process information in tests of cognition and intelligence and perform well in them (Anderson, 1992; Bornstein 1985a; 1989; Colombo & Mitchell, 1988; 1990; Slater et al., 1989).

Rose, Gottfried, Melloy-Carminar, and Bridger (1982) tested 3- and 5-month-olds and found that study time affects familiarity/novelty preferences: very short study times resulted in familiarity preferences, slightly longer ones gave no preferences, and still longer ones produced novelty preferences. These effects were consistent across age, except that the study times (in all conditions these were only a few seconds) needed to be longer for the younger infants in order to produce the same effects. Rose et al.'s findings suggest that measures of recognition memory are likely to reflect the extent to which infants "process" the stimulus during familiarisation: Those infants who give familiarity preferences have not formed a coherent "memory" or engram of the "familiar" stimulus, whereas those infants who give novelty preferences have learned enough about the familiar stimulus to appreciate that the novel stimulus, in some sense, differs from it. We might surmise from this observation that the duration of the study time is critical: if the infant's study time is too long (as it would be if infants were taken to a criterion of habituation), then novelty preferences will not relate to "amount of processing" (a ceiling effect because all infants have learned enough about the familiar stimulus to "recognise" the novel one as being new), and if study time is too short infants are unlikely to base their responses to the novel stimulus on what they have learned about the "familiar" one (a floor effect). The most efficacious study time also appears to depend on the stimuli: thus, in Rose and Feldman (1987) it was only 5 seconds for abstract patterns, but 20 seconds for faces.

In turn, several different possible mechanisms could contribute to individual variation in information-processing efficiency (Colombo, 1995). *First*, it could be that individual differences in information processing reflect individual differences in some aspect of central nervous system functioning, such as speed of neurotransmission, depending on myelinisation, extent of dendritic branching, and neurochemical or biophysical parameters. *Second*, processing information may depend on whether or not infants typically focus on the task. This possibility in turn presumably reflects some combination of attention and temperament. If, for example, some babies are easily arousable or poorly self-regulated, and information processing is inhibited by high arousal level or poor self-regulation, those factors would consistently interfere with performance. *Third*, a knowledge based on experience with different kinds of stimulation and information may consistently underlie better performance. Of course, these hypotheses about mechanisms underlying information processing are not exhaustive, nor are they mutually exclusive, and individual variation in infant information processing is likely to have multiple determinants.

Memory abilities. A second possibility for explaining predictive validity is that individual variation exists in memory capability and that consistency in *memory abilities* underlies both the infant and child/adult measures (Colombo, 1993; Larson & Alderton, 1992). Certainly, many of the infant tasks depend on memory as do the child and adult intelligence and cognitive tasks. Other measures of memory in the first year also predict IQ at 2 to 3 years of age (see Fagen & Ohr, 1990).

Inhibition of attention. A third process that has been posited to underlie both the infant measures and the child and adult measures is *inhibition of attention* (McCall, 1994; McCall & Mash, 1995). This view posits that superior mental performance and stability reflect the ability of infants, children, and adults to inhibit attention and action toward low-salient, familiar, or irrelevant stimulation. For example, children's performance in a variety of cognitive domains (including verbal self-regulation, lexical and discourse processing, and memory) can be accounted for by their improving ability to inhibit attention to irrelevant or distracting stimulation (Dempster & Brainerd, in press). Dempster (1991) has also argued that such inhibitory processes are "integral and fundamental" to adult intelligence. It is important to recognise, too, that such inhibition of attention can be observed in the A- not-B paradigm where children must inhibit responding to the stimulus behind which they previously found an object (Diamond, 1985; 1988). McCall (1994, p. 114) argued that "it is the failure to inhibit the reaching response that explains the anomalous but common observation that some infants look in the correct location but nevertheless do not inhibit reaching to the place where they reached before." Indeed, in their longitudinal project Sigman et al. (1991) included two verbal analogy tasks in which a pre-cue was presented that consisted of novel information either relevant or irrelevant to solving a verbal analogy problem. For example, a novel *relevant* pre-cue was "Lakes are dry" followed by the question "Trail is to hike as lake is to [blank] (swim, walk, water, or dust)." *Walk* is correct in this case (because one cannot swim in a dry lake!). A novel but *irrelevant* pre-cue was "Water runs up hill," in which case *swim* is the correct answer. The strongest predictions they obtained fell between habituation and IQ as well as the irrelevant pre-cue analogies test score, *rs* = –0.38 and –0.29. That is, attention in infancy predicted IQ and also the ability to inhibit attention to irrelevant novelty at 12 years. McCall (1994) points out that this finding is consistent with the inhibition of attention mediation view.

Summary. Several possible common threads to the fabric of individual stability have been woven. These include speed or efficiency of information processing, memory skills, attention inhibition, and supportive experience. Although it would be parsimonious to believe that a single mechanism underlies stable performance, that clearly need not be the case. There is nothing to say that these processes are exhaustive or mutually exclusive. Each mechanism has some face validity and supporting empirical evidence, but each also has penetrating questions and unresolved issues. For example, if they are mediating processes, what underlies their commonality? Is each of these processes equally applicable to explaining the connection between the several infant predictors and the several child/adult outcomes?

SOME INTERIM CONCLUSIONS

Measures of infants' information processing and causal understanding have been shown to predict measures of later cognitive ability, the latter in the age range of 2 to 12 years, and this predictive validity has recurred across many laboratories, with many procedural, age, and stimulus variations. In summary of the above considerations and findings, we can draw several conclusions which, because of their number and nature, are, however, interim:

1. *The predictive measures.* Two classes of paradigms have been distinguished thus far: visual information processing measures and understanding causal relations, and within each class different measures can be distinguished: (a) habituation, (b) the duration of individual fixations to visual stimuli, independent of habituation, and (c) visual recognition memory; as well as (d) means–end problem solving and (e) enabling relations. Each of these gives similar prediction coefficients, and there is no pressing reason to suppose that one is a better predictor than the others.

2. *Predictive power.* Thus far, the predictive correlations that have been reported occasionally approach 0.6, but are usually in the range 0.3 to 0.5, and sometimes lower. These are not great, and may be of more theoretical than practical value (McCall, 1994). McCall (1989, p. 179) has pointed out that, "The maximum predictive correlation equals the square root of the reliability of the predictor and the criterion". This means that, if the reliability of an IQ test is 0.80 and the reliability of infant measures is 0.50, the maximum predictive correlation will be 0.63, a value that is only slightly higher than many of the predictive correlations reported. The combination of poor infant-test reliability and moderate predictive correlations leads to the reasonable supposition that, if more reliable measures of infant cognition could be found, predictive correlations may be much higher: "Future efforts to increase the reliability of infant recognition scores are worth pursuing since one may expect appreciable gains in predictive validity" (Fagan & McGrath, 1981, p. 128).

3. *Failures to replicate.* Lécuyer (1989, p. 149) referred to "the 0.05 syndrome" and continued: "It is difficult to publish an experimental paper if no statistical tests reach this magical level of significance. So, how many studies exist that show no correlation between infancy and childhood measures?" One failure to replicate was reported recently: Laucht, Esser, and Schmidt (1994) used a fixed-trial habituation–dishabituation paradigm with a sample of 226 3-month-old "at risk" infants, and extracted eleven measures of looking. Very few of these measures correlated with either Bayley MDI at 2 years or with cognitive tests at 4 years: the highest coefficient was 0.21, which accounts for only approximately 4% of the variance in the intelligence test scores. They echo Lécuyer and "wonder about the proportion of unpublished studies with equally low correlations as ours which were insignificant because of small sample size". In some of the more complex longitudinal studies to be found in the contemporary literature, infants have been tested at several ages on several different tasks, and on several tasks at later ages, and it is not unusual to find, amongst printouts of large numbers of correlations, some that appear to be failures to replicate others' predictive correlations. Whether these (and maybe many more unpublished) failures to replicate result from inappropriate techniques, use of unreliable measures,

skewed sample characteristics, or other variables that affect these types of predictive relations is unknown.

4. *Sample size.* It has been known for some time that the size of predictive correlations, as they are derived from measures of visual information processing at least, are themselves negatively correlated with sample size—the smaller the sample size, the larger the reported predictive correlation. McCall and Carriger (1993, p. 73) discussed possible reasons for this finding: if one or two individuals give extreme scores these will have more of an effect on correlations with small samples, or maybe "extremely high as well as extremely low correlations are more likely to be found in small than in large samples, but only extremely high correlations will be significant and therefore likely to be published. In contrast, smaller correlations are more likely to be significant in large samples and will be published."

Unfortunately, scatter plots of data from predictive studies are rarely published, so that it is difficult to know whether extreme scores cause higher correlations for smaller samples. However, we can be reasonably sure that prediction is not merely an artifact resulting from chance effects found in a few selected studies: if the data resulted from chance, there would presumably be equal numbers of significant positive and negative correlations. Thus, for example, quick habituators' later IQs would be just as likely to be low ("negative prediction") as to be high ("positive prediction"). However, we are unaware of reports of such "negative predictions".

5. *Developmental window of opportunity.* McCall and Carriger (1993) observed that correlations appear to be strongest when prediction originates in measures of infant performance on visual information-processing tasks between 2 and 8 months. Above that age, predictive correlations attenuate to nonsignificance for several paradigms. It may not be difficult to find a reason for this: from about 4 months of age, infants become increasingly adept at visually-directed reaching, crawling, object manipulation, exploration, problem solving, and so on, and to keep them interested in tasks which merely involve looking at patterns (like habituation and VRM) needs careful attention to stimulus and procedural details. Tasks that are too easy or too difficult yield little or no variation in cognitive processing. After the middle of the first year or thereabouts, therefore, we need alternative measures of cognitive abilities.

Thus, there may be an age-related developmental "window of opportunity" such that the best predictive measures turn out to be useful when taken from younger or older infants depending on the task. For means–ends problem solving, as we have seen, there may be something special about the ages 8 and 9 months. At 6 and 7 months, infants seem simply unable to do the task, meaning that their intention scores are low and are subject to error variance (a floor effect). At 10 months, almost all infants can solve the problem without difficulty (a ceiling effect). Therefore, the predictive age for this task occurs when the component cognitive skills are emerging and improving; that is, around 8 and 9 months.

6. *Detection of infants "at risk".* One of the primary aims of research into the predictability of measures of infant cognitive abilities is to provide tests to discriminate among infants in terms of their intellectual development, with a special emphasis on the detection of infants at risk for delayed development. The considerations already mentioned, of low short-term reliability, poor long-term stability, the occasional failure to replicate, and relatively poor prediction coefficients, mean that we can often make good group estimates based on measures of visual information processing, but extreme caution is called for in attempting to make predictions for individual infants.

In short, predictive research in infancy has considerable theoretical significance, but the search must continue for a greater number of reliable measures of infant cognitive performance before a useful test of infant mental or cognitive development will emerge.

ACKNOWLEDGEMENTS

This chapter summarises selected aspects of our published research, some of which was supported by research grant R000232967 from the Economic and Social Research Council. Portions of the text appear in previous scientific publications. We thank C. S. Tamis-LeMonda and B. Wright.

REFERENCES

Anderson, M. (1992). *Intelligence and development: a cognitive theory*. Oxford: Blackwell.

Baillargeon, R. (1993). The object concept revisited: New directions in the investigation of infants' physical knowledge. In C. E. Granrud (ed.), *Visual perception and cognition in infancy*. Hillsdale, N.J.: Lawrence Erlbaum Associates Inc.

Bauer, P.J. (1992). Holding it all together: How enabling relations facilitate young children's event recall. *Cognitive Development*, *7*, 1–28.

Bayley, N. (1949). Consistency and variability in the growth of intelligence from birth to eighteen years. *Journal of Genetic Psychology*, *75*, 165–196.

Bayley, N. (1993). *The Bayley scales of infant development*. New York: Psychological Corporation.

Bertenthal, B.I., Haith, M.M., & Campos, J.J. (1983). The partial-lag design: A method for controlling spontaneous regression in the infant-control habituation paradigm. *Infant Behavior and Development*, *6*, 331–338.

Bornstein, M.H. (1981). Psychological studies of color perception in human infants: Habituation, discrimination and categorization, recognition and conceptualization. In L.P. Lipsitt (ed.), *Advances in infancy research*, Vol. 1, pp. 1–40. Norwood, N.J.: Ablex.

Bornstein, M.H. (1985a). Habituation of attention as measure of visual information processing in human infants: Summary, systematization, and synthesis. In G. Gottlieb & N.A. Krasnegor (eds), *Measurement of audition and vision in the first year of postnatal life: a methodological overview*. Norwood, N.J.: Ablex.

Bornstein, M. (1985b). How infant and mother jointly contribute to developing cognitive competence in the child. *Proceedings of the National Academy of Sciences*, U.S.A., *82*, 7470–7473.

Bornstein, M.H. (1988). Mothers, infants, and the development of cognitive competence. In H.E. Fitzgerald, B.M. Lester, & M.W. Yogman (eds), *Theory and research in behavioral pediatrics*, Vol. 4, pp. 67–99. New York: Plenum.

Bornstein, M.H. (1989). Information processing (habituation) in infancy and stability in cognitive development. *Human Development*, *32*, 129–136.

Bornstein, M.H. (1992). Perception across the life span. In M.H. Bornstein & M.E. Lamb (eds), *Developmental psychology: an advanced textbook*, pp. 155–209. Hillsdale, N.J.: Lawrence Erlbaum Associates Inc.

Bornstein, M.H. & Benasich, A.A. (1986). Infant habituation: Assessments of individual differences and short-term reliability at five months. *Child Development*, *57*, 87–99.

Bornstein, M.H. Pêcheux, M.-G., & Lécuyer, R. (1988). Visual habituation in human infants: Development and rearing circumstances. *Psychological Research*, *50*, 130–133.

Bornstein, M.H. & Sigman, M.D. (1986). Continuity in mental development from infancy. *Child Development*, *57*, 251–274.

Bornstein, M.H. & Tamis-LeMonda, C. (1994). Antecedents of information-processing skills in infants: Habituation, novelty responsiveness, and cross-modal transfer. *Infant Behavior and Development*, *17*, 371–380.

Bouchard, T.J., Lykken, D.T., McGue, M., Segal, N.L., & Tellegen, A. (1990). Sources of human psychological differences: The Minnesota study of twins reared apart. *Science*, *250*, 223–228.

Campione, J.C., Brown, A.L., & Ferrara, R.A. (1982). Mental retardation and intelligence. In R.J. Sternberg (ed.), *Handbook of human intelligence*, pp. 392–492. Cambridge: Cambridge University Press.

Caron, A.J. & Caron, R.F. (1969). Degree of stimulus complexity and habituation of visual fixation in infants. *Psychonomic Science*, *14*, 78–79.

Clarke, A. (1978). Predicting human development: Problems, evidence, implications. *Bulletin of the British Psychological Society*, *31*, 249–258.

Cohen, L.B. (1981). Examination of habituation as a measure of aberrant infant development. In S.L. Friedman & M. Sigman (eds), *Preterm birth and psychological development*, pp. 241–253. New York: Academic Press.

Colombo, J. (1993). *Infant cognition: predicting later intellectual functioning*. Newbury Park, Calif., London, & New Delhi: Sage.

Colombo, J. (1995). *Some hypotheses about speed of processing in infancy*. Paper presented at the meeting of the Society for Research in Child Development, Indianapolis.

Colombo, J. & Mitchell, D.W. (1988). Infant visual habituation: In defense of an information-processing analysis. *European Bulletin of Cognitive Psychology/Cahiers de Psychologie Cognitive*, *8*, 455–461.

Colombo, J. & Mitchell, D. W. (1990). Individual differences in early visual attention: Fixation time and information processing. In J. Colombo & J.W. Fagen (eds), *Individual differences in infancy: reliability, stability, and prediction*, pp. 193–228. Hillsdale, N.J.: Lawrence Erlbaum Associates Inc.

Colombo, J., Mitchell, D.W., O'Brien, M., & Horowitz, F.D. (1987a). Stimulus and motoric influences on visual habituation to facial stimuli at 3 months. *Infant Behavior and Development*, *10*, 173–181.

Colombo, J. Mitchell, D.W., O'Brien, M., & Horowitz, F.D. (1987b). The stability of visual habituation during the first year of life. *Child Development*, *58*, 474–487.

Colombo, J., Mitchell, D.W., Coldren, J.T., & Freeseman, L.J. (1991). Individual differences in infant visual attention: Are short lookers faster processors or feature processors? *Child Development*, *62*, 1247–1257.

Cooper, L.A. & Regan, D.T. (1986). Attention, perception, and intelligence. In R.J. Sternberg (ed.), *Handbook of human intelligence*, pp. 123–169. Cambridge: Cambridge University Press.

Deary, I.J. (1992). *Auditory inspection time and intelligence.* Unpublished doctoral dissertation, University of Edinburgh, Edinburgh.

Dempster, F.N. (1991). Inhibitory processes: A neglected dimension of intelligence. *Intelligence, 15*, 157–173.

Dempster, F.N. & Brainerd, C.J. (in press). *New Perspectives on interference and inhibition in cognition.* Orlando, Fla.: Academic Press.

Diamond, A. (1985). The development of the ability to use recall to guide action, and indicated by infants' performance on A-B. *Child Development, 56*, 868–883.

Diamond, A. (1988). Differences between adult and infant cognition: Is the crucial variable presence or absence of language? In L. Weiskrantz (ed.), *Thought without language*, pp. 337–369. Oxford: Oxford University Press.

DiLalla, L.F., Plomin, R., Fagan, J.F., Thompson, L.A., Phillips, K., Haith, M.M., Cyphers, L.H., & Fulker, D.W. (1990). Infant predictors of preschool and adult IQ: A study of infant twins and their parents. *Developmental Psychology, 26,* 759–769.

Eysenck, H.J. (1987). Speed of information processing, reaction time, and the theory of intelligence. In P.A. Vernon (ed.), *Speed of information processing and intelligence*, pp. 21–67. Norwood, N.J.: Ablex.

Fagan, J.F. & McGrath, S.K. (1981). Infant recognition memory and later intelligence. *Intelligence, 5*, 121–130.

Fagen, J.W. & Ohr, P.S. (1990). Individual differences in infant conditioning and memory. In J. Colombo and J. Fagen (eds), *Individual differences in infancy: reliability, stability, prediction*, pp. 155–192. Hillsdale, N.J.: Lawrence Erlbaum Associates Inc.

Friedman, S. (1975). Infant habituation: Process, problems, and possibilities. In N. Ellis (ed.), *Aberrant development in infancy: human and animal studies*, pp. 217–239. New York: Halstead Press.

Hoff-Ginsberg, E. & Tardif, T. (1995). Socioeconomic status and parenting. In M.H. Bornstein (ed.), *Handbook of parenting*, Vol. 2, pp. 161–188. Hillsdale, N.J.: Lawrence Erlbaum Associates Inc.

Hunt, E.B. (1983). On the nature of intelligence. *Science, 219*, 141–146.

Jensen, A.R. (1982). Reaction time and psychometric g. In H.J. Eysenck (ed.), *A model for intelligence*, pp. 93–132. Berlin: Springer-Verlag.

Kessen, W., Haith, M.M., & Salapatek, P. (1970). Human infancy: A bibliography and guide. In P. Mussen (ed.), *Carmichael's manual of child psychology*. New York: Wiley.

Larson, G.E. & Alderton, D.L. (1992). The structure and capacity of thought: Some comments on the cognitive underpinnings of g. In D.K. Detterman (ed.), *Current topics in human intelligence*, Vol. 2, pp. 141–156. Norwood, N.J.: Ablex.

Laucht, M., Esser, G., & Schmidt, M. (1994). Predicting later cognitive functioning from infancy: Visual attention measures vs traditional developmental tests. *Journal of Child Psychology and Psychiatry, 35*, 649–662.

Lécuyer, R. (1989). Habituation and attention, novelty and cognition: Where is the continuity? *Human Development, 32*, 148–157.

Lehrl, S. & Fischer, B. (1990). A basic information psychological parameter (BIP) for the reconstruction of concepts of intelligence. *European Journal of Personality, 4*, 259–286.

Lester, B.M. (1975). Cardiac habituation of the orienting response to an auditory signal in infants of varying nutritional status. *Developmental Psychology, 11*, 432–442.

Lewis, M. & Brooks-Gunn, J. (1981). Visual attention at three months as a predictor of cognitive function at two years of age. *Intelligence, 5*, 131–140.

Malcuit, G., Pomerleau, A., & Lamarre, G. (1988). Habituation, visual fixation and cognitive activity in infants: A critical analysis and attempt at a new formulation. *European Bulletin of Cognitive Psychology, 8*, 415–440.

Mandler, J.M. & McDonough, L. (1995). Long-term recall of event sequences in infancy. *Journal of Experimental Child Psychology, 59*, 457–474.

Mayes, L.C. & Bornstein, M.H. (1995). Infant information-processing performance and maternal education. *Early Development and Parenting, 4*, 91–96.

McCall, R.B. (1977). Childhood IQs as predictors of adult educational and occupational status. *Science, 197*, 482–483.

McCall, R.B. (1979). Qualitative transitions in behavioral development in the first two years of life. In M.H. Bornstein & W. Kessen (eds), *Psychological development from infancy: image to intention*, pp. 183–224. Hillsdale, N.J.: Lawrence Erlbaum Associates Inc.

McCall, R.B. (1981). Early predictors of later IQ: The search continues. *Intelligence, 5*, 141–147.

McCall, R.B. (1983). Environmental effects on intelligence: The forgotten realm of discontinuous nonshared within-family factors. *Child Development, 54*, 408–415.

McCall, R.B. (1989). Commentary. *Human Development, 32*, 177–186.

McCall, R.B. (1994). What process mediates predictions of childhood IQ from infant habituation and recognition memory? Speculations on the roles of inhibition and rate of information processing. *Intelligence, 18*, 107–125.

McCall, R.B. & Carriger, M.S. (1993). A meta-analysis of infant habituation and recognition memory performance as predictors of later IQ. *Child Development, 64*, 57–79.

McCall, R.B. & Mash, C.W.(1995). Infant cognition and its relation to mature intelligence. *Annals of Child Development, 10*, 27–56.

McDonough, L. & Mandler, J.M. (1984). Very long-term recall in infancy. *Memory, 2*, 339–352.

Mitchell, D.W. & Colombo, J. (in press). Infant cognition and general intelligence. In M. Welko & J. Kingma (eds), *Prospectives on intelligence*. Greenwich, Conn.: JAI Press.

O'Connor, M.J., Cohen, S., & Parmelee, A.H. (1984). Infant auditory discrimination in preterm and full-term infants as a predictor of 5-year intelligence. *Developmental Psychology, 20*, 159–170.

Pêcheux, M.-G. & Lécuyer, R. (1983). Habituation rate and free exploration tempo in 4-month-old infants. *International Journal of Behavioral Development, 6*, 37–50.

Pêcheux, M-G. & Lécuyer, R. (1989). A longitudinal study of visual habituation between 3, 5, and 8 months of age. *British Journal of Developmental Psychology, 7*, 159–169.

Piaget, J. (1953). *The origins of intelligence in the child.* London: Routledge & Kegan Paul.

Plomin, R. (1986). *Development, genetics, and psychology.* Hillsdale, N.J.: Lawrence Erlbaum Associates Inc.

Plomin, R. (1989). Environment and genes: Determinants of behavior. *American Psychologist, 44*, 105–111.

Rescorla, R.A. & Wagner, A.R. (1972). A theory of Pavlovian conditioning: Variations in the effectiveness of reinforcement and nonreinforcement. In A. H. Black & W. F. Prokasy (eds), *Classical conditioning II: current research and theory.* New York: Appleton-Century-Crofts.

Rose, S.A. & Feldman, J.F. (1987). Infant visual attention: Stability of individual differences from 6 to 8 months. *Developmental Psychology, 23*, 490–498.

Rose, S.A., Feldman, J.F., Wallace, I.F., & McCarton, C. (1991). Information processing at 1 year: Relation to birth status and developmental outcome during the first 5 years. *Developmental Psychology, 27*, 723–737.

Rose, S.A., Feldman, J.F., & Wallace, I.F. (1988). Individual differences in infants' information processing: Reliability, stability, and prediction. *Child Development, 59*, 1177–1197.

Rose, S.A., Feldman, J.F., & Wallace, I. F. (1992). Infant information processing in relation to six-year cognitive outcomes. *Child Development, 63*, 1126–1141.

Rose, S.A., Gottfried, A.W., Melloy-Carminar, P., & Bridger, W.H. (1982). Familiarity and novelty preferences in infant recognition memory: Implications for information processing. *Developmental Psychology, 18*, 704–713.

Rose, D.H., Slater, A.M., & Perry, H. (1986). Prediction of childhood intelligence from habituation in early infancy. *Intelligence, 10*, 251–263.

Sigman, M., Cohen, S.E., Beckwith, L., Asarnow, R., & Parmelee, A.H. (1991). Continuity in cognitive abilities from infancy to 12 years of age. *Cognitive Development, 6*, 47–57.

Slater, A. (1995). Individual differences in infancy and later IQ. *Journal of Child Psychology and Psychiatry, 36*, 69–112.

Slater, A., Cooper, R., Rose, D., & Morison, V. (1989). Prediction of cognitive performance from infancy to early childhood. *Human Development, 32*, 137–147.

Slater, A. & Morison, V. (1985). Selective adaptation cannot account for early infant habituation: A reply to Dannemiller and Banks (1983). *Merrill-Palmer Quarterly, 31*, 99–103.

Slater, A.M., Morison, V., & Rose, D. (1983). Locus of habituation in the human newborn. *Perception, 12*, 593–598.

Tamis-LeMonda, C.S. & Bornstein, M.H. (1989). Habituation and maternal encouraging attention in infancy as predictors of toddler language, play, and representational competence. *Child Development, 60*, 738–751.

Tamis-LeMonda, C.S. & Bornstein, M.H. (1993). Antecedents of exploratory competence at one year. *Infant Behavior and Development, 16*, 423–439.

Thompson, L.A., Fagan, J.F., & Fulker, D.W. (1991). Longitudinal prediction of specific cognitive abilities from infant novelty preference. *Child Development, 62*, 530–538.

Thompson, R.F. & Spencer, W.A. (1966). Habituation: A model phenomenon for the study of neuronal substrates of behavior. *Psychological Review, 73*, 16–43.

Vernon, P.A. (ed.) (1987). *Speed of information-processing and intelligence*. Norwood, N.J.: Ablex.

Willatts, P. (1989). Development of problem solving in infancy. In A. Slater & G. Bremner (eds), *Infant development*. Hove: Lawrence Erlbaum Associates Inc.

Willatts, P. (1992). *Relations between infant cognitive ability and early childhood intelligence*. Final report: The Nuffield Foundation.

Zigler, E., Abelson, W.D., & Seitz, V. (1973). Motivational factors in the performance of economically disadvantaged children on the Peabody Picture Vocabulary Test. *Child Development, 44*, 294–303.

3 SOCIAL AND LANGUAGE DEVELOPMENT

Social and Language Development: Introduction

Infancy is, by definition, the period in human development prior to the acquisition of speech. To explain how human infants acquire language we need to understand not only their perceptual abilities but also the social abilities on which pre-verbal communication and ultimately speech is founded. The perceptual systems allow infants access to auditory and visual information from very early in development. Their social abilities support the interpersonal relationships on which communication by means of a spoken language can be built. In recent years the intricate interweaving of the perceptual and social processes has become apparent through new empirical evidence and this, in turn, has given impetus to the task of theoretical integration. It is no longer tenable to characterise the infant as asocial, or as totally dependent on the social skills of the caretaker for socialisation. The infant is now seen to be engaged in a partnership with others, contributing to her own social development through her influences on others. In fact, the infant and the social partner constitute a unit of analysis in themselves. The question is no longer one of how babies become social. Rather, the issue is how best to characterise the intrinsic sociality apparent in early human relations so that emerging phenomena, such as spoken language, can be explained.

Fundamental to the specifically human aspects of this process is the ability to discriminate and relate to significant social partners. Recent research on face perception, reviewed in the chapter by Slater and Butterworth, suggests that babies may be born with the ability to perceive faces as a "special" category within experience. Newborn infants find faces particularly interesting and they may be predisposed to attend to them, both visually and through audition. Initially, visual attention to the face may be determined by a very general preference but it has been shown that babies soon learn to recognise specific other people. The ability to imitate facial gestures, such as tongue protrusion or lip movements, may also be inborn. This ability to imitate must be considered an important process in the elaboration of social relationships as well as having particular implications for shaping vocal communication.

Evidence is reviewed that babies are highly tuned to information about people. They are soon capable of subtle discriminations, as demonstrated in their preference to look at beautiful faces, in their ability to discriminate the gender of a speaker and in their ability to register emotional expressions of faces. All of these perceptual abilities may be considered component processes in the social development of the infant.

The chapter by Reddy elaborates this theme extensively. She argues that the starting point for social development is already social, in the sense that babies can be shown from the outset to engage in a process of communication with the caretaker. She characterises this process as reciprocal and mutual, rather than as the one-sided accomplishment of the more skilled adult. Infants are not blind to the psychological nature of the persons in their world. Reddy's theoretical approach does not, however, entail a preformation of adult social relationships in the infant. It merely asserts that, from the outset, adequate and mutual socio-emotional links can be postulated from which, with development, new forms of mutuality can emerge. The case is made that babies' emotional attunement to people is the foundation for communication. Although the attachment of the infant for her parent may contribute to the emotional attunement underlying communicative abilities, Reddy suggests that an even more fundamental motive for communication is the need for companionship which can be observed even between babies.

There are important links between this chapter and Hobson's psychoanalytic analysis of infancy. Hobson reminds us of the importance, for Freud and the more recent psychoanalytic schools, of social relationships formed in infancy. He argues that identification with significant others is a fundamental process in the formation of self. Whether the self is perceived as desirable or undesirable is a function of the quality of the relationship between parent and child. The question Hobson raises is whether the recent evidence from infancy might show that innately given forms of interpersonal relatedness are the foundation for social development. Psychoanalysts consider such aspects of self knowledge to arise only after the capacity for symbolic reasoning; and, indeed, symbolic functioning, may be a prerequisite for fantasy and dreams. However, Hobson suggests that the pre-symbolic infant's social experience is nevertheless affectively charged and anchored in the basic facts of embodiment. This anchoring of interpersonal relations in bodily processes need not entail the traditional oral, anal and phallic developmental stages of classical Freudian theory. However, the more general principle that social relationships in very early life may operate through the facts of embodiment may still be a useful contribution to developmental psychology from the psychoanalytic perspective. Hobson's particular concern is to make links with contemporary research on babies which may help in understanding some of the phenomena observed in adult psychopathology. He does so by examining the capacity even of babies to feel threatened or insecure, under conditions of faulty relationships.

Messer builds on the evidence that infants are pre-attuned to the social world in his chapter on the origins of referential communication. Reference, a process whereby significant objects are singled out to become the focus of joint attention by the partners in a communicative exchange, is a complex matter. Philosophers have long been puzzled about how we can know to which attribute adult speech refers. Messer considers three possibilities :

1. Objects may be singled out according to invariant features so that when we hear the word "apple", for example, we can identify the object referred to in terms of the characteristic features of apples.
2. Objects may be identified according to common functional properties revealed in how they engage with actions, as, for example, in the case of cutlery and its use in eating.
3. Objects may also be grouped together because they serve common social purposes, as, for example, in play with toys

Messer argues that the infant's ability to perceive the physical and social world according to such categories enables the baby to discover the common referent of the adult's speech across the varying contexts in which utterances are made. The infant must be alert to what the adult is interested in, so that she can bring her attention to the same focus and hence "crack" the linguistic code.

Messer discusses an alternative to this socially based view which is that babies may be predisposed to consider adult speech to refer to whole objects. Such a constraint on perceptual processing, however, leaves unexplained the reciprocal problem of how the subsidiary properties of whole objects come to be singled out in the child's early speech. Messer argues that it is most likely that the philosopher's problem of ambiguity of reference is readily solved by the baby. He makes the case that the adult and infant share a social history which has given them repeated and mutual experience of the characteristics of the world that are perceptually, functionally and socially salient. These common aspects of experience readily lend themselves to a common language of description.

The apparent ease with which babies slip into language belies the complexity of the process, as Harris shows in her chapter. Babies are innately attuned to perceive the sounds of speech. They rapidly develop selective perception for the particular phonemes of their own language and they selectively "forget" phonetic contrasts that may interfere with speech perception in their native language. This sensitivity to phoneme boundaries is a precursor to the segmentation of the sound stream into words. Recent studies show that babies begin to comprehend some words as early as 6 months of age. Comprehension of speech generally proceeds in advance of speech production, although there are very large individual variations in both processes. Manual pointing, the species' typical means of referring using the index finger and arm, may be closely linked with acquisition of nominals. The development of comprehension in some children may proceed mainly by acquisition of object names but for others object names form only a minor proportion of the early comprehension vocabulary.

Recent research on the effects of brain lesions on acquisition of speech suggests that in babies, unlike in adults, the comprehension and production of speech may respectively be located in right and left hemispheres of the brain. This evidence raises the possibility that the earliest comprehension of speech may be a function of global processing and integration of socially derived information. This view would be consistent with the idea that entry into language depends upon the redundancy of everyday social relationships. Once the infant's entry into the meaning of speech has been achieved, however globally, the way is clear for the further refinement of speech comprehension and its eventual production. The shift from global to specific comprehension of speech might entail a further development in the cortical localisation of speech comprehension from right to left hemisphere, since (in right-handed people) speech comprehension and production systems are typically located in separate centres in the left cerebral hemisphere.

These chapters illustrate the vibrant condition of contemporary research on the social development of babies. Nothing that is said here denies social development occurs but contemporary theorists are characterising the social process in radically different ways than in the past. This break with tradition promises not only to give a better foundation to our understanding of the origins of social relations but it is already pointing the way forward in explaining how infants enter the linguistic community.

9 Perception of Social Stimuli: Face Perception and Imitation

Alan Slater
Department of Psychology, Washington Singer Laboratories, University of Exeter, UK.
George Butterworth
Division of Psychology, University of Sussex, Brighton, UK.

INTRODUCTION

Human infants are born to be social individuals. They need to form attachments to, and to communicate and interact with, significant others. A primary requirement for the establishment of social interactions is the ability to distinguish between people and objects, to distinguish one person from another, and to learn about the characteristics of people. In making these distinctions, knowledge about the human face is of particular importance. Imagine I say to you "I have a beautiful baby", and offer to show you photographs for you to confirm my (perhaps prejudiced!) opinion: you would be able to agree with me if the photos were of my baby's face, but if it were of some other part of her anatomy you would be most surprised!

It is important to investigate the infant's ability to understand and to learn about faces, in order that we can better understand early social development. There are various theoretical positions to be discerned with respect to face perception in infancy. One view is that infants are attracted to faces from birth because of the varied stimulation they provide to the visual system (Slater, 1993). Another argument is that "faces are special", and that infants have an innate predisposition to respond to faces as faces, over and above the stimulation they offer (Johnson & Morton, 1991). Whatever the outcome of these arguments, it must be true that infants have to learn to discriminate between different faces, and we can surmise also that they have to learn about the many types of information faces provide: for example, information about emotion, attention, and physical attractiveness.

In this chapter we review evidence to do with infants' understanding of faces. In the next section, *Prerequisites for face perception*, evidence relating to the ability to detect and respond to faces is briefly discussed, and in *Are faces special?*, the argument that innately available "face detectors" direct and control infants' attention to, and learning about faces is presented. The following section, *Imitation*, reviews the remarkable abilities of infants, from birth onwards, to imitate a variety of the facial gestures they see. The final section, *Learning about "faces in general"*, discusses some of the ways in which infants learn about attentional, gestural and emotional cues that faces provide.

PREREQUISITES FOR FACE PERCEPTION

The human face is one of the most complex stimuli encountered by the human infant. It is three-dimensional, has areas of both high and low contrast, and contains features that can appear both in invariant relationships (the positions of eyes, mouth, hair, etc.), and in changing ones (perhaps with changes of expression). It also moves, both back and forth and from side to side, with respect to the infant, and from frontal to side (profile) views. In order for us to understand the origins and development of infants' responses to faces it is necessary to understand their responses to these aspects of stimulation: if a face were perceived as a formless blur, or as an unconnected combination of separate elements, then face perception, in any meaningful sense, could not exist. A logical place to begin is with the visual abilities of the newborn infant.

Basic Visual Functions

Acuity, movement, depth and form. It is not surprising to find that the visual information detected by the infant at birth is very impoverished compared with that detected by the adult. Visual acuity, the ability to detect fine detail, is typically measured by showing to infants two patterns side by side: one of these contains alternating black and white stripes, the other a gray patch. Infants will usually look at something (the stripes) rather than nothing, and when they cannot discriminate the stripes (which get finer and finer) from the gray patch they no longer look more at the stripes, indicating that their acuity threshold has been reached. Measured in this way acuity in the newborn infant is somewhere between 10 and 30 times poorer than in the adult: curiously, this level of acuity is close to that of the adult cat (whose acuity is 10 times poorer than ours). Figure 9.1 shows how a face might look to a newborn baby at a distance of about 30cm from the eyes: while the image is considerably blurred, there is sufficient information to detect most

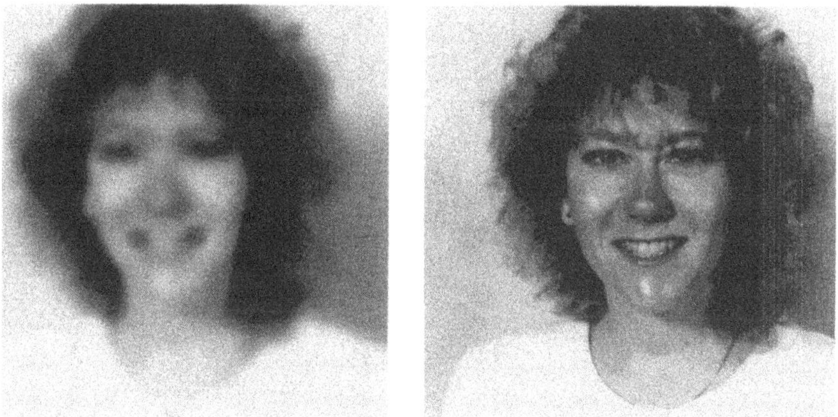

FIG. 9.1. A face as it might appear to a newborn, and to us.

of its important features. We can note that high levels of acuity are important to adults, for distance vision, for reading, and for making fine discriminations: for the young prelocomotor infant, whose world is confined to a zone extending only a foot or so away from its body, and who does not need to make fine visual discriminations, poor acuity is not a particular handicap. Acuity develops rapidly, so that by the time the infant starts to crawl, from about six months, acuity is at near-adult levels.

Infants of all ages will spend more time looking at some stimuli when these are shown paired with other stimuli, and one such preference is shown towards moving stimuli. Slater, Morison, Town, and Rose (1985) found that a moving stimulus, when paired with its stationary counterpart, would attract more than two-thirds of newborn infants' looking time (see Fig. 9.2). Slater et al. (1985) also found that if newborns were habituated to a moving stimulus they demonstrated, by subsequent preferences for a novel shape, that they could remember the shape or pattern of the stimulus they had previously seen moving. This suggests that, when they see a face in movement they will detect its features, and not simply respond to its movement *per se*.

In some sense the immediate visual input is that which impinges upon the flat, two-dimensional retinae. However, neither adults nor infants perceive a two-dimensional world. For example, newborn infants will look more at a three-dimensional object in preference to its photograph, even when they have one eye covered and the only difference between the two is provided by the kinetic cue of motion parallax (Slater, Rose, & Morison, 1984). Newborn infants also fail to recognise a three-dimensional object after having been shown its photograph (and vice versa), and it seems that, for the

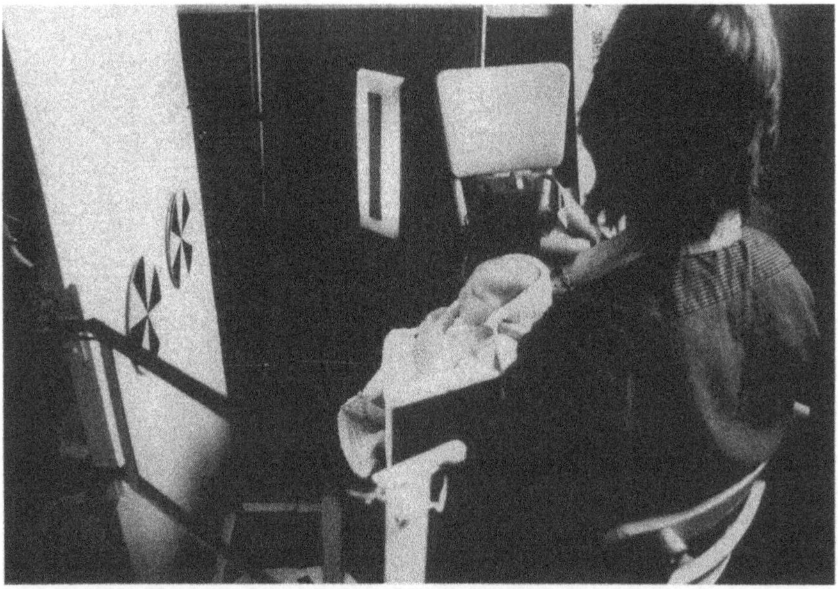

FIG. 9.2. A newborn baby being tested. If one of the identical patterns shown the infant is rotating, it will be looked at in preference to the static pattern.

newborn, the *differences* between objects and their two-dimensional representations are more detectable or obvious than their similarities (Slater et al., 1984). These findings are evidence both that infants detect at least some depth cues from birth, and that three-dimensional stimuli are highly attention-getting, adding further to the view that infants respond to depth cues from birth.

The newborn baby can discriminate between a variety of stimuli that differ in pattern, orientation, contrast, form and size. The typical procedures used to demonstrate these abilities are habituation and subsequent testing for novelty responses to a new pattern, or familiarisation to a series of stimuli which have one invariant property in common, followed by presentation of a stimulus which does not have the invariant property. Some of the findings from the use of these procedures are the following: newborn infants (1) discriminate between the simple outline shapes of a square, triangle, circle and cross, and between complex abstract shapes; (2) discriminate between gratings that differ only in orientation; (3) discriminate between acute and obtuse angles, which may be the basic "building blocks" of form perception; (4) detect the real shapes and real sizes of stimuli that differ in their slant or orientation, and distance from the infant; (5) have a preference for looking at high-contrast patterns (these and other findings are reviewed by Slater, 1995).

Overview

The findings described above lead to two major conclusions. The first is that the human face will be highly attention-getting to the infant at birth and beyond. It moves, has areas of high contrast, and is three-dimensional, and these aspects of stimulation are strongly preferred to static, low-contrast, and two-dimensional comparisons. The second conclusion is that even the newborn infant has sufficient abilities to perceive a face as unchanging across changes in its distance from the baby, and as a coherent whole rather than as a collection of separate elements.

In sum, the face is highly salient to the infant, sufficiently so to make it the most attractive visual stimulus infants are likely to encounter in their world, and it is also potentially comprehensible to the infant. That is, those perceptual abilities that are prerequisites for the infant to begin an understanding of the face are in place at birth. This does not mean, of course, that infants *do* make sense of faces from birth, and there is a long period of learning about them. Some theoretical views and evidence about infants' responses to faces are presented next.

ARE FACES SPECIAL?

As adults we are able to recognise thousands of faces, and it can be argued that "our ability to process information about faces is greater than that for any other class of visual stimuli" (Johnson & Morton, 1991, p. 23). How does this ability develop? One view is that it is a product of years of experience of observing faces, resulting from perceptual learning mechanisms that can be applied to any context where complex discriminations between visual stimuli are needed: thus, experienced dog-show judges can make very fine discriminations between individual dogs of their specialised breed (Diamond & Carey, 1986); chicken sexers can achieve 99.5% accuracy of sorting despite the fact that the necessity to discriminate very subtle differences is confounded by considerable variations within and between pullets and cockerels in their genital eminences (Gibson, 1969, p. 7).

An alternative view is that infants are born with some innately-specified, species-specific mechanism(s) that causes them both to orient towards, and to learn about, faces: that is, faces are special and our ability to process and understand faces results from face-specific mechanisms. Several types of evidence can be adduced to give support to these various, and contrasting, theoretical views. We shall begin by looking at a couple of case studies with adults which illustrates what can happen when face perception goes wrong.

Prosopagnosia: A Face-Specific Disorder?

The term prosopagnosia is derived from the Greek (proso = face, and nosia = knowledge) and refers to individuals who have severe difficulties in recognising faces. The term is used in particular to refer to patients whose visual problems are specific to faces. Two cases described here are a woman (called AB, which are not her real initials), and a male patient, WJ.

AB suffers from *developmental* prosopagnosia, and she was first seen when she was 12 years and 9 months. She said that she has always had difficulties in recognising faces, and that she recognises people by their clothing and mannerisms instead of using facial information. When tested as an adult the full severity of her handicap became apparent. She is a fluent reader, which is evidence of an ability to make fine visual discriminations, but she gave chance results when deciding whether photographs of people were famous or not, or were familiar to her or not: she is quite unable to name *any* famous face reliably. A long-haired man's face is easily mistaken for that of a woman, and she confuses facial expressions such as surprise and disgust. However, additional testing demonstrated that her visual problems are not specific to faces. For example, she is very poor at recognising silhouettes of familiar objects such as rabbits and guns, she is unable to recognise any make of automobile, and she confuses similar objects like donkeys and horses, or a violin with a guitar (Campbell, 1992).

Thus, for AB it seems that her difficulty with faces is simply one manifestation of a general inability to discriminate between objects that resemble each other. The majority of cases of prosopagnosia are *acquired*, rather than developmental, in the sense that they result from a neurological insult, such as a stroke. McNeil and Warrington (1993) summarise the findings from a number of such patients, and describe their ability to make other within-category discriminations for visually complex stimuli that were previously familiar to them. These include a former bird watcher who could no longer recognise birds, a farmer who could not recognise his cows, and another farmer who could not recognise faces but *could* recognise his dogs and cows. One further case, yet another farmer, showed the converse effect: he recovered his ability to recognise faces, but remained unable to recognise his cows. McNeil and Warrington describe the case of patient WJ, a 51-year-old professional man who, after strokes, had profound prosopagnosia. This disorder is not inevitably associated with farming, but WJ became a farmer and, despit the continuation of his prosopagnosia, displayed a remarkable ability to distinguish and recognise the individual faces of his flock of sheep.

For AB it is clear that her visual disorder is not specific to faces, while for WJ, a reasonable case can be made that it is: McNeil and Warrington argue that, for WJ, "other visually complex and difficult-to-discriminate stimuli (the faces of sheep) were processed normally, indicating that prosopagnosia cannot be seen as a more general impairment for within-category discriminations", and they conclude that "for some cases, at least, prosopagnosia appears to be a face-specific impairment" (p. 9).

If a case *can* be made for developmental and/or acquired impairments of visual function which are face-specific we can then suppose that the impairment results either from the failure to develop, or lesions to, brain areas or functions that are specialised for face processing. This "neural specificity" could arise in one of two ways: it could be that our intensive experience with faces, from birth on, causes specialised areas of the brain to "concentrate" on face processing; alternatively, there could be innate brain mechanisms, or "face modules" which are present at birth and are provided by evolution in order to ensure that the infant has a uniquely human start to life. Certainly, evolution has used a variety of means to ensure that individuals will become members of their own species. For example, the chicks of finches (*fringillidae*) can be individually hand-reared by humans, but as adults they will (fortunately) court members of their own species; the cuckoo chick, reared by a different species, does not imprint on its host species, and when adult it seeks out another cuckoo to mate with. Both of these examples point to the presence of innately determined mechanisms that ensure conspecific recognition. Is there evidence for the presence of such mechanisms in the human infant?

Recognition of individual faces by infants

The role of contrast and externality. In a study by Melhuish (1982) 1-month-old infants were shown pictures of the mother's face and female strangers' faces, one at a time for 30 second periods, and the time the infants spent looking at the pictures was measured. Melhuish found no differential attention to the mother's versus the strangers' faces, but there was one significant finding: the infants looked longest at the faces with the highest contrast. We know that contrast is very important in directing infants' attention in the first 2 or 3 months from birth, and its role is further indicated by an habituation study by Bushnell (1982), again looking for discrimination between mothers' and strangers' faces. Bushnell's results suggested that infants as young as 5 weeks of age could discriminate between the photographed faces of their mother and a stranger, but it seemed probable that the basis for the discrimination was the outer boundary of the face, probably the hair–face boundary, with internal features becoming more important only from 4 to 5 months. Maurer and Barrera (1981) used preferential looking and habituation procedures to see if infants could discriminate between natural and schematic arrangements of two-dimensional schematic faces, and found that while 2-month-olds could make the discriminations, 1-month-olds could not.

One possible reason for the younger infants' apparent inability to discriminate between faces is in terms of what is called the "externality effect", which was described by Bushnell (1979). In Bushnell's studies infants were habituated to a compound stimulus in which one shape was enclosed by another; for instance, a small circle might be inside a larger square. Following habituation to such a pattern, new combinations were shown, which might be a small circle inside a triangle (external change), or a small triangle inside a square (internal change). A clear age-related effect was found: infants older than 2 months detected changes both to the internal and the external features, while younger infants noticed only changes to the external shape; hence the term "externality effect".

Other researchers have reported age differences in infants' attention to faces. Kleiner (1987; Kleiner & Banks, 1987) compared newborns' and 2-month-olds' preferences between two-dimensional face-like and abstract patterns. She reported that newborns preferred to look more at an abstract pattern whose high amplitude components were near to their peak contrast sensitivity rather than at a face-like pattern, suggesting that their "preferences are governed primarily by stimulus energy and not by the familiarity or social significance of such patterns" (Kleiner, 1987, p. 47). In this context the expression "stimulus energy" relates to the amount of contrast in the stimulus. In comparison, the 2-month-olds looked more at the face-like patterns, suggesting the emergence of sensitivity to faces by this age. Dannemiller and Stephens (1988) reported a similar age-related trend: 3-month-olds showed a clear face preference, while 6-week-olds did not.

These studies combine to tell what seems to be a coherent story about infants' responses to faces. For the first month or two, infant attention is dominated by response to contrast, stimulus energy, and external features of faces, meaning that there is no response to faces *per se*. From about 2 months of age, responses to faces begin to differ from responses to other visual stimuli; and perhaps as infancy progresses the invariant features of the face gradually differentiate, and recognition of individual faces and of facial expressions becomes possible (Gibson, 1969; Fagan, 1976). However, the literature on infants' responses to faces is both extensive and complex, and with reference to other studies a different story can be told.

Recognition of mother in early infancy

The "externality effect" described earlier seems to work primarily with stimuli where the internal element is static. If the internal element moves or jitters, infants younger than 2 months will detect changes to its shape (Bushnell, 1979; Girton, 1979). Maurer (1983) recorded newborn and 1-month-olds' scanning and visual fixations when shown two compound stimuli, these consisting of features inside a frame. One of these was a small square framed by a larger one, and she found the externality effect in that babies rarely looked at the smaller one. However, when the stimulus was a schematic face, they showed no external bias, and looked at its internal features at least half of the time. We also have evidence that when a face is moving this affects young infants' scanning of faces: Haith, Bergman, and Moore (1977) found that 9-11-week-olds were more likely to look at the eyes of a talking face than other features such as the mouth and hairline when compared with looking at a static, silent face. These findings suggest that the externality effect may not apply to young infants' visual attention to faces, and that any tendency for it to occur is likely to be nullified when the internal features move and when the baby is spoken to. Hence, it is possible that even newborn infants attend to faces' internal features, leading to the further possibility that they learn about the characteristics of important faces.

Many habituation studies have shown that the newborn infant quickly learns about, and discriminates between, a range of visual stimuli; and three studies suggest that neonates learn about the specific characteristics of the mother's face within hours from birth. Field, Cohen, Garcia, and Greenberg (1984), and Bushnell, Sai, and Mullin (1989) reported statistically reliable preferences for the mother's face, compared with that of a female stranger, at 45 hours, and 49 hours from birth, respectively. Bushnell et al. were careful to use pairings where mother and stranger were matched for hair colour and overall brightness, suggesting that these discriminations were made on the basis of differences in the faces' internal features. Walton, Bower, and Bower (1992) reported that infants aged between 12 and 36 hours of age produced more sucking responses in order to see a videotaped image of their mother's face, as opposed to an image of a stranger's face.

Such early learning testifies to the importance of the face to the infant, and it seems likely that the infants were attending to the internal features in order to make their discriminations, although we do not know exactly what features they were attending to.

Conspec and Conlern

The above evidence of early learning about faces, impressive though it may be, is perhaps only a specific example of a more general learning ability: it is possible that the infants could have learned to discriminate between "other visually complex and difficult-to-discriminate stimuli" (to select a quote from the earlier section on prosopagnosia!) if they had had lengthy exposure to these stimuli. We therefore need to look elsewhere for convincing evidence of a special response to the human face.

In a well-known study Goren, Sarty, and Wu (1975) presented laterally moving stimuli to newborn infants. They reported that their infants, who averaged only 9 *minutes* from birth at the time they were tested, turned their heads and eyes significantly more to follow (i.e. track) a two-dimensional schematic face-like stimulus than either of two stimuli consisting of the same facial features in different arrangements. There were some methodological problems with this study; for example, the observer who presented the stimuli was not "blind" as to which one was being shown. This and other problems were removed by Johnson, Dziurawiec, Ellis, and Morton (1991) who carried out a partial replication of Goren et al.'s study, and ensured that no unconscious bias on the part of the experimenter could affect the results. The stimuli they used, referred to as *Face*, *Scrambled*, and *Blank*, were three of those used by Goren et al., and are shown in Fig. 9.3: each was head-sized. Each infant was placed on its back on the experimenter's lap, and as soon as the baby looked at the stimulus (these were shown in a random order), it was moved in an arc, back and forth in front of the baby's head, at a rate of about 5° per second, and the amount of looking and head-turning to each was recorded.

They substantially replicated Goren et al.'s results; that is, the *Face* elicited more looking and tracking than the *Scrambled* pattern, which in turn was preferred to the *Blank*. Johnson and Morton (1991) use these findings to argue that we now "have more confidence that new-borns do show a discriminatory response toward a face-like pattern" (p. 33) and suggest that two cognitive mechanisms, Conspec and Conlern are found in the human infant, which serve to orient the infant to faces, and to facilitate learning about individuals of the species. We know that visual orienting responses are often mediated by subcortical mechanisms, such as the

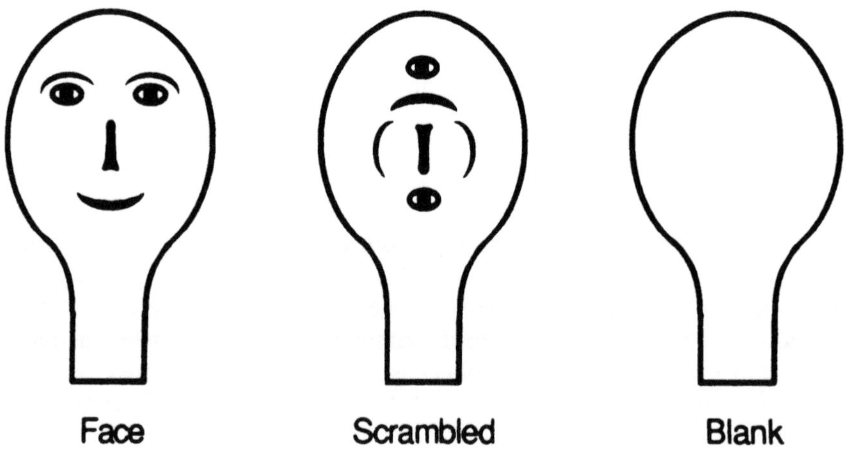

FIG. 9.3. The three stimuli used by Johnson et al. (1991) in their replication of Goren, Sarty and Wu (1975).

superior colliculus in the midbrain; and they argue that the first of these mechanisms, Conspec (referring to conspecifics), is subcortical and its sole purpose is to orient the infant to faces. The other mechanism, Conlern, has a two-fold function: (1) to detect similarities between faces, and (2) to detect differences between faces. A problem with this mechanism is that it is cortically driven, and is not supposed to make its appearance until the baby is two months old. As we have seen, however, babies from about 12 hours from birth show a preference for the mother's face which suggests that infants are learning about faces from birth onwards.

In summary, the evidence for Conspec seems to be more compelling than that for Conlern. We can note, however, that Conlern does not need to be face specific: "Rather, the mechanism becomes specialized for faces as a result of massive experience of them provided by the species-typical environment. We see this view as entirely consistent with the adult literature indicating that expertise in recognizing and processing faces is similar to that of expertise with other classes of stimuli with similar properties." (Johnson & Morton, 1993, p. 249). Thus, Conlern becomes a general perceptual learning mechanism that allows the infant (and adult) to learn about, and make fine and complex discriminations between similar stimuli. Johnson and Morton would presumably agree with the view that prosopagnosia is *not* a face-specific disorder.

IMITATION

Imitation may be defined as establishing a correspondence between one's own behaviour and that of another person. To the extent that imitation involves facial expressions this topic may offer an alternative approach to the question of face perception in babies. Baldwin (1890) wrote one of the earliest descriptions; he argued that imitation begins in the repetitive activities of babies. The basic mechanism of imitation, he argued, was the circular reaction, a repetitive cycle of activity in which achieving the goal of the act initiates a new cycle of activity. On this argument, imitation begins by imitation of self; for example, as the baby repeatedly sucks her own hand, before it is possible for the baby to imitate the actions of another person. Piaget (1962) shared Baldwin's view that imitation only slowly becomes truly social. He argued that for the infant to comprehend the relationship between her own behaviours and those of another person it is necessary to be able to represent the self in memory. He described a series of achievements culminating in representation whereby the baby infers the correspondence between self and other. For example, the infant at 6 months may see the mother move her hand and imitate the movement. Piaget argued that because the infant can see that her own hand resembles her mother's hand, the visual information allows her to place her own actions into correspondence. To imitate facial movements is considered a much more advanced achievement, possible only from about one year. The infant cannot see her own face and the ability to match facial movements is thought to require mental representation (a mental model) of the appearance of the face. Piaget describes the baby from about 8 months touching her mother's face and then touching her own, as if to establish the correspondence between invisible parts of her own body and visible parts of the mother's face. On these traditional theories, imitation of facial expressions develops late because the infant must first establish, through inference, the relationship between visible and invisible movements. If it were the case that imitation of movements of the face is not possible before the end of the first year, it would follow that little could be learned about face perception by the study of early imitation.

There have been other accounts of facial imitation, however. For example, McDougall (1931) described his nephew imitating tongue movements at 3 months. Such anecdotal observations did not carry much weight because it is always possible that the infant might have been trained (perhaps inadvertently) to make a response with the tongue simply by the adult rewarding the behaviour of tongue protrusion. This might make it seem that the baby is actually imitating when he has merely learned to respond in a particular way to a particular cue, which need not imply any face perception at all. However, with the discovery of the perceptual abilities of babies the possibility that young infants may indeed be able to imitate facial expressions has received particularly careful study in the last 25 years.

One of the first systematic studies was by Maratos (1973) who studied imitation of finger movements (visible movement) and tongue protrusion (invisible movement) in newborn babies. She reported that babies can imitate both the visible and invisible movements. Meltzoff and Moore (1977) made carefully controlled studies of imitation of tongue protrusion, mouth opening and lip pursing in newborn babies. Babies systematically imitated these stimuli and there was little possibility of explaining the ability to imitate in terms of a learned response to the experimenter's cues. Since these early and controversial demonstrations there have been several replications of newborn imitation of mouth, tongue and facial movements. Evidence for imitation of tongue protrusion in newborns is particularly well established (Kugiumutzakis, 1993; Reissland, 1988; Vinter, 1986) and there is also evidence for innate imitation of emotional expressions (Field et al., 1982) and for auditory imitation of vowel sounds (Kugiumutzakis, 1993).

This research raises fundamental questions relevant to our understanding of early face perception. First, the question whether there is a general, innate ability for imitation in humans, although not fully resolved, is beginning to receive an affirmative answer. However, if imitation does exist, this still leaves two further issues to be resolved concerning the mechanisms and motives for the ability. How can the newborn baby imitate both visible and invisible movements and why does the baby imitate at all?

In the early attempts to explain the mechanism of imitation it was suggested that perhaps the imitative response was released rather automatically by some critical aspect of the stimulus. For example, Hayes and Watson (1981) argued that any moving object (not specifically a tongue) might be sufficient to elicit tongue protrusion in the newborn baby. Such general stimuli are called releasers by ethologists who have described many examples where minimal stimulus input is sufficient to elicit complex behaviour in the young. A well-known example concerns the herring gull chick where the sight of a red dot on the adult's beak is sufficient to elicit the feeding response in the young. Meltzoff (1994) addressed this possibility and showed that tongue protrusion in the newborn is more likely to occur when the stimulus object is a real tongue than when it is a moving but inanimate object. Other aspects of this behaviour have now been carefully studied. For example, the baby often takes some time to respond to the stimulus and appears to make "searching" movements for the tongue, which suggest that the imitative response is rather effortful and not automatically released (Meltzoff 1994). The rather mechanistic explanation of facial imitation in newborns as an indiscriminately released response does not receive strong support on the evidence to date.

A second type of explanation stresses the perceptual abilities of the baby. This argument hinges on how we choose to explain perception and on how babies perceive the equivalence of different types of information obtained through different perceptual channels. Meltzoff (1988) has argued that this problem is logically equivalent to matching information across sensory modalities. Meltzoff and Borton (1979) showed that babies of 1 month would orally explore a dummy which was either knobbly or smooth. They did not see the dummy before it was placed in the mouth, yet they would subsequently prefer to look at a dummy of similar shape and texture placed in the field of view. That is, the baby picked up some information about the visual shape or texture of the dummy just through active oral exploration. Meltzoff argues that the imitation of facial movements involves a similar process of active matching of the visual input to the proprioceptive properties of the motor output.

Further progress with this type of explanation has come from Vinter (1986) who showed that newborn babies imitate tongue protrusion only if they first see the model tongue in motion. That is, information from the dynamics of the movement seems to be necessary for imitation. Kugiumutzakis (1986) has shown that newborns will imitate a repetitive vowel sound "a" and that the baby pays very close attention to the visual and auditory dynamics of the display. These demonstrations also show that it is necessary to take into account rather subtle interpersonal aspects of the testing situation and this may explain why some investigators have failed to replicate newborn imitation (Abranavel & Sigafoos, 1984).

There is therefore evidence that the mechanisms underlying newborn facial imitation may involve matching the dynamic patterns perceptible in the input to the proprioceptive output channel. This matching occurs whether the "translation" is from vision or from audition to the action of the mouth and tongue. The long held distinction between visible and invisible movements proves to have been a red herring, since the dynamic patterns of stimulation that elicit imitation are not specific to the visual modality. A further extension of this argument is that imitation is an expression of an inherent predisposition to recognise the actions and emotions of others as importantly similar to the self (Trevarthen, 1993). This implies that imitation does involve recognition of important similarities between the self and others. Of course, this puts rather a different perspective on what is meant by face perception in very young babies. The argument shifts from thinking of face perception as registering static visual patterns (sometimes presented as two-dimensional pictures) toward a definition of the face as carrying important information through its mobility and species-typical human means of expression.

This leads to the third question which is rarely asked. What is the motive for imitation in the newborn? Why does the infant oblige the curious psychologist and produce an imitative response? Kugiumutzakis (1993) suggests that the ultimate motive is a deep-seated need to communicate. Some of the specific imitative phenomena of newborns, such as mouth or tongue movements, emotional expressions, and hand movements may be understood as the fundamental components of the vocal, gestural and emotional systems characteristic of human communication.

With development in the first year, the capacity for imitation undergoes further changes. Babies can now reproduce a response having seen only the end result: for example, Vinter (1986) showed that a static tongue is sufficient to elicit imitation at 12 months. They can also imitate after a significant delay since observing the stimulus, and imitation can even take on symbolic properties. Piaget (1962) himself observed that imitation at 12 months can take on a symbolic aspect. He described his daughter Jacqueline trying to work out how the drawer of a matchbox operates by systematically sliding her tongue in and out of her mouth. There is also evidence that the capacity for deferred imitation emerges soon after the ability to imitate immediately. Meltzoff and Moore (1994) showed that imitation 24 hours after first seeing the model is possible in babies from 6 weeks. This is significantly earlier than had previously been thought possible and it suggests that the infant is representing the stimulus imitated in memory.

All of this is consistent with the thesis that there may be two basic developmental changes in facial imitation. First, imitation may proceed from reproduction of the dynamics of the facial (or manual) display to reproduction of the end state. Second, development may proceed from immediate imitation based on perception of facial expression (this might be characterised as participation: Baldwin, 1890) to imitation based on a representation which enables the infant to defer a response over time. Certainly, the finding that infants imitate facial gestures from birth provides the clearest evidence that they come into the world with a rudimentary knowledge about the face.

LEARNING ABOUT "FACES IN GENERAL"

As infants become familiar with individual faces, and as they see a variety of different faces, they acquire information about "faces in general". Some of the ways in which this can be demonstrated is in the formation of prototypes, the "inversion effect", acquisition of gender categories, and the recognition of facial expressions and emotions.

Prototype Formation

Babies quickly form a prototype, or averaged version, of the face. Samuels and Ewy (1985) showed pairs of black and white slides of same-gender faces (equal numbers of male and female faces were used) to 3- and 6-month-old infants. The slides were constructed so that each of the members of a pair were as similar as possible in other respects, but they differed in attractiveness as rated by adults: attractive and unattractive faces were paired together. Both age groups looked longest at the attractive face for all of the 12 pairings. This finding of preference for attractive faces was replicated and extended by Langlois et al. (1987; 1991), with infants as young as 2 months. They found that the effect generalised across faces differing in race (black and white), gender, and age (adult and infant faces). Most people's faces are asymmetrical, and the two faces that can be constructed from the mirror images of the left half and of the right half of a face often look quite different from each other. Since infants are sensitive to symmetry, the possibility exists that perhaps attractive faces are preferred because they tend to be more (or less) symmetrical than less attractive ones. Samuels et al. (1994) tested this suggestion, but found that vertically symmetrical faces did not receive any more or less visual attention than the same faces in their natural form.

A possible interpretation of these infant preferences is the following: if faces are created by combining or averaging the features of a number of individual faces, these "averaged" or prototypical faces are rated as significantly more attractive than the ones they were derived from: and such averaged faces become even more attractive as more faces are added (Langlois & Roggman, 1990; Langlois, Roggman, & Musselman, 1994). An example of an averaged face is shown in Fig. 9.4. Thus, the babies' preferences for attractive faces can be interpreted as a prototype effect: these faces are preferred because they are simply more "face-like" than the less attractive ones. Alternatively, however, preference for attractive faces may be innate rather than the result of averaging over a large number of faces. If this should prove to be the case, the notion of prototype formation through experience would need to be modified to allow for an "archetype", or ideally proportioned facial configuration against which the relative attractiveness of the faces encountered are evaluated. This hypothesis awaits experimental investigation.

FIG 9.4. An average or prototypical face produced by computer-averaging of several faces (photograph by Phil Benson).

The Inversion Effect

Faces are typically seen in only one orientation, and it has been known for many years that pictures of well-known human faces are extremely difficult to recognise when viewed upside down. Memory and recognition for inverted faces seems to be disproportionately affected when compared with that for other classes of familiar and complex (and similarly mono-oriented) inverted objects, such as houses, aeroplanes, etc., leading once again to the suggestion that unique face-processing mechanisms underlie face perception (Yin, 1969). In theoretical debates (similar to those discussed earlier for prosopagnosia), however, some researchers have argued that the "inversion effect" is not specific to faces. This view is supported by the finding that experienced dog-show judges show the "inversion effect" when judging their own specialist breed, whilst inexperienced judges do not (Diamond & Carey, 1986).

A similar "inversion effect" has been well documented in infants' perception of faces. Familiar faces were shown to 8- and 14-week-old infants by Watson (1966), and the older, but not the younger, infants, produced more smiling, with a shorter latency, to upright faces than to faces rotated through 90° or 180°, which suggests a sensitivity to facial orientation by around 3 months of age. In a series of studies Fagan (reviewed by Fagan, 1979) has shown that infants younger than 4 months have little difficulty in discriminating between two faces that are presented either upright or upside down, but after this age the discrimination becomes orientation-specific: "When upright faces were discriminated by 5- to 6-month-old infants, the same stimuli inverted 180° were not" (Fagan, 1979, p. 97).

Irrespective of whether the "inversion effect" is specific to faces, or whether it is a consequence of more general mechanisms of perceptual learning, there is complete agreement that it is found only with perception of stimuli with which the subjects are familiar. For example, "It took the dog judges many years of experiencing a breed before they developed an inversion effect" (Johnson & Morton, 1991, p. 24). The experimental designs used in testing adults' and infants' recognition of upside down faces are, of course, quite different, but the presence of an "inversion effect" from about 3 or 4 months is clear evidence of the importance of, and of early learning about, faces in infancy.

Learning About Gender

Infants display categorical knowledge of male and female voices as early as 2 months of age. This was shown by Jusczyk, Pisoni, and Mullenix (1992), who habituated 2-month-olds to several male (or female) voices uttering a particular syllable. Their habituation procedure used high-amplitude sucking: the infants heard the syllable contingent upon the rate of sucking, and they were judged to have habituated when the sucking rate fell below a given criterion. After habituation they recovered interest (shown by an increase in sucking rate) when they heard the same syllable produced by speakers of the opposite sex to the original syllable-utterer.

Gender-based categorical responding seems to appear for faces in later infancy. Cohen and Strauss (1979) habituated infants to a series of female faces, and found that 6-month-olds recovered attention to a new female face, while 7-month-olds generalised what they had learned to the new face. However, Leinbach and Fagot (1993) report that infants as young as 5 months can distinguish between the categories of male and female faces. In their study, infants were habituated to a series of male or female faces, and then they were found to generalise habituation to a new face of the same category, and to recover visual attention to an opposite-sex face. This demonstrates categorical perception, that is, the infants clearly had separate categories for male and female faces. In a second study, they obtained evidence suggesting that by 1 year of age, infants' categories for men and women may include information about sex-typical hair length and clothing style, since the infants were less likely to recover attention to the opposite-sex face when unisex clothing and short hair were presented with the male and female faces shown.

The results from these studies demonstrate that by 5 months infants have some clear categorical knowledge of male and female faces and voices, and the basis of a gender schema has become established. Since the distinction between male and female is of fundamental importance to all societies, it is perhaps not too surprising to find these distinctions in infants' early categorical knowledge.

Facial Expressions and Emotions

Infants are able to discriminate between different facial expressions from a very early age. For example, Field, Woodson, Greenberg, and Cohen (1982) reported that newborn infants, only 1 to 2-days-old, discriminated and imitated the expressions sad, happy and surprise, when these were posed by a live model, and Barrera and Maurer (1981) found that 3-month-olds discriminated between these expressions, and also between smiling and frowning. The research described earlier demonstrates that categorical knowledge of gender differences is available to infants by at least 5 months, and categorisation of facial expressions emerges around the same time. Thus, Caron, Caron, and Myers (1982), and Nelson and Dolgin (1985), found that 7-month-olds generalised habituation to facial expressions of fear and happiness between and across male and female faces, although in Caron et al.'s study 6-month-olds generalised across different happy faces, but not across fear expressions. Categorisation of any set of perceptual stimuli results from experience with that set, and infants will have had much more exposure to happy faces than to fearful ones: Malatesta and Haviland (1982) reported that 3 to 6- month-olds rarely saw a negative expression on their mother's face, and never a fearful one. In one part of Nelson and Dolgin's study, they showed their 7-month-olds two pictures of the same model posing happy and fear expressions, and they looked overwhelmingly at the fearful face, a preference that almost certainly results from the novelty of this expression.

Another preference between expressions was reported by Kuchuk, Vibbert, and Bornstein (1986), which is that 3-month-olds preferred to look at happy faces rather than neutral ones, and that the greater the intensity of the smiling face the more it was looked at. These preferences, together with the other findings discussed earlier, tell us that very young infants discriminate between a variety of facial expressions, and that they soon learn to categorise at least some of the different expressions.

This does not, of course, tell us whether the infants are aware that different emotional states underly the different expressions. In some respects, for the prelocomotor infant, the detection of underlying emotional states may not be of great importance—unlike, say, the infant monkey, the human baby does not have the physical independence to approach smiling people or to avoid fearful or sad ones. However, by the time they are able to crawl, such facial messages can assume great importance. A study by Sorce, Emde, Campos, and Klinnert (1985) provides a clear demonstration of this. They tested 12-month-olds on a visual cliff, and looked to see under what conditions the babies could be coaxed by their mothers to cross the deep side, which gave the appearance of a drop. When the mothers posed fear none of the 17 infants crossed, and when she posed anger only 2 (of 18) crossed. However, when she appeared either interested or happy the majority crossed the deep side (12 of 18, and 14 of 19, for "interested" and "happy", respectively). Additionally, the infants were more likely to retreat from the cliff edge and to look distressed when the negative expressions were posed.

Nelson (1987) argues that the ability to recognise and understand facial expressions of emotions undergoes a long incubation period in humans, and that "infants by the end of the second year are still developing a working knowledge of facial expressions" (p. 906). Nevertheless, we can see that considerable development occurs in early infancy. Soon after birth infants can discriminate a variety of expressions, and they begin to represent them categorically some time after 4 months. When they begin to crawl, if not before, infants are clearly aware that different expressions mean different things, and that they have consequences both for their own and for others' actions.

OVERVIEW AND CONCLUSIONS

Faces possess several salient stimulus characteristics, such as movement, contrast, three-dimensionality, (and they talk!), which ensure that they will be attention-getting and attention-holding for the infant. Add to this a possible species-specific mechanism such as Conspec, which gives an additional incentive to orient towards the face, and it is little wonder that faces are so attractive to the infant, and that they learn so readily about them. One of the main issues in the literature on face perception concerns the question "Are faces special?", which for our purposes divides into two interrelated questions: (1) do humans have special neural mechanisms ("face modules") for learning about, remembering and understanding faces?; and (2) do infants come into the world with some innately specified knowledge of faces? From the literature we have surveyed, particularly that to do with cases of prosopagnosia, we have no unambiguous answer to the first of these questions. However, the recent work on imitation, in particular, suggests that the answer to the second question is "yes". Much of our knowledge about early face perception comes from studies that have presented static, two-dimensional stimuli to infants; and the work on facial imitation is important because it emphasises the importance of the dynamic aspects of the displays shown to infants: the dynamic, animate qualities seem most important for early infant perception, imitation and communication.

Soon after birth infants discriminate between different facial expressions, and they quickly learn to distinguish their mother's face from others. By 3 months infants prefer to look at attractive rather than unattractive faces, which may be innate, or alternatively might be interpreted in terms of the extraction of a prototype resulting from seeing a number of different faces. Experience soon makes itself apparent in other ways: in the early appearance of the "inversion effect" where upside-down faces become difficult to recognise, and in the development of categories for gender and for some facial expressions. Understanding of the various types of information conveyed by faces continues throughout childhood, and throughout life, but it is clear that by the end of the first year infants have acquired a good working knowledge of some of the more important aspects of this information.

REFERENCES

Abranavel, E. & Sigafoos, A.D. (1984). Exploring the presence of imitation during early infancy. *Child Development*, *55*, 381–392.

Baldwin, J.M. (1890). *Mental development in the child and the human race*. London: Macmillan.

Barrera, M.E. & Maurer, D. (1981). The perception of facial expressions by the three-month-old. *Child Development*, *52*, 203–206.

Bushnell, I.W.R. (1979). Modification of the externality effect in young infants. *Journal of Experimental Child Psychology*, *28*, 211–229.

Bushnell, I.W.R. (1982). Discrimination of faces by young infants. *Journal of Experimental Child Psychology, 33*, 298–309.

Bushnell, I.W.R., Sai, F., & Mullin, J.T. (1989). Neonatal recognition of the mother's face. *British Journal of Developmental Psychology, 7*, 3–15.

Campbell, R. (1992). Face to face: Interpreting a case of developmental prosopagnosia. In R. Campbell (ed.), *Mental lives: case studies in cognition.* Oxford: Blackwell.

Caron, R.F., Caron, A.J., & Myers, R.S. (1982). Abstraction of invariant face expressions in infancy. *Child Development, 53*, 1008–1015.

Cohen, L.B. & Strauss, M.S. (1979). Concept acquisition in the human infant. *Child Development, 50*, 419–424.

Dannemiller, J.L. & Stephens, B.R. (1988). A critical test of infant pattern preference models. *Child Development, 59*, 210–216.

Diamond, R. & Carey, S. (1986). Why faces are and are not special: An effect of expertise. *Journal of Experimental Psychology: General, 115*, 107–17.

Fagan, J.F. (1976). Infants' recognition of invariant features of faces. *Child Development, 47*, 627–638.

Fagan, J.F. (1979). The origins of facial pattern recognition. In M.H. Bornstein & W. Kessen (eds), *Psychological development from infancy: image to intention*, pp. 83–113). Hillsdale, N.J.: Lawrence Erlbaum Associates Inc.

Field, T.M., Cohen, D., Garcia, R., & Greenberg, R. (1984). Mother–stranger face discrimination by the newborn. *Infant Behavior and Development, 7*, 19–25.

Field, T.M., Woodson, R.W., Greenberg, R., & Cohen, C. (1982). Discrimination and imitation of facial expressions by neonates. *Science, 218*, 179–181.

Gibson, E.J. (1969). *Principles of perceptual learning and adaptation.* New York: Appleton-Century-Crofts.

Girton, M.R. (1979). Infants' attention to intra-stimulus motion. *Journal of Experimental Child Psychology, 28*, 416–423.

Goren, C.C., Sarty, M., & Wu, P.Y.K. (1975). Visual following and pattern discrimination of face-like stimuli by newborn infants. *Pediatrics, 56*, 544–549.

Haith, M.M., Bergman, T., & Moore, M. (1977). Eye contact and face scanning in early infancy. *Science, 198*, 853–855.

Hayes, L.A. & Watson, J.S. (1981). Neonatal imitation: Fact or artifact? *Developmental Psychology, 17*, 655–660.

Johnson, M. & Morton, J. (1991). *Biology and cognitive development: the case for face recognition.* Oxford: Basil Blackwell Limited.

Johnson, M., Dziurawiec, S., Ellis, H.D., & Morton, J. (1991). Newborns' preferential tracking of face-like stimuli and its subsequent decline. *Cognition, 40*, 1–19.

Johnson, M.H. & Morton, J. (1993). Authors' response. *Early Development and Parenting, 2*, 248–249.

Jusczyk, P.M., Pisoni, D.B., & Mullenix, J. (1992). Some consequences of stimulus variability on speech processing by two-month-old infants. *Cognition, 43*, 253–291.

Kleiner, K.A. & Banks, M.S. (1987). Stimulus energy does not account for 2-month-olds' face preferences. *Journal of Experimental Psychology, 13*, 594–600.

Kleiner, K.A. (1987). Amplitude and phase spectra as indices of infants' pattern preferences. *Infant Behavior and Development, 10*, 49–59.

Kuchuk, A., Vibbert, M., & Bornstein, M.H. (1986). The perception of smiling and its experiential correlates in three-month-old infants. *Child Development, 57*, 1054–1061.

Kugiumutzakis, G. (1986). The origin, development and function of early infant imitation. Unpublished doctoral dissertation, Department of Psychology, University of Uppsala, Sweden.

Kugiumutzakis, G. (1993). Intersubjective vocal imitation in early mother–infant interaction. In J.Nadel & L.Camioni (eds), *New perspectives in early communicative development*, pp 23–47). London & New York: Routledge.
Langlois, J.H. & Roggman, L.A. (1990). Attractive faces are only average. *Psychological Science, 1*, 115–121.
Langlois, J.H., Roggman, L.A., & Musselman, L. (1994). What is average and what is not average about attractive faces? *Psychological Science, 5*, 214–220.
Langlois, J.H., Ritter, J.M., Roggman, L.A., & Vaughn, L.S. (1991). Facial diversity and infant preferences for attractive faces. *Developmental Psychology, 27*, 79–84.
Langlois, J.H., Roggman, L.A., Casey, R.J., Ritter, J.M., Rieser-Danner, L.A., & Jenkins, V.Y. (1987). Infant preferences for attractive faces: Rudiments of a stereotype? *Developmental Psychology, 23*, 263–369.
Leinbach, M.D. & Fagot, B.I. (1993). Categorical habituation to male and female faces: Gender schematic processing in infancy. *Infant Behavior and Development, 16*, 317–331.
Malatesta, C.Z., & Haviland, J.M. (1982). Learning display rules: The socialization of emotion expression in infancy. *Child Development, 53*, 991–1003.
Maratos, O. (1973). *The origin and development of imitation during the first 6 months of life.* Unpublished doctoral dissertation, University of Geneva, Switzerland.
Maurer, D. (1983). The scanning of compound figures by young infants. *Journal of Experimental Child Psychology, 35*, 437–448.
Maurer, D. & Barrera, M. (1981). Infants' perception of natural and distorted arrangements of a schematic face. *Child Development, 52*, 196–202.
McDougall, W. (1931). *Social psychology*, 2nd edn. London: Methuen.
McNeil, J.E. & Warrington, E.K. (1993). Prosopagnosia: A face- specific disorder. *Quarterly Journal of Experimental Psychology, 46A*, 1–10.
Melhuish, E.C. (1982). Visual attention to mother's and stranger's faces and facial contrast in 1-month-olds. *Developmental Psychology, 18*, 299–331.
Meltzoff, A.N. (1988). Infant imitation and memory: Nine-month-olds in immediate and deferred tests. *Child Development, 59*, 217–225.
Meltzoff, A.N. (1994). *Representation of persons: A bridge between infants' understanding of people and things.* Paper presented at the International Conference on Infant Studies, Paris, April.
Meltzoff, A. & Borton, R.W. (1979). Intermodal matching by human neonates . *Nature, 282*, 403–404.
Meltzoff, A.N. & Moore, M.K. (1977). Imitation of facial and manual gestures by human neonates. *Science, 198*, 75–78.
Meltzoff, A.N. & Moore, M.K. (1994). Imitation, memory, and the representation of persons. *Infant Behavior and Development, 17*, 83–99.
Nelson, C.A. & Dolgin, K.G. (1985). The generalized discrimination of facial expressions by seven-month-old infants. *Child Development, 56*, 58–61.
Nelson, C.A. (1987). The recognition of facial expressions in the first two years of life: Mechanisms of development. *Child Development, 58*, 889–909.
Piaget, J. (1962). *Play, dreams and imitation in the child.* New York: Norton.
Reissland, N. (1988). Neonatal imitation in the first hour of life: Observations in rural Nepal. *Developmental Psychology, 24*, 464–469.
Samuels, C.J., Butterworth, G., Roberts, A., Graupner, L., & Hole, G. (1994). Facial aesthetics: Infants prefer attractiveness to symmetry. *Perception, 23*, 823–831.
Samuels, C.J., & Ewy, R. (1985). Aesthetic perception of faces during infancy. *British Journal of Developmental Psychology, 3*, 221–228.
Slater, A.M. (1993). Visual perceptual abilities at birth: Implications for face perception. In B. de Boysson-Bardies, S. de Schonen, P. Jusczyk, P. McNeilage & J.Morton (eds), *Develop-*

mental neurocognition: speech and face processing in the first year of life. Dordrecht, Boston, London: Kluwer Academic Publishers.

Slater, A.M. (1995). Visual perception and memory at birth. In C.K. Rovee-Collier & L.P. Lipsitt (eds), *Advances in infancy research*, Vol. 9, pp. 105–155. Norwood, N.J.: Ablex.

Slater, A.M., Morison, V., Town, C., & Rose, D. (1985). Movement perception and identity constancy in the new-born baby. *British Journal of Developmental Psychology, 3*, 211–220.

Slater, A.M., Rose, D., & Morison, V. (1984). New-born infants' perception of similarities and differences between two- and three-dimensional stimuli. *British Journal of Developmental Psychology, 2*, 287–294.

Sorce, J.F., Emde, R.N., Campos, J.J., & Klinnert, M.D. (1985). Maternal emotional signaling: Its effects on the visual cliff behavior of 1-year-olds. *Developmental Psychology, 21*, 195–200.

Trevarthen, C. (1993). The functions of emotions in early infant communication and development. In J.Nadel and L.Camioni (eds) *New perspectives in early communicative development*. London: Routledge.

Vinter, A. (1986). The role of movement in eliciting early imitation. *Child Development, 57*, 66–71.

Walton, G.E., Bower, N.J.A., & Bower, T.G.R. (1992). Recognition of familiar faces by newborns. *Infant Behavior and Development, 15*, 265–269.

Watson, J. (1966). Perception of object orientation in infants. *Merrill-Palmer Quarterly, 12*, 73–94.

Yin, R.K. (1969). Looking at upside-down faces. *Journal of Experimental Psychology, 81*, 141–145.

10 Communication in Infancy: Mutual Regulation of Affect and Attention

Vasudevi Reddy
Department of Psychology, University of Portsmouth, UK.
Dale Hay
Faculty of Social & Political Sciences, University of Cambridge, UK.
Lynne Murray
Winnicott Research Unit, Department of Psychology, University of Reading, UK.
Colwyn Trevarthen
Department of Psychology, University of Edinburgh, UK.

Beginning in the 1970s, a view has been expressed that young infants exhibit a natural ability for "intersubjectivity", or an effective mind knowledge, and show an early ability to engage in communication with other psychological beings. This view has caused vigorous debate amongst psychologists who argue that early social interaction by human infants cannot be called true communication for a variety of reasons. Infant communication seen as entailing a perception of the other as a psychological recipient and partner is clearly antithetical to prevailing cognitive developmental approaches which view communication as mediated by late developing cognitions about mental states. Recently some writers have attempted a *rapprochement* by positing infant communication at the very end of the first year and in the second year as revealing good evidence of mental state understanding. However, the intersubjective status of infant communication in the first year, and especially in the first half of the first year, is still viewed with extreme scepticism. This scepticism is especially interesting given the wide acceptance of claims about the infant's knowledge of physical realities in the early months. Part of the resistance is due to a prevailing discomfort with the idea that early sociality originates from anything other than a starting point of asociality. It is also due in part to our continuing acceptance of the proposition that things mental, being invisible, are graspable only conceptually and with difficulty. The approach favoured in this paper views intersubjectivity as possible through an engagement of affects and attention.

It sees communication in the first year as skilled in and motivated by such engagement, rather than motivated by the drive to seek simple, behavioural and "non-mental" reactions.

In this paper, we describe patterns of early communication and then re-examine three issues fundamental to understanding the psychological significance of early communication: First, we review the evidence that communicative behaviour in the first year, and even in the first two months of life, can be truly mutual—i.e. that infants indeed regulate their actions and feelings in accordance with the actions and feelings of others. This being so, mutual regulation is not merely an illusion created by the skill and imagination of an accomplished partner. Evidence for mutual regulation is provided by three sets of studies: experimental disruptions of normal mother-infant interaction; studies of infants whose mothers suffer from depression; and studies of the interaction of infants with other infants. Second, we examine the proposition that what we have been calling communication in the early months of life is merely some reflexively driven expression of bodily states or behaviour which just happens to be communicative but is not intentional. The criteria conventionally used for deciding the onset of intentional communication are critically considered and found wanting. Finally, we consider the larger theoretical context in which to place observations of communication in infancy. We ask whether attachment as a motive is sufficient for explaining these early communicative behaviours. We argue that the current pre-occupation of attachment research with the strange situation has led to the neglect of such behaviour within much theorising. An exclusive focus on attachment as the motive for explaining early communication is insufficient. A more general motive for companionship beyond the single relationship is needed to explain the *why* of early communication.

INTERACTION IN THE FIRST MONTHS

Readiness for Communication

The human neonate appears to be adapted to an environment of consistent interpersonal contacts. Numerous studies reveal a preferential responsiveness for human over non-human stimuli shortly after birth. Such perceptual discriminations and preferences are evident in every modality—e.g., face-like features are preferred to scrambled shapes (Goren, Sarty, & Woo, 1975; others), the sound of the human voice is preferred to non-human sounds of similar pitch and intensity (Friedlander, 1970; Eisenberg, 1975), human milk taste is preferred over cow's milk, etc. Within the first few days and weeks preferences are shown for the particular characteristics (voice, face and smell) of the persons involved in the infant's care (DeCasper & Fifer, 1980; Bushnell, Sai, & Mullin, 1989; Cernoch & Porter, 1985).

Such preferences demonstrated experimentally appear to reveal a static "recognition" of stimulus characteristics; but the neonate's adaptation to things human is a dynamic and communicative one. The most impressive, as well as the most resisted, evidence of the human neonate's adaptedness to other humans is that of neonatal imitation. Carefully solicited, newborns can focus on and imitate, with voluntary and exploratory effort, a wide range of expressions, including facial, vocal and gestural movements (Maratos, 1973; 1982; Meltzoff & Moore, 1977; 1983; 1992; Field et al., 1982; Kugiumutzakis, 1985; 1993; Heimann & Schaller, 1985). These imitations are not reflexes. They are produced with effort (Kugiumutzakis) and reveal self-corrective changes in the imitation of the model's actions (Meltzoff, 1994). Neonatal imitations are most likely to appear in a reciprocating communication with the "model"; they are difficult to elicit in rigidly controlled conditions with adult actors who are offering pre-programmed expressions in repeating sequences and who are not supporting the infant's interest in a reciprocal affective interaction (Kugiumutzakis, 1993). In other words, outside an affectively regulated communicative interaction, imitation is harder to elicit from neonates. Further, once "taught", an imitation can be elicited by the reappearance of a partner in communication even with a delay of many hours. Thus the imitated expressions are clearly associated with some kind of "representation" that can be stored in the mind of the young infant (Meltzoff & Moore, 1992).

Notwithstanding these remarkable demonstrations of the capacity of human interpersonal awareness soon after birth, a newborn's contribution to interactions of a conversational kind are fragmentary, and the responses in reciprocal exchanges of expression are comparatively slow and inconsistent for several weeks.

Infants Maintaining Communication

When observing what happens between a 2-month-old infant and an adult partner who is attentive and solicitous, the impression of a mutual, conversation-like exchange can be vivid. Detailed analysis of interactions confirms the impression of co-ordination and reveals precise regularities in the timing of interactions (Brazelton, Koslowski, & Main, 1974; Trevarthen, 1974; 1975; 1977; 1979). The infant is likely to look attentively to the partner's face, to react with smiles and "coos", and to make active "pre-speech" movements of lips and tongue, wide open shapings of the mouth synchronised with a wide range of emotions and active gesturing of the hands (Trevarthen, 1993a). The adult, in turn, will typically address the infant with repeated calling in a relaxed high-pitched voice and will mark particular infant expressions and actions with smiles and vocalisations, often "attuning" to or complementing what the infant has done with enhanced mimicry (Snow, 1977; Trevarthen, 1977; Stern, 1985; Papousek & Papousek, 1989). This display is clearly regulated by both infant and adult; indeed, the adult is the more imitative or accommodating, taking cues from the infant's responses (Trevarthen, 1977). A rhythmic turntaking is set up, with chains of brief "utterances" by the infant stimulating the adult to join in a pattern of address and reply (Trevarthen, 1993b).

The most detailed analyses of these interactions have come from the more tightly regulated exchanges that occur after the first month, between 6 and 12 weeks after a full-term birth. Following the pioneering reports of M.C.Bateson (1975; 1979) these have been called "proto-conversations", because the behaviours by which the adult and infant interact exhibit many of the dynamic and physiognomic characteristics of the paralinguistic part of adult conversation: they resemble "utterances" emitted in turn that integrate vocalisations, smiling, eye-contact and hand gestures (Stern, 1974; Trevarthen, 1979). In fact, early advances in research on the regulation of mother–infant interactions was aided by application of techniques of "conversational analysis" developed for adults (Stern et al., 1977; Stern & Gibbon, 1980; Beebe et al., 1985). The timing of moves in protoconversations has proved to be remarkably close to that of adult–adult interactions. It has been established that the dynamic co-operation results from adult and infant taking complementary emotional positions from moment to moment. At any given moment they are likely to have expressions with differing emotional valence or interpersonal intensity of animation (Trevarthen, 1979; 1993a; 1993b). Each appears from time to time to challenge or invite the other and the force of these initiatives is reflected in a watchful or intimidated and retreating attitude of the other. Equilibration in a sharing of communication is signalled by reciprocal smiling and "utterances" (speech or imitative sounds by the adult and coos or prespeech lip and tongue movements by the infant) are exchanged at the mid level of animation, when the two subjects have set up a dynamic balance of initiatives (Trevarthen, 1979).

Infants Initiating Communication

One way in which the development of communication and communicative intentions can be explored and better understood is through an examination of the manner in which initiatives towards obtaining psychological responses from others are made by infants. That is, it is harder to conceive of interaction as non-communicative when the infant is not "merely responding" to others' communicative behaviour, but is herself initiating interaction. Fogel (1993) has argued that even in early communication there is a constant micro-level creation on both sides, through a continuous process of modification of current acts in the light of the other's behaviour. However, both the main gestures and expressions obvious to a casual observer, and those details of expression revealed in micro-analyses (Stern, 1974; Trevarthen, 1977; 1979; 1993a; 1993b) show that clear initiatives by the infant towards a partner who is inactive or unresponsive can appear quite early in infancy. The infant's expressiveness is not always just cued by the partner.

The 3-week old may appear to do little to invite interaction beyond broadcast signals of mood and an attentiveness, which can, nevertheless, exercise strong influence over others' efforts to join in communication. At first the infant seems to be drawn into a co-operative game by the recurrent, rhythmical and musical patterns of the partner's behaviour, which tend to match the spontaneous rhythms of the infant's movements. Soon the infant is responding to the emotions and intentional or attentional dynamics that are carried in the beat and rhythms, melody or pitch variation and timbre or quality of the partner's voice. By 6 weeks infants appear much more obviously social: smiling to a partner readily occurs and eye-to-eye contact is reliably maintained during interaction.

Then, soon after the beginning of this phase, when protoconversations appear at around 6 to 8 weeks, two clear types of communicative initiatives by infants become apparent. Firstly, following disruptions in the other's communicative behaviour, infants attempt a series of other-directed acts, including vocalisations and arm movements with gaze on the other's face (Cohn & Tronick, 1989; Murray, 1980) . If the adult is unresponsive the infant may increase the intensity of the normal "proto conversational" expressions (Trevarthen, 1990). Secondly, when the other is looking elsewhere, or the interaction has gone quiet, infants develop ways of "calling" the other, sometimes with a shrill vocalisation with a pleasant expression and gaze on the other's face (Reddy, personal observations). The infant gives the impression at this age of becoming a bolder and more confident partner in face-to-face interactions. In both cases, the initiatives appear to be directed towards and succeed in re-engaging the other's communicative attention to self.

Infants Avoiding Communication

That the communicative attention of others has a powerful effect on the infant can be seen not only from infants seeking to re-engage such attention when it is missing, or from infants revelling in it with confidence, but also from infants seeking to avoid it. Thus avoidance of attention may be seen as one of the infant's earliest devices for regulating interactions with others, and thus evidence for the mutuality of those interactions (Robson, 1967; Jaffe, Stern, & Peery, 1973; Stern, 1974; Murray & Trevarthen, 1985; Trevarthen, 1993b).

Three different affective tones to gaze avoidance can be identified within the course of an ongoing interaction in the early months. From at least as early as 6 weeks infants can turn their heads and gaze away repeatedly from mutual gaze in a self-contained and sober-faced way, even when their head turn brings them to a new visual field with no interesting content rather than some particular thing they may want to keep gazing at. As Brazelton et al. (1974), Stern (1985) and others have shown, this withdrawal of gaze can be caused by intrusive and insensitive demands for interaction from the other, and then neutral gaze avoidance becomes distressed gaze avoidance.

In addition to such neutral and negatively toned withdrawals of gaze, one can also find positive gaze aversion where, following an interaction initiative from a familiar other such as a greeting or even a smiling renewal of mutual gaze, the infant smiles deeply and averts head and gaze briefly, sometimes bringing its arms up in a complete movement with the fists curved near the face, then often turns back to the other (Reddy, 1992; 1994a). Such smiling gaze aversions have been recorded from about 10 weeks of age, following interaction initiations by familiar others, as well as in response to mutual gaze with the self in a mirror, a few weeks after the infant has been confidently "chatting" with friendly others. This behaviour looks to the naïve human viewer like shyness or coyness. It is reminiscent of coy reactions to intimate compliments in old-fashioned romances and meets the behavioural criteria for shyness and related self-conscious affective behaviour (Amsterdam, 1972; Amsterdam & Greenberg, 1977; Izard & Hyson, 198?; Lewis et al.,1989). It functions briefly to control the strong positive affect aroused in the infant by the familiar other's greetings or eye contact at the beginning of an interaction; and functions also to charm those who observe such intense reactions in the infant to themselves. The significance of such shy or coy behaviour is not that it indicates any conceptual or articulate awareness of self, but that it demonstrates an early perceptual awareness of the other's attentiveness to self which undoubtedly develops further within the particular contexts of attention exchanges and responses obtained and given. Further, gaze withdrawal may bear some relation to the genesis of a "topic" in speech or thought. In protoconversations, the infant's expressive "utterance" is usually accompanied by a brief withdrawal of gaze from the partner. Adults, too, turn the gaze from the interlocutor when making a statement or thinking of a topic (Trevarthen 1993b).

CHANGES IN THE SECOND HALF OF THE FIRST YEAR

Active participation in co-operative games

By 6 months of age infants demonstrate a more facile awareness and a keen pleasure in relating to the way familiar playmates respond to their creative expressions. They react with eager enthusiasm to often-repeated games that have a regular pattern of predictable changes in emotional force and tension (Stern, 1974; Trevarthen & Hubley, 1978; Trevarthen, 1986; 1987). Parents use this responsiveness to create joyful action games, chants, nursery songs, and the like, and make exaggerated facial expressions, nonsense speech and body movements that both challenge the infant's initiatives and confer "affect attunement" to reinforce and shape them (Stern et al., 1985). Bruner (Bruner & Sherwood, 1976; Ratner & Bruner, 1978) and Dore (1983) have related these games to the acquisition of grammatical rules, and Papousek and Papousek (1991) have drawn attention to the importance of the prosodic patterns of mothers' vocalisations. Increasing attention is being given to the responses of infants for musical forms of vocalisation with movement, and to their sensitivities to music and to the prosodic and poetic aspects of speech (Trevarthen & Marwick, 1986; Trevarthen, 1986; 1987; Trehub, Trainor, & Unyk, 1993).

The infant's participation in others' action games, nursery songs, etc., although beginning at about 3 months, becomes much more active during the last quarter of the first year (Bruner, 1977; Gustafson, Green, & West, 1979). More strikingly, however, the infant begins to establish his or her own games from this time (eg. Papousek & Papousek, 1981; 1989).

Directing Attention to Acts by Self

In the last quarter of the first year infants demonstrate an observed awareness of "being an actor" by showing off in comical ways to a mirror, treating their own image as a provocative partner, posturing what Wallon (1934) called a "prestance" or "impressive bearing". The "boldness" or pride of an infant's playful jokes and appreciation of teasing by a partner is a reliable indication of health and emotional well-being.

After about 7 or 8 months infants display unmistakable initiatives in soliciting attention not just *to* the self, but to *acts by* the self (Bates et al., 1979; Hubley & Trevarthen, 1979; Trevarthen, 1990). Clowning involves the repetition of odd or extreme behaviour (such as grimaces, postures, odd locomotion) which succeeds in eliciting laughter from others. Showing-off involves the repetition of a behaviour, often a conventional act, which elicits approval and attention from others. Clowning often begins with solitary explorations of extreme sensations produced by things such as shaking the head vigorously from side to side, screwing up the face, walking or breathing in a funny way, shouting in an extremely shrill shriek, and so on. The infant's sensitivity to laughter and attention then allow the detection of the specific oddities in their actions that others are laughing at, or the specific achievements which others are appreciatively attending to (Reddy, 1990).

Use of objects as topics.

Parents and siblings profit from the infant's imitations of comical movements and presentations of objects, involving the infant in person-person-object games (Trevarthen & Hubley, 1978; Bakeman & Adamson, 1984).

Before 6 months, infants often become totally absorbed in exploration of objects using hands and mouth, and are apparently oblivious to other people. In the second half of the first year they become more willing to mix social signs or demonstrations with their self-centred "work", aiming gestures to show what they are handling, seeking eye contact, or making vocal "comment" on what they do and the sounds they produce by banging, shaking or throwing objects. That is, before attaining the kind of curiosity about disappearances that is taken as evidence for "object permanence", infants bring objects into communication.

Around 8 months of age, infants begin to offer food and other objects to their mothers and other companions, including siblings and even dogs (Rheingold, Hay, & West, 1976). Over the next few months, infants characteristically use the offering gesture as a vehicle for co-operative games of give-and-take; the partner's requests for objects, followed by an offer back, dramatically increases the frequency of this early form of sharing (Hay & Murray, 1982). Around 12 months of age the basic give-and-take framework expands to include such exchanges as ballgames and using cups and jugs to pour imaginary liquids back and forth between partners (Hay, 1979).

Infant Initiated Novel Games

Apart from co-operating in conventional cultural routines or games, infants in the second half of the first year also reveal a clear ability to create novel games. The clearest examples of such games are provocative actions, or teasing, which are repeated, often for days on end, for their emotional effect on the other (Hubley & Trevarthen, 1979; Reddy, 1991; 1994b). Sometimes teasing acts can originate in accidental and/or meaningless acts which obtain their meaning solely from the response they subsequently obtain from others. These "proto-teasing" acts nonetheless reveal the infant's interest in focusing on the other's exaggerated protests and repeating the provocation in the prolonging of the new game. There are more striking examples of teasing which also emerge towards the end of the first year which originate as deliberate provocation either in order mischievously to disrupt the other's ongoing actions, or not to comply with a previously accepted prohibition, or to disrupt normally accepted gestures and routines. For example, gestures relating to use of objects such as offering, are very often followed by playful withdrawal rather than giving of the object. Even these deliberate provocations—i.e. otherwise meaningful and non-accidental actions—sometimes develop into games, depending on the other's response and the individual child's interests, often changing the motivational function of the act from disruptive provocation to seeking of the game. Sometimes, however, provocative teasing occurs in one-off episodes, with no game developing at all. For example, where compliance had previously been established on the issue, the infant might smile cheekily and partially non-comply on a single occasion with evidence of greater interest in the other's reactions than in the apparent object of non-compliance itself, and with no ensuing game. Such episodes are rarer than the teasing games, and are harder to observe and remember. However, they too are present in some infants' communicative behaviour before the end of the first year.

Social and emotional referencing

From around 9 months on, infants seem both to become sensitive to others' attentions and reactions to external objects and to seek to elicit such reactions by looking at the other (Bretherton & Bates, 1979; Trevarthen & Hubley, 1978; Trevarthen, 1987). This happens in cases where the infant is in an uncertain or ambiguous situation such as when confronted with a visual cliff (Klinnert et al., 1983), or with a toy that could potentially be either frightening or enjoyable (eg. Gunnar, Leighton, & Peleaux, 1984). Referencing, however, also occurs in cases where the infant is in a happy situation and looks around with a smile to an other who is not involved in the situation. Emotional referencing—checking the mother to perceive what she feels, within the context of flexible mutual orientation and joint awareness of physical surroundings and their potentialities—guides the infant to accept the same evaluations of the world as the partner holds. Bindra (1974) has argued that, as infants follow their mothers about the world, they become aware of the objects and events the mothers find interesting, distressing and pleasant, and that this form of social learning is more important than the more behavioural processes of social reinforcement and modelling. Through their sensitivity to the feelings and communicative attentions of their partners, infants are displaying special motives for learning how to share experiences of the world with other persons.

IS EARLY INTERACTION TRULY MUTUAL?

The evidence just reviewed, focusing primarily on infant–mother relationship, calls attention to an early capacity for the negotiation of harmonious interaction as well as important developments over the first 12 months of life. Nonetheless, although parents and "naïve" observers readily perceive a mutually regulated process in such episodes, the status of the infant's role has remained controversial. Thus, it has been proposed that the apparent two-way nature of the interchange is just that—apparent and not real—and that what is actually happening is that the adult partner, seeking to find communicative significance in the infants' activity, merely fills in gaps in an autonomous flow of infant behaviour. Eventually, it is alleged, the infant comes to register the connections between her own activity and the adult response, and by a process of association builds up a repertoire of communicative gestures (Kaye, 1982; Schaffer, 1984). Perhaps the intensity of the mother's own attachment to her infant provides a context in which the infant looks more skilful than he or she really is.

In this section we discuss three lines of research that examine infants outside the normal, harmonious relationship with the mother and thus provide additional opportunities to measure the infants' own contributions to such mutual exchanges. These areas of research are (1) experimental perturbations of mother–infant interaction; (2) studies of depressed mothers with their infants; and (3) studies of infants with other equally unskilled infants.

Perturbation Studies

An important source of data bearing on the issue of the extent to which early face-to-face contacts are mutually regulated has been a series of experimental studies involving brief perturbations to the adult partner's communication (Brazelton et al., 1975; Papousek & Papousek, 1975; Tronick et al., 1978; Murray & Trevarthen, 1985). Several of these studies have used the procedure of asking the mother to cease communicating with her infant and adopt a still, or blank, face. All have reported that infants between 6 and 12 weeks old have become quickly disturbed. Typically, an initial form of response is shown that has the characteristics of protest, the infant looking at the mother, frowning, thrashing the arms, and making effortful negative vocalisations. As the blank-face presentation continues the infant appears to cease efforts to solicit maternal responsiveness, and instead becomes withdrawn and self-absorbed, darting occasional glances in the mother's direction as though to check her availability. Over the years more sophisticated disruptions to the adult partner's communication have been effected in experimental studies, and one of the principal findings to emerge from this subsequent body of work is the specificity of the infant's response to different forms of disrupted contact (Murray & Trevarthen, 1985; Cohn & Tronick, 1989). For example, if, instead of simply presenting a blank face, the mother ceases to respond to the infant by turning to speak to another adult, and in so doing changes several parameters of her behaviour (voice pitch and contouring, rate of movement, and a profile rather than *en face* presentation), the infant shows neither distress, nor self-absorbed withdrawal, but quite appropriately, ceases to show the former active engagement with the mother (rates of smiling and active mouthing fall) and instead watches her, or the person with whom she is conversing, with quiet interest (Murray 1980; Murray & Trevarthen, 1985).

In a further experiment mother and infant communicated with each other via a closed circuit television or "double video" system (Murray, 1980;

Murray & Trevarthen, 1985). The image of the mother seen by the infant was displayed in either real, live time,where the mother could respond to the infant, or else in replayed time. In this replay condition the form of the other's response is held constant while its relationship in time to the infant's activity is disrupted. During the live sequences 6- to 12-week-old infants showed the full range of communicative behaviours seen in normal face-to-face interactions. But when the infants were presented with the same video sequence of the mother in replayed time they rapidly appeared confused and eventually became avoidant. This evidence of the sensitivity of infants as young as 6 weeks to the quality of the partner's response, and the specificity of the form of the infant behaviour in the face of the different forms of perturbation argues against an account of early mother–infant contacts in terms of the infants being passive and autonomous.

Even more compelling evidence of the active role of the infant in mother–infant communication derives from an experiment, again using the double video technique, but complementary to that described above, in which the timing of the mother's behaviour in relation to the infant's was perturbed (Murray, 1980; Murray & Trevarthen, 1985). In this second double video experiment, the mother experienced the perturbation, being presented with either live or replay video sequences of the infant in interaction with her. An analysis was conducted of maternal speech in the two conditions and consistent differences were found. In live sequences mothers showed all the usual characteristics of "motherese"; for example, speech was focused on infant experience and showed a predominance of interrogative and imperative syntactical forms. By contrast, in the condition where the infant communication video sequence was replayed, and therefore unresponsive to whatever the mother did, the characteristics of normal motherese were lost. These results are not consistent with a model of mother–infant engagement in which the adult's task in such situations is simply to fill in the gaps in the flow of infant behaviour. If this were so, there should be no difference in maternal response to live and replay conditions since the demands on the mother, according to this model, would be identical. The fact that the usual quality of infant-focused communication occurred only in live sequences attests to the fact that infant responsiveness, present only in the latter condition, is itself a key component of maternal communicative structure.

The conclusions arising from these experimental studies employing perturbations to either maternal or infant communication are the following: firstly, and most simply, from the first weeks of life infants are highly sensitive to the quality of adult communication. Further, they respond not only to simple alterations in form (for example, from an active and responsive partner to a still, blank face), but appear to process manifold parameters of adult displays in unison, treating each complex whole as specifying distinctive interpersonal positions. The strong affective quality of infant response to the adult's unavailability or incomprehensible behaviour attests, too, to the fact that infant emotionality is intimately bound up with the state of mutual engagement, and that there is a focused investment in achieving particular forms of contact. Finally,the finding that the quality of maternal behaviour depends on whether or not there is the potential responsiveness on the infant's part indicates that early mother–infant contacts are essentially mutually regulated, rather than arising as artefacts of one sophisticated and active partner (the adult) creating the illusion of communication with a simple, unresponsive infant.

Maternal Depression

Although communication is significantly disturbed in the context of depression, the infant still retains a repertoire of behaviours serving the purpose of social engagement (Cohn et al.,1990; Murray et al., 1994) that may be flexibly adapted to different communicative partners (Murray et al., 1994). However, studies involving rather older infants (4- to 6-month-olds) report significant differences in the communicative behaviour of infants of depressed and well mothers, depressed mothers' infants manifesting behaviour that resembles in many respects the response of the infants in normal populations to the experimental blank-face perturbation (Cohn et al., 1986; Field 1984; Field et al., 1988). In addition, Field and her colleagues have found that the more withdrawn and distressed behaviour of these older infants generalises to interactions with other, non-depressed adults, and even causes these adults to behave in a depressed-like fashion (Field et al., 1988). This latter finding provides compelling evidence for the infant's own contribution to early interaction.

Longitudinal follow-up of such samples (Murray et al., 1993) shows that the quality of mother–infant communication in the early postpartum months is strongly predictive of the infant's later cognitive performance. Assessments of the infant communicating with someone other than her mother, however, are not so (Murray et al., 1994). This body of work suggests, therefore, that a pattern of engagement between mother and infant evolves over the first months postpartum in which, in the context of maternal depression, there appears to be a progressive deterioration and growing inflexibility in infant responsiveness, which may have long-term consequences for cognitive functioning. Thus, although infants do, in fact, make their own important contributions to interactions with their mothers, and those interactions thereby qualify as mutually regulated, continued development of interactional as well as cognitive skills seems to depend on the mother's active, non-depressed participation and scaffolding of the infant's developing abilities.

Peer Interaction

On the face of it, early peer relations seem quite different from those between mothers and infants on almost every front. Mothers, even mothers who are depressed or modifying their behaviour according to experimental instructions, are more skilled, engaged and committed social partners than other infants could possibly be. Observations of infants with each other thus provide an extreme test of their capacities for social interaction, further along on the continuum represented by the perturbation studies or the studies of infants with mothers who are ill.

Before a resurgence of interest in the 1970s, the topic of peer relations in infancy was last examined in detail by investigators such as Charlotte Buhler and Lois Murphy in the 1930s. The longstanding disregard of early peer relations probably derived from two key accounts of early interaction: Parten's characterisation of toddlers' interactions as being dominated by "parallel play" in which the children might be in physical proximity but engaged in quite independent activity, and Maudry and Nekula's (1939) description of the infant as "socially blind"—i.e. participating in interaction with peers as part of an individualistic quest for toys, not as a goal in its own right. These earlier characterisations were echoed by Bronson (1981) in an influential monograph.

Nonetheless, observations of pairs of infants interacting with each other suggest that the communication with peers follows a developmental pathway roughly similar to that followed by infants with their mothers, and that the lag between attainments being shown firstly with the mother and subsequently with peers is a matter of months, not years (for a review and a general model with which to chart the development of social relationships in infancy and early childhood, see Hay, 1985).

Initially it appears that 2- and 3-month-old infants respond to each other's presence with diffuse arousal. Experimental studies have contrasted young infants' reactions to their peers v. their mothers (Fogel, 1979) or to peers v. their own reflections in a mirror (Field, 1979). In these studies, infants were reported to show diffuse excitement in the presence of peers, as opposed both to more discrete social actions such as smiling to the mother and quiet contemplation of self in a mirror. More recent research has, however, suggested that, given regular familiarity with their own face in a mirror, even three-month-olds will begin to interact joyfully with themselves (Reddy, 1993). There may be an inhibition of responses to an unfamiliar partner from early in infancy, comparable to the frank fear of strangers shown later.

At this early point in development, whilst infants are unable to locomote, dyadic peer interaction is actually nested within the interaction of a quartet of infants and caregivers. Thus infants' capacities for interaction with peers are largely supported by the interaction between the caregivers, which thus may lead to the sort of conceptual problems already discussed concerning the creation of social illusions. Nonetheless, by 6 months of age, discrete social actions such as smiling or vocalising whilst looking at the peer or reaching out to touch the peer can be discerned (Hay, Nash, & Pedersen, 1983; Vandell et al., 1980). Furthermore, over the course of an interaction between 6-month-old peers, mutual regulation can be discerned; for example, infants whose peers fuss or cry for a minute or two are reliably likely to start to fuss or cry themselves (Hay, Nash, & Pedersen, 1981).

We noted earlier that, when interacting with their mothers, young infants often regulate the flow of interactional information by averting their gaze or temporarily withdrawing from the interaction. Mothers' behaviour then changes accordingly, confirming that they are indeed interacting with a more or less responsive partner, not simply acting autonomously in a way that creates the illusion of interaction; the perturbation experiment in which mothers were required to interact with delayed-time video images of their infants is simply an extreme version of this process (Murray & Trevarthen, 1985).

A similar sort of responsivity to a partner's failure to interact was found in observations of pairs of 6-month-old infants, in terms of the infants' reactions to being touched by their peers (Hay et al., 1983). About half of the time infants reacted passively to being touched by the peer; however, if they did respond more actively, they were reliably more likely to continue the interaction by reaching for or touching the peer in turn than to terminate it by fussing or withdrawing from the mutual contact. Furthermore, the partner's initial reaction to being touched–touching back or not—seemed to serve as feedback to the initiator. When the recipient of a touch touched back, the first infant was about equally likely to continue the interaction with another touch or not. However, when the peer did not reciprocate the touch, the first infant was reliably less likely to touch again. Thus, just as 6-month-olds are sensitive to their mother's reactions in terms of continuing or withdrawing from a particular exchange, so they seem sensitive to the reactions of their peers.

Over the second half of the first year, just as in the case of interaction with the mother, infant peers seem to become more able to use objects as topics for interaction. Initially the presence of toys in the environment seems to be somewhat distracting; in the experiment just described, infants were reliably more likely to touch their peers when toys were absent (Hay et al., 1983), a finding also remarked upon by other investigators (e.g. Eckerman & Whatley, 1977; Vandell et al., 1980). Given the earlier characterisation of young infants as "socially blind" one might be tempted to conclude that they use each other as toys when more conventional toys are absent; nonetheless, the extent to which 6-month-olds touch toys when present does not predict the extent to which they touch peers when toys are absent (Hay et al., 1983), suggesting that the two tendencies are not indeed measures of the same general trait.

It also appears that the peer's holding of an object may make it more attractive. This was seen in the interactions of older toddlers when duplicate copies of toys were available; a child holding one toy wheelbarrow might drop it in order to go over and grab on to an identical wheelbarrow held by the peer (Hay & Ross, 1982). Even at 6 months of age, the factors that predict touching toys in general do not seem to be the same as those that predict interest in toys held by peers: 6-month-old boys are reliably more likely than six-month-old girls to touch toys held by peers, even though there are no overall gender differences in the tendency to touch toys in general.

Over the next 6 months of life, as in the case of mother–infant interaction, the protodeclarative gestures of pointing, showing, and offering toys come to be directed to peers as well as to adult companions. Twelve-month-old infants, tested in groups of three with all three mothers presented, offered objects to each other at a rate that did not differ significantly from that of peers a year older (Hay, Caplan, Castle, & Stimson, 1991; see also Franco, Perucchini, & Butterworth, 1992). Indeed, by 12 months of age, the interactions of peers show sequences of both co-operative and conflictual exchange that are virtually identical to the interactions of much older children (Caplan, Vespo, Pedersen, & Hay, 1991). What changes over the second year of life is the use of words and certain strategies in such encounters, not the basic capacity for co-operation or conflict. Co-operation and conflict with peers would seem to emerge around 9 months of age, at about the same time that, in the context of the mother–infant relationship, infants are becoming aware of separations and disappearances and are showing more signs of self-awareness in relation to others' awareness, as described above. Six-month-olds simply do not react to their peers' behaviours with protest or other signs of annoyance, even though the peers may be toppling over on top of them or yanking on their hair. Such overtures are likely, however, to meet with protest, resistance, or retaliation at 12 months of age. Even 12-month-olds, however, are reliably more likely than 24-month-olds to respond to their peers' expressions of interest in an object with sharing, rather than protest or self-defence (Hay et al., 1991). Therefore, the early emergence of conflict between peers is interesting in that it shows co-ordinated exchange with objects as topics; nevertheless, although most 12-month-olds do sometimes engage in conflict, the rates are low, and sharing and co-operative use of resources seem developmentally prior to conflict and aggression.

In general, then, much would seem to develop between 6 and 12 months of life in the use of objects as a topic for sustained communication between peers as in communication with adults. Nevertheless, even 6-month-olds betray considerable interest in their peers, emotional responsiveness to peers' distress, positive rather than negative reactions to physical contact and mutual use of toys, and a sensitivity to feedback from their peers that guides subsequent interaction. These observations further confirm the infant's capacity for mutual interaction in the first year of life.

WHEN DO COMMUNICATIVE INTENTIONS APPEAR? A CRITIQUE OF CURRENT CRITERIA OF INTENTIONAL COMMUNICATION

One issue which has for years intermittently bedevilled the literature on preverbal communication has been the question of the intentionality of communicative acts. The current form of the debate has adopted the language of knowledge of mental states to tackle this difficult problem. There are many reasons to avoid re-opening this debate, the simplest one being that semantic and definitional problems constantly confound developmental ones. The issue of intentionality is in itself interpretable in a multitude of ways: as goal directedness (where the end state may be seen as stable and anticipated prior to action or as constantly unfolding during interaction); as object directedness (Vedeler, 1991); or as purposive or motivated action (Trevarthen, 1979; 1980).

However, there is also a strong reason to confront it now, arising from a current effort to find a more or less single point in developmental time as the beginning of intentional communication. These attempts are motivated by a desire either to differentiate it from some earlier and lesser form of interaction (eg. to emphasise the special status of communication at 12 months as different from that at 10 months), or to liken an early form to later more sophisticated behaviour (eg. to show how communication at 12 months is similar to that in older children). Whichever the reason, there is an underlying assumption that communicative intentions are cognitive activities, emerging in development at a discrete point in time after which the organism's interactions are categorically different from before. This quest for a point in time when communicative intentions appear is rather like the proverbial search for the moment when the soul enters the body! Far from clarifying differences between levels of communication and thus enhancing our understanding of development, such categorical before and after distinctions seem to exaggerate differences, and in fact conceal the process of change. Focusing on categorical differences rather than continuities clouds rather than illuminates our understanding of the development of communication.

If one were to accept current criteria, none of the interactions described thus far would qualify as evidence of communicative intentions in the infant.

Three clear (but ultimately arbitrary) criteria for establishing the achievement of intentional communication are generally used (Bates et al., 1979; Bretherton et al., 1981): (1) the presence of gaze alternation between the receiver and the external referent of the communicative act; (2) the repair of failed messages by augmenting the intensity of communicative behaviour or substituting a new gesture or "means" for the first; and (3) the ritualisation of gestures—i.e. behaviours that previously served purely instrumental functions which are transformed into ritualised signals.

The age at which these various criteria are met by infants is, however, a difficult one to pinpoint. The three criteria may not be achieved at one time by an infant. Nor do the norms for the three average down to a narrow time window: they are achieved on average between 9 and 15 months. Nonetheless, these criteria assume some coherent cognitive shift in understanding which underpins the onset of intentional communication.

Camaioni (1993) argues that even these criteria are inadequate for demonstrating intentional communication. According to her, gaze alternation "certainly does not mean that intentional communication has been achieved"; it merely creates an external focus of attention, providing a basis from which topics of conversation can emerge. Camaioni argues against a conflation of intentionality in communication with instrumentality or agency. What is necessary for intentional communication according to Camaioni is: (1) evidence of a "non-instrumental interest in the other as an end in itself", (2) evidence of the child's view of the other person as having intentions; and (3) evidence of the child's view of the other as understanding one's communicative intentions. Accordingly, she criticises the Bates et al. (1979) "tool-use hypothesis" of the origins of intentional communication, arguing that it is only sometime after the emergence of instrumental or imperative use of persons that communicative intentions can be visible in proto-declarative acts, i.e. at 12 months (or even 14 months; see Franco & Butterworth, 1988).

But what of infant interactions before 12 months? We are now in the odd position of admitting that before meeting these criteria, infant actions towards other persons are clearly intentional and clearly communicative, but are not intentionally communicative. What, then, are the intentions of the other-directed acts of the 3-month-old or the 6-month-old or indeed even of the 10-month-old? The conclusion would have to be that if the actions were intentional at all, then their intentions must be to achieve instrumental ends of a purely behavioural kind.

This assumption of the blindness of the infant to the psychological nature of the other is a commonly accepted implication of the fundamental Cartesian tenet about the invisibility of mind. However, it is intensely problematic for explaining the development of mind understanding (Hobson, 1991; Butterworth, 1994). One implication of this mind–behaviour dualism is that it posits minds as unreal entities to be hypothesised from behaviour. We would argue on the contrary, that the other's intentions and understandings are a part of the other's behaviour, and as such need to be observed, understood in context and perhaps abstracted, but not invented as theoretical entities (Newton, 1994). The evidence of early sensitivity, even at 2 months, to the appropriateness, relevance, emotionality and force of the other's communicative responses, already demonstrates that infants show sensitivity to the mentality of others. Thus, rather than argue that communicative intentions originate somehow in the "discovery" of minds which some put at 3 years, and some at 12 months, we argue that even the newborn seeks to find communicative contact with other persons. We have presented evidence that as early as 2 months, infants not only seek to communicate with others, but also discriminate others' psychological responses to such attempts. It is upon this basis that both communicative understanding and the communicative intentions themselves are elaborated in development.

Criteria such as the externality of a referent in communication are interesting reflections of developmental change, indicating the growing articulateness of communicative behaviour around "topics". But such criteria can neither be sensibly used to determine the origins of communicative intent, nor can they be used to indicate a single point of achievement. The fact that infants' earliest affective exchanges are not "about" something outside of the organism makes these emotional acts components of a different level of communication, but does not necessarily disqualify them as non-accidental and non-reflexive communication. Consider the emotional communing of lovers: there is an exchange of looks and smiles and affects there without any clear "object" to their communication (see Stern, 1985, for a discussion of core relatedness). This is nonetheless intentional communication. And it is in this sense that infants at 2 months can be said genuinely to be showing communicative intentions at a directly interpersonal level (Trevarthen, 1993b). Further, the emergence of external referents does not happen as one shift. The contents of infant communicative acts change gradually, from being simply affective (at 2 months) to including controlled expressions of affect (at 5 or 6 months), acts by the self and acts on the body (from 7 or 8 months in showing-off and clowning), and acts on the external world (from 9 or 10 months in giving, or after 12 months in protodeclarative pointing). The attainment of externality, and indeed of a non-instrumental interest in the other, can thus equally well be fixed at 6 months or at 9 months or at 12 months.

The question we are trying to answer is about the beginnings of communicative intentions. The conventional criteria, in attempting to pinpoint the cognitive prerequisites and indeed co-requisites for intentional communication, say very little about the origins of such intentions, beyond positing parental mis-attributions as a possible cause. However, communicative intentions cannot originate in a cognitive clarification of the nature of other persons as mental beings. They necessarily originate in motivations. While an understanding of what it means to communicate undoubtedly develops in complexity throughout life, such an understanding cannot be responsible for the emergence of the motive to communicate. We may wish to pick up particular points in the understanding to evaluate communicative interactions differently. However, there are many such time points rather than a single one that are of relevance to intentionality in communication.

Just as it is wrong to assume that the first birthday, or any other point in infancy, is the point at which communicative intentions emerge, so also is it wrong to assume that by this point in time they have emerged in full. If we adopt a genuinely mutualist approach to the emergence of communication we have to accept that, although the infant is predisposed to be a genuine participant in communication with the right partners from very early in life, nonetheless both knowledge about the effects of communicative acts on others, and the very communicative intentions themselves—i.e. the what and how and why of communicating—are changing and diversifying within interaction throughout life.

COMPANIONSHIP OR ATTACHMENT?

What are the broader interpretations of the infant's tendency to engage in, affectively relate to and control communicative exchanges with others? Is early communication motivated and sufficiently explained by the development of focused attachment relationships?

The current preoccupations of attachment research are largely with the strange situation, and with individual differences in patterns of attachment and their sequelae. Further, although Bowlby (1969) acknowledged that infants may be attached to persons other than their biological mother, it is the single attachment relationship that has received the most attention. A general motive for companionship beyond and before attachment relationships has by and large been neglected.

This neglect is a feature of the way in which attachment research has progressed rather than a necessary conclusion from the original theory. It might be argued that the early theory did not preclude the wider motivational focus that we are arguing for. Winnicott's perspective (Winnicott, 1960) can, for example, be extended to explain the readiness of infants to form companionable, playful relationships with familiar persons other than the mother, and independently of their provision of food and comfort. In Winnicott's view, early communication might be motivated either by the infant's attachment needs or by a broader need for companionship with other familiar humans.

A focus on the infant's striving for companionship with a number of other persons, with attachment relationships emerging as part of that more general human capacity for mutual, intentional communication, forms one of the major criticisms of the evolutionary, as opposed to the developmental, aspects of Bowlby's attachment theory (see Nash, 1988; Nash & Hay, 1993). Current evolutionary thinking rejects groups selection arguments (which Bowlby's theory was premised upon) in favour of individual cost–benefit arguments. We are not persuaded that an analysis of individual costs and benefits captures the fundamental nature of evolution. Nonetheless, the emphasis it has placed on the human infant's adaptation for social relations in general, as opposed to a single relationship, mirrors the emphasis in this paper on a motive for companionship as well as for attachment.

An emphasis on the development of communication in the first months of life rests on a characterisation of infants as beings who are acutely aware of and interested in their companions and in the world they can share with them. In the course of their daily encounters with caregivers, especially their mothers, that interest and motivation gradually translates into a capacity for mutual and co-operative interaction. As infants turn attention to the environment and come to regulate their emotions about experiences with reference to the emotions of their caregivers, they clearly become motivated to seek the comfort and protection of their mothers and other important adults in times of difficulty or stress. Thus particular attachment motivation may be developing in the second half of the first year of life, perhaps growing out of but still perceptibly distinct from the earlier, more basic foundation of the infant's fundamental desire for companionship.

Throughout the history of psychology, it has been notoriously difficult to pin down motives for particular forms of action, and the case of early communication will prove no exception to that rule. Communicative behaviours no doubt have multiple functions and complex motivation. Nonetheless, it is very important not to study early forms of communication in a very narrow theoretical context, merely as precursors to later attachment behaviours. Rather, a broader analysis of the range of variation in early communication, with rather more attention to individual differences in infants than has been paid to date, might elucidate the development of patterns of attachment over the first year of life.

Contemporary attachment theory has placed the greatest emphasis on differences in maternal sensitivity in the early months as a major cause of secure v. insecure patterns in the second year (Ainsworth & Wittig, 1969; Ainsworth et al., 1978). Yet the studies of early communication reviewed in this chapter show that the 6-week-old infant, or even the neonate, is not a passive partner, but rather has an important role to play in even the earliest exchanges. In view of the infant's active role in early communicative interactions, the notion that attachment patterns are derived solely from maternal sensitivity or insensitivity seems untenable. Analyses of infants' contributions to their own attachment relationships need to move beyond gross assessments of temperamental features (see Belsky & Cassidy, 1994). Studies of infants' own tendencies to initiate and avoid communication with their mothers may prove much more fruitful (Trevarthen & Aitken, in press). And, in seeking to document meaningful individual differences amongst infants in the first months of life, the studies of infants of depressed mothers will serve to highlight important patterns of variation.

SUMMARY AND CONCLUSIONS

The present paper has presented evidence of the nature and developments in communication through the first year of infancy. We have affirmed that infants are born with a readiness for communicative interactions, shown in behaviours such as neonatal imitation, and that they are capable of complex ways of maintaining, initiating and regulating communicative interactions as early as 2 and 3 months of age. These interactions are characterised by subtle engagement of affect and attention on the part of both participants. In the second half of the first year, the early affective engagement develops into interactions in which games, both conventional and novel, are dominant, and in which "topics" enter into the dyadic communication. From as early as 7 or 8 months, objects as well as the actions of the infant and of the other become topics for obtaining and regulating the other's affects and attention by the infant. Further, the other's affects and attention become read by the infant as related to the topics under attention.

The paper has discussed issues concerning the mutuality, the intentionality and the motivational basis of such communication. The mutuality of early communication may now be taken as read, given the converging evidence from experimental perturbation studies, clinical studies of depressed mothers and their infants, and observations of infants with like-aged peers. The infant is an active partner seeking both to initiate and influence the course of communication. In discussing criteria for determining the intentionality of infant communication we have argued that communicative intentions emerge from innate motivations to engage psychologically with others, rather than from a late appearing cognitive restructuring of the nature of persons, and a discovery of their minds. It seems imperative to abandon strictly dualistic, stage theories that posit a switching on of communicative intentionality at a particular point around the first birthday, and instead to study its emergence and elaboration as a continuous, multi-faceted process. We have argued that contemporary attachment theory is insufficient on its own for providing a motivational explanation of early infant interest in and communicative behaviour towards people other than attachment figures. We have posited, along with Winnicott among others, that there is a motive for companionship as well as for attachment, both of which are evident in the first year.

REFERENCES

Ainsworth, M.D.S. & Wittig, B.A. (1969). Attachment and exploratory behaviour of one-year-olds in a strange situation. In B.M. Foss (ed.), *Determinants of infant behaviour*, Vol.4. London: Methuen.

Ainsworth, M.D.S., Blehar, M.C., Waters, E., & Wall, S. (1978). *Patterns of attachment: a psychological study of the strange situation*. Hillsdale, N.J.: Lawrence Erlbaum Associates Inc.

Amsterdam, B. (1972). Mirror self-image reactions before age two. *Developmental Psychobiology*, *5* (4), 297–305.

Amsterdam, B. & Greenberg, L.M. (1977). Self-Conscious Behaviour of Infants. *Developmental Psychobiology*, *10*(1), 1–6.

Bakeman, R. and Adamson, L. B. (1984). Coordinating attention to people and objects in mother–infant and peer–infant interaction. *Child Development*, *55*, 1278–1289.

Bates, E., Benigni, L., Bretherton, I., Camaioni, L., & Volterra, V. (1979). *The emergence of symbols: cognition and communication in infancy*. New York: Academic Press.

Bateson, M.C. (1975). Mother–infant exchanges: The epigenesis of conversational interaction. In D. Aronson & R.W. Rieber (eds), *Developmental psycholinguistics and communication disorders*. Annals of the New York Academy of Sciences, Vol. 263. New York: New York Academy of Sciences.

Bateson, M.C. (1979). The epigenesis of conversational interaction: A personal account of research development. In M. Bullowa (ed.), *Before speech: the beginning of human communication*, pp. 63–77. London: Cambridge University Press.

Beebe, B., Jaffe, J., Feldstein, S., Mays, K., & Alson, D. (1985). Inter-personal timing: The application of an adult dialogue model to mother–infant vocal and kinesic interactions. In T.M. Field & N. Fox (eds), *Social perception in infants*. Norwood, N.J.: Ablex.

Belsky, J. & Cassidy, J. (1994). Attachment: Theory and evidence. In M.Rutter & D.F. Hay (eds), *Development through life: a handbook for clinicians*. Oxford: Blackwell.

Bindra, D.A. (1974). A motivational view of learning, performance and behaviour modification. *Psychological Review*, *81*, 199–213.

Bowlby, J.W. (1969). *Attachment and loss*. London: The Tavistock Institute of Human Relations.

Brazelton T.B., Koslowski, B., & Main, M. (1974). The origins of reciprocity: The early mother–infant interaction. In M. Lewis & L.A. Rosenblum (eds), *The effect of the infant on its caregiver*, pp. 49–76. New York & London: Wiley.

Brazelton, T.B., Tronick, E., Adamson, L., Als, H., & Wise, S. (1975). Early mother–infant reciprocity, pp. 137–154. In E. Hofer (ed.), *Parent–infant interactions*. Ciba Foundation Symposium, 33. Amsterdam: Elsevier.

Bretherton, I., McNew, S., & Beeghly-Smith, M. (1981). Early person-knowledge as expressed in gestural and verbal communication: When do infants acquire a "theory of mind"? In M.E. Lamb and L.R. Sherrod (eds), *Infant social cognition*. Hillsdale, N.J.: Lawrence Erlbaum Associates Inc.

Bretherton, I. & Bates, E. (1979). The emergence of intentional communication. In I.C. Uzgiris (ed.), *New directions for child development*, Vol. 4. San Francisco: Jossey-Bass.

Bronson, W.C. (1981). Toddlers' behaviour with agemates: Issues of interaction, cognition and affect. In L.P. Lipsitt (ed.), *Monographs on infancy*, Vol. 1. Norwood, N.J.: Ablex.

Bruner, J.S. (1977). Early social interaction and language acquisition. In H.R. Schaffer (ed.), *Studies in mother–infant interaction*. London: Academic Press.

Bruner, J.S. & Sherwood, V. (1976). Early rule structure: The case of "peekaboo". In: R. Harre (ed.), *Life sentences: aspects of the social role of language*. New York & London: Wiley.

Bushnell, I.W.R., Sai, F., & Mullin, J.T. (1989). Neonatal recognition of the mother's face. *British Journal of Developmental Psychology*, *7*, 3–15.

Butterworth, G. (1994). Theory of mind and the facts of embodiment. In C. Lewis & P. Mitchell (eds), *Children's early understanding of mind: origins and development*. Hove, U.K.: Lawrence Erlbaum Associates Ltd.

Camaioni, L. (1993). The development of intentional communication: A re-analysis. In J.Nadel and L.Camaioni (eds), *New perspectives in early communicative development*. London: Routledge.

Caplan, M., Vespo, J., Pedersen, J., & Hay, D.F. (1991). Conflict over resources in small groups of one- and two-year-olds. *Child development*, *62*, 1513–1524.

Cernoch, J.M. & Porter, R.H. (1985). Recognition of maternal axillary odors by infants. *Child Development*, *56*, 1593–1598.

Cohn, J.F., Matias, R., Tronick, E.Z., Connell, D., & Lyons-Ruth, D. (1986). Face-to-face interactions of depressed mothers and their infants. In E.Z. Tronick and T. Field (eds), *Maternal depression and infant disturbance: new directions for child development*, *34*, San Francisco: Jossey-Bass.

Cohn, J.F. & Tronick, E.Z. (1989). Specificity of infants' response to mothers' affective behaviour. *Journal of the American Academy of Child and Adolescent Psychiatry*, *28*, 242–248.

Cohn, J.F., Campbell, S.B., & Matias, R. (1990). Face-to-face interactions of postpartum depressed and non-depressed mother-infant pairs at two months. *Developmental Psychology*, *26*, 15–23.

DeCasper, A.J. & Fifer, W.P. (1980). Of Human Bonding: Newborns prefer their mothers' voices. *Science*, *208*, 1174–1176.

Dore, J. (1983). Feeling, form and intention in the baby's transition to language. In R. Golinkoff (ed.), *The transition from prelinguistic communication*. Hillsdale, N.J.: Lawrence Erlbaum Associates Inc.

Eckerman, C.O. & Whatley, J.L. (1977). Toys and social interaction between infant peers. *Child Development*, *48*, 1645–1656.

Eisenberg, R.B. (1975). *Auditory competence in early life: the roots of communicative behaviour*, Baltimore: University Park Press.

Field, T.N. (1979). Differential behavioural and cardiac responses of 3-month-old infants to a mirror and a peer. *Infant Behaviour and Development*, *2*, 179–184.

Field, T., Woodson, R., Greenberg, R., & Cohen, D. (1982). Discrimination and imitation of facial expression byneonates. *Science*, *218*, 179–81.

Field, T.N. (1984). Early interactions between infants and their postpartum depressed mothers. *Infant Behaviour and Development*, *7*, 517–522.

Field, T.N., Healy, B., Goldstein, S., Perry, S., Bendell, D., Schanberg, S., Zimmerman, E.A., & Kuhn, C. (1988). Infants of depressed mothers show "depressed" behaviour even with non-depressed adults. *Child Development*, *59*, 1569–1579.

Fogel, A. (1979). Peer v. mother-directed behaviour in 1- to 3-month-old infants. *Infant Behaviour and Development*, *2*, 215–226.

Fogel, A. (1993). Two principles of communication:co-regulation and framing. In J. Nadel and L. Camaioni (eds), *New perspectives in early communicative development*. London: Routledge.

Franco, F. & Butterworth, G. (1988). *The social origins of pointing in human infancy*. Paper presented at the Annual Conference of the Developmental Psychology Section of the BPS, Coleg Harlech, Wales.

Franco, F., Perucchini, P., & Butterworth, G. (1992). *Pointing for an age-mate in 1–2-year-olds*. Presented at the 5th European Conference on Developmental Psychology, Seville.

Friedlander, B. (1970). Receptive language development in infancy. *Merrill-Palmer Quarterly, 16*, 7–51.

Goren, C.G., Sarty, M., & Wu, P.Y.K. (1975). Visual following and pattern discrimination of face-like stimuli by newborn infants. *Paediatrics, 56*, 544–549.

Gunnar, M.R., Leighton, K., & Peleaux, R. (1984). Effects of temporal predictability on the reactions of 1-year-olds to potentially frightening toys. *Developmental Psychology, 20*, 449–458.

Gustafson, G.E., Green, J.A., & West, M.J. (1979). The infant's changing role in mother–infant games: The growth of social skills. *Infant Behaviour and Development, 2*, 301–308.

Hay, D.F. (1979). Cooperative interactions and sharing between very young children and their parents. *Developmental Psychology, 15*, 647–653.

Hay, D.F. (1985). Forming relationships in infancy: Parallel attainments with parents and peers. *Developmental Review, 5*, 122–161.

Hay, D.F. & Ross, H.S. (1982). The social nature of early conflict. *Child Development, 53*, 105–113.

Hay, D.F. & Murray, P. (1982). Giving and requesting: Social facilitation of infants' offers to adults. *Infant Behaviour and Development, 5*, 301–310.

Hay, D.F., Nash, A., & Pederson, J. (1981). Responses of six-month-olds to the distress of their peers. *Child Development, 53*, 557–562.

Hay, D.F., Nash, A., & Pederson, J. (1983). Interactions between six-month-old peers. *Child Development, 54*, 557–562.

Hay, D.F., Caplan, M., Castle, J., & Stimson, C.A. (1991). Does sharing become increasingly "rational" in the second year of life? *Developmental Psychology, 27*, 987–993.

Heimann, M. & Schaller, J. (1985). Imitative reactions among 14–21-day-old infants. *Infant Mental Health Journal, 6*(1), 31–39.

Hobson, R.P. (1991). Against the theory of "Theory of Mind." *British Journal of Developmental Psychology, 9*, 33–51.

Hubley, P. & Trevarthen, C. (1979). Sharing a task in infancy. In I. Uzgiris (Ed.), *Social interaction during infancy: new directions for child development*, pp. 57–80. San Francisco: Jossey-Bass.

Izard, C. & Hyson, M. (1986). Shyness as a discrete emotion. In H.J. Warren, J.M. Cheek, & S.R. Briggs (eds), *Shyness: Perspectives on research and treatment*. N.Y.: Plenum Press.

Jaffe J., Stern D.N., & Peery, J.C. (1973). Conversational coupling of gaze behaviour in prelinguistic human development. *Journal of Psycholinguistic Research, 2*, 321–330.

Kaye, K. (1982). *The mental and social life of babies*. Brighton: Harvester Press.

Klinnert, M.D., Campos, J.J., Sorce, J.F., Ende, R.N., & Svejda, M. (1983). Emotions as behavior regulators: Social referencing in infancy. In R. Plutchik and H. Kellerman (eds), *Emotion: theory, research and experience*, Vol. 2. New York: Academic Press.

Kugiumutzakis, G. (1985). The origins, development and function of early infant imitation. Doctoral dissertation Uppsala University. *Acta Universitatis Uppsaliensis, 35*.

Kugiumutzakis, G. (1993). Intersubjective vocal imitation in early mother–infant interaction. In J. Nadel & L. Camaioni (eds), *New perspectives in early communicative development*. London: Routledge.

Lewis, M., Sullivan, M.W., Stanger, C., & Weiss, M. (1989). Self-development and self-conscious emotions. *Child Development, 60*, 146–156.

Maratos, O. (1973). The origin and development of imitation in the first six months of life. Doctoral dissertation, University of Geneva.

Maratos, O. (1982). Trends in development of imitation in early infancy. In T.G. Bever (ed.), *Regressions in mental development: basis phenomena and theories*, pp. 81–101. Hillsdale, N.J.: Lawrence Erlbaum Associates Inc.

Maudry, M. & Nekula, M. (1939). Social relations between children of the same age during the first two years of life. *Journal of Genetic Psychology*, *54*, 193–215.

Meltzoff, A.N. & Moore, M.K. (1977). Imitation of facial and manual gestures by human neonates. *Science*, *178*, 75–78.

Meltzoff, A.N. & Moore M.K. (1983). Newborn infants imitate adult facial gestures. *Child Development*, *54*, 702–709.

Meltzoff, A.N. & Moore, M.K. (1992). Early imitation within a functional framework: The importance of personal identity, movement and development. *Infant Behavior and Development*, *15*, 479–505.

Meltzoff, A. (1994). *Foundations for the notion of self*. Paper presented in symposium on Early Sense of Self, 9th International Conference on Infant Studies, Paris 2–5 June.

Murray, L. (1980). The sensitivities and expressive capacities of young infants in communication with their mothers. Doctoral dissertation, University of Edinburgh.

Murray, L. & Trevarthen, C. (1985). Emotional regulation of interactions between two-month-olds and their mothers. In T. Field, & N. Fox (eds), *Social perception in infants*, 177–197. Norwood, N.J.: Ablex.

Murray, L., Kempton, C., Woolgar, M., & Hooper, R. (1993). Depressed mothers' speech to their infants and its relation to infant gender and cognitive development. *Journal of Child Psychology and Psychiatry*, *34*, 1083–1101.

Murray, L., Fiori-Cowley, A., Hooper, R., & Cooper, P.J. (1994). The impact of postnatal depression and associated adversity on early mother–infant interactions and later infant outcome. Manuscript submitted for publication.

Nash, A. (1988). Ontogeny, phylogeny and relationships. In S. Duck (ed.), *Handbook of personal relationships*, pp. 121–141. Chichester: Wiley.

Nash, A. & Hay, D.F. (1993). Relationships in infancy as precursors and causes of later relationships and psychopathology. In D.F. Hay and A. Angold (eds), *Precursors and causes of development and psychopathology*, pp. 199–232. Chichester: Wiley.

Newton, P. (1994). *Preschool prevarication: An investigation of the cognitive prerequisites for deception*. Doctoral dissertation, University of Portsmouth, U.K.

Papousek, H. & Papousek, M. (1975). Cognitive aspects of pre-verbal social interaction between human infants and adults. In E. Hofer (ed.), *Parent–infant interaction, Ciba Foundation Symposium*, *33*. Amsterdam: Elsevier.

Papousek, M. & Papousek, H. (1981). Musical elements in the infant's vocalization: Their significance for communication, cognition, and creativity. *Advances in Infancy Research*, *1*, 163–224.

Papousek, M. & Papousek, H. (1989). Forms and functions of vocal matching in interactions between mothers and their precanonical infants. *First Language*, *9*, 137–158.

Papousek, M. & Papousek, H. (1991). The meanings of melodies in motherese in tone and stress languages. *Infant Behaviour and Development*, *14*, 415–40.

Ratner, N. & Bruner, J.S. (1978). Games, social exchange and the acquisition of language. *Journal of Child Language*, *5*, 391–401.

Reddy, V. (1990). *Humorous communication in infancy*. Paper presented in symposium on Communication in Infancy at the European Developmental Conference, Stirling, August 1990.

Reddy, V. (1991). Playing with others' expectations: Teasing and mucking about in the first year. In A. Whiten (ed.), *Natural theories of mind*. Oxford: Blackwell.

Reddy, V. (1992). *The rudiments of shyness in two month-olds? Visual cutoff, head turning and arm curving in intimate interactions.* Poster presented at the European Developmental Conference, Seville, August–September 1992.

Reddy, V. (1993). *Shy behaviour in infancy.* Paper presented at the 2nd meeting of the British Infancy Research Group, Ambleside, July 1993.

Reddy, V. (1994a). *The origins of self-consciousness in consciousness of other.* Paper presented in symposium on Self as Process at Annual Conference of the BPS, Brighton, March 1994.

Reddy, V. (1994b). *Negotiating playful intentions: Teasing in infancy.* Paper presented at symposium on Interpreting and Negotiating Intentions at the 9th International Conference on Infant Studies, Paris 2–5 June.

Rheingold, H.L., Hay, D.F., & West, M.J. (1976). Sharing in the second year of life. *Child Development, 47,* 1148–1158.

Robson, K.S. (1967). The role of eye-to-eye contact in maternal-infant attachment. *Journal of Child Psychology and Psychiatry, 8,* 13–25.

Schaffer, H.R. (1984). *The child's entry into a social world.* London: Academic Press.

Snow, C.E. (1977). The development of conversation between mothers and babies. *Journal of Child Language, 4,* 1–22.

Stern, D.N. (1974). Mother and infant at play: The dyadic interaction involving facial, vocal and gaze behaviours. In M. Lewis and L. Rosenblum. (eds), *The effect of the infant on its caregiver.* New York: John Wiley.

Stern, D.N. (1985). *The interpersonal world of the infant: view from psychoanalysis and development psychology.* New York: Basic Books.

Stern, D.N. & Gibbon, J. (1980). Temporal expectancies of social behaviours in mother–infant play. In E. Thoman (ed.), *Origins of Infant Social Responsiveness,* pp. 409–429. Hillsdale, N.J.: Lawrence Erlbaum Associates Inc.

Stern, D.N., Beebe, B., Jaffe, J., & Bennett, S.L. (1977). The infant's stimulus world during social interaction: A study of caregiver behaviours with particular reference to repetition and timing. In H.R. Schaffer (ed.), *Studies in mother–infant interaction,* pp. 177–202. London: Academic Press.

Stern, D.N., Hofer, L., Haft, W., & Dore, J. (1985). Affect attunement: The sharing of feeling states between mother and infant by means of inter-modal fluency. In T.M. Field & N.A. Fox (eds), *Social perception in infants,* pp. 249–268. Norwood, N.J.: Ablex.

Trehub, S.E., Trainor, L.J., & Unyk, A.M. (1993). Music and speech processing in the first year of life. *Advances in Child Development and Behaviour, 24,* 1–35.

Trevarthen, C. (1974). The psychobiology of speech development. In E.H. Lenneberg (ed.), *Language and brain: developmental aspects* (Neurosciences Research Program Bulletin, 12, pp. 570–585). Boston: Neurosciences Research Program.

Trevarthen, C. (1975). Prespeech in communication of infants with adults: Project report. *Journal of Child Language, 1,* 335–338.

Trevarthen, C. (1977). Descriptive analyses of infant communication behaviour. In H.R. Schaffer (ed.), *Studies in mother–infant interaction: The Loch Lomond Symposium,* pp. 227–270. London: Academic Press.

Trevarthen, C. (1979). Communication and cooperation in early infancy: A description of primary intersubjectivity. In M. Bullowa (ed.), *Before speech: the beginning of human communication,* pp. 321–347. London: Cambridge University Press.

Trevarthen, C. (1980). The foundations of intersubjectivity: Development of interpersonal and cooperative understanding in infants. In D. Olson (ed.), *The Social foundations of language and thought: essays in honor of J.S. Bruner,* pp. 316–342. New York: W.W. Norton.

Trevarthen, C. (1986). Development of intersubjective motor control in infants. In M.G. Wade & H.T.A. Whiting (eds), *Motor development in children: aspects of coordination and control,* pp. 209–261. Dordrecht: Martinus Nijhof.

Trevarthen, C. (1987). Sharing makes sense: Intersubjectivity and the making of an infant's meaning. In R. Steele & T. Threadgold (eds), *Language topics: essays in honour of Michael Halliday*. Amsterdam & Philadelphia: John Benjamins.

Trevarthen, C. (1990). Signs before speech. In T.A. Sebeok & J. Umiker-Sebeok (eds), *The semiotic web*, pp. 689–755. Berlin, New York, Amsterdam: Mouton de Gruyter.

Trevarthen, C. (1992). An infant's motives for speaking and thinking in the culture. In A.H. Wold (ed.), *The dialogical alternative: towards a theory of language and mind* (Festschrift for Ragnar Rommetveit), pp. 99–137. Oslo/Oxford: Scandinavian University Press/Oxford University Press.

Trevarthen, C. (1993a). The function of emotions in early infant communication and development. In J. Nadel & L. Camaioni (eds), *New perspectives in early communicative development*, pp. 48–81. London: Routledge.

Trevarthen, C. (1993b). The self born in intersubjectivity: The psychology of an infant communicating. In U. Neisser (ed.). *The perceived self: ecological and interpersonal sources of the self-knowledge*, pp. 121–173. New York: Cambridge University Press.

Trevarthen, C. (1993c). Playing into reality: Conversations with the infant communicator. *Winnicott Studies*, *7*, Spring 1993, 67–84 (London: Karnak Books).

Trevarthen, C. & Hubley, P. (1978). Secondary intersubjectivity: Confidence, confiding and acts of meaning in the first year. In A. Lock (ed.), *Action, Gesture and Symbol*, pp. 183–229. London: Academic Press.

Trevarthen, C. & Marwick, H. (1986). Signs of motivation for speech in infants, and the nature of a mother's support for development of language. In B. Lindblom and R. Zetterstrom (eds), *Precursors of early speech*, pp. 279–308. Basingstoke, Hampshire: Macmillan.

Trevarthen, C. & Aitken, K.J. (1994). Brain development, infant communication and empathy disorders: Intrinsic factors in child mental health. *Development and Psychopathology*, *6*, 597–633.

Tronick, E.Z., Als, H., Adamson, L., Wise, S., & Brazelton, T.B. (1978). The infants' response to entrapment between contradictory messages in face-to-face interaction. *Journal of American Academy of Child Psychiatry*, *17*, 1–13.

Vandell, D.L., Wilson, K.S., & Buchanan, N.R. (1980). Peer interaction in the first year of life: An examination of its structure, content and sensitivity to toys. *Child Development*, *51*, 481–488.

Vedeler, D. (1991). Infant intentionality as Object Directedness: An alternative to representationalism. *Journal for the Theory of Social Behaviour*, *21* (4), 431–448.

Wallon, H. (1934). *Les origines du charactère chez l'enfant*. Paris: Presses Universitaires de France.

Winnicott, D.W. (1960). The theory of the parent–infant relationship. *International Journal of Psychoanalysis*, *41*, 585–595. (Republished in Winnicott, D.W., *The maturational process and the facilitating environment London*, 1990. The Institute of Psychoanalysis, Karnak Books.)

11 Psychoanalysis and Infancy

R. Peter Hobson
Developmental Psychopathology Research Unit, Tavistock Clinic and UCL Medical School, London, UK.

INTRODUCTION

To many people who pick up this book, it will seem incongruous or even perverse that a volume on infancy research should contain a chapter on psychoanalysis. Do not advances in developmental psychology and child psychiatry reflect a progressive move *away* from the unscientific methods and outmoded "hydraulic" theory of Freud and his followers? Whither progress?

Such attitudes are understandable and in some ways justifiable; but they also embody prejudice and ignorance. I take the view that one sign of progress in infancy research is new-found academic interest in and respect for psychoanalytic perspectives, which seem far less outlandish and far more relevant for our understanding of infancy than they might have done two decades ago. In this chapter, I shall be taking a fresh look at selected aspects of psychoanalytic practice and theory, in an attempt to illustrate how the approach is both accessible and innovative—and by no means divorced from contemporary concerns in research on infancy.

Although our focus is on infancy, I need to begin by saying something about psychoanalysis with older children and adults.

PSYCHOANALYSIS

Psychoanalysis is concerned not so much with explaining the present in terms of the past, but rather with exploring the patterning of a person's interpersonal relatedness and relationships, and alongside this, with understanding how the person's mind functions. The underlying idea is that each individual has a finite, indeed a relatively small number of dominant relationship patterns which shape his or her current interpersonal relations *and* exercise a powerful influence on his or her modes of thinking and feeling. These very same patterns are also discernible in the patient's accounts of his or her early life, in dreams, and in a variety of additional clinical manifestations. What happens in analysis, is that the analyst comes to experience what it is like to be a figure *within* one of the stereotyped relationship patterns which are somehow represented in the patient's mind: the analyst is ascribed various roles, and is made to feel things and sometimes to do things that also have a specificity *vis-à-vis* any particular patient. For example, an adopted male patient of mine who was highly sensitive to any sign of denigration or rejection from others, would frequently respond to weekends or breaks in treatment by arriving late, avoiding or mistaking my name, finding other undertakings more important than his analysis, and otherwise making me feel useless and left out. I once protested that my name was not Hobbs, as he had indicated when leaving a message about a missed session, but Hob*son*! I was experiencing and reacting to being orphaned or abandoned by the patient as (seemingly) powerful and in control, but in so doing I was also living out an aspect of his own potential experience *vis-à-vis* others. It is the analysis of this kind of *intersubjective* encounter between patient and analyst that yields the analytic perspective on the structure and functioning of the mind.

Now when Freud launched psychoanalysis towards the end of the last century, he was intent upon formulating a scientific account of psychology, and adopted for this purpose concepts from the physical sciences and neurology that seemed appropriately objective and impersonal. The psychological theory that emerged was one couched in terms of energy, its conservation, displacement and discharge. The style of such theorising is markedly in contrast to Freud's clinical case descriptions, which are altogether more human in their concerns with patients' wishes, anxieties, conflicts, and the like. Even in his theoretical writings, however, Freud was pointing toward a quite different view of mental structure and function. This was prefigured in his paper on Mourning and Melancholia (1917) in which he suggested that psychotic depression arises when an individual reacts to the loss of an ambivalently loved-and-hated person by internalising the relationship. That is, a part of the patient identifies with the lost person, and now the patient directs his or her newly-inflamed hatred towards this part of the self in relentless self-denigrating attacks. Freud came to suggest that it is through such processes of identification that a young child establishes the functions of external figures within the mind: interpersonal relationships and attitudes become intrapsychic relationships and attitudes (compare Vygotsky, 1978).

I am now going to leap forward from Freud to consider how these ideas have been developed in the work of the two most influential architects of "object-relations" theory, Melanie Klein and W.R.D. Fairbairn. It may help if I summarise what is at stake by considering the notion of "object" in psychoanalytic theory. As Rycroft (1968) has put it, an object is "that towards which action or desire is directed; that which the subject requires in order to achieve instinctual satisfaction; that to which the subject relates himself. In psychoanalytic writings, objects are nearly always persons, parts of persons, or symbols of one or the other". Freud's focus was on the "object" as the object of instinct or drive, a relatively impersonal concept: the "object" of object-relations theory is the very same object, but one that is now reconceptualised in terms of personal or quasi-personal (so-called "part-object") relationships and qualities.

First, the contribution of the Scottish psychoanalyst Fairbairn. For Fairbairn (1952), the infant's aim is to establish satisfactory relationships with objects, and Freud's ideas of oral aims, anal aims and so on need to be reconceptualised as channels whereby personal aims may be achieved. Fairbairn emphasised the "specificity of instinctive object-seeking, which is best observed in animals, but which is in no sense compromised, although it may be obscured, by human adaptability. The nesting-habits of birds may be cited in this connection ... a nest is no less an object to a bird ... because it is an object which has to be constructed. It is an object which is sought, even if, to be found, it has first to be made" (Fairbairn, 1952, p. 141). It is worth holding on to this notion of what it might mean to construct an object. Thus Fairbairn, like his contemporary Melanie Klein, viewed the infant's self as whole at birth and capable of relating to external objects on the basis of its constitutional endowment. On the other hand, the self so constituted can then become split so that parts of the self may be experienced in relation to aspects of the caretaker or to other parts of the self in relatively separate constellations of experience. For example, the infant may experience herself as satisfied and in harmonious relation with a source of goodness and succour (although obviously, this way of putting it imports adult-style concepts to a realm of experience for which such concepts are only loosely applicable), but she may switch into states of frustration or neediness in relation to an object experienced as wholly frustrating or malign, or into states of excitement in relation to a tantalising object. This gives rise to a picture of internal object relations between active semi-autonomous agencies within a single personality—the good self related to the bounteous object, the frustrated self in relation to the withholding object, and so on. The internal figures have specific characteristics which are then organised and registered as stable mental representations (Ogden, 1983). In other words, the mind functions like a theatre with various *dramatis personae*; or, to put it more strongly, the mind is structured rather like dreams are structured. That is, a basic structural unit of the mind is some form of self-representation, an object representation, and a representation of the affectively charged interaction between self and object.

Broadly speaking, much of what I have been saying is compatible with Kleinian theory. Klein supposed the first five months or so of life involved the infant in experiences and "phantasies" of relationships with aspects or functions of other persons (for example, what we might loosely call "the breast" as provider of good feelings) rather than with whole persons recognised as having their own integrity or experiences. The Kleinian view is that inherent in the bodily impulses and sensations of infants is some kind of apprehension of objects distinct from the self, and that the earliest objects are largely configured by split-off parts of the self that are "projected" and experienced as being directed towards the self from outside. For example, an angry or hungry infant may encounter an object that is attacking and devouring, in so far as attacking and devouring qualities are partly displaced from the infant's self-experience to become characteristics of the object-as-experienced. As Guntrip (1961) observed, Klein was confronted by an abundance of phantasies in which her child patients fought with or were persecuted by soldiers, burglars and robbers, fierce wild animals, and so on, who used activities such as sucking, biting, eating, and stabbing in destructive ways. Note again, the infant's experience of others is seen to arise on the basis of projected experiences of the infant's own bodily activities. Such infant-created objects might then be experienced as taken inside the body, on the model of oral incorporation of food, and there form the substrates for the kind of dramatic "internal world" I referred to earlier. As Susan Isaacs (1948) expressed it: "The earliest phantasies, then, spring from bodily impulses and are interwoven with bodily sensations and affects. They express primarily an internal and subjective reality, yet from the beginning they are bound up with an actual, however limited and narrow, experience of objective reality" (p. 86). Thus the emphasis is on what is, as it were, self-generated from the infant's way of experiencing its own body—this is important for the analytic view of the origins of interpersonal understanding—but also dependent on the infant's perception of reality. Development over the first year is envisaged as an integrative process by which the loved and hated objects become aspects of a single, whole object—a person—with a new status and value, such that after the earliest months an infant comes to feel guilt and to experience the impulse to make reparation for hostility.

In support of this position was the clinical material gained in the psychoanalysis of neurotic and more disturbed adults, and especially in the play-based psychoanalysis of little children from two years old and upward. If, as Isaacs and other Kleinian analysts maintained, phantasies such as those of oral incorporation of objects or part-objects were clearly evident in young children only a little beyond infancy, then by the principle of genetic continuity, these might be taken to have existed in *some* form in the earliest oral phase of development. One of Isaac's illustrations was of a small boy who said of his mother's nipple when he saw her feeding a younger child: "That's what you bit me with." Another example related to a somewhat older but still preverbal child of 20 months, who developed an intense phobia of her mother's shoe from which the sole had come loose, and was flapping about. This phobia resolved, but 15 months later, the child anxiously enquired: "Where are Mummy's broken shoes?... They might have eaten me right up." Of course, such examples do not establish that infants as well as toddlers experience part-objects in ways that are coloured by the children's projected oral aggression or whatever, but the form and content of such experiences illustrate how psychological mechanisms of the relevant kinds are operative from early in life.

In addition, there was the evidence from detailed observations of infants in context. Such observations were taken to confirm, or at least support, the idea that an infant's modes of relatedness to its caretaker reflected complex and by no means fully reality-based experiences and activities. It is hardly surprising that in the "controversial discussions" of the 1940s within the British Psychoanalytical Society, such critics as Anna Freud and Edward Glover saw this latter kind of reasoning as circular, with the theories determining the inferred phantasies rather than these being derived from theory-free observation. For Glover, the Kleinians "confused larval origins with organised phantasy proper"; or as another analyst, Sylvia Payne, remarked: "We don't call a foetus 'a man'".

Now my purpose in covering this ground is to illustrate the *kinds* of theory that object-relations theories are. The central notion is that there are innate principles, or at least early-developing principles, for an infant's structuring and representation of social experience in terms of affectively-charged and bodily-anchored exchanges between self and object.

I shall now draw out how certain themes that have long been central to the psychoanalytic perspective may be brought to bear on non-analytic developmental research.

DEVELOPMENTAL PSYCHOPATHOLOGY

The first point concerns the theoretical stance which psychoanalysts adopt towards disturbed and abnormal psychological functioning. I have already illustrated how Freud drew upon observations of psychotically depressed patients to evolve a theory about the structuring of a person's mind. This theory brings with it a perspective on developmental *changes* in psychological functioning. In the quotations I cited, the processes of identifying a part of the self with an ambivalently loved-and-hated person and taking in a sadistic relationship with that person within the psyche, were the pathogenetic mechanisms that Freud delineated. Yet such processes are not restricted to the pathological case: they are also considered to be central for normal personality development and even for the capacity to think coherently (Bion, 1962; Urwin, 1989). So, too, Freud's view of the perversions as developmental abnormalities on a continuum with normality opened out a radically new perspective on the plasticity of sexual development. I am emphasising the nature of this stance not only because it accounts for the psychoanalytic position on the development of interpersonal relations—that is, certain clinically abnormal states of mind in children and adults are seen to be related to what is normal in the early months of life—but also because it is controversial. For example, Daniel Stern (1985) and Colwyn Trevarthen believe that analysts' preoccupations with abnormal states of mind actually lead to distorted views of normal development. Yet psychoanalysts would respond by claiming that as in the case of so-called perverse sexuality, so with regard to supposedly abnormal or disturbed interpersonal experience, we can see tell-tale indicators of what is said to be abnormal even in normal people: consider myths and fairy tales as well as children's play; consider the contents of our dreams; and consider the nature of psychopathology in normal people. Correspondingly, analysts would hold that the scope of what needs to be explained in theories of normal development includes quite a lot of supposedly *abnormal* phenomenology. Even more radically, and controversially, what seems abnormal in adults may correspond with what is normal in infants, and thus may reveal the bases for normal social development and interpersonal understanding.

BODIES, FEELINGS AND THE FOUNDATIONS FOR INTERPERSONAL DEVELOPMENT

I shall now consider the ways in which psychoanalysts characterise the foundations for interpersonal experience, for self–other representation, and for social development. I have already noted that they highlight how one prerequisite for normal development in this domain is a sufficiently available (i.e. intersubjectively available) other person, what Winnicott called a good-enough caregiver and what is now generally referred to as a psychologically "containing" person. Many, but not all, psychoanalysts believe that either at the very beginning or near to the very beginning of life, an infant has experiences of self in relation to not-self, and both registers and represents self-in-relationship-with-other. As we have seen, Fairbairn and others have seen infants as *basically* object-seeking; more than this, it is supposed that the infant establishes representations of self, other, and transactions between the two. (I myself have misgivings about the use of the term "re-presentation", but let that be). I think it is important that even such early representations are of transactions that entail *attitudes* between self and other.

It may be appropriate to cite two strands of Lynne Murray's work to exemplify the potential importance of this approach. Murray and Trevarthen (1985) sat individual two- and three-month-old infants in front of a television monitor which showed the mother's live face, looking towards the infant. The mother herself was situated in another room, but she too could relate to a TV monitor showing her baby facing her, close up. Through such an arrangement, mother and baby were able to engage with each other via television in a surprisingly natural and fluent way. A perturbation was achieved by employing a videotape feedback system to introduce a delay of 30 seconds in the time when the mother's responses were relayed to the baby over the TV link. This meant that from each participant's point of view, what should have been a co-ordinated to-and-fro became almost totally desynchronised. The effect was considerable infant distress, with the infants turning away from and darting brief looks back towards the mother's image, and with other signs of confusion as well as self-directed behaviour. On the other hand, changes in an infant's direction of gaze were linked with changes in facial expression and communication, and the patterning of gaze was sensitive to the quality of maternal response. Such observations, as well as those concerning young infants' protests and wariness when confronted with mothers assuming a "blank face" posture (e.g. Cohn & Tronick, 1983), attest to the patterning and emotional significance of caregiver–infant relatedness. Person-with-person configurations of mutual gaze and of facial, vocal, and gestural interchange seem to involve not merely the co-ordination of behaviour between infant and caregiver, but also some kind of emotional linkage which when established has consequences for both participants. There is a sense in which the infant seems to *expect* appropriate forms of response from the other person.

The second strand of Murray's work I shall cite concerns the implications that early interpersonal relations might have for subsequent social and cognitive development. Murray (1991) offers an overview of a research programme in which she has been studying the effects of maternal postpartum depression. When compared with a control group at two months postpartum, depressed mothers were more preoccupied with their own experiences than with those of their infants, they expressed more hostility, and they were less likely to acknowledge the infant as an active subject or agent. Even though most maternal episodes of depression had remitted within three or four months of onset, at 18 months of age the infants of these mothers differed from control subjects in being less likely to be securely attached, more likely to have sleep disturbance, and less proficient in object concept tasks. In a separate study, Alan Stein and colleagues reported that even when there had been remission of maternal depressive symptoms, one-and-a-half year-old infants of post-natally depressed mothers showed less affective sharing towards their mothers than infants in a control group (Stein, et al., 1991). It is worth noting that according to a psychoanalytic view, postpartum depression might be an index of maternal "internal object relations" that would exert an influence on mother–infant relations well past the episode of depression *per se*. So although these results do not *require* a psychoanalytic explanation—for example invoking specific forms of defense against infantile anxieties and conflict to explain patterns of attachment—they are certainly compatible with long-established (and oft-derided) psychoanalytic propositions concerning the potentially far-reaching effects of emotionally sensitive or unresponsive and/or intrusive caregiving in an infant's life.

I have observed how, in somewhat differing ways, psychoanalysts have attempted to characterise the features of *un*developed or maldeveloped experiences of the personal world in, for example, the paranoid-schizoid (nightmarish, psychotic, black-and-white, potentially malevolent or beatific) world of part-objects described by Melanie Klein and others. The object relationships represented in an infant's mind are likely to correspond very partially with what people are objectively like, since infants under the sway of powerful needs and emotions would seem to have relatively little anchorage in what *we* call objective reality (not least because they do not yet recognise its status as objective). In a thoughtful and original paper that relates Kleinian theory to research in the Piagetian tradition, Hopkins (1987) brings out how, before infants have acquired a working grasp of the nature of enduring entities around the middle of the first year of life, they are very likely to have unintegrated, episodic experiences of other people (corresponding to Kleinian part-objects) which are powerfully shaped by the infants' own intense feelings and bodily impulses. Very early awareness of the environment as 'out there' is sufficient to structure experiences according to an apprehension of the self–other distinction, but the emergence of feelings of concern for another person and anxieties about dependency and loss (Klein's depressive position) appears to correspond with infants' growing understanding of the identity and enduring nature of objects, both personal and non-personal. If this represents a coherent argument, then it makes sense to suppose that somewhere in human psychology, we might find evidence for fragmented and perhaps bizarre modes of experience that seem to correspond with the unintegrated elements of primitive mental life. It is here that psychoanalysts draw upon evidence from psychopathology to derive propositions about the givens of human psychology in the interpersonal realm.

It is also here that we find a radical alternative to most academic developmental psychology of infancy. Consider paranoid states of mind—typical of many disturbed children and adults, familiar to most of us in dreams and, according to many psychoanalysts, ubiquitous as a *potential* from time to time in infancy. There is a view prevalent among developmental psychologists (and also entertained by some analysts such as Stern) that infants *could not* have experiences of a person with malign intents towards the self (for instance, being invasive and potentially annihilating) until certain cognitive capacities have developed—at least until the period of secondary intersubjectivity towards the end of the first year of life, and very probably until the capacity to symbolise has emerged at around 18 months. As I see it, the alternative psychoanalytic view is that even very young infants are prone to experiences of being threatened, and moreover that these experiences contribute to their later conceptualisations as well as experiences of persons. Sure enough, these are not experiences exactly like those of 2-year-old children or 30-year-old adults, but nor do they need to be based on a cognitively elaborated understanding of people as such. Rather, they are experiences that have genetic continuity with what we adults describe as feelings of persecution, invasion and threat, only they are less well-defined or circumscribed, and more powerful and potentially overwhelming. In fact, they may be rather like a psychotic person's persecuting experiences, or like certain experiences in dreams. Experiences such as these occur when the needy infant is *not* responded to or contained adequately, and their form is determined by the in-built emotional propensities of human beings.

If we supplement this kind of account with a handful of additional factors that can operate from early in life, then we have the essentials of *a* psychoanalytic view (and, for partly contrasting and partly complementary integrative perspectives, see Mahler, Pine, & Bergman, 1975; and the exceptionally lucid contemporary work of Stern, 1985). Firstly, there is the idea (again informed by observations of disturbed adults) that there can be splits in the mind, whereby given states of mind or even aspects of the personality can be segregated off from other parts of the self. Secondly, there is the idea that in infancy and beyond, mental functioning can be experienced on the model of physical functioning, so that not only physical but also mental contents can be treated as if they were expelled from the self, or taken into the self from outside. It is relevant to note that we all tend to think of the mind as a place (Wollheim, 1969). Thirdly, and connected with all this, an infant's experiences of others may at times be coloured by what the infant has "projected" from his or her own mental life. Finally, an infant's capacity to integrate these fragmented and partitioned representations, a capacity that itself depends upon the emotional availability of a caregiver, is what leads to a transformation in interpersonal relatedness and with this, a newly emerging appreciation of and concern for other persons as beings with their own value, their own capacity to be harmed, and with their *own* subjective mental life.

Therefore psychoanalytic perspectives offer something novel in drawing our attention to forms of interpersonal relatedness, and corresponding modes of psychological structure and representation, that may amount to primitives for social-psychological development (but aberrant, perhaps, in early childhood autism; Hobson, 1990). I do not think it is a coincidence that in Mandler's (Chapter 7, this volume) attempts to characterise the basic forms of perceived meaning, we find a number of features such as agency and containment that are already familiar in psychoanalytic accounts of early infant experience. Whilst it is important not to be facile in seeking correspondences across different theoretical traditions, there seems to be something that is far from trivial here. To perceive agency is very close to perceiving something like agents-with-emotional/intentional-colouring (the "colouring" often being provided by the infant, as well as having contributions from direct perception); to perceive containment is not the same as experiencing emotional containment, but it is an available perceptual structure to give form to experiences of being emotionally held. Therefore one upshot of the psychoanalytic account is that in certain (not all) respects, we may have got it the wrong way round when we suppose that an infant has to demonstrate an awareness that embodied people have intentions and attitudes, or has to exhibit creative symbolic play, *before* he or she can have anything like experiences of being threatened or nourished from outside agencies. If it is true that a child's understanding of what persons *are*, which includes an understanding of person's minds (so-called "theory of mind"), is founded upon the child's experiences in relation to persons, then these psychoanalytic perspectives might prompt us to reconsider the forms that these early interpersonal experiences take. We might also reflect on factors that foster the integration of an infant's fragmented and primitive representations of people (objects), so that the child can think as well as feel about self and others in a coherent, integrated way.

In the final section of this chapter, I shall pursue these issues by illustrating an especially important area of contemporary research at the interface between psychoanalytic and nonanalytic approaches to development: the study of how an individual comes to mentally represent early attachment relationships, and of how such representations correspond with the individual's later experiences and behaviour in relation to people.

THE MENTAL REPRESENTATION OF EARLY SOCIAL EXPERIENCE

I opened this chapter by characterising the psychoanalytic view that from very early childhood, patterns of intersubjective relationship are somehow represented in the mind, in such a way as to exert a formative influence on subsequent relationships. In fact, this mapping can take a number of complex forms, in so far as defensive manoeuvres may disguise, distort or otherwise transform an individual's experiences in relationships. For example, a person may maintain psychic equilibrium by inducing other people to carry unmanageable anxieties, wishes, or other states of mind. Such defensive processes may also interfere with the individual's capacity for coherent, self-reflective thought. This kind of developmental account has acquired fresh significance with the recent advent of a body of research linking caregivers' ways of thinking and feeling about their own early attachment figures, and these caregivers' relationships with their infants. This work is also unravelling the impact of caregiver–infant relationships on the early development of children's personality and modes of mental representation, with increasing evidence of continuity from infancy through to early childhood and beyond (Main, 1991).

As so often in areas of progress, methodological innovation has provided the impetus for the elaboration of new theoretical perspectives, and in this case for *rapprochement* between psychoanalytic and non-analytic perspectives on early development. The approach has involved a convergence between studies of adults' ways of talking about their early relationships in a semi-structured interview, the *Adult Attachment Interview* of George, Kaplan, and Main (1985), and observations of caregiver-infant relations as recorded in the *Strange Situation* of Ainsworth, Blehar, Waters, and Wall (1978). Indeed, transcripts from such interviews were originally studied with reference to the patterns of attachment that had been observed between the interviewees and their infants four years earlier. From its very inception, therefore, this approach explored the link between adults' mental representations of early relationships on the one hand, and observed styles of adult infant relations, with their associated patterns of infant interpersonal responsiveness, on the other.

The Adult Attachment Interview (AAI) is a semi-structured interview in which a person is asked to reflect on aspects of his or her childhood relationships with caregivers. As a part of the interview, subjects are asked to give adjectives describing each parent, and then to back these up with specific memories; to recall specific experiences of parental responsiveness to upset, accidents and illness; and to relate how these relationships have changed over time and how they have influenced their adult personality. Transcribed interviews are classified on the basis of scales that evaluate an individual's state of mind with respect to early relationships. In all, seven scales are normally considered. Examples of these are scales that concern idealisation of a parent, where the patient gives a very positive view at a general level that is either unsupported or contradicted by actual memories; persistence of not remembering, reflected in repeated failure to recall supporting memories for generalisations made about the parent–child relationship; and perhaps most importantly, coherence of discourse across the interview as a whole, which encompasses how far the individual is able to acknowledge and integrate contradictory experiences and memories. Thus the emphasis is on the "how" rather than the "what" of the individual's memories and attitudes.

Transcripts are ultimately classified into three major categories (with a total of twelve subcategories): free to evaluate attachments, where people talk coherently and objectively about their early relationships; dismissing of attachments, characterised by a dismissiveness towards the likelihood that early attachment experiences have affected personal development; and preoccupied (or enmeshed) in attitudes towards attachment, where the influence of parents or attachment-related experiences can neither be coherently described or dismissed, and where such relationships seem to preoccupy attention. In these latter transcripts, patients may also oscillate between good and bad evaluations of the past or of their parents (Main & Goldwyn, 1991). More recently a further group, unresolved/disorganised/disorientated with respect to loss and trauma, has been described. Unresolved status is considered on separate scales, based primarily upon the notion of cognitive disorganisation and/or disorientation as signs of a particular kind of unresolved experience. This is shown most often in lapses in an individual's reasoning, in unfounded fear, unfounded guilt, or in irrational thought processes when the individual is talking about loss or trauma. In other areas such accounts may be quite coherent (Main & Goldwyn, 1991).

Why am I devoting so much space in a chapter on infancy, to describing a measure of adults' ways of organising thoughts and feelings about their own childhoods? One reason is that the kind of discourse analysis employed to classify AAI transcripts yields a picture of mental functioning closely allied to the psychoanalytic view of people's defensive strategies and intellectual characteristics (Patrick et al., 1994). More than this, there is evidence for direct *transmission* of representational styles from caregivers to infants. This strongly suggests that a person's style of mentally representing his or her own childhood relationships—how that person organises and often defensively structures his or her thoughts and feelings about significant parenting figures—has implications not only for the person's own behaviour in relation to his or her infant, but also for the *infant's* subsequent psychodynamic development and interpersonal relations. The evidence I mentioned comes not only from studies confirming an impressive association between maternal AAI classifications and concurrent mother–infant Strange Situation classifications (reviewed in Van IJzendoorn, 1992), but also from prospective studies by Fonagy, Steele, and Steele (1991) in which pregnant mothers' representations of their own attachment histories predicted the organisation of infant–mother attachment at one year of age. For example, autonomous versus dismissing or preoccupied categories of maternal interview predicted secure versus insecure infant–mother attachment patterns 75% of the time, whereas a number of other variables such as personality and marital satisfaction had little predictive power. Subsequent work by this research team (Fonagy et al., 1991; Fonagy et al., 1993) has suggested that for mothers who have themselves experienced childhood deprivation, a capacity to reflect upon the mental states of themselves and others (corresponding to high reflective-self ratings) significantly increases the chance of the mother's relationship with her own infant as being rated secure. This reflective capacity is thought to correspond with the mother's ability to assimilate and contain the infant's emotional states (see also Haft & Slade, 1989; Main, 1991).

So, too, when one turns to psychopathology and considers the case of adult patients with a proneness to just the kinds of disturbed (primitive) psychological functioning discussed earlier—relationships fluctuating between overidealisation and devaluation, persecutory states of mind, unstable identities frequently admixed with features of perverse sexuality, affective instability, bodily self-destructive acts, and so on—a study from our own research team has yielded evidence for characteristic abnormalities in AAI ratings. This study involved blind ratings of AAI transcripts from 12 female patients with borderline personality disorder who manifest such clinical features, and 12 less disturbed female patients with dysthymia (neurotic depression). Although the two groups of patients were closely comparable in intellectual achievement and in current levels of depression at the time of interview, all 12 of the borderline women but only 4 of the dysthymic women were preoccupied, confused and mentally entangled (E) with respect to significant early attachment relationships. Indeed, 10 out of 12 of the borderline patients but none of the 12 dysthymic patients were classified as fearful and overwhelmed in relation to such early interpersonal experiences (subcategory E3 of the AAI). The borderline patients' thinking in these areas exhibited marked oscillations in attitude that seemed to correspond with observed swings between idealisation and denigration in their current relationships. They were unable to locate or contain significant early experiences within a coherent mental framework. Although the overall rates of reported traumata and loss were almost exactly the same in each group, the majority of dysthymic patients but none of those with borderline personality disorder had managed to assimilate these experiences in a psychologically coherent and reflective way. It was also the case that on a separate self-report questionnaire, the *Parental Bonding Instrument* of Parker, Tupling, and Brown (1979), the borderline patients reported significantly lower maternal care and higher maternal overprotection (intrusiveness). This is of additional interest in the light of suggestive evidence that individuals' ratings of parents on the Parental Bonding Instrument reflect a degree of veridical perception, in that they represent a perception of circumstances shared by others (Mackinnon, Henderson, & Andrews, 1991; McCrae & Costa, 1988; Parker, 1983). Although it would be premature to conclude too much about these patients' "actual" childhood experiences (or about how such experiences might have arisen), there now appear to be opportunities for empirical as well as theoretical exploration of developmental interconnections among an infant's experiences of interpersonal relations, the infant's evolving representations of those relationships, and the dynamic psychopathology and phenomenology of disturbed psychological functioning in later life. Psychoanalytic perspectives on the nature and developmental significance of an infant's object relations seem to have much to offer in this domain.

CONCLUSION

In this chapter, I have tried to present, and hopefully to demystify, a psychoanalytic perspective on infancy. This perspective sets the patterning of infants' intersubjective experience at the centre of a theory of social development, a theory that also has important implications for the development of personality and certain cognitive abilities. This theory holds that there are innately given configurations of interpersonal experience that are foundational for, rather than supervenient upon, a cognitively elaborated understanding of the nature of persons with minds. It also suggests that specific forms of insufficiently sensitive caregiving may result in infants failing to integrate person-related experiences, with far-reaching effects on the structuring of those individuals' subsequent interpersonal relations, capacity for coherent thinking, personality and psychiatric status.

Psychoanalysis continues to be a radical intellectual tradition, yet the points of congruence with recent advances in infancy research are increasingly impressive. It is no longer easy for mainstream psychologists and psychiatrists to caricature the practice and theory of psychoanalysis, nor to dismiss psychoanalytic propositions about infant mental life as "inconceivable". True, we have to be circumspect about the way in which our adult concepts are applied to an infant's experiences in the earliest stages of development, a period for which such concepts are necessarily inadequate (Hamlyn, 1974). This said, it is in the psychoanalytic field that we can find ideas rich enough to encompass emergent findings in the field of developmental psychopathology, findings that may prompt a renewed appreciation of psychoanalytic insights into the course of normal as well as abnormal development.

ACKNOWLEDGEMENTS

Sections of this paper were presented at a meeting of the British Infancy Research Group, Ambleside, July 1993, and to the Conference of the Developmental Section of the BPS, in a symposium entitled, *Conceiving minds in developmental psychology*, Birmingham, September 1993.
I am grateful to my colleague Matthew Patrick for his advice on this chapter.

REFERENCES

Ainsworth, M.D., Blehar, M., Waters, E., & Wall, S. (1978). *Patterns of attachment.* Hillsdale, N.J.: Lawrence Erlbaum Associates Inc.

Bion, W.R. (1962). *Learning from experience.* London: Heinemann.

Cohn, J.F. & Tronick, E. (1983). Three-month-old infants' reaction to simulated maternal depression. *Child Development, 54*, 185–193.

Fairbairn, W.R.D. (1952). Object-relations and dynamic structure. In *Psychoanalytic studies of the personality*, pp.137–151. London: Routledge & Kegan Paul.

Fonagy, P., Steele, H., & Steele, M. (1991). Maternal representations of attachment during pregnancy predict the organisation of infant–mother attachment at one year of age. *Child Development, 62*, 891–905.

Fonagy, P., Steele, M., Steele, H., Leigh, T., Kennedy, R., & Target, M. (1993). *The predictive specificity of Mary Main's Adult Attachment Interview: Implications for psychodynamic theories of normal and pathological emotional development.* Paper presented at conference on John Bowlby's Attachment Theory: Historical, clinical and social significance, Toronto, October.

Fonagy, P., Steele, M., Steele, H., Moran, G. S., & Higgitt, A. (1991). The capacity for understanding mental states: The reflective self in parent and child and its significance for security of attachment. *Infant Mental Health Journal, 13*, 200–217.

Freud, S. (1917). Mourning and melancholia. In J. Strachey (ed.), *Standard edition of the complete psychological works of Sigmund Freud Volume XIV*, 243–258. London: Hogarth.

George, C., Kaplan, N., & Main, M. (1985). *The attachment interview for adults.* Unpublished manuscript, University of California,Berkeley.

Guntrip, H. (1961). *Personality structure and human interaction.* London: Hogarth Press.

Haft, W.L. & Slade, A. (1989). Affect attunement and maternal attachment: A pilot study. *Infant Mental Health Journal, 10*, 157–172.

Hamlyn, D.W. (1974). Person-perception and our understanding of others. In T. Mischel (ed.), *Understanding other persons*, pp.1–36. Oxford: Blackwell.

Hobson, R.P. (1990). On psychoanalytic approaches to autism. *American Journal of Ortho psychiatry, 60*, 324–336.

Hopkins, J. (1987). Synthesis in the imagination: Psychoanalysis, infantile experience and the concept of an object. In J. Russell (ed.), *Philosophical perspectives on developmental psychology*, pp.140–172. Oxford: Blackwell.

Isaacs, S. (1948). The nature and function of phantasy. *International Journal of Psychoanalysis, 29*, 73–97.

Mackinnon, A., Henderson, A., & Andrews, G. (1991). The Parental Bonding Instrument: A measure of perceived or actual parental behaviour? *Acta Psychiatrica Scandinavica, 83*, 153–159.

Mahler, M.S., Pine, F., & Bergman, A. (1975). *The psychological birth of the human infant.* London: Hutchinson.

Main, M. (1991). Metacognitive knowledge, metacognitive monitoring, and singular (coherent) vs multiple (incoherent) models of attachment: Findings and directions for future research. In P. Marris, J. Stevenson-Hinde, & C. Parkes (eds), *Attachment across the life cycle*, pp.127–159. New York: Routledge.

Main, M. & Goldwyn, R. (1991). *Adult attachment rating and classification system.* Unpublished scoring manual, Department of Psychology, University of California, Berkeley.

McCrae, R. & Costa, P. (1988). Recalled parent–child relations and adult personality. *Journal of Personality, 56*, 417–434.

Murray, L. (1991). Intersubjectivity, object relations theory and empirical evidence from mother–infant interactions. *Infant Mental Health Journal, 12*, 219–232.

Murray, L. & Trevarthen, C. (1985). Emotional regulation of interactions between two-month-olds and their mothers. In T.M. Field & N.A. Fox (eds), *Social perception of infants*, pp.177–197. Norwood,N.J.: Ablex.
Ogden, T. H. (1983). The concept of internal object relations. *International Journal of Psycho-Analysis, 64*, 227–241.
Parker, G. (1983). *Parental overprotection: a risk factor in psycho-social development*. New York: Grune & Stratton.
Parker, G., Tupling, H., & Brown, L. (1979). A parental bonding instrument. *British Journal of Medical Psychology, 52*, 1–10.
Patrick, M., Hobson, R.P., Castle, D., Howard, R., & Maughan, B. (1994). Personality disorder and the mental representation of early social experience. *Development and Psychopathology, 6*, 375–388.
Rycroft, C. (1968). *A critical dictionary of psychoanalysis*. Harmondsworth, Middlesex: Penguin.
Stein, A., Gath, D. H., Bucher, J., Bond, A., Day, A., & Cooper, P.J. (1991). The relationship between post-natal depression and mother–child interaction. *British Journal of Psychiatry, 158*, 46–52.
Stern, D.N. (1985). *The interpersonal world of the infant*. New York: Basic Books.
Urwin, C. (1989). Linking emotion and thinking in infant development: A psychoanalytic perspective. In A. Slater & G. Bremner (eds), *Infant development*, pp.273–300. Hillsdale, N.J.: Lawrence Erlbaum Associates Inc.
Van IJzendoorn, M.H. (1992). Intergenerational transmission of parenting: A review of studies in nonclinical populations. *Developmental Review, 12*, 76–99.
Vygotsky, L.S. (1978). Internalization of higher psychological functions. In M. Cole, V. John-Steiner, S. Scribner, & E. Souberman (eds), *Mind in society: the development of higher psychological processes*, pp.52–67. Cambridge,Mass.: Harvard University Press.
Wollheim, R. (1969). The mind and the mind's image of itself. *International Journal of Psycho-Analysis, 50*, 209–220.

12 Referential Communication: Making Sense of the Social and Physical Worlds

David Messer
Department of Psychology, University of Hertfordshire, Hatfield, UK.

By the end of the first year infants are starting to use recognisable words to refer to aspects of their world and by 18 months infants have acquired a large vocabulary that they can employ to communicate with others. How do infants come to achieve so much in a comparatively short space of time? In other words how do infants come to put both the social and physical worlds together so that they can use words to communicate about objects and events? In this chapter I shall take a chronological look at topics related to this issue. The chapter starts of with a consideration of the nature of early social interaction and the way this may allow infants to begin to understand and relate to their social world. This is followed by a consideration of the beginnings of interest in the physical world which culminates in the use of and response to referential gestures at about 9 months. Next the role of joint attention in vocabulary acquisition is discussed. This leads to an evaluation of the role of cognitive constraints in early vocabulary development: a contrast is draw between this approach and ones that discuss similar phenomena from a social-based problem-solving perspective. A theme running through my chapter is the way that infants' social environment is structured in ways that facilitate these achievements and the way that cognitive abilities both limit and enable development to take place.

THE EARLY SOCIAL WORLD

Infants start life with a preference for the stimuli coming from humans, their face, their voice and perhaps their movement. Whatever the outcome of the debate about the basis for infants' preference for faces over other comparable stimuli in the first few months of life (see Chapter 9), it is clear that the human face is very attractive to young infants. A comparable finding has come from studies which indicate that infants find human speech very attractive, and that the modified speech that adults use with young children is preferred over typical adult-to-adult speech (see Messer, 1994). Furthermore, 3-month infants have a preference for the movement of humans over comparable stimuli (Bertenthal, Proffitt, Spetner, & Thomas, 1985), but whether younger infants show these preferences is not yet known. All these studies indicate that infants, at least by 4 months, pay special attention to the people in their world.

Not only are infants attracted to people in general, but they also show a special preference for the sight, sound and smell of their mother (Messer, 1994). As has been discussed in Chapter 9, the work of Bushnell, Sai, and Mullin (1989) suggests that infants less than a day old prefer to look at their mother's face rather than that of another woman. Similarly, newborn infants prefer to listen to the sound of their mother's voice rather than that of another woman (DeCasper & Fifer, 1980), and this seems to be based on a preference for sounds heard while in utero. Within the first 10 days of life infants also show a preference for the odour of their mother in comparison with that of other women (MacFarlane, 1975). There is a suggestion that this preference for the odour of the mother is the result of familiarity; female infants (but not males) preferred the smell of peppermint or ginger after they had been exposed to this in their cot (Balogh & Porter, 1986).

Thus, from the first few days of life infants are attracted, probably on the basis of familiarity, to the person who is typically going to play the most important part in their social lives. As a result, young babies appear to be cued into the characteristics of certain individuals and are likely to pay more attention to their actions and behaviour. Such preferences mean that infants begin life with an orientation to the people who are likely to provide a continuity of experience and with whom shared perspectives can develop. However, it is important to remember that these preferences are not the same as attachment: it is not until about 8 months that infants start to be upset at the absence of their mother and show a strong preference for their mother over other individuals (see Messer, 1995).

So far I have discussed the way that infants show a preference for the physical stimuli emanating from their social world. However, there is also evidence which suggests that infants appreciate the significance of people at a more profound level. This work seeks to move away from the conception of infants responding to people as a collection of interesting stimuli to a conception which involves infants recognising that people are social beings who need to be responded to in social ways.

It is extremely difficult, if not impossible, to convince a sceptic that an organism without speech understands the difference between people and other entities not just in terms of differences in the stimuli that they produce, but also in terms of their having some common and shared knowledge of each other as communicative and conscious partners (e.g. Moore & Corkum, 1994). Despite the difficulty of substantiating these claims, they constitute a very important alternative to a mechanistic view of social development.

Trevarthen's notion of intersubjectivity has provided a focal point for these ideas (see previous chapter). In addition, more recent formulations of Meltzoff and Gopnik (1993) have suggested that infants may react to other entities in relation to how similar the entity is to them, a "like me" response. They believe that the ability of very young infants to imitate the actions of another person may be due to their recognition that the model is similar to themselves ("like me"). In other words, Meltzoff and Gopnik are claiming that from a very early age, infants recognise the similarity between themselves and other humans. Another related viewpoint, is that of Hobson (1991; 1993) who believes that young infants are attuned to the emotional expressions of others. In this way they can make sense of their social world by interpreting the emotions and feelings of adults. An interesting question in relation to all these perspectives is whether infants" notions of communicative beings is limited to humans, and if not, how far the notions are extended to other animals such as the family cat, dog, or goldfish?

What evidence do we have to support these claims? The first set comes from observations of interaction where investigators such as Reddy et al. have recorded the apparent fine tuning of responses between infant and adult (see Chapter 10). Other evidence comes from the studies of imitation by Meltzoff and his colleagues. If young infants can imitate the actions of adults then one explanation (among others) is that they do so because they can relate the actions of others to their own self. A third source of evidence is the way that young infants respond to emotion, and the way children with autism fail to make these responses (Hobson, 1986; but see Baron-Cohen, 1993).

To summarise: I have argued that from birth infants are tuned to their social world; they find the stimuli coming from the social world interesting, and they have a preference for the social stimuli with which they are accustomed. Furthermore, there are suggestions that infants' preferences are not based merely on physical stimuli, but also on a deeper appreciation of people as similar beings who can be influenced by the infants' own behaviour. In contrast to these early social abilities, infants' access and control of their physical environment is limited by poor vision and poor manipulative abilities. Thus, it is no surprise that various theorists have characterised the first 5 or 6 months as a period when caregiver and infant interact with one another, and largely ignore the wider physical world. Their interactions are about each other and their reactions to each other. Such a period may be important in allowing mutual knowedge to develop, and for infants to start to become attuned to some of the characteristics of their culture. For example, even by 3 months there are differences in the way that American and Japanese mother–infant pairs interact with one another (Fogel, Toda, & Kawai, 1988). In addition, it is important to bear in mind that these early interactions may be part of the process of attachment formation, and may influence the type of attachment that is formed.

THE CO-ORDINATION OF THE PHYSICAL AND SOCIAL WORLDS

A number of investigators have identified a change in social interaction that occurs at about 5 to 6 months (Kaye, 1982; Schaffer, 1984; Trevarthen, 1982). Infants appear to move their interest to physical objects and events outside of the previous focus of person-based social activity. This change may be due to physical developments such as increasing manipulative control or postural control (Fogel, 1993), better vision, or to neurological developments. The change means that social interaction starts to involve topics other than the adult–infant pair themselves, what is touched and what is looked at becomes a topic of interaction and adult speech.

The new orientation to the physical world has been commented upon by various investigators. Sylvester-Bradley and Trevarthen (1978) have provided a detailed investigation of one mother–infant pair between 2 and 5 months. Across these ages there seemed to be a decline in sociability of the infant, as assessed by the reduction of the infant's positive looking at the mother in the absence of crying. There was also an increase in the amount of maternal speech, although the proportion of contentless utterances (i.e. with no referent) increased to a peak at about 4 months, and then declined. Thus, across this age there was a change in both infant functioning and maternal speech.

Penman, Cross, Milgrom-Friedman, and Meares (1983) provide similar observations with a larger sample. They studied infants and maternal speech at 3 months and at 6 months. Between these ages they identified a change in the infants' focus of attention, from being engaged in communication or reflective activities at 3 months, to praxic activities at 6 months. The praxic activities involved using and relating to objects: at 3 months 27% of the session was made up of this; the figure at 6 months was 61%. In addition, there were comparable changes in maternal speech: over this age the number of utterances involving affect-related speech declined, and the amount of informative speech increased. In particular, there was an increase in the number of references to the external environment and a decrease in the number of utterances without a referent.

There are also reports of a continuing change beyond 6 months. Between 5 and 7 months maternal speech becomes even more concerned with infant activities and events and less concerned with internal states and feelings, (Snow, 1977); and between 9 and 18 months becomes more marked for semantic features and less marked for affect, (Blount & Padgug, 1976). In addition, across a wider age band, Rabain-Jamin and Sabeau-Jouannet (1989) have described the way that maternal uterances to 3-month-olds concern mood and physiological activity, those to 7-month-olds concern perception, volition and psychological activity, while utterance to 10-month-olds are about goal directed activities.

Other studies have provided detailed observations of small numbers of individual cases. Ratner and Bruner (1978) observed, in two mother–infant pairs from 5 to 14 months, the development of a routine involving a clown that could be made to disappear and reappear in a cloth cone. During this time one mother reduced the amount of attention obtaining and maintaining activities she produced. At 5 months she marked every change in the game with a comment (e.g. "Where's he gone?"), but by 9 months she marked only a quarter of these features. During the same period, the infant's participation changed from trying to manipulate the clown to watching the game and responding with laughter and smiles at appropriate points as he started to appreciate the regularities in the game. Interest in the game waned between 9 and 14 months, to reappear when the infant was able to control the puppet himself. Thus, during this period, social interaction appeared to provide experiences which allow infants to become entrained with the game, and to later be able to take over the mother's role in the game.

Another group of advances at about 9 months involve behaviours which concern adult's and infant's interest in objects and events. Here we see the beginnings of behaviours which allow adults and infants to be much more efficient in the establishment of joint topics of interest. The ostentive theories of reference assume that infants are able to make sense of words because they see an object to which their attention has been directed by a point, and relate the word they hear to that object. It is now reasonably well established that towards the end of the first year, there are a number of procedures in addition to pointing which allow the co-ordination of attention. Furthermore, it would appear that these behaviours are bi-directional: not only can infants' attention be directed, but infants' attention or gesture directs adult interest to establish a joint topic for speech. Pointing, gaze and manipulation are three forms of behaviour that are used to co-ordinate infant and adult attention.

In the case of pointing it would appear that by 9 months infants are capable of following simple points to near objects and objects directly in front of them. By 14 months infants are capable of following points where the index finger and the target object are not in the same visual field

(Murphy & Messer, 1977; Lempers, 1976; Butterworth & Grover, 1991). Gaze direction is another important procedure which results in the co-ordination of attention. At about 8 months of age, if adults turn their head and look to the right or left, then infants who are facing the adult consistently look in the same direction (Scaife & Bruner, 1975). However, it is still unclear whether the same phenomenon occurs in non-experimental situations where cues are less obvious. There is better evidence that the reverse process—adults following the infant's gaze—often occurs in naturalistic circumstances, occurs from an earlier age, and results in adult speech being linked to infant interest (Collis, 1977). Manipulation of objects also provides a way of establishing the interest of the partner and allows the adult to link attention to the focus of infant interest. My own work has suggested that maternal speech is usually related to an object that either the mother or the infant is holding. References are comparatively rare to other objects, and as time from the manipulation increases, so the likelihood of a reference decreases (Messer, 1978; 1983).

In addition to these three behaviours which can be used to establish joint attention by following the interest of the partner, there are other features which mark out the structure of interaction. For example, I have argued that the way interaction is organised can provide non-verbal cues about when a topic of interest has been changed (Messer, 1981; 1983). Adult speech to infants seems to be organised into verbal episodes; that is, sequences of utterances which all refer to the same object. This redundancy could be of considerable help in identifying the referent of interaction if infants can locate the start of new verbal episodes. My investigations revealed that utterances about the same referent tend to occur temporally closer together than utterances about different referents. In addition, utterances about a new referent tended to occur after a new object had been picked up by the child or adult, and the first utterances about a new referent tended to contain its name. All these sources of information provide assistance in relating what is said to referents in the environment.

So far I have discussed the way in which infants are able to identify the referent of adult speech. To make the link between the referent and a word also requires infants to be able to identify the referential word in an utterance. Such a process is likely to be considerably assisted by an understanding of the pragmatic force of the utterance (which is discussed later). In addition, there may be a number of devices which aid the identification of referential words. Such words are often produced as single word utterances so that infants are provided with a very simple association between word and referent. In addition, words about objects tend to be the loudest word in an utterance and produced at the end of an utterance (Messer, 1981; Fernald & Mazzie, 1991).

Thus, we can see that there are a variety of ways that adults and infants can register their interest in the environment to their partner, and also there are a variety of behavioural cues that can be used to help identify the referent of adult speech. However, understanding reference is not just a matter of physical co-ordination; there also has to be mental co-ordination. This issue of developing a shared understanding of the world is considered in the next section.

SHARING THE PHYSICAL AND SOCIAL WORLDS

Another perspective which is important to consider in relation to the understanding of reference is the development of a shared understanding. According to this perspective, during the first year, infants are not only acquiring ways to identify the referent of utterances, they are also developing an understanding of what are the important and relevant aspects of their cultural world. For example, in most instances, to be able to follow a point involves not only a response to the gesture, but also involves the ability to identify what is likely to be a salient object from an array of stimuli. This issue has taken on important theoretical significance in relation to the way infants can relate a word they hear to an object they see. As philosophers have argued, there is no way of knowing whether a new word refers to the whole object, its colour, shape or some other property of the object (e.g. Quine, 1969). From such a perspective, acquiring a new vocabulary becomes virtually impossible because of the difficulty of resolving such uncertainties. However, if we can accept that throughout the first year infants and adults are developing a shared understanding of the world then such uncertainties about reference can be minimised.

One claim about early shared understanding is the relationship between the suprasegmental characteristics of adult's speech (i.e. sound patterns that cross word boundaries) and infant reactions. Papousek, Papousek, and Symmes (1991) have proposed that there are universal patterns of sound which have similar functions. These include, a rising pitch, which is associated with adults encouraging a response from an infant, and a falling pitch, which is associated with soothing an infant. Furthermore, by 4 months, approving sounds can increase attention to a face (Papousek et al., 1990). In addition, the different types of infant vocalisations appear to be responded to in a predictable way by adults (Papousek & Papousek, 1989). Thus, early in life, vocalisations seem to provide ways of understanding each other, and ways of developing shared understanding about objects and events.

During the first year it also seems likely that infants, through social interaction, come to identify the salient aspects of their environment. Through their experience of joint interaction, adults and infants are likely to build up a recognition of procedures which allow them to identify significant objects and events; for example, marking an event or object by using a loud voice is something that most people and many animals recognise. In addition, as has just been outlined, there are specific claims about innate capacities to recognise the pragmatic functions of utterances from their acoustic form. However, it is also likely to be the case that the ways of marking attentional focus will be influenced by cultural conventions. For example, Moriwaka, Shand, and Kosawa (1988) report that there are differences between the interaction patterns of pre-linguistic infants and their Japanese or American mothers.

Thus, I believe that during the first year of life both adults and infants are coming to understand and agree on methods of marking out significant objects and events (remember that even young infants will wave their arms in excitement and squirm with pleasure at something that pleases them). What I would also argue is that the use of communicative devices which identify that something is significant can then play a part in the understanding of reference. For example, a ball is interesting because adults roll and bounce it. In this way certain functional properties are identified and given significance through the process of social interaction. In this situation it is likely that an adult would draw attention to the action of the ball by a mock suprised expression, by a vocalisation which marks the event as unusual, and by speech which is integrated with the movement of the ball so that attention-worthy movements coincide with the crucial words in the utterance (i.e. the word "ball" might be said at the moment a ball is rolled). In these and similar ways, adults mark out to infants the significant aspects of their environment; infants learn that balls are important because of what they do and may learn that different balls can be treated in equivalent ways. They learn that the same procedures are used with different sized and shaped balls and in this way different balls are treated as equivalent during the process of interaction.

Nelson (1974) in her theory about acquiring a vocabulary drew attention to the way that common functional properties could provide the basis for identifying category membership, so that objects are identified on the basis of their common functional properties (e.g. a ball on the basis of rolling, throwing, etc.). However, a problem with the theory is that it is not clear on what basis infants can identify a set of functional relations relevant to a ball from the many different examples of throwing, rolling etc. This issue has been a central problem in theories about the development of categories and concepts: how can a concept be formed from different examples of the target, when there are so many functional and perceptual dimensions on which items of a category differ? (Think about all the different types of spherical object an infant might see.) I am suggesting that one way out of this impasse is to suggest that infants appreciate the intentional significance of adult actions and use these as a basis for identifying commonalities between different objects. In other words, the discovery of categories is not simply a result of attunement to the physical world as some have suggested (e.g. the semantic feature hypothesis of Clark or a Gibsonian view of affordances), but also a result of attunement to the social world.

It is certainly the case that an appreciation of perceptual features may play a part in category formation (see Mandler, Chapter 7, this volume), but I do not believe that they provide a complete explanation of the understanding of reference. Without infants possessing an understanding of the intentions and the objectives of social interaction it is difficult to explain the way they are able to link the range of words to referents in their environment; I believe that they are able to do this because they can identify objects which are similar because they are involved in similar *purposes*. Of course, such a proposal moves the problem of identifying concepts elsewhere, to the understanding of social purposes, but its importance is that the suggestion involves not simply an analysis of the physical world, but also an analysis of the social world. Nor would I want this claim to be interpreted as a suggestion that all concepts are formed as a result of identifying similar social purposes. Rather, it may be that we should admit that concepts are formed by infants on the basis of a variety of forms of information, and a variety of ways, much as adults form new concepts.

JOINT ATTENTION AND THE ACQUISITION OF SPEECH

There is now considerable evidence that the relationship of adult speech to objects that are the focus of infant interest is related to the development of vocabulary and speech. A number of studies have indicated that mothers who link their speech to infant interest have children who at a later age have a larger vocabulary (Tomasello & Todd, 1983; Tomasello & Farrer, 1986) and are more lingusitically advanced (Harris, 1993; Wells & Robinson, 1982). However, there are uncertainties with such non-experimental studies. It can always be argued that maternal behaviour could be a product of child characteristics, so that the relation between adult speech to infant interest is a result of infants having certain abilities, rather than a cause of these abilities. Thus, it is reassuring that experimental studies also indicate that there is better comprehension of words spoken to a child during periods of joint attention than at other times (Tomasello & Farrer, 1986). Indeed, Tomasello and Farrer (1986) report that infants are better at comprehending words when an adult refers to an object that the infant is already looking at, than an object which is introduced to the infant by the experimenter (see also Dunham, Dunham, & Curwin, 1993).

More recent research about these issues has revealed that by 16 months infants are remarkably adept in using non-verbal cues to help them understand the referent of adult speech. Baldwin (1993b) has documented the way that between 14 and 19 months there is a change from instability in linking words and referents, to the ability to make sophisticated deductions about the identity of the referent. Baldwin (1991) has examined what occurs when an adult refers to an object which is the focus of her own interest, but the child is looking elsewhere. On testing afterwards, 16 month old, infants, when asked, accurately pointed to the appropriate object from an array. Thus, the infants did not simply link the word with the object of their interest, but linked the word with the object of the *adult's* interest. Tomasello and Barton (in press) also found that 24 month infants will "skip over" irrelevant information and appropriately link a word with its referent. In this situation an adult said an utterance like, "Where's the toma?", the adult then picked up two objects with a disappointed expression, and eventually there was pleasure when a target object was picked up. When the comprehension of children was tested afterwards they tended to pick out the target object as a "toma". Here again it is apparent that children are not simply linking a word with the concurrent object they see, but have a more sophisticated understanding of the purpose and context of the adult utterance, which enables them to understand the meaning of unfamiliar words.

Thus, not only is joint attention assoicated with vocabulary development in the second year, but also by the end of the second year infants already have in place quite advanced understanding of reference which allows them to use non-verbal cues and pragmatic information to identify the referent of an utterance. In the future, research is likely to provide answers to questions about the age at which these skills emerge and the developmental course of these abilities.

DOUBTS ABOUT THE SIGNIFICANCE OF JOINT ATTENTION

There are a number of reports of circumstances which seem to indicate that speech can develop without the establishment of joint attention. The cross-cultural studies reported by Ochs and Schieffelin (1984) suggest that children develop language without the experience of the modified and supportive social interaction that is typical of Western middle-class families. Some of these findings will be briefly reviewed. For example, the Kaluli of Papua New Guinea are reported to sit their infants on their laps seated outwards, and the mothers speak *for* their infants, so that it appears that the infant is taking part in conversation with other adults. The mother does not typically engage in conversation with her young infant. Furthermore, the modifications present in Western speech to young infants are not supposed to take place (e.g. higher pitch, shorter utterances, and baby terms). Infants of between 6 months and 12 months are expected to start to respond to commands; and when words are produced, mothers engage in tutorial sessions where they will supply a model utterance which the child is expected to imitate. However, these reports do not necessarily constitute a problem for arguments about the importance of joint attention. Ochs and Schiefflin themselves argue that children become adapted to the procedures and social organisation of their culture, and that speech then becomes tied into this cultural perspective. Furthermore, there have been questions raised about the accuracy of reports about childrearing in these and other circumstances (Fernald et al., 1989; Harris, 1992). In addition, it seems likely that taking care of any infant must involve some element of shared understanding, even if it is concerned only with matters such as feeding, soothing and cleaning. What may differ between cultures is the extent to which adults adapt to the needs of the infant, and the frequency of interactions where there is a shared understanding.

The studies of children who are blind and of children who are deaf reveal that, in the absence of cognitive disabilities, speech develops at a very similar rate to that in other children (Messer, 1994). At first sight such studies suggest that joint attention, and in particular visual joint attention is not essential for the development of vocabulary and language. Children who are blind cannot establish visual joint attention, and children who are deaf have the problem of seeing a referent and the adult's sign at the same time. Given the remarkable resilience of language development in both these circumstances, can a claim about the importance of joint attention be sustained? I would argue that there are a number of reasons for believing that joint attention is important for development with these children.

In the case of children who are blind, joint attention can be established by adults talking about objects that the child is manipulating. Fraiberg (1979) in her pioneering work emphasised this very point. She encouraged parents to watch their infant's hands to gain information about his or her interest and to speak about the objects that infants are manipulating. Urwin (1978) in her work has suggested that shared routines, such as the use of nursery rhymes, can fullfill a similar function. Thus, in both these ways the social and physical worlds can be integrated despite the lack of co-ordination provided by the visual channel. Interestingly, the development of communication of children who are blind is different from that of sighted in a number of respects; and these differences are consistent with children who are blind having less experience of attending to topics established by their conversational partner. Children who are blind tend to talk about their own actions and feelings; they have problems about using the personal pronouns "I" and "you"; and they often introduce topics at inappropriate points in the conversation (Anderson, Dunlea, & Kekelis, 1993).

Children who are deaf, as has already been mentioned, are likely to have difficulty in integrating the physical and social world simply because both sources of information about reference come in the visual channel.

Obviously this could create difficulties, because, instead of having a simultaneous presentation of speech with referent, there is a problem of relating a visual sign with the physical object when the two may not occur in the same visual field. Despite this, children who are deaf can acquire signs at about the same age as hearing children acquire words, and the rate may even be faster and earlier (Folven & Bonvillian, 1991). One factor which may aid the acquisition of signs is the way adults modify their signing with deaf infants. Harris (1992) has reported that parents often sign so that the gesture occurs in the same visual field as the target object.

This optimistic picture does not seem to apply to all children who are deaf. Those children who are born to hearing parents seem to be more at risk for long-term problems related to communication. This is usually related to the fact that hearing parents have to acquire a sign language to be able to communicate with their child, and they will not be as fluent when using this second language. However, Gregory and Barlow (1989) have argued that these difficulties also may stem from parents having to use a different mode of communication, with different constraints, and with the child having different needs. Consistent with this argument are findings which indicated that in relation to a deaf child, more time is spent in joint attention by deaf mothers than by hearing mothers (Gregory & Barlow, 1989). Consequently, it would appear that there are ways to overcome the difficulties of establishing joint attention when there is sensory disability; and the findings indicate that joint attention may be important for communicative development.

Thus, vocabulary and language can emerge in circumstances where there is apparently little opportunity for joint visual attention to take place. However, a closer inspection of these reports suggest that we may need to extend the notion of joint attention from the joint visual regard of an object or event, to other circumstances and other sets of behaviours which can ensure that an infant understands the relation between a referent and a referential word. Once this extension is carried out, then confidence in the importance of joint attention for development is reinforced rather than diminished.

ASSUMPTONS AND CONSTRAINTS.

The postulation of assumptions and constraints that aid the vocabulary acquisition process minimises the role of joint attention and in particular the role of shared understanding in development. According to this perspective, children have a number of cognitive strategies which enable them to understand the meaning of words they hear, and to develop categories for these words. The most relevant assumption to our discussion is the *whole object assumption*. This involves children assuming that a word refers to a whole object rather than a part or attribute of the object (i.e. it is assumed that "ball" refers to the whole thing rather than its colour or shape). If children make such an assumption, there would be none of the uncertainty discussed earlier about the exact identity of the referent of a word (whether the word refers to the whole object, its shape, colour or so on). At a stroke centuries of discussion about the difficulties of identifying can be eliminated! Several versions of the whole object assumption have been put forward in various forms and by various investigators (MacNamara, 1972; Clark, 1991; Markman, 1991). My worries about the whole object assumption (and about similar proposals) are that there is also a tendency to believe that this is a product of an innate bias, and that the term is a description rather than an hypothesis.

Although it is possible that infants automatically assume a word they hear is related to the whole object they see, this claim largely ignores the social and cultural information that enables infants to identify this relationship. Thus, a cognitive ability in the shape of a constraint is attributed to the infant, but the operation of the cognitive ability can be accomplished only if there is substantial understanding of as cognitively demanding, if not more demanding, array of social information For example, locating an object in the environmental depends on information from the social context being used to locate the referent before the whole object assumption could come into operation. Such social information is in itself a complex array, the understanding of which depends on experience and inference. Furthermore, a related assumption appears to operate in primates. Savage-Rumbaugh (1990) taught apes to communicate using different discs (lexigrams). When presented with a known disc which related to a known food, together with a new disc and a new food, the apes assume the new disc refers to the new food. Furthermore, Carpenter Tomasello, and Savage-Rumbaugh (1995) have reported that chimpanzees raised by humans show many child-like behaviours and attention patterns when dealing with novel objects during problem solving, and their behaviour is often closer to that of children than to that of chimpanzees raised by their biological mothers.

However, I am not arguing against the idea that children employ such assumptions but against the idea that it is necessary to claim that this is an innate ability. A more parsimonious explanation is that children, because of their previous social experiences, come to recognise that communication is usually about the whole object rather than one of its properties. In this way there is a symmetry between the social processes used to identify the referent and the social processes which enable children to identify the relevant property of the referent. Already, these types of criticism have been taken on board by Golinkoff, Mervis, and Hirsh-Pasek (1994) who have proposed that vocabulary acquisition principles are a result of developmental processes.

The idea of a constraint on information processing also encounters problems with explaining the way that verbs are acquired; if children simply assume that words always refer to objects, they would never acquire verbs. Obviously another set of constraints is required to pull the hypothesis out of these difficulties. Equally seriously, the whole object assumption does not allow children to acquire the meaning of properties of objects (hence a child will refer to a cooker as "hot", presumably having heard the expression "No, it's hot"). This has been recognised and has resulted in proposals of a *mutual exclusivity assumption,* that different words will refer to different aspects of the world (Markman, 1991). From this it follows that if children already know the name of the object and they hear the object referred to by a new word, they will come to the conclusion that the new word refers to a property of the object. However, there is not a clear specification of when the mutual exclusivity assumption starts to operate and of the developmental relationship it has with the whole object assumption (but see Golinkoff et al., 1994 for an interesting set of proposals about the emergence of these principles). Such uncertainties mean that there have been very great problems in testing this hypothesis.

Consequently, I believe that it is difficult to maintain that these assumptions are innate or are aspects of cognitive functioning which are isolated from social understanding. Instead, a broader view of the evidence points to these assumptions being part of a perspective that children have acquired from their social experience and which are brought to bear on identifying the relation between words, intention, and reference. Rather than supposing that children apply these assumptions in a mechanistic way, it seems more reasonable to claim that children utilise their knowedge of communication to make sense of the relationships they detect between words and objects. The studies of Baldwin and of Tomasello and his colleagues, already described, point to the flexibility and sophistication of children when attempting to understand these relationships.

It has to be admitted that the claim that children are working out the relationship between words and referents from their prior understanding of the world does not constitute a clear and testable hypothesis. However, neither do the claims about assumptions and constraints provide a clear set of testable hypotheses. One difference between the two positions is that children should be more flexible in their strategies according to a problem-solving approach. In relation to this, it is interesting that 2-year-old children when given a solid object appear to treat a new word as the name for the shape, but when given a shape made of Nivea cream treat a new word as the name of the substance (Soja, Carey, & Spelke, 1990). Thus, they make a link between word and referent according to the characteristics of the object being referred to, and knowledge of the relevance of such characteristics is likely to be based on prior experience. It would be interesting to know whether similar behaviour occurs at younger ages.

THE WIDER SIGNIFICANCE OF JOINT ATTENTION

I hope I have argued convincingly that the procedures involved in establishing joint attention are significant in assisting the development of shared understanding and in developing children's vocabulary. However, the development of vocabulary is not the same as the development of language. The controversy surrounding teaching "language" to primates centres on this difference. It has repeatedly been shown that primates can acquire a vocabulary to describe their world, made up of either the signs used by the deaf or arbitary discs given distinctive attributes. Some maintain that this vocabulary is merely instrumental and does not involve any wider understanding of communication, although, such a view seems to be at variance with the flexibility and creativity of the production of these signs. What is in greater dispute is whether these communicative signs can be considered to consititute a language. From a linguistic perspective, language is usually considered to involve a rule based ordering of elements and structural dependency (the agreement between different elements in an utterance such as between the subject and the verb, "I swim", "he swim*s*"). Greenfield and Savage-Rumbaugh (1991) claim that Kanzi, a pygmy chimpanzee, shows evidence of such ordering, by tending to place a name at the beginning of an utterance when another animal was the actor, and at the end of the utterance when the other animal was the receiver of an action. Although this appears to represent the beginnings of a linguistic structure, such an organisation is relatively unsophisticated, and consequently the debate about whether or not this is language is likely to continue.

Whatever one's position about whether or not primates can produce language, it is apparent that they cannot produce communication which has the complexity and sophistication of a 3-year-old. Thus, it is important to recognise that having a vocabulary does not necessarily entail being able to use morpho-syntax (the grammar for language). Such a conclusion implies that though joint attention is related to the acquisition of vocabulary it is not necessarily involved in the development of the more complex aspects of language abilities.

Currently there is a debate related to this issue. The debate concerns the connectionist and symbolic accounts as explanations of language acquisition. Connectionist accounts usually suppose that there is a single mechanism underlying the acquisition and development of vocabulary and morpho-syntax. Thus, continuity is predicted to exist between the acquiring of words and the development of linguistic rules, involving, for instance, using the past tense on verbs (in English this commonly involves adding -ed to a verb; walk*ed*). Symbolic accounts tend to stress the discontinuity in development, because such models suppose that children's acquisition of linguistic rules is a separate and different process from the acquisition of vocabulary items (e.g. Marcus et al., 1992).

Marchman and Bates (1994) have described evidence in support of the continuity position. One piece of evidence is that the best predictor of a 28-month-old's mean length of utterance (often taken as a good measure of linguistic ability) is the size of the child's earlier vocabulary (Bates, Bretherton, & Snyder, 1988), suggesting that a child with a larger vocabulary will later be more linguistically advanced. Marchman and Bates also present evidence that the development of past tense forms of verbs is related to the size of children's vocabularies. Thus, there are some findings which suggest that earlier vocabulary acquisition processes may be related to the development of linguistic forms. This controversy is likely to continue, but it does point to the possibility of vocabulary providing an important basis for linguistic progress.

SUMMARY

In this chapter I have examined the development of reference to objects. This process involves children being able to integrate the social and physical worlds. In the first 6 months, social processes put infants in a position to begin to appreciate the communication of others. From a very early age they are exposed to communication which marks out significant parts of their physical environment; and adults comment on the physical environment with increasing frequency during the first year. Towards the end of the first year infants and adults have a number of procedures which allow the co-ordination of interest. As a result, infants can start to relate words to objects, but such understanding is not a trivial process. Infants need to be able to select the appropriate characteristic of the target object, and I argue that such selection is made possible by a shared history of what is significant and salient. Adults and infants, through a history of shared experiences, have a continually growing awareness of the salient and significant parts of their environment for each other. Evidence has also been reviewed which indicates that adult–infant shared interest in the world is related to vocabulary acquisition, and this in turn may be related to later lingusitic processes.

REFERENCES

Anderson, E. S., Dunlea, A., & Kekelis, L. (1993). The impact of input: Language acquisition in the visually impaired. *First Language*, *13*, 23–49.

Baron-Cohen, S. (1993). *Origins of theory of mind: The eye-direction detector*. Presentation at the Society for Research in Child Development Conference, New Orleans.

Balogh, R.D. & Porter, R.H. (1986). Olfactory preferences resulting from mere exposure in human neonates. *Infant Behaviour and Development*, *9*, 395–401.

Baldwin, D.A. (1991). Infants' contribution to the achievement of joint reference. *Child Development*, *62*, 875–890.

Baldwin, D.A. (1993a). Early referential understanding: Infants' ability to recognize referential acts for what they are. *Developmental Psychology*, *29* (5), 832–843.

Baldwin, D.A. (1993b). Infants' ability to consult the speaker for clues to word reference. *Journal of Child Language*, *20*, 395–418.

Bates, E., Bretherton, I., Snyder, L. (1988). *From first words to grammar: individual differences and dissociable mechanisms.* Cambridge: Cambridge University Press.

Bertenthal, B.I., Proffitt, D.R., Spetner, N.B., & Thomas, M.A. (1985). The development of infant sensitivity to biomechanical motions. *Child Development*, *56*, 531–543.

Blount, B.G., & Padgug, E.J. (1976). Prosodic, paralinguistic, and interaction features in parent–child speech: English and Spanish. *Journal of Child Language*, 67–86.

Bushnell, I.W.R., Sai, F., & Mullin, J.T. (1989). Neonatal recognition of the mother's face. *British Journal of Developmental Psychology*, *7*, 3–15.

Butterworth, G.E. & Grover, L. (1990). Joint visual attention, manual pointing and preverbal communication in human infancy. In M. Jeannerod (ed.), *Attention and performance*, *13*. Hove: Lawrence Erlbaum Associates Ltd.

Carpenter, M., Tomasello, M., & Savage-Rumbaugh, S. (1995). Joint attention and imitative learning in children, chimpanzees, and enculturated chimpanzees. *Social Development*, *4* (3), 217–237.

Clark, E.V. (1991). Acquisition principles in language development. In S.A. Gelman & J.A. Byrnes (eds), *Perspectives on language and thought*. Cambridge: Cambridge University Press.

Collis, G.M. (1977). Visual co-orientation and maternal speech. In H.R. Schaffer (ed.), *Studies in mother–infant interaction*, pp.355–375. London: Academic Press.

DeCasper, A.J. & Fifer, W.P. (1980). Of human bonding: Newborns prefer their mothers' voices. *Science*, *208*, 1174 1176.

Dunham, P.J., Dunham, F., & Curwin, A. (1993). Joint-attentional states and lexical acquisition at 18 months. *Developmental Psychology*, *29*, (5), 827–831.

Fernald, A. & Mazzie, C. (1991). Prosody and focus in speech to infants and adults. *Developmental Psychology*, *27* (2), 209–221.

Fernald, A., Taeschner, T., Dunn, J., Papousek, M., Boysson-Bardies, B., & Fukui, I. (1989). A cross-language study of prosodic modications in mothers' and fathers' speech to preverbal infants. *Journal of Child Language*, *16*, 477–501.

Fogel, A. (1993). *Developing through relationships.* Hemel Hempstead: Harvester Wheatsheaf.

Fogel, A., Toda, S., & Kawai, M. (1988). Mother–infant face-to-face interaction in Japan and the United States: A laboratory comparison using 3-month-old infants. *Developmental Psychology*, *24*, 398–406.

Folven, R.J. & Bonvillian, J.D. (1991). The transition from nonreferential to referential language in children acquiring American sign language. *Developmental Psychology*, *27* (5), 806–816.

Fraiberg, S. (1979). Blind infants and their mothers: An examination of the sign system. In M. Bullowa (ed.), *Before speech.* Cambridge: Cambridge University Press.

Golinkoff, R.M. (1993). When is communication a "meeting of minds"? *Journal of Child Language*, *20*, 199–207.

Golinkoff, R.M., Mervis, C.B., & Hirsh-Pasek, K. (1994). Early object labels: The case for a developmental principles framework. *Journal of Child Language*, *21* (1), 125–155.

Greenfield, P.M. & Savage-Rumbaugh, E.S. (1991). Imitations, grammatical development, and the invention of protogrammar by an ape. In N.A. Krasnor, D.M. Rumbaugh, R.L. Schiefelbusch, & M. Studdert-Kennedy (eds). Biological and behavioral determinants of language development. Hillsdale, N.J.: Lawrence Erlbaum Associates Inc.

Gregory, S. & Barlow, S. (1989). Interaction between deaf babies and hearing mothers. In B. Woll, (ed.), Language development and sign language. *Monographs of the International Sign Linguistics Association.* University of Bristol.

Harris, M. (1992). *Language experience and early development.* Hillsdale, N.J.: Lawrence Erlbaum Associates Inc.

Harris, M. (1993). The relationship of maternal speech to children's first words. In D. Messer & G. Turner (eds), *Critical influences on language acquisition and development.* London: Macmillan.

Hobson, R.P. (1986). The autistic child's appraisal of expressions of emotion. *Journal of Child Psychology and Psychiatry, 27,* 321–342.

Hobson, R.P. (1991). Against the theory of "Theory of Mind". *British Journal of Developmental Psychology, 9,* 33–51.

Hobson, R.P. (1993). Perceiving attitudes, conceiving minds. In C. Lewis & P. Mitchell (eds), *Origins of an understanding of mind.* Hillsdale, N.J.: Lawrence Erlbaum Associates Inc.

Kaye, K. (1982). *The mental and social life of babies.* Chicago: University of Chicago Press.

Lempers, J.D. (1976). *Production of pointing, comprehension of pointing and understanding of looking behavior in young children.* Unpublished doctoral dissertation, University of Minnesota.

MacFarlane, A. (1975). Olfaction in the development of social preferences in the human neonate. In Ciba Foundation Symposium (ed.) *Parent–infant interaction.* New York: Elsevier.

MacNamara, J. (1972). Cognitive basis of language learning in infants. *Psychological Review, 79* (1), 1–13.

Marchman, V.A. & Bates, E. (in press). Continuity in lexical and morphological development: A test of the critical mass hypothesis. 1994: *Journal of Child Language, 21* (2), 339–366.

Marcus, G.F., Ulman, M., Pinker, S., Hollander, M., Rosen, T.J., & Xu, F. (1992). Over regularization in language acquisition. *Monographs of the Society for Research in Child Development, 57*(4), Serial No. 228.

Meltzoff, A. & Gopnik, A. (1993). The role of imitation in understanding persons and developing a theory of mind. In S. Baron-Cohen, H. Tager-Flushberg, & D. Cohen (eds), *Understanding other minds: perspective from autism.* Oxford: Oxford University Press.

Markman, E.M. (1991). The whole-object, taxonomic and mutual exclusivity assumptions as initial constraints on word meanings. In S.A. Gelman & J.A. Byrnes (eds), *Perspectives on language and thought.* Cambridge: Cambridge University Press.

Messer, D.J. (1978). The integration of mother's referential speech with joint play. *Child Development, 49,* 781–787.

Messer, D.J. (1981). The identification of names in maternal speech to infants. *Journal of Psycholinguistic Research, 10,* 69–77.

Messer, D.J. (1983). The redundancy between adult speech and non-verbal interaction: A contribution to acquisition? In R. Golinkoff (ed.), *The transition from prelinguistic to linguistic Communication.* Hillsdale, N.J.: Lawrence Erlbaum Associates Inc.

Messer, D.J. (1994). *The development of communication.* Wiley: Chichester.

Messer, D.J. (1995). Attachment and care. In D.J. Messer & C. Meldrum (eds), *Psychology for nurses and health care professionals.* Hemel Hempstead: Harvester Wheatsheaf.

Moore, C. & Corkum, V. (1994). Social understanding at the end of the first year of life. *Development Review, 141* (4), 349–72..

Moriwaka , H., Shand, N., & Kosawa, Y. (1988). Maternal speech to prelingual infants in Japan and the United States: Relationships among functions, forms and referents. *Journal of Child Language, 15,* 237–256.

Murphy, C.M. & Messer, D.J. (1977). Mothers, infants and pointing: A study of a gesture. In H.R. Schaffer (ed.) *Studies in other–infant interaction.* London: Academic Press.

Nelson, K. (1974). Concept, word and sentence: Interrelations in acquisition and development. *Psychological Review*, *81*, 267–285.

Ochs, E. & Schieffelin, B.B. (1984). Language acquisition and socialization. In R.A. Shweder & R.A. Levine (eds), *Culture theory*. Cambridge: Cambridge University Press.

Papousek, M., Bornstein, M.H., Nuzzo, C., Papousek, H., & Symmes, D. (1990). Infant responses to prototypical melodic contours in parental speech. *Infant Behaviour and Development*, *13*, 539–545.

Papousek, M. & Papousek, H. (1989). Forms and functions of vocal matching in precanonical mother–infant interactions. *First Language*, *9* (26), 137–158.

Papousek, M., Papousek, K. H., & Symmes, D. (1991). The meanings of melodies in mothers in tone and stress languages. *Infant Behaviour and Development*, *14*, 415–440.

Penman, R., Cross, T., Milgrom-Friedman, J., & Meares, R. (1983). Mothers' speech to prelingual infants: a pragmatic analysis. *Journal of Child Language*, *10*, 17–34.

Quine, W.V.O. (1969). *Ontological relativity and other essays*. New York: Columbia University Press.

Rabain-Jamin, J. & Sabeau-Jouannet, E. (1989). Playing with pronouns in French maternal speech to prelingual infants. *Journal of Child Language*, *16*, 217–238.

Ratner, N. & Bruner, J. (1978). Games, social exchange and the acquisition of language. *Journal of Child Language*, *5*, 391–401.

Savage-Rumbaugh, E.S. (1990). Language as a cause–effect communication system. *Philosophical Psychology*, *3*, (1), 55–76.

Scaife, M. & Bruner, J.S. (1975). The capacity for joint visual attention. *Nature*, *253*, 265–266.

Schaffer, H.R. (1984). *The child's entry into a social world*. London: Academic Press.

Snow, C.E. (1977). Mothers' speech research: From input to interaction. In C.E. Snow and C.A. Ferguson (eds), *Talking to children*. Cambridge: Cambridge University Press.

Soja, N.N., Carey, S., & Spelke, E.S. (1990). Ontological categories guide young children's inductions of word meaning: Object terms and substances terms. *Cognition*, *38*, 179–211.

Sylvester-Bradley, B. & Trevarthen, C.B. (1978). Baby-talk as an adaptation to the infant's communication. In N. Waterson & C.E. Snow (eds), *The development of communication*. New York: Wiley.

Tomasello, M. & Barton, M. (in press). Learning words in non-ostensive contexts. *Developmental Psychology*.

Tomasello, M. & Todd, J. (1983). Joint attention and lexical acquisition style. *First Language*, *4*, 197–212.

Tomasello, M. & Farrar, J. (1986). Joint attention and early language. *Child Development*, *57*, 1454–1463.

Trevarthen, C. (1982). The primary motives for co-operative understanding. In G. Butterworth & P. Lights (eds), *Social cognition*. Brighton: Harvester.

Urwin, C. (1978). *The development of communication between blind infants and their parents: Some ways into language*. (Unpublished). Doctoral dissertation, University of Cambridge.

Wells, G. & Robinson, W.P. (1982). The role of adult speech in language development. In C. Fraser and K. Scherer (eds), *The social psychology of language*. Cambridge: Cambridge University Press.

13 Language and its Pathology

Margaret Harris
Department of Psychology, Royal Holloway and Bedford New College, UK.

INTRODUCTION

The study of infancy has traditionally given little attention to the development of language. Indeed, Piaget saw the emergence of language as a main achievement of the sensorimotor period—an accomplishment which, along with other kinds of symbolic representation, marked the transition into preoperational thought. Piaget's view of the non-linguistic nature of infancy arose from his assumption that language is synonymous with speech as is implied by the term "infancy" itself, which comes from the Latin *infans* meaning "unable to speak".

It is easy to see why the emergence of speech should be seen as such an important milestone in development both by psychologists and by parents. Once children produce their first word they are seen as having mastered the first step towards a significant human achievement. However, although the utterance of the child's first word does mark the beginning of an important new stage in language, this event should also be seen as the culmination of a series of important developments that have occurred in the first months of infancy.

The first part of this chapter is concerned with two important developments that occur in the first year of life and are essential for the acquisition of spoken language. These are speech perception and the development of lexical comprehension. The second part considers the relationship between early language comprehension and production and the wide range of individual variation shown by children in both the content and the rate of their early development. The final section is concerned with recent evidence about the way in which the development of language comprehension and production is affected by early focal brain injury.

SPEECH PERCEPTION

Evidence for innate abilities

Research into the abilities of young infants to perceive speech has produced some very remarkable results in the past two decades (see Mehler & Dupoux, 1994 for an excellent overview). One of the most striking findings is that hemispheric lateralisation for perception of speech sounds rather than non-speech sounds appears to be present at birth. Using a dichotic listening task, in which syllables are presented in both ears, Bertoncini et al. (1989) showed that infants less than four days old respond more to a syllable change presented to the right ear than to the left ear. They obtained the opposite pattern with musical notes: babies reacted more when a change in note was presented to the left ear than the right.

This very early specialisation for perception of speech sounds is further demonstrated both by abilities present at birth and by the rapid learning that takes place over the first months of life. There is very wide variation among languages in the acoustic distinctions that are linguistically significant. Research on infant abilities to perceive speech has shown that the first year of life is very important for the development of specific awareness of those phonemes that are present in the language or languages used in the infant's speech community. There appears to be a critical period for setting phoneme boundaries and, once these have been set in one way, it is very difficult for an adult to master a different set of phonemes particularly if they draw phoneme boundaries that are incompatible with those of the mother tongue. For example, in English, /r/ and /l/ are two different phonemes but, in Japanese, both sounds are variants of a single phoneme which is why Japanese people who learn English as adults typically have great difficulty in hearing the difference between the two.

Pioneering research by Eimas and his colleagues (Eimas, Siqueland, Jusczyk, & Vogirito, 1971) demonstrated the remarkable ability of the young infant to distinguish between phoneme pairs. Using a sucking paradigm, in which young infants sucked on a dummy in order to hear a sound, Eimas et al. were able to demonstrate that babies of 1 to 4 months could distinguish between pairs of sounds that were also different phonemes. Having established a baseline of sucking for each baby, Eimas first played a single synthesised sound, /pa/. An initial increase in rate of sucking followed; then, as the infants habituated to the sound, their sucking rate returned to baseline. The neonates were then presented with a new synthesised sound. For half of them this was a different phoneme, /ba/. The other babies heard a sound that differed acoustically from the original by an equal amount but did not cross the phoneme boundary and so would still be heard as /pa/ by an adult. The babies in the first group, who heard /ba/, started to suck rapidly again in order to hear the new sound but the second group did not increase their rate of sucking, suggesting that the "new" sound did not appear to differ from the original one.

Subsequent studies have shown that infants of 1 month or less are able to discriminate phonemes on the basis of all possible kinds of phonetic contrast. These include studies by Eimas (1974) contrasting place of articulation (/p/, /t/, /k/) and two studies by Miller and Eimas contrasting manner of articulation: Miller and Eimas (1983) compared /d/ with /n/ (an occlusive with a nasal) and Eimas and Miller (1980) compared /d/ with /l/ (a liquid). A study by Trehub (1976) showed that infants could also discriminate between vowel pairs such as /a/ and /i/ or /i/ and /u/.

As Mehler and Dupoux (1994) note, these impressive findings strongly suggest that babies are born with the potential to discriminate all possible phonetic contrasts. However, what has begun to emerge from more recent studies is that, over the first year of life, infants' discriminatory abilities become more and more finely tuned by the language of their speech community.

Learning language specific discriminations

By about 8 months of age, infants begin to show a marked decrease in their ability to distinguish phonetic contrasts that are not present in the language (or languages) that they hear around them. This early effect of language exposure was first demonstrated by Werker and Tees in a series of studies. One of the best known (Werker & Tees, 1984) compared groups of babies from monolingual English, Hindi (Indian) and Salish (North American Indian), communities in a cross-sectional study. At 6 months, babies who had heard only English could distinguish equally well between phoneme pairs in each of the three languages. However, at 8 months, babies began to show signs of a decrease in ability to discriminate phonetic contrasts that occurred in either Hindi or Salish but not in English. At 1 year, babies who had heard only English were completely accurate in distinguishing between English phoneme pairs but were unable to perform above chance in discriminating phonemes that were specific to the other two languages. However, 1-year-old babies who had heard only Salish were 100% accurate with Salish phonemes and babies who had heard only Hindi were 100% accurate with Hindi phonemes.

A longitudinal study with monolingual English babies (Werker, Gilbert, Humphreys, & Tees, 1981) also demonstrated the gradual loss of ability to discriminate phonetic contrasts that are unique to Hindi and Salish. At 6 to 8 months of age the English babies could discriminate these contrasts with 100% accuracy but, between 8 and 10 months, this ability was almost completely lost. By the end of the first year, the infants were behaving in the same way as monolingual English-speaking adults in being totally unable to discriminate the Hindi and Salish phonemes.

It is important to note that the loss of ability to detect phonetic contrasts that are not present in the language of the infant's speech community arises when the contrasts overlap with those of the language with which the infant is becoming familiar. Best, McRoberts, and Sithole (1988) showed that the "clicks" used in the Zulu language remain detectable by 1-year-old infants and adults who have learned English. These clicks do not involve the same phonetic contrasts as Western languages and so there is no possible source of interference between the perception of clicks and the perception of phonemic boundaries in any Indo-European language. Thus it would appear that the "unlearning" of phonetic distinctions is a biproduct of the way that the infant learns to categorise a range of speech sounds as being realisations of a single phoneme. This categorical ability is an essential part of being able to perceive a particular language because there is very wide acoustic variation in the way in which a particular phoneme is pronounced by different speakers on different occasions. In order to identify a phoneme correctly the infant has to disregard phonetic contrasts that are not phonologically significant in the language of the speech community. As Mehler and Dupoux (1994) put it, speech perception is very much a case of "learning by forgetting".

A recent study by Kuhl et al. (1992) suggests that the age at which speech perception starts to become language specific is even earlier than the 8 months suggested by the Werker et al. studies. Kuhl et al. compared the ability of Swedish and American infants to discriminate vowel pairs. The vowels of Swedish and English are not identical and, when confronted with vowels from both languages, babies of 6 months were more sensitive to vowel contrasts in their native language. This is strong evidence that the process of extracting language specific information about phoneme boundaries is well under way as early as 6 months. As we shall see later, this fits in very neatly with data on the emergence of lexical comprehension.

Segmenting speech

So far our discussion of speech perception has concentrated on the infant's development of phonemic sensitivity which is, as we have seen, achieved through the development of selective sensitivity to phonetic contrasts. However, in order for the child to be able to recognise words it is necessary that information about speech sounds be perceived in such a way that sequences can be recognised and remembered.

There has been considerable debate both about the unit of analysis that is used in speech segmentation and about the age at which such segmentation becomes language specific. A series of elegant experiments by Mehler and his colleagues suggests that the unit of analysis used by young infants in the segmentation of speech may vary according to the language of their speech community.

In French, the syllable is an important unit in the segmentation. This is because French has a very regular syllabic structure as the duration of vowels is more or less constant and the stress pattern is fixed. Italian is also a syllabic language but stress patterns are variable. Two words, with different meanings, may differ only in stress and so it might be expected that the segmental unit for Italian would be sensitive to stress. Information about stress is also important in English although, unlike Italian, it is a non-syllabic language.

A comparison of French and English speaking adults (Cutler, Norris, & Segui, 1986) found that French speakers showed evidence of syllabic segmentation when listening to French, English and nonsense words, whereas the English subjects did not show syllabic segmentation even when listening to English words. Japanese speakers also show evidence of non-syllabic segmentation but of a different kind from that of English and Italian speakers. Otake, Hatano, Cutler, and Mehler (1993) found that Japanese adults segment speech at the level of the mora, a unit longer than a phoneme but shorter than a syllable.

The interesting developmental question that arises from these cross-linguistic comparisons concerns the age at which infants first begin to show language specific perception of segmentation. Four-day old French babies are sensitive to syllables and can detect the difference between bisyllabic and trisyllabic words even when the words are manipulated so that their duration is the same (Bijeljac-Babic, Bertoncini, & Mehler, 1993). Sansavini, Bertoncini, and Gionanelli (1994) have shown that Italian neonates are sensitive to stress. They can distinguish between two bisyllabic words that differ only according to which syllable is stressed (such as *ma*ma and ma*ma*). A recent study reported by Mehler (1994) has shown that Japanese neonates are sensitive to morae.

It is not yet clear at what age infants begin to develop selective sensitivity to the segmental features of their mother tongue. Evidence from phonetic development suggests that, at birth, babies will be equally sensitive to syllables, stress patterns and morae, but at what age do they lose the ability to perceive distinctions that are not salient in their own language? Definitive evidence will be provided only by longitudinal studies that compare abilities to make these different distinctions over the first year of life. However there is a high probability that such learning will have begun well before the end of the first year since Jusczyk, Cutler, and Redanz (1993) have shown that, by 9 months, English infants prefer to listen to words that follow the stress pattern occurring most frequently in English.

Access to information about segmental structure is an essential first step to recognising the boundaries of words. Indeed, Cutler and Mehler (1993) now argue that the infant's phonetic development is actually driven by processes that underpin lexical acquisition. This suggests that babies should have developed the appropriate segmental skills for word perception well before the end of the first year and so be in a position to acquire their first understanding of word meaning.

THE DEVELOPMENT OF LEXICAL COMPREHENSION

By comparison with the huge number of studies of early word production, there are relatively few studies of comprehension. This discrepancy stems, to a great extent, from the relative difficulty of obtaining reliable data on early comprehension. Assessing the competence of infants, using the traditional methods of vocabulary testing such as picture choice or object selection, is notoriously difficult and requires considerable familiarity with the child being tested. Bates (1993) also notes that the both the inter-correlations of different measures of early comprehension and split-half correlations within the same measure tend to be low. She found that correlations among laboratory measures of lexical comprehension at 13 months never rose above 0.50 (accounting for only 25% of the variance) and were sometimes as low as 0.10. The comparable range for intercorrelations of production measures was 0.50 to 0.75 and, by 20 months of age, production measures had become more reliable. The intercorrelation of comprehension measures, however, remained low.

Although there are significant problems in the use of laboratory methods for assessing early comprehension, there were several ways in which the reliability of assessment can be improved. Structured parental reports using checklists as well as spontaneous observation have provided one important method. The checklists of the Communicative Development Inventories (Fenson et al., 1990) have proved particularly valuable as a standardised assessment of early comprehension development.

Another important factor in obtaining reliable data on comprehension is to carry out detailed longitudinal studies which allow follow-up testing of information obtained from parental report or completion of checklists. Such testing is often essential for obtaining detailed information about the precise context in which a word is initially understood. It can also be helpful to ask parents to provide detailed information about the situation in which their child understands a particular word.

Studies of early comprehension

The first major investigation of comprehension was carried out by Benedict (1977; 1979). She studied the first 100 words comprehended and the first 50 words produced by eight infants, classifying the words using a modified version of Nelson's (1973) system which divides words into several categories including specific nominals (personal names such as "mummy"), general nominals (object names) and action words.

Benedict found that the largest categories in both domains were object names and action words. However, marked differences emerged in their distribution across the two modalities, and there were also changes in the proportion of different classes of word with increasing lexical size. Most notably, the proportion of object names in comprehension increased once the children had understood 50 words. Benedict thought that the 50-word level in comprehension marked an important boundary in language development as a considerable vocabulary spurt occurred at that time.

Benedict did not take account of the context in which words were understood and she based her classification on the adult use of words which is not always the same as the young child's. For example, a child may understand the word "bird" only in the single context of going over to the window to look out onto the garden, as reported by Harris et al. (1995b). When comprehension is restricted to a single behavioural context this should not be taken as evidence that the child understands the word as a specific nominal or object name.

A recent study by Gunzi (1993) investigated the early lexical comprehension of three children taking context into account and also testing comprehension as a follow-up to maternal diary reports. The findings of Benedict and Gunzi were comparable in many respects. For example, both studies found that comprehension generally preceded production and that, while there was considerable variation in the size of individual pre-production vocabularies, all children showed evidence of understanding object names in their first 50 words. Gunzi also replicated Benedict's finding that the proportion of object names increased between 50 and 100 words. However, there was a degree of disagreement between the studies concerning the relative proportion of object/action words in comprehension vocabularies. For example, Benedict found that object names constituted 39% of the first 50 words understood, while action words accounted for 36%. In Gunzi's study, object names accounted for only 25% of the first 50 words, while the proportion of action words was 43%. Similar discrepancies were also found at the 100-word level. Part of this difference in findings can be put down to Gunzi's use of contextual information in her classification which tended to demonstrate that some early object words were not comprehended as object names but were, instead, associated only with a single behavioural routine.

Individual difference in early comprehension

One important finding to emerge from both the studies of Benedict and Gunzi was that there were large individual differences in the proportion of object names understood. Bates, Bretherton, and Snyder (1988), who studied 27 children, found a similar pattern of individual variation. Object names were found to account for an average 34% of the words understood at 10 and 13 months, but this proportion ranged from 14% to 66% for individual children. The considerable variation in the proportion of object names appearing in early production vocabularies has led Bates et al. to suggest that Nelson's (1973) referential/expressive style dimension in the acquisition of production vocabulary is also evident in early comprehension. Significantly, Bates et al. found that the number of object names understood at 10 months was positively related to comprehension vocabulary size several months later. In other words, children who acquired more object names at the outset of acquiring a comprehension vocabulary—those who might be thought of as more "referential"—had generally more precocious comprehension vocabulary development.

Changes in the composition of comprehension vocabulary

The proportion of object names that children have in their comprehension vocabulary tends to increase with vocabulary size. This trend was first noted by Benedict (1977; 1979) and it has recently been studied in more detail by Harris and Chasin (1993). They compared the proportion of words of different types that children understood at various vocabulary sizes.

Harris and Chasin (1993) divided the first 100 words that children understood into four different types. Two of these categories have already been mentioned: object names and action words. The other two categories were personal names (that is, names of people, toys and family pets) and context-bound object words.

Context-bound object words are those which the child understands only as part of a fixed behavioural routine involving an object. For example, one of the children studied by Harris and Chasin (Harris et al., 1995b) first responded to the word "bird" by going over to the window and looking out at the garden of his house (presumably to see if there was a bird). He did not respond to "bird" in any other situation by, for example, looking or pointing. His response to "bird" was thus classified as an instance of context-bound object comprehension rather than as an instance of object name comprehension. This distinction between object names and context-bound object words is analogous to that made between contextually flexible object naming and context-bound object word use in production (see Harris et al., 1988, Barrett, Harris, & Chasin, 1991). Some examples of words in each of the four categories can be seen in Table 13.1.

In line with both Benedict (1977; 1979) and Gunzi (1993), Harris and Chasin found that the proportion of words of each type changed as the size of the comprehension vocabulary increased (see Table 13.2). Most notably, the proportion of object names gradually increased.

At the 20-word level, the number of personal names and object names was almost equal and together they accounted for two thirds of the total. The remaining two categories—context-bound object words and action words—each made up about one sixth of the total. At 60 words the proportion of object names and action words had both increased, while there was a marked decrease in the proportion of personal names. By the 100-word level the proportion of personal names had decreased even further and there was a corresponding rise in the proportion of object names. The proportion of action words remained the same as did the proportion of context-bound object words which was identical at all three points.

There was considerable individual variation in the number of object names and action words understood at each stage of vocabulary development. At the 60-word stage, for example, the range in number of object names understood was from 18 to 31 while the corresponding range for action words was from 9 to 22. In line with the findings of Bates et al. (1988), Harris and Chasin also found that there was a relationship between the proportion of object names in the 60-word comprehension vocabulary and the size of comprehension vocabulary at 16 months. However, the

TABLE 13.1
Examples of Categorisation of Early Comprehension Vocabulary

Word	*Classification*	*Context of Comprehension*
Lamby	Personal name	To woollen toy lamb used as comforter
Dylan	Personal name	To family cat
cat	Object name	To family cat and novel picture of cats
nose	Object name	To teddy's nose, own nose, mother's nose
down	Action word	Squats down on haunches
lunch	Action word	Goes to kitchen and attempts to climb into high chair
bird	CB object word	When indoors, looks out of window to garden
car	CB object word	Waves on hearing word or sound of car

NOTE:
CB = context-bound

TABLE 13.2
Percentage of Words in Each Category with Increasing Size of Comprehension Vocabulary

Vocabulary Size	*Word Category*			
	Personal Names	*Object Names*	*Context-bound Object Words*	*Action Words*
20	32.5	35.0	15.0	17.5
60	18.0	40.0	15.0	27.0
100	15.0	43.0	15.0	27.0

correlation between this first measure and the total number of words produced at 16 months did not reach significance, nor did the correlation between the two measures of vocabulary at 16 months (see Table 13.3).

Put simply, these findings and those of Bates et al. (1988) show that children who understand a large proportion of object names typically build up a comprehension vocabulary more quickly than children who understand fewer object names and more action words and personal names. However, neither the composition nor the size of comprehension vocabularies reliably predicts the size of production vocabularies. (It is relevant to note here that, within production, there is no simple relationship between the proportion of object names acquired and rate of vocabulary development. See Bates et al. (1994) for a detailed discussion of this issue.)

This finding of a dissociation between measures of early comprehension and production is in line with the argument of Bates et al. (1988) that there are two different—and separable—strands in the development of early

TABLE 13.3
Correlations between Proportion of Object Names in 60-word Comprehension Vocabulary and Size of Comprehension and Production Vocabularies at 16 months

	% object names in 60 word vocabulary	Comprehension vocabulary size at 16 months	Production vocabulary size at 16 months
% object names in 60 word vocabulary	1.00		
Comprehension vocabulary size at 16 months	0.86 $p=0.029$	1.00	
Production vocabulary size at 16 months	0.71 $p=0.115$	0.70 $p=0.122$	1.00

language. One strand—unanalysed production—consists of words and phrases that the child has learned to produce by rote whereas the other—analysed production—consists of words and phrases that the child also understands. Thus there will not be a simple relationship between the development of comprehension and production since the size of the production vocabulary is determined not only by the number of words that the child understands before first using them but also by the number of words that are produced without prior understanding.

Object name comprehension and the development of pointing

Given that object name comprehension has a key role in early lexical acquisition, it is appropriate to ask what factors might be associated with the emergence of this ability. Messer (Chapter 7, this volume) reviews the complex series of factors that are associated with the establishment of reference and with the child's developing understanding of the relationship between verbal and nonverbal ways of referring. There is also evidence of a very specific relationship between developing object name comprehension and the use of pointing.

Pointing is crucial to arguments about the development of referential communication—of which object naming forms a key part—because this gesture provides an important nonverbal procedure for picking out an object in the environment both for the benefit of another person and for oneself. The ability to point is uniquely human: even chimpanzees are incapable of using an outstretched arm and index finger to indicate (Butterworth, 1994).

What one might assume is that there is something common to the development of the ability to produce and understand pointing and the ability to understand and later produce object reference. Harris, Barlow-Brown, and Chasin (1995a) showed that there was a very high correlation ($r_s = 0.94$) between the age at which infants understood their first object name and the age at which they first pointed. This relationship was a very specific one in that there was no correlation between the first use of pointing and more general measures of comprehension development such as the age at which the first word was understood and the age at which a comprehension vocabulary spurt occurred.

The close coincidence between the emergence of object name comprehension and the first use of pointing was further evidenced by the fact that the mean age at which these two events occurred was separated by only one day with the mean age of pointing being 1;0.21 and the mean age of object name comprehension being 1;0.22. The author's own daughter, Francesca, produced her first point at 0;9.25 and showed evidence of understanding her first object name, "nose", a few days later at 0;10.0 (Harris, 1994).

Other authors have argued for a relationship between the child's own production of pointing and early language development. Bates et al. (1979) showed that both spontaneous giving of objects and communicative pointing (pointing followed by checking) were predictive of early vocabulary development; and Folven, Bonvillian, and Orlansky (1984/85) found that the frequency with which children produced communicative pointing between 9 and 12.5 months was positively correlated with the size of both spoken and signed lexicons during the second year of life.

Taken together these findings about the relationship between pointing and vocabulary development suggest that important stylistic differences emerge in the early stages of acquiring a comprehension vocabulary. Some children are highly object-oriented both in their vocabulary acquisition and their use of pointing whereas others are much less so. These individual differences are related to a wider issue concerning the young child's mastery and use of reference. What gives rise to this difference is still not clear and many different factors will almost certainly prove to be of importance. These are likely to include both individual differences in the infant's predisposition as well as differences in the opportunities that are made available for infants to derive information about object reference and the verbal and nonverbal ways in which such reference is made (see Chapter 7 by Messer for a discussion of these issues).

THE RELATIONSHIP BETWEEN COMPREHENSION AND PRODUCTION

The traditional view of the relationship between comprehension and production is that children begin to produce their first words when they have a comprehension vocabulary of between 20 and 30 items (see, for example, Nelson, 1988). More recently, however, it has become clear that the lag between comprehension and production is another source of individual variation in early language development.

Variations in the lag between comprehension and production

The clearest picture of variation in the comprehension–production lag comes from data emerging from the large-scale use of the Communicative Development Inventories (Fenson et al., 1990). Bates (1993) reports that, in a cross-sectional sample of 659 children, the overall correlation between comprehension and production was 0.45 when age was partialled out. Production began for most children when their comprehension vocabulary was between 11 and 50 words but production continued to lag behind comprehension. At a comprehension vocabulary of between 101 and 150 words, the median production vocabulary contained fewer than 20 words.

Although comprehension tended to follow behind production fairly consistently for the majority of children, there was a clearly identifiable subgroup of children who had a comprehension vocabulary in excess of 150 words but almost no intelligible speech. The existence of such children, who acquire a very large comprehension vocabulary before they produce their first word, was also noted by Bates et al. (1988), and there is a single-case study of Matthew (described in Harris, 1992) who also showed this pattern.

A third pattern was evident in a longitudinal study by Harris et al. (1995b) of six children, two of whom (Ben and Katy) understood only one and two words, respectively, at the point when they first began production. They also showed a lag of less than 1 month between the onset of comprehension and that of production whereas the other children showed a more typical lag of between 2 and 5 months. Figure 13.1 shows the pattern of comprehension and production vocabulary development for Ben over the next few months. His comprehension and production continued to follow one another closely; this pattern contrasts with the more typical pattern shown by Andrew.

There would thus appear to be three different patterns evident in the relationship between comprehension and production. The majority of children show a consistent lag in the acquisition of comprehension and production vocabularies, with comprehension being some way ahead of production. A significant number of children, however, build up an extensive comprehension vocabulary before beginning production. A third group

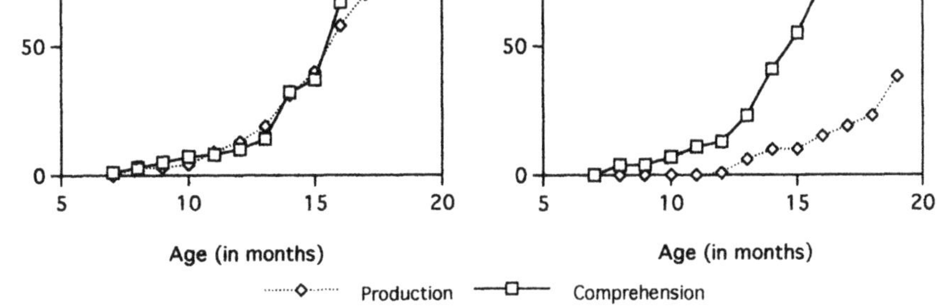

FIG. 13.1. Two patterns of developing lexical comprehension and production. Graphs show cumulative number of words acquired each month.

of children, who are probably fairly rare, do not show any significant lag between early comprehension and production.

In spite of this individual variation, there appears to be one aspect of development that is similar for normally developing children. In Harris et al. (1995b) all children began to understand their first word, usually their own name, between 7 and 8 months of age. This finding, that comprehension begins about half way through the first year of life, is entirely consistent with the data on speech perception that was reviewed earlier. Since both segmental and phonetic analyses have become language specific by about 6 months, it is entirely possible that infants can begin to recognise and respond to highly frequent words, such as their own name, by 7 months of age.

Comprehension and production of individual words

There is another important issue concerning the interrelation of comprehension and production that has not been touched upon so far. This concerns the extent to which the early understanding and production of words is symmetrical. In other words, does the young child's initial production of a word mirror the way in which that word is understood?

Harris et al. (1995, b) carried out a study to investigate the symmetry of early comprehension and production, focusing on the first 20 words that were produced. They found that there was a very close relationship between early production and comprehension of words: words that were contextually flexible in production tended also to be so in comprehension, and words that were context-bound also tended to be so in both modalities.

At first sight these data appeared to contradict the claim of Bates et al. (1988) that there are two strands evident in early language development which are distinguished by the extent to which comprehension underpins production. According to Bates et al., "analysed production"—the first strand—consists of words that have previously appeared in the child's comprehension vocabulary. Analysed production is characterised by contextually flexible word use; that is, the use of words in more than one behavioural context (see Harris et al., 1988). On the other hand, "unanalysed production"—the second strand—is characterised by an independence from comprehension since it consists of words and phrases that the child has learned by rote or in fixed routines.

One implication of the two-strand model is that context-bound words and contextually flexible words should differ in the extent to which they are rooted in comprehension: only words that are initially produced in a contextually flexible manner should have their basis in comprehension.

Close inspection of the Harris et al. data revealed some evidence that initially context-bound and initially contextually flexible words differed in the extent to which comprehension preceded their production. For words that were contextually flexible in both production and comprehension, there was clear evidence of comprehension occurring before the first instance of production in 78% of cases. The pattern for context-bound words was rather different: in only 35% of cases was there a record of comprehension prior to production. This is good evidence that words that are produced in a contextually flexible way from the outset are more likely to have been understood in the period prior to production than initially context-bound words.

EFFECTS OF FOCAL BRAIN INJURY

A new source of ideas about the developing relationship between lexical comprehension and production has come from recent studies of the effects of early focal brain injury. The children who have been studied come from a rare group who suffer a localised brain insult either prenatally or within the first 6 months of life. The main cause of such focal brain injury is a stroke and, in some babies, it is marked either by partial paralysis on one side of the body or by neonatal seizures. In other cases, the lesion is not detected until the baby is given routine ultrasound scanning. The extent and site of the lesion is confirmed through neuroimaging using either a CT scan or Magnetic Resonance Imaging (MRI).

Several studies have now been completed or are ongoing (see Bates, 1993 and Stiles & Thal, 1993 for useful overviews) but there is one study by Thal et al. (1991) that is particularly relevant to our present discussion of the relationship between lexical comprehension and production in infancy.

Focal brain injury and language development in infancy

Thal et al. present data on 27 children between the ages of 12 and 35 months, ten of whom were studied longitudinally. Their study also included data from five subjects studied by Marchman, Miller, and Bates (1991). The children varied in the severity and site of their lesion although the majority (19 out of 27) had a left hemisphere injury.

The children's communicative and linguistic development was assessed using the MacArthur Communicative Development Inventories (CDI) which have checklists to be completed by parents indicating which words the child can comprehend and produce (Fenson et al., 1990). There are two scales, the Infant Scale, covering the period between 8 and 16 months, and the Toddler Scale which covers the 16 to 28 month age range. The Infant Scale assesses the development of communicative gestures as well as vocabulary. The Toddler Scale focuses on vocabulary production as well as the beginning of grammatical competence. The norms for the CDI were derived from a sample of over 1700 children taken from three different sites in the United States. As such, the norms provided appropriate comparison data for the focal brain lesion subjects.

Thal et al. found delays in the early stages of lexical production for the focal brain lesion group as a whole throughout the 12 to 35 month age range covered by the study. The pattern for comprehension delays was rather different. Only the younger age group (12 to 16 months) showed a delay by comparison with the MacArthur norms. Quite correctly, Thal et al. point out that this finding has to be treated with some caution because the CDI Toddler Scale does not have norms for comprehension and so the comparison of the older group with focal brain lesions, whose age ranged from 17 to 22 months, was with normal 16-month-old infants. Comprehension vocabulary accrues at a very fast rate after 16 months—it is not measured on the Toddler Scale precisely because experience has shown that parents find it almost impossible to keep track of the huge number of new words that the child understands—so the difference between 16 and 22 months is a significant one in terms of vocabulary size.

The picture for comprehension became a little clearer when the site of the lesion was considered. All children, irrespective of lesion site, showed evidence of impairment in early lexical production. However, within the 12 to 16 month age range (the subgroup for whom comprehension measures were available), comprehension impairment was mainly associated with right hemisphere (RH) damage. The sample was small since there were only six infants with RH damage within the age range so, again, the results are suggestive rather than conclusive. However, a second, more robust, finding is compatible with the view that the main hemispheric involvement for early comprehension is different from that for production: children who showed persistent production difficulties were those who had a lesion involving the left posterior (LP) cortex. There was no association between comprehension deficits and LP damage. This pattern is consistent with the finding of Marchman et al. (1991) that LP damage was associated with delay in the development of phonological production.

A comparison of the pattern for infant and adult

Although there is clearly need for further research into the effects of focal brain injury, involving more subjects and a greater use of longitudinal assessment, the data so far suggest that the pattern of hemispheric involvement in early language development is rather different from that revealed by studies of adult aphasias. For right-handed adults, left anterior lesions give rise to Broca's aphasia, where comprehension is spared but production is halting and effortful, whereas left posterior lesions give rise to Wernicke's aphasia where production is fluent but empty and patients typically show word finding difficulties, substitution errors and impairment in comprehension. Thus, in adults, both comprehension and production deficits are associated with left hemisphere (LH) damage, with production being seen as localised mainly in the left anterior region. Neither pattern of association is shown in the infant data where it is LP damage that gives rise to production delays and RH damage that is associated with comprehension delays. So it would appear that the regions that mediate early language development are not the same as those that mediate adult language processing.

This marked difference between cortical involvement in infant and adult language does not appear in the case of spatial analysis and drawing ability where there is a high degree of similarity between the adult pattern and that shown by young children with focal brain lesions (Stiles & Nass, 1991; Stiles & Thal, 1993). For both groups, LH damage is associated with an analytic deficit (involving difficulty with the extraction of local perceptual detail) whereas RH damage typically gives rise to deficits in spatial integration (where local detail is preserved but global information is lost).

Bates (1993) has argued that the data from focal brain lesion studies of language and spatial cognition can be explained by considering the task that confronts the infant who is attempting to understand and produce words for the first time.

The right hemisphere of both adult and young child has an important role in sensory integration; and one way of viewing early lexical comprehension is to see it as a process of precisely this kind. In order to understand what a word means, particularly at the outset of development, the child has to integrate various different kinds of sensory information including, at a minimum, spoken language and salient information from the nonverbal context. Thus early comprehension development is likely to involve the right hemisphere.

Phonological development and lexical production, on the other hand, requires the extraction of very precise acoustic detail. This is the kind of task that generally involves the left hemisphere, as the data on spatial tasks shows. More specifically to language, the very early use of the LH for the task of phonetic analysis is supported by the finding of Bertoncini et al. (1989) of a right ear advantage for speech perception at birth.

CONCLUSION

This chapter has reviewed recent research in four areas: speech perception, early word comprehension, the relationship between comprehension, and the effects of early focal brain injury. Together they provide a picture of the important developments that occur in language comprehension and production during infancy.

The work on speech perception shows that, well before the end of the first year, the infant has become selectively attuned to the phoneme boundaries and segmental structure of the language of the speech community. This selective attunement occurs through a process of "unlearning" in which the infant gradually loses the ability to perceive phonemic distinctions and segmental regularities that are not salient for the target language.

Once an infant's perception of speech has become tuned to the language of the speech community the stage is set for the first understanding of words to emerge. Language comprehension typically begins at around 7 months of age when infants begin to respond reliably to their own name (Harris et al., 1995b). The study by Kuhl et al. (1992) shows that, by this age, sensitivity to vowel contrasts has been established, so it is entirely possible that the infant can begin to recognise frequently used words. However, in order for the infant to develop a real understanding of the meaning of words it is essential that other important developments have occurred. One key development concerns the understanding of reference.

The emergent understanding of reference arises in a context of joint attention between the infant and communicative partner which is brought about by several different mechanisms (see Chapter 7 by Messer). However, from the perspective of using language to refer, the infant's own production of pointing seems to be of particular significance. There is a striking similarity in the age at which children first begin to point and first begin to understand object names (Harris et al., 1995a). Furthermore, children who acquire a large proportion of object names in their early vocabulary tend to acquire new words at a faster rate. This is perhaps because understanding the notion of "object nameness" allows many new names to be acquired whereas, for a child who is learning a greater proportion of action words or context-bound object words, a common strategy cannot be applied so easily.

Another theme to emerge from this chapter concerns the relationship between comprehension and production. The research on infant focal brain injury reinforces the view that there are important dissociations between the two. Studies by Bates et al. (1988) and Harris et al. (1995a) showed that measures of early comprehension do not reliably predict early production. Data from the first studies of focal brain injury go some way to explaining why this pattern is evident: in the early stages of language development, the right hemisphere plays a major role in comprehension whereas the left hemisphere appears to be mainly implicated in early production. The reason for this differential location appears to lie in the rather different requirements of understanding and producing language at the outset of development.

A different kind of dissociation between comprehension and production is evident in the wide individual variation in the lag between the two. Although the most common pattern is for early production to lag behind comprehension is a fairly consistent manner, two other, less frequent, patterns have been observed. Some children understand as many as 200 words before producing their first word while others appear to show no lag at all between comprehension and production. At the moment it is not clear what gives rise to these different patterns but they are symptomatic of a consistent finding in recent studies of early language development that individual variation is the norm rather than the exception. What this chapter has shown is that these individual differences first appear in infancy.

REFERENCES

Barrett, M.D., Harris, M., & Chasin, J. (1991). Early lexical development and maternal speech: A comparison of children's initial and subsequent uses of words. *Journal of Child Language, 18*, 21–40.

Bates, E. (1993). Comprehension and production in early language development. *Monographs of the Society for Research in Child Development, 58*, 222–242.

Bates, E., Benigni, L., Bretherton, I., Camaioni, L., & Volterra, V. (1979). *The emergence of symbols: cognition and communication in infancy*. New York: Academic Press.

Bates, E., Bretherton, I., & Snyder, L. (1988). *From first words to grammar: individual differences and dissociable mechanisms*. Cambridge: Cambridge University Press.

Bates, E., Marchman, V., Thal, D., Fenson, L., Dale, P., Reznick, J.S., Reilly, J., & Hartung, J. (1994). Developmental and stylistic variation in the composition of early vocabulary. *Journal of Child Language, 21*, 85–123.

Benedict, H. (1977). *Language comprehension in the 10–16-month-old infant*. (Unpublished). Doctoral dissertation, Yale University.

Benedict, H. (1979). Early lexical development: comprehension and production. *Journal of Child Language, 6*, 183–200.

Bertoncini, J., Bijeljac, R., McAdams, S., Peretz, I., & Mehler, J. (1989). Dichotic perception of laterality in neonates. *Brain and Language, 37*, 591–605.

Best, C.T., McRoberts, G.W., & Sithole, N.M. (1988). Examination of the perceptual reorganization for nonnative speech contrasts: Zulu click discrimination by English-speaking adults and infants. *Journal of Experimental Psychology: Human Perception and Performance, 14*, 345–360.

Bijeljac-Babic, R., Bertoncini, J., & Mehler, J. (1993). How do 4-day-old infants categorize multisyllabic utterances? *Developmental Psychology, 29*, 711–721.

Butterworth, G. (1994). Infant perception and the explanation of intelligence. In F. Khalfa (ed.), *Intelligence*. Cambridge: Cambridge University Press.

Cutler, A. & Mehler, J. (1993). The periodicity bias. *Journal of Phonetics, 21*, 103–108.

Cutler, A., Norris, D., & Segui, J. (1986). The syllable's differing role in the segmentation of French and English. *Journal of Memory and Language, 25*, 385–400.

Eimas, P. (1974). Auditory and linguistic cues for place of articulation by infants. *Perception and Psychophysics, 16*, 513–521.

Eimas. P. & Miller, J. (1980). Discrimination of the information for manner of articulation. *Infant Behavior and Development, 3*, 367–375.

Eimas, P.D., Siqueland, E., Jusczyk, P., & Vogirito, J. (1971). Speech perception in infants. *Science, 171*, 303–306.

Fenson, L., Dale, P., Resnick, S., Bates, E., Thal, D., Reilly, J., & Hartung, J. (1990). *MacArthur communicative development inventories: Technical manual*. San Diego: San Diego State University.

Folven, R.J., Bonvillian, J.D., & Orlansky, M.D. (1984/5). Communicative gestures and early sign language acquisition. *First Language*, *5*, 129–144.

Gunzi, S. (1993). *Early language comprehension and production.* Unpublished doctoral dissertation, University of London.

Harris, M. (1992). *Language experience and early language development: from input to uptake.* Hove: Lawrence Erlbaum Associates Ltd.

Harris, M. (1994). *The emergence of referential understanding: Pointing and the comprehension of object names.* Paper presented at the 9th International Conference on Infant Studies: Paris.

Harris, M., Barlow-Brown, F., & Chasin, J. (1995a). The emergence of referential understanding: Pointing and the comprehension of object names. *First Language*, *15*, 19–34.

Harris, M., Barrett, M., Jones, D., & Brookes, S. (1988). Linguistic input and early word meaning. *Journal of Child Language*, *15*, 77–94.

Harris, M. & Chasin, J. (1993). Developing patterns in children's early comprehension vocabularies. In J. Clibbens & B. Pendleton (eds), *Proceedings of the 1993 Child Language Seminar.* University of Plymouth.

Harris, M., Yeeles, C., Chasin, J., & Oakley, Y. (1995b). Symmetries and asymmetries in early lexical comprehension and production. *Journal of Child Language*, *22*, 1–18.

Jusczyk, P.W., Cutler, A., & Redanz, N. (1993). Preference for the predominant stress patterns of English words. *Child Development*, *64*, 675–687.

Kuhl, P.K., Williams, K.A., Laard, F., Stevens, K.N., & Lindblom, B. (1992). Linguistic experience alters phonetic perception in infants by 6 months. *Science*, *255*, 606–608.

Marchman, V.A., Miller, R., & Bates, E. (1991). Babble and first words in children with focal brain injury. *Applied Psycholinguistics*, *12*, 1–22.

Mehler, J. (1994). *The acquisition of phonology.* Paper presented to the Royal Society Meeting on "The acquisition and dissolution of language". The Royal Society: London.

Mehler, J. & Dupoux E. (1994). *What infants know.* Oxford: Basil Blackwell.

Miller, J. & Eimas, P. (1983). Studies on the categorisation of speech by infants. *Cognition*, *13*, 135–165.

Nelson, K. (1973). Structure and strategy in learning to talk. *Monographs of the Society for Research in Child Development*, *143*, 38.

Nelson, K. (1988). Constraints on word learning? *Cognitive Development*, *3*, 221–246.

Otake, T., Hatano, G., Cutler, A., & Mehler, J. (1993). Mora or syllable? Speech segmentation in Japanese. *Journal of Memory and Language*, *32*, 258–278.

Sansavini, A., Bertoncini, J., & Gionanelli, G. (1994). *Italian newborns discriminate stress patterns in phonetically complex Italian words.* Paper presented at the 11th International Conference on Infant Studies: Paris.

Stiles, J. & Nass, R. (1991). Spatial grouping ability in young children with congenital right or left hemisphere brain injury. *Brain and Cognition*, *15*, 201–222.

Stiles, J. & Thal, D. (1993). Linguistic and spatial cognitive development following early focal brain injury: Patterns of deficit and recovery. In M. H. Johnstone (ed.), *Brain development and cognition: a reader.* Oxford: Basil Blackwell.

Thal, D., Marchman, V., Stiles, J., Aram, D., Trauner, D., Nass, R., & Bates, E. (1991). Early lexical development in children with focal brain injury. *Brain and Language*, *40*, 491–527.

Trehub, S.E. (1976). The discrimination of foreign speech contrasts by infants and adults. *Speech Development*, *13*, 466–472.

Werker, J.F., Gilbert, J.H.V., Humphreys, G.W., & Tees, R.C. (1981). Developmental aspects of cross-language speech perception. *Child development*, *52*, 349–355.

Werker, J.F. & Tees, R.C. (1984). Cross-language speech perception: Evidence for perceptual reorganization during the first year of life. *Infant Behavior and Development*, *7*, 49–63

Author Index

Subject Index

For Product Safety Concerns and Information please contact our EU
representative GPSR@taylorandfrancis.com
Taylor & Francis Verlag GmbH, Kaufingerstraße 24, 80331 München, Germany

www.ingramcontent.com/pod-product-compliance
Ingram Content Group UK Ltd.
Pitfield, Milton Keynes, MK11 3LW, UK
UKHW022215190926
475702UK00003B/373

Contents